PREGNANCY,
BIRTH &
THE NEWBORN
BABY

The Boston Children's Medical Center

PREGNANCY, BIRTH &
THE NEWBORN BABY
A Complete Guide for Parents and Parents-to-be
Members of the Staff of the
Boston Children's Medical Center

NO MORE DIAPERS!
Joae Graham Selzer, M.D.,
and Members of the Staff of the
Boston Children's Medical Center

BELTS ON, BUTTONS DOWN
What Every Mother Should Know about Car Safety
Edward D. Fales, Jr., and Members of the Staff
of the Boston Children's Medical Center

KEEPING YOUR FAMILY
HEALTHY OVERSEAS
James P. Carter, M.D., M.S., Dr.P.H.,
Eleanora de Antonio West, M.A.,
and Members of the Staff of the
Boston Children's Medical Center

THE EMERGING PERSONALITY
Infancy through Adolescence
George E. Gardner, M.D., Ph.D.,
and Members of the Staff of the
Boston Children's Medical Center

Publications for Parents

PREGNANCY, BIRTH & THE NEWBORN BABY

A PUBLICATION FOR PARENTS

The Boston Children's Medical Center

A Merloyd Lawrence Book

DELACORTE PRESS / SEYMOUR LAWRENCE

Copyright © 1971, 1972 by The Children's Hospital Medical Center

PHOTO CREDITS: Figures 1–4, 7–11 Lennart Nilsson; Copyright © 1965
by Albert Bonniers Forlag, Stockholm
Figures 5 and 6 By courtesy of
Carnegie Institution of Washington

All rights reserved. No part of this book may be
reproduced in any form or by any means without
the prior written permission of the Publisher, excepting
brief quotes used in connection with reviews written
specifically for inclusion in a magazine or newspaper.
Library of Congress Catalog Card Number: 71–175649
Manufactured in the United States of America
Sixth Printing—1978

Library of Congress Cataloging in Publication Data

Boston. Children's Hospital Medical Center.
Pregnancy, birth & the newborn baby.
(A Publication for parents)
"A Seymour Lawrence book."
1. Pregnancy. 2. Childbirth. 3. Infants—Care
and hygiene. I. Title.
RG525.B645   613   71–175649

To Leonard W. Cronkhite, Jr., M.D.

EXECUTIVE-VICE-PRESIDENT OF
THE BOSTON CHILDREN'S MEDICAL CENTER

*without whose vision this volume
could never have been written.*

Contributors

RICHARD CHASIN, M.D.
Assistant Clinical Professor in Psychiatry
Boston University Medical School

Lecturer in Psychiatry
Harvard Medical School

Director of James Jackson Putnam
Children's Center

MARCIA H. CHASIN, ED.D.
Clinical and Research Associate
Laboratory of Behavioral Psychiatry
Massachusetts Mental Health Center

SHIRLEY STENDIG EHRLICH, M.S.W.

RICHARD I. FEINBLOOM, M.D.
Assistant Professor in Pediatrics
Harvard Medical School

Acting Medical Director
Family Health Care Program
Children's Hospital Medical Center

ARTHUR GORBACH, M.D.
Instructor in Obstetrics and Gynecology
Harvard Medical School

Obstetrician and Gynecologist
Boston Hospital for Women

HOWARD S. KING, M.D.
Clinical Instructor in Pediatrics
Harvard Medical School

Assistant in Medicine
Children's Hospital Medical Center

MARGARET MEAD, PH.D.
Curator Emeritus of Ethnology
American Museum of Natural History
New York

Adjunct Professor of Anthropology
Columbia University

NILES ANNE NEWTON, PH.D.
Associate Professor
Division of Psychology
Department of Psychiatry
Northwestern University Medical School

PETER WOLFF, M.D.
Professor in Psychiatry
Harvard Medical School

Director of Psychiatric Research
Children's Hospital Medical Center

Children's Hospital Medical Center

Chiefs-of-Service

CHARLES F. BARLOW, M.D., Neurologist-in-Chief
M. JUDAH FOLKMAN, M.D., Surgeon-in-Chief
MELVIN J. GLIMCHER, M.D., Orthopedic Surgeon-in-Chief
ROBERT E. GROSS, M.D., Surgeon-in-Chief, Cardiovascular Surgery
JOHN E. HALL, M.D., Chief of Clinical Services in Orthopedic Surgery
BURTON F. JAFFE, M.D., Otolaryngologist-in-Chief
CHARLES A. JANEWAY, M.D., Physician-in-Chief
ROBERT T. McCLUSKEY, M.D., Pathologist-in-Chief
ALEXANDER S. NADAS, M.D., Chief, Department of Cardiology
EDWARD B. D. NEUHAUSER, Radiologist-in-Chief
JULIUS B. RICHMOND, M.D., Psychiatrist-in-Chief
RICHARD M. ROBB, M.D., Ophthalmologist-in-Chief
ROBERT M. SMITH, M.D., Anesthesiologist-in-Chief
LENNARD T. SWANSON, D.M.D., Dentist-in-Chief
KEASLEY WELCH, M.D., Neurosurgeon-in-Chief

Board of Editors

John H. Durston, Editor-in-Chief
Joanne B. Bluestone
Harriet H. Gibney
Patricia Nelson
Merloyd Lawrence
Betty Hannah Hoffman
Philip C. Ward

Acknowledgments

Grateful acknowledgment is made to Harriet H. Gibney,
former Director of Health Education at The Children's Hospital Medical Center,
who first thought of the idea for this book,
selected the contributors and developed the project
with such patience and skill.

The following persons framed the first outline
and helped with the conceptualization of the book:

JOEL J. ALPERT, M.D.
Senior Associate in Medicine;
Director, Family and Child Health Division,
The Children's Hospital Medical Center;
Associate Professor of Pediatrics,
Harvard Medical School

GRETE L. BIBRING, M.D.
Professor Emeritus, Harvard Medical School;
Psychiatrist-in-Chief Emeritus,
Beth Israel Hospital

T. BERRY BRAZELTON, M.D.
Coordinator of Patient Care,
The Children's Hospital Medical Center;
Clinical Assistant Professor,
Harvard Medical School

WILLIAM COCHRAN, M.D.
Acting Pediatrician-in-Chief,
Boston Hospital For Women; Assistant
Clinical Professor, Harvard Medical School

ERIK H. ERIKSON
Professor Emeritus, Human Development,
Harvard University; Lecturer on Psychiatry,
Harvard Medical School

LEON E. KRUGER, M.D.
Director, Martin Luther King, Jr. Clinica
Campesini; Associate Professor of Pediatrics,
University of Miami (Florida)

MALKAH T. NOTMAN, M.D.
Associate Psychiatrist, Beth Israel Hospital;
Clinical Instructor,
Harvard Medical School

PETER WOLFF, M.D.
Director of Psychiatric Research,
The Children's Hospital Medical Center;
Professor in Psychiatry, Harvard Medical School

Thanks go also to those who aided the project
by reading and reviewing material in their specialities:

THOMAS E. CONE, JR., M.D.
Chief, Medical Ambulatory Service,
The Children's Hospital Medical Center;
Clinical Professor of Pediatrics, Harvard Medical School

WILLIAM CROWELL, M.D.
Staff Psychiatrist, The Children's Hospital Medical Center;
Clinical Instructor in Psychiatry,
Harvard Medical School

CHESTER C. D'AUTREMONT, M.D.
Senior Associate in Psychiatry,
The Children's Hospital Medical Center;
Instructor in Psychiatry, Harvard Medical School

JAMES E. DRORBAUGH, M.D.
Senior Associate Physician,
The Children's Hospital Medical Center;
Assistant Clinical Professor of Pediatrics,
Harvard Medical School

L. J. FILER, M.D.
Professor of Pediatrics,
University of Iowa Hospitals and Clinics

ROBERT M. FILLER, M.D.
Associate Chief of Surgery,
The Children's Hospital Medical Center;
Associate Clinical Professor of Surgery,
Harvard Medical School

JOHN GROVER, M.D.
Chief of Clinics, Vincent Memorial Hospital;
Assistant Clinical Professor,
Harvard Medical School

JOHN P. HUBBELL, JR., M.D.
Associate in Medicine,
The Children's Hospital Medical Center;
Instructor of Pediatrics, Harvard Medical School

CHARLES A. JANEWAY, M.D.
Physician-in-Chief,
The Children's Hospital Medical Center;
Thomas Morgan Rotch Professor of Pediatrics,
Harvard Medical School

ELLEN KANG, M.D.
Assistant in Clinical Genetics,
The Children's Hospital Medical Center;
Assistant Professor of Pediatrics,
Harvard Medical School

SAMUEL L. KATZ, M.D.
Chairman, Department of Pediatrics,
Duke University Medical Center;
Professor, Duke School of Medicine

ROBERT B. KELLER, M.D.
Assistant in Orthopedic Surgery,
The Children's Hospital Medical Center;
Instructor of Orthopedic Surgery,
Harvard Medical School

DONALD W. MacCOLLUM, M.D.
Senior Associate in Surgery,
The Children's Hospital Medical Center;
Assistant Clinical Professor in Surgery,
Harvard Medical School

ALAN D. PERLMUTTER, M.D.
Chief, Division of Pediatric Urology,
Children's Hospital of Michigan;
Professor of Urology,
Wayne State University School of Medicine

JOHN SHILLITO, JR., M.D.
Senior Associate in Neurosurgery,
The Children's Hospital Medical Center;
Associate Professor of Surgery,
Harvard Medical School

DAVID H. SMITH, M.D.
Senior Associate in Medicine
and Chief, Division of Infectious Diseases,
The Children's Hospital Medical Center;
Associate Professor of Pediatrics,
Harvard Medical School

IRVING UMANSKY, M.D.
Associate in Medicine,
The Children's Hospital Medical Center;
Instructor of Pediatrics, Harvard Medical School

MARY ELLEN WOHL, M.D.
Associate in Medicine,
The Children's Hospital Medical Center;
Assistant Professor of Pediatrics,
Harvard Medical School

And thanks go to George E. Gardner, M.D.,
Psychiatrist-in-Chief Emeritus, the Children's Hospital
Medical Center, for his wisdom and guidance; to
Roger Bibace, Ph.D., Professor of Psychology, Clark
University, for his special consultation; to Robert J.
Haggerty, M.D., Professor and Chairman, Department
of Pediatrics, University of Rochester School of
Medicine and Dentistry, and Pediatrician-in-Chief,
Strong Memorial Hospital, who was one of the earliest
supporters of our Health Education Department
and its Publications for Parents series; to Park S.
Gerald, M.D., Chief, Clinical Genetics Department,
The Children's Hospital Medical Center, and
Professor of Pediatrics, Harvard Medical School,
for his special assistance and guidance regarding the
chapter on genetics; and to Joae Selzer, M.D.,
Consulting Psychiatrist at the New England Home
For Little Wanderers, and Instructor in Psychiatry,
Harvard Medical School, for her helpful suggestions
on many questions.

Contents

PART FIVE

SPECIAL PROBLEMS

PART ONE

INTRODUCTION

CHAPTER ONE

Childbearing in Broad Perspective

*P*ARENTHOOD is one of the great events of a lifetime, both physically and emotionally. It is a deep human experience. Whether it is an essentially good experience or a bad one depends not only on the physical course of reproduction but also on the social and emotional impact of childbearing.

Fortunately, there is a growing body of new and fascinating knowledge concerning the behavioral aspects of early parenthood. A science of reproductive behavior exists and can help parents to understand what is happening to them. Anthropology, sociology, animal behavior, and psychology all contribute toward understanding the broader aspects of becoming a parent.

PREGNANCY CHANGES BEHAVIOR IN MAMMALS INCLUDING MAN

Many readers will have heard a story about a pregnant unmarried nurse who strapped herself in a corset to hide her pregnancy and kept on with her normal life, even staying on the job at her hospital. She hid the fact of her pregnancy so convincingly that those around her never knew the difference. The eventual arrival of the baby was a shock to all her colleagues at the hospital and to her friends.

This story is remembered because it is so very, very unusual. For the overwhelming majority of women, pregnant behavior does differ from nonpregnant behavior. Women the world over show the impact of pregnancy by changing the way they act. This fundamental change is not confined to human females. Subhuman mammals often change their behavior in late pregnancy. The lioness in the wild becomes more retiring. In captivity she develops a fondness for a back corner of her cage, which she uses for rest during pregnancy and later to care for her young. Females of various cat species have been observed to change their emotional responses in late pregnancy. They become more irritable, more defensive, more aggressive.

The urge to provide suitable habitation for the future offspring is typical of many mammals besides the human female. The "nesting urge," noticeable in expectant human couples who change their housing arrangements and worry about fixing up a room for the baby, may be based on a biological foundation, as well as on human foresight. The pregnant Shiras moose chooses a home area carefully as labor approaches. She needs a solitary, safe place with food and water nearby, for she will not leave the calf while it is young. She selects a spot near a small stream and a willow hedge for water and for easily available food. The expectant rabbit and the expectant sow, when given nesting materials, will build nests in preparation for the coming event.

The behavior of the pregnant laboratory rat has been studied in scientific detail. During pregnancy her interest centers increasingly on the reproductive parts of her own body; her usual self-licking or "cleaning" concentrates more and more on the parts of the body that will be involved in reproduction. She repeatedly licks her nipples and her genital region. As pregnancy progresses, the homemaking urge hits her. At first the nest-building urge is sporadic, with a little piling up of materials here and there in the cage. But toward the end of her pregnancy, she gets down to business and builds a suitable nest for herself, in a cozy corner if possible. Then the active phase of her pregnancy is over. Most of the day she now rests lethargically in her nest.

Changes of behavior of the human female in pregnancy may be quite as great as those of the female laboratory rat—perhaps even greater. Moreover, these behavior changes are not confined to the expectant mother. Mankind has a strong tradition that males, as well as females, shall support and protect the young. So it is not surprising that the human father's behavior, as well as the mother's, changes in anticipation of parenthood. Change in behavior during pregnancy is so fundamental that it appears among peoples all over the world, in both simple and complex cultures.

Perhaps the most usual behavior change required of expectant mothers (and sometimes fathers too) is submission to dietary rules. The rules change from time to time and from group to group, but the pattern of making rules about what should be eaten occurs again and again. The Maricopa woman, a North American Indian of the Southwest, is warned not to eat fat for fear her baby will be covered with a membrane of fat at birth. In the Northwestern United States the Sanpoil tribe of Indians are supposed to eat sparingly during pregnancy for the sake of their health and an easier childbirth. Salt and sweet things are forbidden to the Jivaro women of Ecuador in the belief that this deprivation prevents the fetus from growing too big. The Ila husband of Northern Rhodesia, as well as his wife, is not supposed to eat the flesh of hartebeest, for the young of this animal are born blind, and these people fear that the baby might likewise be affected.

Although American women usually do not have specifically taboo foods, they are often under strong social pressure to restrict calories and weight gain. For instance, a widely read public health publication on prenatal care had only one illustration in the section on what to eat in pregnancy. It was not a picture emphasizing the scientifically documented need to eat extra quantities of protein, vitamins, and mineral-rich foods in pregnancy. Instead, the sole illustration emphasized the restrictive rules. It was a picture of a woman being weighed and carried the caption "The scale tells the story."

Changes in the *type* of advice given to American mothers about eating may be in the offing. For instance, there is new research suggesting that thin women who gain only a little weight in pregnancy are more likely to give birth to high-risk underweight babies. In recent years doctors writing for the popular press have emphasized the importance of eating sufficient wholesome food during pregnancy.

Nevertheless, regulation of diet in pregnancy stems from fundamental human tendencies quite apart from, and predating by thousands of years, the science of nutrition. It may be that dietary rules arise in so many different societies for the simple reason that the pregnant woman, needing more nourishment at the end of pregnancy, automatically changes her customary patterns of eating. The appearance of change in behavior patterns stimulates an interest in regulation of behavior.

Spontaneous physical activity is another area where behavioral changes occur in the course of pregnancy. Again we find keen interest in making rules and regulations for the expectant mother to follow. Widely scattered primitive peoples have emphasized the importance of exercise to the expectant mother. If the expectant mother of the Ainu primitive tribe on the Japanese Islands exercises in pregnancy, she is supposed to have a short labor for her reward. The Hopi Indian woman of our Southwest is enjoined to get up early every morning and not to sit around all day. The Sanpoil tribe goes even further. For their pregnant women, a regular program of exercise, mainly walking and swimming, is prescribed.

Pushing out the baby in childbirth is a task requiring vigorous muscular effort, so the folkways concerning the need for exercise in pregnancy may well be based on some observation of the outcome. But here again, as in the case of diet, the tendency may be to try to control the natural changes in behavior due to pregnancy. The pregnant woman, like the pregnant laboratory rat, is likely to feel less desire for physical activity in the later stages of pregnancy. In response to this biological lassitude, many peoples may have tried consciously to encourage the pregnant woman's activity.

Another widespread human response to pregnancy is to give the expectant woman special care. Folk sayings about pregnancy emphasize this solicitude. Among the Chagga of Tanganyika, Africa, the saying goes, "Pay attention to the pregnant woman! There is no one more important than she." The Jordan villagers of the Middle East say, "As people are careful of a chicken in the egg, all the more so should they be of a child in its mother's womb." On the opposite side of the world, the Aymara people, in the highlands of Bolivia, surround a woman with protective and kindly rules. The concern for the future baby is so strong that the family dog may be given away or killed for fear the dog might become jealous of the baby.

Even people who profess not to fuss over pregnant women often do so indirectly, showing definite changes of behavior. For instance, the Bulgarian village people have a matter-of-fact attitude toward pregnancy, summed up as follows: "The woman is born to be a mother. She knows it, and as her duty, should not expect anything from others." Nevertheless, they give the expectant mother things she asks for lest the baby die if she is not satisfied. She is also protected from bending and lifting heavy objects.

Similar feelings can be noted in our own society. Many families are quite open in their solicitude for expectant mothers. While others may seem on the surface to take things in a matter-of-fact way, underneath there is usually a feeling of extra concern. Gone are the days when gallantry required well-brought-up young men to give up their seats in overcrowded buses or streetcars to *any* woman, but even today the girl who looks as if her baby is about due can usually count on a seat from the first person who notices her condition.

Protectiveness toward expectant mothers is not superficial behavior. It is deep-rooted and occurs again and again all over the world. Indeed, should a society develop that gave no help or consideration whatsoever to the expectant woman, that particular group would be unlikely to survive. Successful human reproduction requires adaptations in behavior, not only of mother and father, but also of the wider group in which the young couple live.

GLAD OR SORRY TO BE PREGNANT

Traditionally, the missed menstrual periods are supposed to be a time of joy, especially after suspicions of pregnancy are confirmed by the physician. Actually, pregnancy, planned or unplanned, causes mixed feelings in most expectant mothers. It is a rare mother who is totally joyful, all the time and in all facets of her personality, at the prospect of having a baby. On the other hand, the mother who, by the end of pregnancy, is still totally unadjusted to the idea of having a baby is also rare.

If the pregnancy was a "planned" one, the expectant mother sometimes feels that she is obliged to feel glad. Psychiatric interviews in depth have shown, however, that this is not always true. In fact, one study found that about one out of every eight women with planned conceptions developed very strong regrets about being pregnant.

Unplanned pregnancies, of course, are often harder to accept, but not always. It depends on the circumstances surrounding the birth as well as the health and adaptability of the mother. Some women take it philosophically, recognizing that there really is *no* completely convenient time to have a baby—so they might as well accept what comes. Such women soon look forward to the satisfactions of being a mother. Others find it harder to accept their condition. From a number of research studies we can get some indication of the circumstances in which pregnancy is joyfully accepted and those in which pregnancy is likely to be regretted. The number of children and the space between them are two very important factors in determining how a woman will feel about conception. For instance, Dr. Edwin Gordon asked expectant mothers, "Are you happy to be pregnant?" Most of the women who had no baby or just one baby said they were happy, but only about half who were expecting a third child said they were happy. And it was hardly surprising to learn that none of the few women who already had five or more children said they were happy about the new one coming along.

Another study concentrated on space between children. Only about one in eleven mothers whose babies had been born less than twenty-one months apart described themselves as delighted to find themselves pregnant the second time. The longer the space between babies, the more likely the mothers were to report pleasure at the idea of a new baby. Those with the traditional two-year gap were still not as likely to be delighted as those with a three- or four-year gap. (For a further discussion of the factors that make pregnancy welcome or unwelcome, see chapter 22 on abortion.)

Although babies conceived before marriage are often assumed to be unwelcome, this is by no means always the case. The response to a baby conceived out of wedlock depends on the attitude of the social group, the personality of the individual, and the reaction of the girl's family. In some societies premarital pregnancy is the natural first step toward marriage. Others, of course, have insisted that marriage must come first.

Even within the same society the different social classes tend to have different feelings about premarital pregnancy. For instance, in England, a study of women having first babies revealed that more than one in four of the poor mothers had a prenuptial pregnancy, whereas the rate among the most affluent mothers was only one in fifty. Naturally, the feelings evoked by a baby due to arrive "too soon" will not be the same for a girl with many friends who have had the same experience, as for a girl who does not know anyone else in the same situation.

In America girls find themselves under strong emotional pressures if they become pregnant without a husband. Nevertheless, one study showed that one-third of all babies born in the United States in a two-year period had in fact been conceived out of wedlock, whether premaritally or otherwise. Although it is difficult to get accurate statistics, one nationwide study indicates that more than four out of five of the college women who become pregnant out of wedlock have abortions. The well-educated girl who goes through with her out-of-wedlock pregnancy is the exception. She has chosen motherhood and the preservation of her future baby despite considerable pressure to do otherwise.

One might expect that the career girl, even more than the home-body, would have a difficult time getting used to the idea of pregnancy. A statistical study has found that among middle-class women the problem is not this simple. True, the girls eager to start a family reported delight in pregnancy more often than did girls who were immersed in careers and reluctant to give them up for children. On the other hand, those who were indifferent about their work also tended to report indifference about their prospective motherhood. The girls who found some nice things to say about their work often tended also to express happiness at being pregnant. The research suggests that perhaps the woman who enjoys work may also enjoy motherhood, because this is her characteristic style in dealing with all of life's situations.

Real financial worries may also be a factor in the frequent "I wish it hadn't happened" feeling about pregnancy. Children in modern American society evoke deep human satisfaction, but, viewed candidly, they also mean economic sacrifice. The impact of the Industrial Revolution has been to take work out of the home and into the factory. The helping hands of children plowing, picking, milking, weaving, sewing are no longer needed. Instead, now that our system extends schooling over so many years, having children requires the continuing expenditure of money over a long period of time.

There was a time when the family with many children was economically blessed; now children are financial liabilities. It is a cliché that the most expensive possession of most families is a house. That may have been true in great-grandmother's day, but today for the couples who hope to see their children through college and professional school the most expensive acquisition may be a baby.

The giving up of one's own desires for those of the future generation begins immediately with practical decisions, such as foregoing a new car because of the looming obstetrical and hospital bills or trading at less expensive stores because the housing expenses are going up. Even harder for some parents is having to deprive an older child in order to provide for the coming needs of the yet unborn.

Besides the obvious monetary stresses, there are other changes in social customs that contribute to the difficulty of accepting pregnancy. It used to be that girls grew up in families where mother continued to have babies until she was over forty, where older sisters lived close by and had babies regularly too, and where a growing girl spent many hours helping to care for babies.

One hundred and fifty years ago the pregnant figure was not restricted to two or three periods in a woman's lifetime. A large proportion of adult women up to the age of menopause had burgeoning tummies. The young girl became accustomed early to the fact of birth because it occurred regularly in her own home and the homes of neighbors.

The shrinking in size of the usual family has been so gradual that we seldom realize that the modern girl no longer has the opportunity to become thoroughly familiar with the facts of childbearing and mothering. U.S. Census reports show that in 1810 every thousand white women between twenty and forty-four had thirteen hundred children *under five* to look after. By the late Victorian era the comparable number of preschool children had shrunk to around seven hundred. The current ratio is probably about the same as that of 1940, with only about four hundred babies and preschoolers for every thousand women of childbearing age. Thus, the modern girl sees less than one-third as much of pregnancy, babies, and young children in the home as did her counterpart in 1810. No wonder young women often see pregnancy, not as the usual female routine, but as something quite individual and unusual! With little experience of babies and expectant mothers in the immediate family, it is easy for the modern girl to develop a "This-thing-never-happened-to-anybody-but-me" feeling. Her ancestor of 150 years ago would tend to see pregnancy as the normal way of life for most women because she herself was constantly surrounded with expectant mothers, birth, and babies.

There is still another change in social custom that may detract from the wholehearted welcome supposedly awaiting all new babies. Conservatives would say it is somehow linked to the freedom women now enjoy. Their fate is no longer the inevitable homecraft, marriage, and children or the nunnery—there are any number of life patterns available. Not only can a girl choose among various types of educational and job opportunities and boyfriends—she has the right to change her mind. Even marriage is usually considered revocable to a certain extent, but motherhood is not. There are former husbands and in-laws, but mothers are mothers "till death do them part." It is not possible to "divorce" a child, and society puts the strongest condemnation on any mother who refuses the unceasing care and responsibility for her child through babyhood to adulthood. In short, pregnancy is the start of a long-term *irrevocable* responsibility that may be particularly hard to accept for the modern woman who has had so much previous freedom to change the other aspects of her life.

Dr. Grete Bibring tells of an expectant mother who put the feeling this way: "I was quite excited last night, quite anxious! It suddenly struck me that I won't be Jeanie much longer but mother forever and ever after!"

Fortunately, regardless of individual hesitations and doubts about pregnancy and the many reasons for it, the pride, wonder, and joy of motherhood usually come to predominate in the long run. Women are the link between the aeons past and the ages to come. It is the process of pregnancy, birth, and mother-care that gives future to the human race and all the cultural heritage it represents. Childbearing can give a deep feeling of basic biological fulfillment.

Most peoples all over the world, even sophisticated Americans living in the materialistic 1970s, recognize, however obliquely, this basic contribution of childbearing women. The woman who is a mother has a special status. Women without children tend to be defensive. Women who have earned the right to be called mother are usually proud of the fact.

But status and preservation of the species are not the only rewards of becoming a mother. Perhaps the deepest satisfaction of all is learning to give of oneself. It is not just that "giving is more blessed than receiving"; giving also yields the deepest and longest lasting satisfaction that human beings can feel. Motherhood is, for most women, a maturing process, bringing out their best by helping to turn their emotions and attention outside themselves and to focus them on the welfare of other human beings. Motherhood fulfills the need to give and the need to be needed.

For most women recognition of the satisfactions of motherhood is not delayed until after the baby arrives. Researchers have repeatedly found a remarkable shift in feelings from negative to positive as pregnancy progresses. One study of sixty-six pregnant women reports that only a few really welcomed pregnancy at the start, and a few continued to regret they were going to have the baby. The great majority of the women—almost two-thirds of them—at first were not particularly pleased about the prospect of the baby, yet as pregnancy progressed they began to want the baby. Another study covers the reaction of thirty Air Force wives who started pregnancy with resentment. Only two of them were unreconciled by the last three months of pregnancy. Even unwed mothers, as pregnancy continues, tend to have a shift in feeling. In one group studied, only about one-third of the unmarried mothers continued to be totally unaccepting of their babies as they approached term.

One crucial time for the shift of feeling toward the baby may come at around the time of quickening—when the mother can begin to feel the baby move. At this time, the interpersonal relationship between mother and baby starts. The baby is clearly alive and separate from her. The baby begins to become a person. It is no doubt easier to love a reacting being than an idea. Then, too, physical changes in the expectant mother may help her to feel more maternal. There is no reason to think that human beings are exempt from the biological drives that influence the motherly behavior of other pregnant mammals. In fact, some obstetricians are almost surprised at how predictably the "nesting urge" begins to show around the middle of pregnancy.

If the idea of having a baby continues to be very upsetting during the *last* two or three months of pregnancy, then a real problem may exist. Sometimes the physical condition may be the cause. When mothers who were healthy in pregnancy were matched with similar mothers who had elevated blood pressure and albumin in their urine or related symptoms, it was found their long-term reactions to the idea of having the baby were quite different. All the healthy mothers got used to the idea as their delivery date approached. The unhealthy ones often remained unreconciled to pregnancy—they felt so strongly, in fact, that some sought abortion or tried to arrange for adoption of the baby.

Emotional health may also be a factor in a continuing resentment of pregnancy. If an expectant mother continues to be upset when she is six or seven months pregnant, it is time to think in terms of discussing her worries with a professional counselor. Her physician can often suggest someone he knows who has been helpful to other expectant mothers with the same sort of problem or he or his nurse may be skilled in providing such help themselves.

EMOTIONAL CHANGES IN PREGNANCY

In human pregnancy emotions and behavior may change as markedly as the shape of the body. The basic tendencies remain the same, but variations and exaggerations of previous behavior can sometimes be expected. There are several reasons for this. First of all, in comparison with the nonpregnant state, the pregnant woman is under the influence of different reproductive hormones. Many women (and their husbands as well) already know from practical experience that the hormonal variations of the menstrual cycle can have a marked effect on behavior.

Then, too, pregnancy places an additional burden on most parts of the body. The weight of carrying the baby is an added strain on muscles; there is need for more blood and more oxygen, and for more nourishment; the kidneys, the heart, the lungs, and even the skin have added burdens. Growing a baby and preparing the body for the stress of childbirth require extra quantities of protein, vitamins, and minerals. The increased physical stress in pregnancy, although often merely challenging to a woman who has maintained good health habits, can be devastating to one already chronically short of sleep, short of exercise, and short of balanced meals.

Along with pregnancy also come changes in day-to-day behavior, and these changes may cause stress. The expectant mother is learning to play a new social role involving greatly increased dependency. Her role is now quite different from that of the unmarried girl or even the married girl who has supported herself in a job to which she has been able to devote most of her energies. A woman late in pregnancy or one with a new baby to care for cannot easily support herself without risking possible harm to the baby. She needs someone else to supply her basic needs for monetary support, while her physical and emotional resources turn toward the baby.

Nor is her new financial need the only dependency of her new role. As her energies go into growing and carrying the increasingly heavy baby within her, she is also physically and emotionally less able "to take care of herself." Adapting to this more dependent role constitutes an emotional stress that comes just when gestation is giving increased bodily stress.

In addition to physical and social stresses, basic psychological shifts may also be under way. Dr. Bibring has pointed out the existence of a developmental crisis in pregnancy of the same sort that is faced by women at the start of menstruation and again at the menopause. The outcome of this emotional crisis of pregnancy, she emphasizes, will be of profound importance to the future psychological health of women. The stresses of gestation appear to cause a disintegration of behavior. This is especially true in our society where many helpful props of traditional societies may be missing. Old conflicts and problems of adjustment that each person normally lives with may become intensified and aggravated in the expectant mother. Unsolved emotional problems with parents and brothers and sisters are likely to reassert themselves. Family conflict may become more intense. In addition, there seems to be a tendency to regress to former patterns of behavior, attitudes, and wishes held when the expectant mother was younger. This time of disequilibrium, in fortunate circumstances, can also be an opportunity for the woman to go on to reorganize herself on a new, more mature level.

Dr. Bibring points out that the relationship between the expectant mother and her own mother is particularly likely to undergo change. The pregnant girl no longer sees her own mother with the same eyes. When successful maturation occurs, the expectant mother begins to develop a "conflict-free, useful identification with the mother as the prototype of a parental figure." The prospect of motherhood may be easier for a girl who admires and likes her own mother and wants to be like her. If the mother-daughter relationship has been a stormy or strained one, the prospect of becoming a mother herself may activate old fears and resentments and make maturation more difficult.

Sexual desires tend to change in pregnancy to some extent, but re-actions are variable and may depend on the period in pregnancy. Mothers carrying their first baby have sometimes noted some lessening of sexual tensions during the first three months of pregnancy. The middle months of pregnancy are often the most active and fatigue-free months, so it is not surprising to see research reports suggesting that the middle months of pregnancy may be sexually active and fulfilling months for many women.

Toward the end of pregnancy there may be a definite waning of sexual feelings in many women. One study of five hundred women found that by the final month of pregnancy half of the women had stopped having sexual relations. Some women stopped coitus quite a bit earlier. On the other hand, a sizable minority continue to report that in pregnancy sexual enjoyment continues undiminished. In fact, one study found that about one in six women reported increased sexual desire in pregnancy. Those continuing sexual relations until a few days before delivery had no more complications of birth than those who stopped early.

The sexual attitudes in pregnancy may find oblique expressions. Some women find it embarrassing to look pregnant. The bulging abdomen announces to the world that sexual relations have taken place. Those who have been brought up with Victorian attitudes toward sexuality may be surprisingly sensitive on this point. Other women growing up with other social traditions more accepting of coital function see the enlarging tummies instead as badges of honor. They are showing their fundamental, wonderful fertility to the world!

Sexual feelings may also be involved in severe cases of nausea and vomiting. Perhaps you have heard it said that a mother who vomits is trying to get rid of her baby symbolically. Newer statistical studies indicate a quite different explanation. Mothers seeking abortions actually appear to vomit less than mothers who are uncertain or of two minds about the prospect of having a baby. Mild cases of temporary queasiness occur in many women, perhaps affecting particularly those who have had a greater tendency to stomach upsets before pregnancy. A dislike of marital relations has been reported in many women who have continuous and serious problems with vomiting in pregnancy. The vomiting may disappear when the woman is admitted to the hospital or when the husband is away. Some writers cite general immaturity as a cause of severe vomiting, but the condition seems too common for this explanation.

Some special guilt feelings may occur in pregnancy. If the baby is interfering with the husband's ambitions, the expectant mother may blame herself for getting pregnant. Then, too, as pregnancy progresses, warm feelings toward the prospective baby tend to become stronger. Girls whose first reaction to pregnancy was strong dislike or attempt at abortion may later feel guilty about these feelings. They might be comforted if they knew how very common their reaction is. In fact, when Dr. P. H. Gebhard and his colleagues questioned a national sample of over five thousand women, they found that actual induced abortions were very common among married women. One in every six reported ending a conception by induced abortion. Unsuccessful attempts at abortion are also very frequent. Interviewing of sixty-six mothers in a prenatal clinic indicated that ten had taken some unsuccessful steps to terminate the pregnancy.

Special food cravings in pregnancy may seem like old wives' tales to some modern girls, but they have been reported by as many as two out of three expectant mothers. Food cravings in pregnancy are not limited to our society. In England a radio program briefly mentioned food cravings in pregnancy, asking for women's experiences. The broadcasters were astonished at the flood of letters telling of real problems with food desires, especially in early pregnancy. Some women reported feeling so ashamed that they had hidden their cravings from their husbands; a few reported desires so strong they were tempted to steal to satisfy them. Food cravings are seen also in primitive societies.

Marked moodiness is often prominent in the psychological changes of pregnancy. One obstetrician had one thousand expectant mothers record their reactions. Six hundred and eighty said that they had crying spells for no apparent reason. Eight hundred and forty reported "blues" lasting more than thirty minutes or occurring more often than once a week. Six hundred and ten described themselves as extremely irritable. Indeed, the pregnant girl who does not cry easily, does not have spells of being blue, and does not think herself irritable may be in the minority.

Feelings of fear, worry, and anxiety are often heightened in pregnancy. General worries, such as money worries, may seem very distressing. But once pregnancy is over, money problems often seem much less troublesome even when the financial situation has not improved. The change in body image bothers some women who have taken pride in their slim shapes. Others fret about what kind of mother they will be—whether they will be able to discharge their new responsibilities adequately. Some women observe a decrease in intellectuality in themselves and resent this.

Fear of nervous breakdown may be quite common in pregnancy. One recent study found this feeling reported in one out of every three expectant mothers. The same study found that the most frequent psychosomatic complaint of expectant mothers was "feeling tired in the morning."

Then there is also a group of more concrete worries, some of which have been catalogued. Here, for instance, is a list of worries expressed by more than half of a group of married women attending a prenatal clinic and expecting their first babies:

> Pregnancy not intended
> Worried about getting too fat
> Frightened by doctors about getting too fat
> Afraid pain will be bad
> Afraid of being cut or torn at birth
> Afraid fall will hurt baby
> Difficulty sleeping

Some of the other common worries were as follows:

> Frightened by babies' movement
> Disliked certain foods
> Worry about figure changing
> Shortness of breath

No sexual desire
Fear sex will hurt baby
Fear sex will lead to loss of baby
Husband thinks sex will lead to loss of baby
Afraid baby will die before birth
Afraid baby will not be normal
Afraid of bleeding during pregnancy
Frightened by bleeding during pregnancy
Frightened by someone about having a baby
Worried that doctor might not be friendly

The readers of this guide will immediately recognize that many of the worries expressed by these mothers could be alleviated by finding out the facts and discussing them with others whose judgment they respect. Talking over a worry or fear helps to get it in the open and clearly thought out. New viewpoints and information can be obtained, and often through discussion with others some practical plan of action develops to help alleviate the problem.

The expectant mother who has previously experienced labor and delivery may want to think about her experience and analyze whether her fears of another labor are realistic. First labors are usually the longest labors, and familiarity with the hospital routines will help the experienced mother feel more relaxed. It may be possible to be anxious about the experience of a previous labor and delivery even if it is not fully remembered. The drug scopolamine, frequently given during labor in some hospitals, does cause memory blackouts when the woman "wakes up," but some memory trace of the labor experience appears to linger. Sometimes the first birth experience is "remembered" con- sciously during the second labor when the mother is under a lighter dose of the same drug.

It is sad that the woman who has experienced labor and delivery may sometimes be just as worried about having her next baby as the woman who has not had the experience, but research indicates this to be the fact. A wholesome satisfying experience should mitigate fear. Fortu- nately, there are now many hospitals and physicians especially con- cerned about giving the woman a good experience from the emotional point of view, as well as caring for her physically.

The cataloging of worries, moods, and adjustment problems of preg- nancy should not make one lose sight of the eventual goal—a new human being and a satisfying parenthood. True, the impact of pregnancy does call for new ways of acting and does impose physical strain as well. Nevertheless, human beings are not only remarkably well equipped to resist the normal stresses of reproduction (as our long survival as a mammalian species testifies) but are also uniquely capable of learning new habits and new concepts quickly and easily. The strains of pregnancy, for most parents, become minor compared to the subsequent satisfactions of parenthood.

In fact, the basic adequacy of many American couples in adapting to their babies is suggested by an extensive research project headed by Dr. Virginia Larsen. After studying couples as they went through their first and third pregnancies, the following basic conclusion was reached: "The greatest single impression of the parents in this study is that they were doing a superb job in adjusting to their first and third babies. . . . Parents in this study, with few exceptions, appeared responsible, loving and flexible."

EXPERIMENTALLY TESTED ADVICE

Most advice given to parents is not scientifically validated, in the strict experimental sense. Suggestions are usually based on current customs, on scientific theories, and on practical everyday experience gathered through working with childbearing women. Such advice has been and will continue to be helpful to expectant parents. Of even greater importance, however, is information that is the result of experimental tests. Advice based on such tests can be accepted with an extra measure of confidence because it is derived from controlled experimental studies that can give clear indications of actual cause and effect.

There are two great experiments that expectant parents especially need to know about. One is in the field of physical health and the other is in the field of mental health. The first one was done at the University of Toronto by J. H. Ebbs and his coworkers, F. F. Tisdall and W. A. Scott. They studied the effect of giving extra food to impoverished mothers who had been on poor diets.

Every other mother was assigned to a special program of receiving added foods. Every day each of these mothers had thirty ounces of milk, one egg, and one orange delivered to her home. Once a week she received, in addition, two one-pound cans of tomatoes and one-half a pound of cheddar cheese. When she came to the clinic, she was given a special palatable dried wheat germ with malt and iron and was urged to take two tablespoonsful daily. Vitamin D capsules were supplied also. The expectant mothers were advised in detail about using the extra food, and were also instructed on how to fill out the nutritional requirements of their diets with foods that could be bought with the family income, small as it might be.

The other poor-diet, low-income mothers were not so fortunate. They were left on their usual diets with no attempt made to change them. To offset the possible psychological factor in pill giving, they did get capsules with plain corn oil instead of the capsules containing vitamin D.

Strenuous efforts were made to make sure that the supplemented group of mothers actually did receive a different diet in keeping with experimental plans. Home visits were made by social workers to look into the use of donated foods. At the time of delivery, chemical blood tests revealed the results of the difference in diets. The vitamin C level of the blood was much higher for the supplemented mothers than for those left on their poor diets.

The differences in the health of the mothers and babies in the two groups was startling. The obstetrician who rated the mothers' progress did not know to which group the mothers belonged. Yet four times as many of the poor-diet mothers were considered to have serious health problems in pregnancy when compared to the mothers whose diets were supplemented with extra nutritious foods. The poor-diet group had seven times as many threatened miscarriages and three times as many stillbirths. Their labors were recorded as lasting about five hours longer. After delivery they had almost twice as many breast infections, three times as many uterine infections, and were much more likely to stop breast-feeding early.

Definite psychological changes were also observed. The researchers state, "We noted a marked improvement in the general mental attitude of the patients in the Supplemented Group; many of them lost their minor aches and pains and no longer had numerous complaints."

The babies were followed for six months after delivery. The babies whose mothers had the food supplements appeared to have benefited even more than their mothers did from nutritional changes experimentally introduced. Babies of poor-diet mothers had more bronchitis, pneumonia, rickets, and anemia. Less than a quarter as many babies whose mothers had received supplemental foods were reported as being subject to "frequent colds." It was in the poor-diet group that the only deaths occurred.

No one experiment gives final proof of anything. In this experiment all psychological influences were not ruled out. While the extra food did introduce physical changes by improving the diet, the gift of food as a symbol of human concern behind the giving would also be likely to have emotional repercussion. Nevertheless, the differences in physical health between the poor-diet group and those receiving extra foods were so great that differences in psychology seem inadequate to account for them. Improved nutrition seems to make a really important difference to the well-being of mother and baby alike. This is one of the most important pieces of advice for any expectant parent.

Just what foods should be added to the expectant mother's diet will depend, of course, on the mother's current habits of eating. There are, unfortunately, many affluent mothers who put themselves on poverty-level diets by snacking on sweets, starch tidbits, and soft drinks instead of eating well-balanced meals at regular intervals through the day. The Toronto experiment suggests such mothers have a very good chance of impairing their own health as well as the health of the baby.

The second remarkable experiment concerning advice to parents is in the field of mental health. Dr. Richard E. Gordon, a psychiatrist in a New York City suburb, and his wife, Katherine K. Gordon, were distressed at the large number of mothers who were having emotional difficulties after the birth of their babies. The Gordons studied some of these mothers carefully and compiled extensive statistical tabulations. They wanted to find out what types of stresses these mothers experienced that differentiated them from other mothers. On the basis of their findings about these problems, the Gordons then formulated some helpful practical advice.

The Gordons did not stop there; they decided to take a further scientific step. They decided to test the value of their advice experimentally. They included two instruction periods containing this advice in a program of regular classes for expectant parents. The parents who had this practical advice were then compared with other parents who were attending the same type of prenatal classes but were not taught the Gordons' material.

The parents who studied the Gordons' material not only changed their behavior to avoid some stresses of parenthood, but also had significantly fewer emotional problems after birth. The effects of the instruction were still noticeable six months after delivery. At this time, the babies of the specially taught mothers were significantly less irritable and had fewer disorders related to sleep or feeding.

Here is the advice the Gordons gave to the experimental groups of expectant patients. It deserves special weight because the Gordons have been able to show that parents receiving this advice got along demonstrably better after the birth of their babies—and so incidentally did their babies.

The words in italics are quoted directly from the Gordons' instruction sheets that were used to teach the experimental groups. The instructions in regular type follow the Gordons' advice but restate it in condensed form. The Gordons explain that parents have to learn how to care for babies, and how to fit babies into their own lives, just as they have to learn to manage at college or on the job. In our society emphasis is on "getting ahead" rather than on the arts of homemaking and baby care. Expectant parents who have had little experience with children may not understand how to go about their new duties and reorganize their own lives.

The Gordons made these basic points:

1. *Get help and advice.* Turn to experienced mothers who can give assistance, advice, and on-the-job training. Grandmothers, relatives, older sisters, grandmothers-in-law, and experienced friends can help. It is not their formal education that counts; it is practical knowledge of baby care and home management combined with love and understanding.

2. *Include husband.* Babies keep women more confined to the home. They are partly cut off from many of the stimulating contacts they once enjoyed. Giving up jobs and moving to new neighborhoods away from families intensifies the problem. The husband has a real responsibility to help his wife adjust to this new situation, seeing that she has the needed companionship, rest, and free time. In order to take on these duties he may have to cut down on some of his usual activities, such as organization work or night school. It is also, however, good to remember that a husband's primary responsibility is that of breadwinner. Most couples feel happier and more secure when they are getting ahead in the world.

3. *Learn to be a mother, not a martyr.* Motherhood is a matter of learning and experience. At first the baby needs feeding, cleaning, and cuddling on a twenty-four-hour basis. Then, too, there are new household duties. Work toward developing a regular routine that will make housekeeping easy. Before the baby comes, talk to others who have developed such a system. Collect ideas on how to manage homemaking

routines. Housewives are expected to make independent decisions about children, repairmen, landlords, and others. These decisions call for more self-confidence and more self-assertiveness than the young mother may previously have shown. Help and advice from her husband and family can enable her to learn without intolerable strain.

4. *Make friends.* If you move into a new neighborhood far away from family and older friends, you will miss companionship. The period before the baby is expected is a good time to work on making new friends. Joining church groups or other organizations can bring you into contact with other persons of similar interests. Neighborhood kaffeeklatsches and mothers' clubs can be helpful. Look for friends with young children, who can share your interests. It is the wife especially who may be cut off from easy social contacts. When cut off from others, she may become confused and begin to doubt herself and her value.

5. *Don't overload yourself.* After the baby is born, it takes a while to get back your strength. Take a cue from how you feel. Rest when you feel tired. Make a point of getting a little relaxation, a cup of coffee with the neighbors, or some other refreshing break. It is good to keep up participation in group activities, but beware of agreeing to take offices or chairmanships or shouldering other major responsibilities when there are young children in the house.

6. *Don't move.* It is natural to think of more space as the family grows but the extra strains of moving had best be postponed until the baby is about six months old. If moving is unavoidable, get to know the new neighborhood well before the baby comes. Learning about the services available in the new neighborhood, as well as making new friends and acquaintances before the baby arrives, can be helpful.

7. *Don't be house proud.* A wife with a new baby and little help cannot be expected to maintain her house as tidily as before. Husbands who dream of a *House and Garden* home may have a surprise, unless they want to start doing some of the work or can hire a maid.

8. *Get rest and sleep.* The need for extra rest and sleep may hang on for many weeks after the return home from the hospital. A regular afternoon nap is recommended. Difficulty with the baby or postdelivery complications in the mother may sap energy. It is helpful to have someone dependable on hand in the first weeks after the mother is home and also someone who can be called on in emergencies for some time after that.

9. *Don't be a nurse.* A new baby is enough of a nursing responsibility for a mother. Arrangements should be made for the care of elderly or

invalid relatives. Let others than the mother with a young baby be responsible. This is not a common problem, but when it occurs, it can result in serious overstrain for the mother.

10. *Line up sitters.* Try to line up experienced and reliable sitters. Once the baby arrives, outings need to be planned in advance. Sometimes friends or neighborhood groups make arrangements to swap baby-sitting.

11. *Get a doctor before you need him.* An advance visit to your chosen pediatrician or family doctor before the baby arrives helps to build confidence.

12. *Learn to drive.* It is easier to get around with a baby if you know how to drive yourself.

13. *Don't give up interests.* Monotony can be a problem for the mother who has developed broad interests and tastes through higher education, responsible jobs, or social and community activities. Put thought on the problem of how to reorganize the work, errands, and daily schedule so that time is available for some outside interest.

14. *Discuss worries.* Helpful information can often be obtained by talking about baby care, home management, and other problems with friends and family. Serious discussion of problems can help a person to formulate sensible plans for meeting them. In years past the roles of women and men were more clearly differentiated, but now in a world where families are small and move often, husbands and wives depend more on each other for discussion and sharing home, community, and financial responsibilities. Individuals who have had family difficulties in the past may have their fears stirred by the prospect of a child. Repeated discussion of past problems with relatives, friends, and experienced advisers can help give new insight into reasons for past difficulties and help to avoid future ones.

You will probably agree that these fourteen points, besides being experimentally validated, represent practical common sense. You may find it helpful to reread them every month or two for a while until you are thoroughly familiar with your new role of parent. And while you are considering measures to avoid the social stresses of childbearing, it is well worthwhile to remember too that many physical stresses can be eased by making sure you have nutritious food during pregnancy. There is a great deal you can do as an individual to make childbearing easier and more enjoyable.

PSYCHOPHYSICAL ASPECTS OF LABOR

The interaction of emotions and pain in labor is well explained by Dr. F. W. Dershimer, who, three decades ago, made these fundamental observations about birth in the *American Journal of Obstetrics and Gynecology.*

> All other physiological functions such as eating, coitus, defecation, and so on are naturally pleasant and easy . . . The usual ease with which they naturally occur may be completely destroyed by the development in the individual of certain emotional attitudes in connection with them. Analogy suggests that labor should be naturally pleasant and easy, and when it is not, the common cause of a similar state affecting other functions should be taken as the most likely cause until proven otherwise . . . Society in general makes every possible effort to prevent the pregnant woman from accepting pregnancy and labor as a natural physiologic function. The same amount of attention to eating would make most of us have nervous indigestion.

Even today most women have "nervous indigestion" at the prospect of labor. To help them, psychophysical methods of pain control have been developed.

You may have heard the term *natural childbirth* and know of the famous work of Dr. Grantly Dick-Read, who insisted that childbirth was meant to be a satisfying experience. The work of Dr. Fernand Lamaze and his psychoprophylactic school of obstetrics, which emphasizes childbirth without pain, is also becoming increasingly known. There are some variations between the two methods, but the principles on which they operate are the same.

Basically, both natural childbirth and psychoprophylaxis take cognizance of what is known about pain and apply it to the problem of making birth a good experience—an event so deeply satisfying that the mother does not wish or need to be "blacked out" by heavy doses of medication and anesthesia.

Pain is a psychosomatic phenomenon. It flourishes with fatigue, loneliness, fear, tension, and bodily dysfunction. Pain is heightened when there is an expectation of pain and dulled when attention is diverted to other matters and when the person is convinced that the pain will not be severe. Psychosomatic methods of pain control aim at controlling the pain in labor by trying to eliminate, as much as possible, the conditions that tend to heighten the feeling of pain.

The principles of psychophysical methods of pain control in labor are:

1. *Knowledge lessens fear.* If you were walking through a park after dark and you suddenly felt a tap on your back, you might have a violent emotional physical reaction. The tap would seem harder than it really was and your body likely would become tense all over. The same tap on the back delivered when you were among friends at a party would probably result in your turning with a friendly smile and relaxed body. Psychosomatic methods of pain control in labor emphasize the importance of familiarity, knowledge, and understanding of the events of childbearing as a method of helping mothers to experience the sensations of birth in a relaxed manner. Information is given through lectures and class discussion, through tours of the hospital delivery suite, and through reading and viewing of films. Actual physical practice of comfortable labor and delivery positions and the type of breathing useful in labor helps to build the familiarity of knowing what to do before it happens.

2. *Emotional support from a concerned person.* Psychosomatic methods of pain control emphasize the importance of going through labor not alone but with someone who really cares—husband, mother, or sympathetic attendant who specializes in helping women in labor. Until rather recently, most deliveries took place in the home, where relatives gave the special friendly loving that a laboring woman needs. When psychosomatic methods of pain control are used in labor, every effort is made to give the laboring woman a companion of the type she might have had in a home delivery. Such a companion can cheer her up by saying encouraging, pleasant things to her, helping her to get into a comfortable position, and reminding her to remember to bulge her abdomen during contractions or to breathe in a special way. When the discomfort is centered in the back, a strong friendly hand pushing on the sore spot can often be a real help.

3. *An environment that is especially pleasant and relaxing.* When psychosomatic methods of pain control are used, the delivery suite is made to look as homelike as possible. If possible, each woman has her own labor room so she will not be disturbed by others. Some hospitals have sitting rooms where women in early labor can play cards and watch TV. Other hospitals have convertible chair-beds for husbands to sleep on in their wives' labor rooms.

The pleasant relaxing environment depends on people as well as things. The delivery suite personnel in hospitals specializing in psychosomatic methods of pain control make extra efforts to treat the patients gently and with courtesy, explaining the need for the various medical procedures. The doctor, aware that his patient feels more relaxed when he is nearby, is in the hospital as much of the time as possible while his patient is in labor.

4. *Avoiding bodily dysfunction that may contribute to pain.* Psychosomatic methods of pain control require attention to correcting bodily dysfunction. During pregnancy special emphasis is placed on building physical fitness to withstand stress. Unusual positions and sudden exercise result in aches and pain for almost everybody. Exercises in pregnancy may help to prevent the usual aches and pains that may come from the sudden use in labor of muscles seldom exercised.

The use of efficient positions can also improve muscular action in labor, and thus make labor proceed more easily. Backrests and triangular pillows are placed behind the backs of women using psychosomatic methods of pain control during second stage labor to help their expulsion mechanisms work more efficiently. From the point of view of mechanics, trying to push out a baby with a flat back is like trying to push out a bowel movement on a bedpan while lying flat in bed. A little curvature adds greatly to comfort and efficiency.

5. *Distraction is used as a shield against pain.* Have you ever heard of a man being knifed and not knowing it for a while because he was concentrating on fighting back? A more ordinary event, illustrating the same phenomenon, has perhaps happened to us all. Pain seems most bothersome when we are resting or at night or other times when we are not occupied. A busy person's mind is concentrating on something else; less discomfort is felt.

This principle works in childbirth too. Psychosomatic methods of pain control involve deliberately distracting the patient's attention by giving her something else to do. A radio and a rocking chair and pleasant conversation with a companion may help through early labor. Later on, counter-stimulations, such as a hot water bottle placed on the lower abdomen, may be used. Concentrating on labor breathing techniques also may help to keep attention focused away from the physical sensations.

6. *Using suggestion to lessen perception of pain.* The millions of dollars a year spent on advertising testify to the fact that most people are influenced by suggestion. Psychosomatic methods of pain control in labor try to build in the mother's mind the expectation of joy and satisfaction in the experience of labor. Some discomfort in labor is a

reality for most women. Nevertheless, conscious participation in the female destiny of birth can be so deeply satisfying to some women that the discomfort seems minor compared with the reward.

Psychosomatic methods shield women from having negative suggestions concerning labor that can increase pain. Uterine contractions are called what they are—contractions, not "labor pains." It is perfectly possible to have uterine contractions in labor that are in no way painful. Efforts are made to keep women in conscious labor away from the sight and sound of heavily drugged women acting out their fears.

Perhaps the most potent positive suggestions concerning labor come from talking to friends or prenatal class teachers who have been through the full experience of conscious labor and can honestly report back, "It wasn't really so bad—and what a joy to be there when the baby came!"

You may have heard of hypnosis for labor pain. Hypnosis uses magnified suggestions; the woman is actually convinced she is not feeling pain. Hypnosis in labor has worked for many women, but the obstetricians who use hypnosis often emphasize other psychosomatic methods of pain control as well. Hypnosis is not as predictable as other methods. A woman can be jarred out of her hypnotic state by upsetting treatment in the hospital.

The reduction of pain in labor does not depend *entirely* on the use of psychosomatic methods of pain control. The physical status of the mother is certainly a factor. Also of real importance is the basic attitude toward childbearing she has learned from her family while growing up.

Feelings about birth are interwoven with feelings about breast-feeding and early baby care. Some years ago, the reactions of women after delivery were analyzed statistically in the book *Maternal Emotions* by Niles Newton. All the mothers interviewed had a rooming-in system of hospital care; the babies were kept with them instead of in the nursery. The women who felt birth was a bad experience tended to complain about having to look after babies and wanted to feed by bottle. In contrast, mothers who felt birth was easy tended to want to nurse their babies and enjoyed caring for them in the hospital.

But mothers' attitudes are only part of the picture. Recent experimental work shows that any disturbances in labor and the environment for labor have a profound effect on the course of reproduction in experimental animals. Because the mechanisms governing the action of the uterus appear to be similar for all mammals, what happens to frightened mice in labor quite possibly can happen to frightened human beings too.

Breeders and veterinarians have long emphasized the importance of keeping mammalian mothers quiet and peaceful during labor. Obstetricians often note a slowing down of labor as women are moved from home to hospital and from labor room to delivery room. The team of Drs. Donald Foshee, Dudley Peeler, Michael Newton, and Niles Newton put these observations to actual experimental test on mice. The details of these experiments are available in *Science* and in obstetrical journals, but the general findings can be of interest to parents seeking to know about the broader aspects of childbearing.

In the first experiment the team decided to see what would happen if mice in labor were disturbed. After each mouse's second pup was born, the mother mouse was picked up and gently held in cupped hands for a minute. Then the time it took to have the next pup was measured. The labor of other mice that were not handled was timed also. The labors of the undisturbed mice were much shorter. The next mouse pups of undisturbed mothers arrived in about twelve minutes, while the mice disturbed in labor took about twenty minutes to deliver.

The team wondered also what would happen if mice were disturbed just before labor began and kept disturbed throughout labor. The disturbance was really quite gentle. Just a few hours before delivery expectant mice were placed in glass fishbowls carrying the odor of cat urine. Others were placed in cages like the ones in which they had grown up. They were also given fluffy absorbent rayon that they could crawl under to "get away from it all."

The mice in the glass bowls delayed delivery of their first pups. It took them an average of more than four hours longer for their first pups to appear. This is quite a difference in time in relation to mouse pregnancy, which lasts only around nineteen days in all. The human equivalent would be about fifty-six hours of delay.

The slowing of labor by fear may actually help the reproducing female to survive. If she is able to delay labor until she is in a relatively safe place, the subhuman mammalian female living in the wild may be more likely to escape being eaten by predators. Probably the same was true of early human females.

It is because of the sensitivity of the mammalian female to her environment that the surroundings can be important in childbirth. In human terms this means it may be worth an extra effort, and even higher medical expenses, to develop maternity care that is not only skilled in obstetrical procedure but also in psychophysical methods of managing labor, with the emphasis on calmness, privacy, and friendliness.

Is it unrealistic to expect birth to be a glowing, totally wonderful experience? Many American hospitals currently are seeking to develop more psychologically oriented labor procedures, but change comes slowly. It is only in a few places in the United States that labors with full use of psychophysical methods of pain control take place. These techniques are new to many physicians. Even if they express interest in natural childbirth or Lamaze method deliveries, they may not fully utilize psychophysical methods of pain control. Then, too, many American women, when their time comes, may prefer to have some drugs. All their lives they may have avoided discomfort, taking a painkiller for each little ache or disagreeable sensation. The frequent use of medication is a national habit that tends to persist in labor.

The value of the psychophysical methods of pain control is *not* that they *eliminate* pharmacological methods of pain control for most American women, but that they *minimize* them so that both mother and baby are subjected to less stress from medication. Labors that have been managed with a special sensitivity to the emotional needs of women may also leave a pleasanter memory and a feeling of greater enjoyment.

AFTER DELIVERY

Under the modern American customs of postdelivery care, the average American baby becomes completely independent of his mother as soon as he is born. Once the cord is cut, his nourishment usually stops coming from his mother and comes instead from a cow via the bottle. Along with this nutritional independence comes separateness in other ways. He spends most of his time out of touch, sight, and smell of his mother, and sometimes out of hearing too. Even for those moments when the mother holds her baby, close skin contact is usually prevented by clothing.

In contrast, most of the babies born a hundred years ago had an entirely different experience. They were kept within sight and sound of their mothers most of the time. The body that brought them nourishment while unborn continued to feed them by producing mother's milk. The baby's body and the mother's body kept a steady interaction going. The baby's sucking and hungry noises brought about a remarkable change in the mother's body. Her nipples came erect. Her pituitary gland released the hormone oxytocin, which acted on her breasts to help push out the milk through the "letdown" reflex. This same hormone also caused her uterus to contract rhythmically during sucking. The baby's body responded in a similarly total manner. Along with the rhythm of sucking, rhythmic motions of hands, feet, fingers, and toes occurred. A happy feeding time ended with both mother and baby relaxed and satisfied.

The question is being asked more and more whether this close physical interaction of baby and mother in breast-feeding made any difference in the way the mother treated the baby in other areas of child care. There is no way to find a sure experimental answer to this question because we cannot order some human mothers to nurse their babies while we stop other mothers from doing so. Dr. Dudley Peeler and the author did test this question using female mice. The nipples were surgically removed from one group of the mice and a different operation performed on a second group to subject them to somewhat the same trauma but without interfering with their ability to nurse. Then all the mice were bred to have litters about the same time. The mice were put in cages in pairs after giving birth to their pups. Each cage contained a mouse without nipples and a mouse with nipples and eight adoptive pups belonging to neither of them.

On following days each pair of mice was subjected to various tests of maternal behavior. Their behavior was very much alike, although only one in each pair was capable of nursing. Both the dry mouse and the mouse giving milk used the same nesting area as the pups and carried the pups back to the nest when they were scattered about. It was only when barriers were put between the mother mice and their adoptive pups that major differences were noted. The nursing mouse made much more strenuous and prolonged efforts to be in physical contact with the young, even to the point of undergoing severe electric shocks to do so.

Exploring this finding further, Dr. Carolyn Rawlins, an obstetrician, and the author studied the behavior of nursing and nonnursing human mothers toward their babies. To make the nursing and nonnursing mothers as nearly comparable as possible in other ways, pairs were matched. Each pair was similar in regard to years of education and number of children and age of the baby. One member of each pair was nursing her baby without the use of solid food or formula while the other one was using no breast milk at all. The nursing and nonnursing mothers acted about the same toward their babies in some ways. Only a few of them spanked their babies. Most of them stayed in the same building with their babies most of the time. The majority of both breast and bottle babies were held a half hour a day or longer when not eating.

Still, one major difference did appear. Seventy-one percent of the nursing mothers reported they sometimes or often rested in bed with the baby, whereas only 26 percent of the mothers giving formula reported this type of cuddling. The nursing human mothers, like the nursing mouse mothers, may have a special drive to have extra physical closeness with their young.

The idea that close contact between mother and baby is not the "natural way" arose in the United States, mostly within this century. Nineteenth-century hospitals placed the babies by the bedsides of even quite seriously sick mothers. Rooming-in went out of fashion only at the beginning of the twentieth century, when feedings regulated by time rather than by the baby's behavior became popular. The first attempts to make schedules were based on the physician's observations of the usual manner of infant feeding. Thus, Dr. T. S. Southworth, in a standard pediatric textbook of 1906, recommended ten nursings a day for most of the first month, eight a day for the second and third months, seven a day for the fourth and fifth months. Cutting out the night feeding by the sixth month was suggested, and about six feedings a day were prescribed for the rest of the first year. Such a large number of nursings represents a great deal more mother-baby interaction than even most breast-fed babies get nowadays. Since sucking stimulates milk production, it is easy to see why the majority of mothers at the turn of the century had an abundance of milk. With night feedings continuing over the first half year, mothers tended to sleep nearer their babies and probably often with them in large double beds—built for cuddling.

Recently there has been a trend to restore some of the closeness between mothers and babies, without interfering with the newest techniques of modern medicine. At some hospitals babies are placed in their mothers' rooms. Since the modern mother often does not feel up to round-the-clock responsibility for her baby right after delivery, a modified rooming-in system has evolved. Mothers can have their babies at the bedside when they want them, while at other times the infants are cared for in a nursery. Just as in the case of psychophysical methods of pain control, hospital routines are not easy to change, and most American hospitals today still require routine separation of mother and baby. It is well worth the extra effort to try to find a hospital that does permit mother and baby to be close to each other when both are in good health and anxious to be together.

How much the current systems of mother and baby care influence what is called "after baby blues" is not known. Many mothers several days after delivery go through a period of feeling weepy and discouraged. Sometimes this blue period does not occur at all, sometimes it is delayed until the time a breast-fed baby is weaned. But for many American mothers it comes so regularly after delivery that it is to be expected as quite usual.

There is a feeling of anticlimax about it all. Months and months of waiting and planning and then it is all over, and the baby, although cute, is quite a responsibility too! It is natural to react with spells of being blue, especially if one is not yet fully recovered from the physical effects of childbirth. Some mothers may have headaches, feel irritable, or have difficulty relaxing. Fatigue is a prominent part of the picture. Getting started in the morning is difficult, and any little activity brings on fatigue. Studies done at Stanford suggest that mothers having their first child, mothers having difficult labors and deliveries, and mothers with the greatest discomfort in the postdelivery period may be the most likely to feel depression.

Episodes of crying are particularly frequent in the period immediately after birth. One detailed study of thirty-nine women indicates that in the first ten days after delivery two out of three had spells of crying lasting at least five minutes. Many of these mothers, puzzled by their own behavior, declared that crying was quite uncharacteristic of them. The crying often seemed to be triggered by a feeling of "increased vulnerability" or "hypersensitivity to possible rejection." Some cried because they felt they had not received enough attention from their doctors on rounds or in the labor room. Others overreacted to their husbands' being a few minutes late or making some seemingly two-edged remark. Some women wept when husbands or roommate left them at the hospital. Others wept from anger at not getting enough help and consideration. Some cried for no discernible reason.

These transient feelings of depression and upset are so common that they should not worry you. As time goes on most mothers feel better. Then, too, it has been shown that efforts to avoid social stress (as outlined by the Gordons, see pages 21–23) help to achieve a calmer and happier postdelivery period. A very few mothers, especially those who have had previous mental health problems, may go on to have more serious problems after the birth of the baby. If depression and crying spells keep on for a long period of time, especially if they are accompanied by real trouble with insomnia, it is best to talk it over with your physician. A little extra help from a psychiatrist at this time may be desirable.

Another problem that some new mothers are troubled with is the fact that mother love does not come all at once with the rush they expect. It takes a while for most mothers to establish basic trust and familiarity and a modus vivendi with their babies. To be sure, it is possible to "fall in love" in an instant, but a sound relationship between two people usually takes a while to develop. In this respect the relationship between mother and baby is like other relationships. When you have had the baby home with you for a while, and have begun to get to know him as a person, and as you take over the day-to-day care of him, you will probably find your love growing tremendously.

Sometimes the baby is so different from what the mother dreamed about and anticipated that it takes a while to become accustomed. Some mothers and some babies are just born different types of people with different rhythms of living. In these cases there is need for more time to adapt and adjust.

Then, too, there may be real physical reasons within the baby that make the early mother-baby relationship difficult. Recently, excessive crying and movement have been observed in babies whose mothers had intensive psycho-active drug therapy during pregnancy. This problem proved temporary. Certain types of medication given in labor may also interfere with the baby's ability to suck for as long as four days after birth. Mothers of such babies need not feel rejected: the refusal to nurse is not a personal matter and will clear up in time.

Even at the very beginning of the relationship, most mothers are far more loving than they realize. Marian Gennaria Morris, in an article in *Trans-action,* has described those mothers who experience real difficulties in their feelings about their children. Perhaps a listing of the combination of behavior traits in these disturbed mothers will convince you that your feelings of doubt about the baby are far from fundamental. These mothers see many aspects of their babies as revolting. They are disgusted by the drooling or the sucking noises or the smell. The mother may let the baby's head dangle, bobbing about without support, and may tend to hold the baby away from her own body instead of close. The mother may worry about the baby's natural relaxation after feeding, and may play with him roughly at this time, even to a point of inducing vomiting. She may not talk or make noises to the baby, and may tend to avoid eye contact. Women having these difficulties often imagine that their babies do not love them and are judging them. They are likely to react strongly to mild disorders in the baby, fearing death or dreadful diseases such as leukemia. They do not see in the baby a single physical trait or facet of personality that they value in themselves.

In contrast, when a satisfactory mother-baby relationship exists, the mother finds pleasure in her baby. Although she may have spells when she resents the constant care, by and large she enjoys being with and caring for her baby. She gradually learns to sense when he is tired, to respond when he is hungry, and to comfort him when he is upset. She does not force too much food or stimulation on him but neither does she supply less than is desired. It takes a while for a new mother to learn the techniques of baby care, but this is natural. When the total picture is one of general enjoyment, the feelings of annoyance, although they sometimes occur, are not serious. An easy responsive relationship, deeply satisfying to both mother and baby, develops.

FATHERS, FAMILIES, AND ADVISERS

So far we have been concentrating on the problems and challenges of childbearing women. In fact, of course, it has been millions of years since reproduction depended on a single individual. Bisexual reproduction is a fundamental biological pattern, and the more complex the organism the greater the interdependence. Homo sapiens has extensive methods of sharing the work of successful reproduction.

In the process of having their children women receive four types of help. First, of course, the help of the male is needed to achieve fertilization. The second type of help, which is also common to many other species, is protection of reproducing females. In particular, the male is often physically equipped to be a more effective fighter, and therefore better able to defend against attackers. The female in turn specializes in gestation, lactation, and maternal care. The burden of reproductive survival is thus shared between male and female in a cooperative way.

The other two types of help given reproducing females appear to be more highly developed in man than in other primates. Human society arranges to give considerable economic help to women physically handicapped by childbearing and child caring. This help is offered in a variety of ways: perhaps sharing hunted food, or having the pregnant woman return to the food supplies of the grandmother, or supplementing her income from government payments. The most common current procedure is to have a male take care of the financial needs of the female and her young.

Still another type of help is needed. Not only does the childbearing woman need money to pay for food and shelter, but around the time of delivery she needs personal assistance, especially if she has older children to worry about. There is need too for help with the usual household chores when late pregnancy and early mothering make the physical performance of these tasks more difficult. Little acts of helpfulness at this time give more than physical assistance. Such actions also give emotional support at a time when the mother is giving a great deal of herself to the new life within her or just born.

When wider family groups stayed in one community and lived near each other, special personal assistance to the childbearing woman was taken for granted. It simply was the thing to do for the women in the family to give help to the pregnant woman and the one burdened with a little baby or many young children. Now, unfortunately, many young reproducing couples find themselves far away from the people who traditionally would give help. They may not even have close friends to turn to. Older female relatives often have full-time jobs that cannot easily be dropped to help daughter, daughter-in-law, or niece. For this reason, the father has additional responsibilities thrust on him. He not only fertilizes, protects, and gives economic support, but increasingly he is called upon to supply the personal assistance and emotional support once given by female relatives.

Many men are responding with an increased interest in the whole process of childbearing. They attend classes during their wives' pregnancies to hear about the physical and emotional aspects of pregnancy, and about labor and the early postdelivery period. Most men enjoy being with their wives in early labor, when the hospital makes them feel welcome. Some men also like to share with their wives the experience of birth. They sit at the head of the delivery table and have the same view of delivery as their wives. Even experienced doctors and nurses often feel a special thrill as a new life comes into the world: the ancient and fundamental drama of birth can have a tremendous emotional impact on the husband seeing the birth of his own child. Such an experience can help him to identify with the wife and baby so that he is more able to give them the solicitous care they need during the especially vulnerable months ahead.

Only a minority of American men, however, wish to participate totally in birth in this way. A study coming from a hospital specializing in family-centered maternity care—St. Mary's Hospital in Evansville—found that most men like being with their wives in early labor and are enthusiastic about being allowed to visit with their babies at their wives' bedsides in the days after delivery. When it came to accompanying their wives into the delivery room, however, about six out of every ten men felt they should not be there. Fathers who do wish the experience will have to seek out a hospital and obstetrician who will permit fathers in the delivery room. Great variations of hospital rules exist. Many obstetricians oppose having fathers accompany their wives, while a few especially encourage it.

The male may feel the impact of parenthood early in the wife's pregnancy. A study of British expectant fathers reported a variety of symptoms beginning about the third month of pregnancy. The complaints included loss of appetite, toothache, and nausea, and afflicted about one in ten expectant fathers. Occasionally, more serious mental symptoms are reported to occur, triggered by the wife's pregnancy.

These reactions of industrialized man to pregnancy are not surprising when it is considered how frequently the custom of couvade is found. In the primitive societies where this custom is followed, the husband takes to his bed before delivery of the wife, subjects himself to various taboos, and goes through simulations of the pangs of childbirth. Among primitive peoples in many parts of the world, the father of the baby is expected to act differently from other men at the time of confinement. The rituals vary, but the symbolism appears to have the same meaning. Basically, this custom indicates the potential for the human male to feel strongly about birth and all it entails. It shows a capacity to identify with the mother and the whole childbearing process.

New expectant fathers, as well as mothers, need special consideration. The physical impact of childbearing falls on the mother, but the economic impact falls mainly on the father. This is a tremendous responsibility for the conscientious middle-class male of modern American society. His success or failure as an individual man and as a member of society is judged in large measure on how well he provides for his children and his wife who bears them. Often it now happens that not until pregnancy does the young man have to rely totally on his own work for support. Parents help during his years of education, and a working wife may contribute. Now he may simultaneously become a father and the sole support of a family. The increased responsibility requires major adjustment. In addition to his increased economic responsibilities, the young husband may find his expectant wife more demanding. Subject to many of the emotional stresses discussed in previous sections, she needs more nurturing attention, and yet she may become increasingly hard to understand. Oversensitivity to little hurts and insults is common. Sometimes the wife seems to act as if she had an inner secret. Her husband reacts by feeling shut out. As pregnancy progresses, new causes of jealousy come to the fore. The baby is kicking and making himself known as a person. Even before birth the wife's emotional life may turn toward her baby. Of course, after birth the needs of the baby for attention are tremendous. The father may feel left out. Then, too, there is sometimes another man in the picture who arouses jealousy. Many women, feeling anxious and especially dependent during pregnancy, turn to their obstetricians for support. They may tend to put their obstetrician on an emotional pedestal and have a warm feeling toward him as a person, as well as a physician.

Time and growing maturity can help the father who is beset with these troubles. The obstetrician tends to lose his special appeal once his medical function is over. As the weeks roll on, the baby becomes less demanding. The older the baby is, the more he is able to interact with the father as well as the mother. The mother-child relationship becomes steadily less exclusive and demanding. Economic worries that once seemed large tend to recede when the techniques of money management are learned, and as successful work and steady income reward the new father.

Fatherhood, like motherhood, can be a wonderfully maturing experience, changing the youth into a fully mature and responsible man. Focus on self tends to be supplanted by an outward flow of emotions, concern, and identification with the family unit, wife, and child. An added bonus often appears. The wife grows more maternal toward her husband as she takes on the role of motherhood. All their lives men need the loving concern of women and may perform best as fathers and husbands when they have wives who are as deeply devoted to their welfare as their mothers were.

The foundations of lifelong happiness in marriage can be built during pregnancy with both husband and wife showing willingness to give a little bit more in view of the extra stresses each is undergoing. Naturally, it is during the first pregnancy that the biggest adjustments are often made. Later, however, especially when faced with an un-planned extra pregnancy, added maturity may be called for.

The period of pregnancy and early parenthood is also a time when renewed contact with relatives, on a mature basis, can be made. Although we as a society tend to think of ourselves as two-generation families, grandparents can wonderfully enrich the lives of grandchil-dren. Grandparents often have time to give to little children that parents rushed with other responsibilities do not have. They also have a broader view of cultural traditions that can give children a sense of the continuity of living. Then, too, grandparents and other relatives can be a real help in the peak periods of stress of illness, childbearing, and economic setback. The old human tradition of childbearing as a total family undertaking, rather than just a job for independent husband and wife, should not be discarded too lightly. There may be wisdom and security in the group approach, provided it is accompanied by mutual respect and affection.

Another aspect of community support is the problem of who outside the family should be chosen as advisers, helpers, and teachers during childbearing. There has been a widespread belief for some years that having registered nurses talk to expectant mothers about the hygiene of pregnancy and the anatomy of reproduction is helpful. Often emphasis is put on answering the mothers' questions instead of presenting a lot of factual material. The trend in medical care in this country is toward increasing the part the nurse is called upon to take. In pediatrics as well as obstetrics we can expect to see the nurse assuming a larger role in educating the expectant mother and the new mother. At medical centers in large cities, group instruction, led by experienced nurses, is becoming extremely popular among not only expectant mothers but also expectant fathers. The success of this kind of instruction may depend on the teacher and the group itself. In choosing the class to attend, the questions to think about are: 1. Is the teacher a warm, motherly woman who accepts childbearing as a desirable and satisfying part of the female sexual role? 2. Is the type of information given practical or just intellectual? For instance, will there be an opportunity to walk through the labor and delivery suite of the hospital where delivery is planned? Will there be an opportunity to see a mother nursing her baby and ask her questions? Will there be an opportunity to see films of normal labor and delivery for an idea of what the experience will be like? Will practical methods of avoiding social stress (see pages 21–23) be studied? The value of classes apart from the instruction may also be important. Preparing for their baby together can bring a special closeness to some husbands and wives. Then, too, a chance to talk with other women who are expecting babies meets the needs of expectant mothers for sociability and reassurance.

Physicians, of course, are the best source of advice on technical matters concerning disease. But some patients do not realize that personal compatibility, as well as medical knowledge, is an important factor in determining the right physician. Some types of physicians tend to do best with some types of patients, whereas other types of physicians seem to click with other types of patients. This may be particularly true in the case of the physician doing obstetrics. The relationship between the doctor and the patient during childbearing is a close and intimate one. She needs to have good rapport with him. The physician in turn needs to understand what having a baby means to the individual patient. Does she want to play an active role, enjoying and learning about the childbearing processes? Does she want to know as little as possible about it? Does she think of herself as "sick," or does she, instead, want to regard her pregnancy and delivery as part of a natural process? Compatibility of attitudes about childbearing helps to make for a better physician-patient relationship, and for easier acceptance of advice.

Another problem arises from the existence of unproved fashions in child care. The author's mother tells of sitting outside the door wringing her hands while her first baby screamed inside the room. The new idea of schedules had just been invented, and "authorities" assured mother that teaching a baby to eat every four hours was important training for the baby and "good" mothering. It was only many years later that actual experiments were carried out on the effect of four-hour schedules on the baby. It was found that breast-fed babies gained much quicker when fed more frequently than every four hours. The advice of "experts" in child care needs to be taken with a grain of salt if it is based only on theory and not on the richness of practical experience or, even better, on experimental, controlled study of the problem. Fortunately, more and more validated information concerning childbearing is becoming available each year.

NILES ANNE NEWTON, PH.D.

CHAPTER TWO

Childbirth in a Changing World

THE BIRTH of a child has always been of great concern to human beings. Every society we know anything about, the most complicated and the most simple, has developed a way of thinking about conception and made rules for protecting the pregnant woman and her unborn child and for the arrangements attending the birth of the new baby. Every society has a pattern of providing for the care of the infant while he learns to eat, to sit up, to recognize his caretakers, to walk, and to talk.

Throughout man's long history, birth has been a matter for magic and for religion, for philosophical speculation, for the expression of the claims both of the family and of the community. And into this mixture of magic, religion, philosophy, and social concern has been incorporated over the centuries a slowly developing knowledge of how the human body functions and a medical means of protecting life and health. All these interests—and today that of industry as well—have been involved in the process of childbirth. Each interest influences the young girl's attitude toward wifehood and motherhood. Society has its say in what the mother herself is to do and what the father's role will be. Community opinion, tempered by advice from neighbors and styles set in magazines and on TV, will decide how much is to be left to obstetrician, pediatrician, hospital, well-baby clinic, child care center, and nursery school professionals.

How to have a baby is something that each generation of women has to learn. Where wild creatures inherit many biological patterns from their forebears, human beings rely on a body of social tradition that they have to learn piece by piece, beginning in childhood and continuing throughout their lives. When the little girl holds her first doll, she is beginning to learn about childbearing and child care. So is the little girl whose doll is broken by an angry and competitive brother. The little girl who is allowed to place her hand on the fluttering life within her mother's body and told to expect a brother or sister is getting a more advanced lesson.

When a society is stable, what the grandmother learned as a child can be passed on to her granddaughter, but when a society is changing rapidly, as almost all societies are today, the grandmother's experience, and even the mother's experience, may be of little help to granddaughters or daughters. It becomes more and more necessary to turn to current sources of advice and help, to magazines and radio and TV, to pamphlets and books, and to the professionals—nurses and doctors and teachers. Today the new mother has to try to reconcile what she learned from her mother, what she learned from her schoolmates and girl friends, what her husband learned from his parents and his friends (who may have grown up in very different circumstances), what her current neighbors bring from their past experiences, what the mass media are saying, and what the doctor or the nurse recommends. Many pieces of all this advice will not quite fit together. Our knowledge is growing so fast that often children born only ten years apart are brought up so differently that it may seem as if they had been born in different centuries or on different continents. In the swiftness of change, bits of the past mingle but do not blend with bits of the present, and for the resulting contradictions, of course, the new mother has to pay a price. Even the mother who already has had several children may find herself confused. But she at least has the advantage, from her experience, of realizing that new knowledge is being developed all the time.

As recently as 1938, for example, we did not know about the Rh factor in blood (see pages 151–56). A developed immunity in the mother's bloodstream from this factor can threaten the mother or her baby, and the situation can become worse if blood from someone of the wrong Rh type is transfused. Today awareness of the necessity of testing the Rh factor for each pregnancy is widespread, and we have methods of replacing the infant's blood supply and of protecting the mother if she gives birth to a baby of contrasting blood type.

Today, for the humblest birth there is a storehouse of knowledge, drugs, and instruments to draw on, and we approach a time in which it will be possible for every baby who is born, and every mother who gives birth, to live. This difference from the past cannot be overstated. When perhaps as many as half the babies born could not be saved and child-birth was a hazard for mother and baby alike, people developed a kind of protective fatalism, and with it a whole series of magical practices to outwit fate. In some societies the baby was not named for several months; instead, it was called Mouse or Caterpillar so as not to attract the malign attention of evil spirits. Or else no one was allowed to see the newborn except very close relatives, and the baby was kept covered up most of the time. Some of these ideas survive in superstitious fears such as the belief that preparing completely for the arrival of a baby is, in fact, tempting fate too much. But mothers in today's society realize for the most part that the most successful way of assuring the baby's safety is to prepare as fully as possible. They have regular checkups and deal with the doctor candidly, giving accurate answers to his questions and following his advice. They find out within what dates the birth can be expected and try to arrange their family affairs accordingly. If the family must move to another house or another town, they schedule the move for a favorable time in the pregnancy, as early as possible. They provide ahead of time for the care of other children in the family and prepare a place for the new baby within the life style of the whole family, into which the new baby can slip easily and comfortably, with the security that can be given by responsible preparation.

To some extent, all human societies have tried to deal with these matters, but lack of knowledge has in the past hampered them. Without science and medicine, it was often a matter of luck whether the practice they hit upon was favorable, such as having a wet nurse present at birth to feed the baby, or finding some form of supplementary feeding that combined blandness and proper nutrients, or developing some rule of kinship that assured that at a birth there would be at least two people present, one to attend to the needs of the new mother and the other to the needs of the new baby. It is very seldom that we can learn from simpler methods of the past, or from today's peasants in remote parts of the world, anything that is directly helpful in our own ways of caring for pregnant women and mothers and babies during childbirth. But some knowledge of how these things were managed in the past and in societies without modern medicine can heighten our appreciation of the ways in which we are fortunate today.

In the very remote past, half a million years ago, the connection between sexual intercourse and conception was probably not understood at all. Even when some connection was made, it was often vague. Some peoples believed that sexual intercourse was necessary to prepare the way for a spirit child to enter the mother's womb; some believed that at the moment of conception an angel brought small bits of earth to become the body of the child, and that the child would be related all through life to the earth from which it was made. The understanding that conception is the result of a single act, and not the result of a whole series of acts that finally result in the coming into existence of a viable child, also had to be arrived at gradually. There are people even today who believe that once it looks as if the process of pregnancy has started, then a great deal of hard work (for sex is now seen as work where before it was seen as play) must be undertaken by both parents to build up the baby. Other peoples believe that as soon as the mother is known to be pregnant, all sex relations must be tabooed.

We do not, of course, even today, understand all that we need to know about all these matters. But we do understand a good deal. We may use tests that are predictive of the time when a baby will be born. We relate the desirability of intercourse in pregnancy to such matters as the particular temperaments of the expectant father and mother, to comfort, and to hygiene—not to the completion of the act of conception. But some of the old beliefs conceived in philosophic ignorance die hard and may appear in new forms.

For instance, the Iatmul of New Guinea had no idea of how long a pregnancy should last. Most primitive peoples have worked out a rough estimate, accurate to the extent that they can keep track of time, and are not misled by various magical practices or beliefs. But the Iatmul believed that a child could be born anytime that the child decided to be born, and this misjudgment led to endless confusion, and sometimes comic situations. It meant that if a man had been away from home for a year and a baby was born three months after his return, he did not question his wife's fidelity, and people said, "The baby hurried up to see its father's face." It also meant that a woman might mistake any kind of cramp for birth pains. False alarms were always disturbing the life of the village as one woman or another would proclaim that her time had come. Only after the other woman had wasted hours waiting for a birth that did not occur would they decide that it had been a false alarm.

We, of course, are better prepared to judge, although the widely held belief that each human fetus should mature in exactly nine months still causes a great deal of unnecessary discomfort, even suffering, to women whose babies are born a few days too promptly for the standards of their religion or community. Rigid adherence to the nine-month theory, without any allowance for the fact that the length of gestation, like all human biological processes, is somewhat variable, can lead also to failures in the way in which a mother or a whole family deals with the last weeks of pregnancy. Literal acceptance of a nine-month pregnancy often finds people woefully unprepared: grandmother has not yet arrived; there is no provision for someone to be on call around the clock because the baby is not expected for at least two weeks; moving is postponed to the last minute and vacations planned too close to the possible time of birth. Or, on the other hand, an unexpected delay of two weeks can set off a chain of utterly unnecessary miseries, especially for the woman who is having her first baby.

Where the mother of a third or fourth child may be quietly certain that the baby is not going to arrive for another two weeks, the mother of a first baby has no such intimate knowledge of her body's signals. She has to learn from experience. If she realizes that the date her obstetrician has given her is an approximation, that the baby may come earlier or later, and for either eventuality she should be prepared, then a great deal of unnecessary anxiety can be avoided. Increased knowledge does give the modern mother more control and more confidence that all will go well, but knowledge applied rigidly like a magic formula becomes only as useful (or useless) as a magic formula. So, among the Iatmul people, who did not know the length of gestation, a husband would get very impatient and quarrel with his wife, abusing her for being so slow in bearing the child, and she would answer: "Is a human being a pig or a dog to be born at a set time? This baby will be born when it feels like being born." And in today's society, as the wife waits, heavy in the last weeks of pregnancy, finding it difficult to buckle her shoes or to sit for long hours on uncomfortable chairs at meetings that seem never to end, it is small comfort to bicker about when the doctor said the baby would come.

Right down the ages and in all sorts of societies, fertility and the sex of the expected baby have been of tremendous concern. Fertility was of course overridingly important, not only for kings but for the humblest farmer needing children to inherit his land and care for him in his old age, but sex of the child was next in importance. In many societies if a woman did not bear children, her husband could divorce her or bring a second wife or a concubine into the house. One of the barriers to the

spread of necessary population controls today is the age-old requirement upon the daughter-in-law, living as a stranger among her husband's relatives, that she produce a proper number of grandchildren,
especially boys. It was also important that these babies should live; the
mother of sickly or vulnerable infants who died was little improvement
on the sterile woman. In many such societies, the whole blame was laid
upon the infertile woman, although sometimes the husband was also
blamed for having incurred the wrath of gods or spirits.

Today the causes of infertility can often be ascertained. They are
never completely conclusive; that is, even if a wife's tubes are found to
be blocked, it does not follow necessarily that if they are opened the
marriage will be fertile, but it does of course mean that no child can be
born to her unless they are opened. Because the husband's sperm count
is so low as to make conception unlikely, it does not follow necessarily
that conception cannot occur. And as we learn more about the biological determinants of sterility, we find also that there are psychological
barriers to conception, though we do not know the biological mechanism through which they operate. It is a fact that some previously
childless couples have conceived after adopting a child, though these
cases are not well studied statistically and seldom controlled by any
careful knowledge of biological changes in husband or wife.

We have come a long way from the position of most peoples on the
importance of fertility—perhaps too long a way. We do not demand, as
many peoples have done, that a couple who propose to marry and who
want children must first demonstrate that they, as a couple, can have
children. On the contrary, experiments of this sort are regarded as
immoral and disapproved by church and state. We prefer the alternative that if a couple, having chosen each other for life, find they cannot
have children, they should be allowed to adopt a child, as early and as
privately as possible, so that they can rear the child as their own.
Emphasis on possessiveness and absolute ownership replaces the emphasis on biological parentage, which has been so important to people
everywhere.

Furthermore, we have relaxed a great deal in our attitude toward the
sex of children. Although a great many peoples' lives are scarred by
their parents' disappointment, still we do say: "We want children," not
"We want sons," and having a child is regarded in most of the modern
world as more important than the sex of the child. Boys and girls can
both inherit property. Except in isolated cases of outmoded aristocracy,
family names are not very important anymore. Girls can achieve dis-

tinction and bring honor to their parents although, even now, less is expected of them than of boys. Grandparents can enjoy both sets of grandchildren equally. Nevertheless, uncertainty about the sex of the unborn child, whether or not it is to be an issue after the child is born, makes it difficult for the parents to adjust fully to this child who is already present, but unknown. The child cannot be named, without prejudging the sex, and mothers today have learned enough psychology so that they do not wish to limit the future happiness of their children by wishing for one sex rather than the other. Further, the more people pay attention to heredity, and the more they know about the families of both husband and wife, the wider range for speculation there is.

Long ago, and among people who do not understand heredity, there were many fears and as many or more devices for allaying the fears. The child might not be human at all—it might be the child of some supernatural being, a god in the shape of an animal, a ghost, a spirit who had decided to take this means of entering the world. And, if the child seemed strange, unexpected, unlike the image that the parents had formed, it could be that it was a changeling, left in the cradle by fairies who had stolen the real child away. The sense of uncertainty about what a child will be like still expresses itself in such fears as the fear that babies will be mixed up in the hospital. Increasingly careful recordings of newborn babies' footprints are more an answer to such uncertainties than they are to real dangers of mixing the newborn up. The fact is that an unborn baby is a stranger, its sex and face unknown but already determined, and it takes great discipline of the imagination, a discipline once expressed in charms and amulets, for the parents to wait, to prepare for the arrival of an unknown stranger who will be their child.

There are also of course hereditary complications that were once explained magically, as harelip was explained as the unfortunate consequence of having a hare cross a pregnant woman's path. Today, some of these physical anomalies have been explored, and nonfelicitous combinations can be predicted, enabling parents who do not wish to take risks to adopt children instead. Heredity clinics are now able to give a good deal of sound negative advice. But often modern couples are as unwilling to give up ungrounded hopes, even with knowledge, as their primitive counterparts were unwilling to accept the evidence that they had no means of interpreting. Where a primitive woman may have to look at a stillborn child and ask, "Why did I anger my father's sister so that she cursed me?", a modern woman who disregards careful medical advice still has her conscience to search. But these are extreme cases; for most parents who have made a responsible survey of each of their hereditary endowments, it is not the reasonable fear of disaster but simply the extraordinary variety of possibilities that confront them as they wait for the child, of unknown sex, blond or brunet, who may be short or tall, a poet or a swimmer, be tone deaf or have the high tenor voice that is as rare as a white blackbird.

The question of how much onlookers—family and friends, children and strangers—are to share in the progress of a pregnancy is an important one. Among primitive peoples often the whole village keeps track—in their minds—of who is pregnant and for how many months. They respond with anxiety to what seems to them some slight abnormality of posture, or they worry whether some newfangled procedure from the outside will take proper account of what medicine can safely be given to a pregnant woman. It was not so very long ago that among Americans, especially the well-to-do, clothes were designed to conceal pregnancy, and pregnant women tended to stay indoors, hidden from the prying eyes of strangers. Today we have gone to the opposite extreme; clothes are designed to proclaim pregnancy even before it would be visible to the untrained eye, and the older children are encouraged to observe the signs that the baby is alive and kicking. Just as the mother receives a blessed reassurance when she first feels her baby move, so the progress of pregnancy is made more real and more shareable with others around her. They all can then begin to form a picture of the coming baby's temperament as he seems to be performing movements like the young man on the flying trapeze, or, at the same hour each day, stubbornly insists on kicking one spot until it is satisfyingly black and blue.

The appearance of life raises theological problems that in turn will affect the way in which the parents regard their unborn baby. At what point in its development may it be said to be a human being, with a personality, with a mind, with a soul? At what point do the parents and society cease to regard it as somehow not quite determined yet, a little prehuman creature, hardly more than a clot of blood, to be dismissed without full recognition? Museum exhibits, films, and carefully illustrated books are substituting knowledge of the actual nature of the fetus for the speculations informed by occasional accidents, which once governed human imagination. Some peoples deeply feared prematurely born infants who had died, and the famous New Zealand greenstone figure, the tiki, is related to the fetus with its disproportionately enlarged head.

Some societies do not treat the infant as though it were fully and definitely human for some weeks after birth, allowing for parental choice as to whether the child is to be allowed to live—perhaps because there are too many children or the children represent a wrong sex balance or because the child is in some way deformed or weak. Among the Ashanti of Ghana the period just after birth was seen as a dramatic contest between the earthly mother of the just born child and a spirit mother trying to take back a spirit baby come to live on earth. Against the spirit mother's desperate efforts, the earthly mother did everything she could to keep her baby with her. Sometimes weeks would pass before the anxious earthly watchers could decide that the baby had indeed come to stay. Among the Balinese, who believe that souls are reincarnated every fourth generation within the same family, people were not permitted to weep at a death, for the soul would be reborn. Only in the case of the death of a very young baby could the mother weep and people lament, "Why did you not stay longer with us, long enough to eat rice with us? The next time you are born stay a little longer."

Whatever the culture, the relationship between birth and the soul is an important one and will affect the way in which the mother cares for her health, the way in which a husband cares for his wife and unborn child. In earlier Christian periods the emphasis on the innocence of baptized infants, their souls cleansed of sin, made it more difficult to arouse interest in keeping all children alive, baptized or not, and it has been only slowly that concern for a good life on earth for all the children has replaced a more exclusive interest in the soul's future in heaven. This ethical problem is highlighted in the case of defective children. How great an effort should be made to teach them so that, in the words of one religious sisterhood devoted to the care of the mentally retarded, "they may make a contribution in time as well as in eternity"?

Prenatal precautions to ensure the safety and well-being of the child take many forms. The mother is almost universally under some restriction not to eat certain foods. In our society the restrictions presumably have a sound medical basis, but primitive peoples can be more imaginative. Some foods, for example, may be tabooed because the shapes of the food suggest images of abnormality or resemble animals that jump too fast and so would produce too rapid a birth or are too slow and so would produce too slow a birth. There is hardly an aspect of pregnancy and childbirth that has not been elaborated upon in taboos governing the behavior of the expectant mother. There are also taboos governing the behavior of expectant fathers. Sometimes these are phrased also as protecting the baby, like taboos against the expectant father's driving stakes into the ground or cutting anything with a knife. Sometimes, however, the taboos are phrased as ways of protecting the expectant father himself, to whom his wife's pregnancy is somehow conceived to be a danger.

It is interesting to compare the attitudes toward children among people who observe many taboos for the child's sake, with the attitudes of people who observe taboos for the sake of the parents. Where the taboos are for the child's sake, children are highly valued and cherished, but where the taboos are not for the child but for the parents, this is not the case. Instead, children are often disliked and harshly treated. It is possible to make some generalizations and suggest that today if measures connected with pregnancy and birth are undertaken in the name of the baby's well-being they make for greater acceptance and greater safety. Consider diet. In some extreme cases where diets have been prescribed primarily to make the birth easier for the mother by keeping the baby's weight down, the nutrition of the pregnant mothers has been found to be woefully deficient. Also, when the question of anesthesia during childbirth comes up, this may be proposed as a measure to save the mother from suffering or as one to assure the optimum conditions for the birth of the baby. The emphasis put upon the prevention of pain has increased women's fear of childbirth, while at the same time diverting attention from possible damaging consequences for the infant. Where the goal is to ensure both optimum health for the mother, so that she can best care for her baby, and optimum conditions for the baby itself, then the full weight of medical scrutiny can be brought to bear on the question of prescribing anesthesia. Distinctions of the same sort apply also, of course, in natural childbirth, for the mother who wants to be conscious at the birth. If this desire is phrased solely as self-fulfillment and the right to experience, rather than as a desire to do what is best for the baby, it may be severely self-defeating. There seem to be certain regularities in human behavior that must be preserved. When children are turned into instruments of their parents' well-being, the adults' capacity to devise and maintain a society in which the well-being of all children is protected seems to be diminished.

The expectation of pain in childbirth and the methods by which the expected pain is treated also vary widely. Some peoples treat childbirth very casually, have no rules about who may be present, call on the mother to continue with her daily tasks up to the last minute. They expect the childbirth itself to be quick, easy, and devoid of much pain.

Among people with this attitude, magical provisions will be invoked if the delivery is long or painful, as these difficulties are felt to be unusual circumstances requiring special care. Or a people may take magical precautions against a birth being too quick. For women who work far from the village, an unexpected birth all alone out in the gardens may be a hazard. Women among nomadic pastoral peoples may hope for and make use of every device imaginable to have their babies born at night when the herds and the tribe are resting.

Other peoples may emphasize pain and the heroism of women who bear pain with never a cry escaping their lips. In some cases, death in childbirth and death in war are equated, as the twin hazards challenging human bravery. It has even been suggested that perhaps customs of human sacrifice came from men's mistakenly looking upon the blood of childbirth as the most creative thing about it; the production of a human being and the production of everything that was most desired both seemed to result from the shedding of blood.

The traditional Christian attitude, in its version of how the burdens of men and women are equalized, equates the heavy toil to which fallen man is condemned with the heavy toil—*labor*—to which women are condemned. Labor, emphasizing the hard, backbreaking, heavy work involved, implies the kind of pain that goes with carrying a load so heavy that it can be endured only for a certain length of time. When ideas of labor and pain are mixed, the particularity of the images is lost. Instead of picturing the pains of labor as involving strain to the point of pain in particular sets of muscles, the emphasis is upon unbearable undifferentiated pain. In societies where men have never been allowed to witness childbirth, their fantasies about its terrible nature may be unbounded. Arapesh men give pantomimed accounts of childbirth in which women are conceived as writhing in screaming agony, whereas in actuality the women of the tribe give birth quietly and matter-of-factly, in difficult and uncomfortable circumstances, on the damp ground of a steep slope, in the dark, with no one to help except one other young woman. The parturient woman is required to take all the care of the newborn herself; she cuts the cord, sets the baby breathing, clears its mouth and nose, and puts it to the breast. The contrast between the men's nightmares and the actuality is striking.

One of the problems that has faced society about the process of childbirth is how much of the care should be entrusted to men, who may have no real empathy with the parturient woman and who may have, moreover, complicated psychological attitudes toward birth in which they feel guilt over the cost of their own births to their mothers or the cost of their children's births to their wives. The present trend is toward greater openness, toward giving boys and men opportunity to see films of birth, whether or not they elect to be present at the birth of their own children. If this trend continues—and although the progress of medicine seems irreversible, all the social practices supporting it are highly fragile and reversible—men's imaginings about childbirth may be replaced by knowledge, and women in consequence be less subject to the images that men have made.

It should be pointed out that natural childbirth, the very inappropriate name for forms of delivery in which women undergo extensive training so that they can cooperate consciously with the delivery of the child, is a male invention, meant to counteract practices of complete anesthesia, which were also male inventions. Contemporary forms of natural childbirth are an attempt to restore to women what women among many peoples once had. When the woman in labor was attended only by women, with no obstetrical tables or anesthetics or forceps, women got down to the business of delivering a baby, using all their muscles and willpower and previous experience of other women's deliveries to help them. But it must also be remembered that under these more, but not completely, natural conditions, in all deliveries that were in any way unusual infants and mothers both died. Under primitive conditions only when the mother and baby were a good fit, during pregnancy, delivery, and the period of suckling, was the baby viable. The others died. Today, in spite of such great discrepancies as the Rh factor we save both mother and child. This advance has required a tremendous amount of invention, apparatus, and intervention and periodic effort to reintroduce some of the natural capacities of the human being back into the process. So natural childbirth has been a valuable corrective for too much emphasis on pain and anesthesia for the avoidance of pain, and too much emphasis on medical convenience and efficiency, appropriate for hazardous cases, but sometimes an impediment to ordinary births.

Insistence on delivery in hospitals, part of the effort to bring the best capacities of modern medicine to bear in childbirth, has raised a series of other problems. Where the baby is to be born, who is to attend the mother, and who is to care for the baby have been matters of concern in most cultures. Overwhelmingly, those societies of which we have records have tended to insist that the most appropriate attendant is the mother of the parturient woman. This custom holds whether the society be patrilineal or matrilineal. In many societies a woman goes home for the birth of her first baby. In others her mother comes to her. Sometimes sisters or even sisters-in-law replace mothers, but whatever the arrangements, there are women who are both close and involved, women who have themselves had children, and who are related to the new baby and concerned with its survival.

In some societies a birth is a pleasant social affair. Many persons, sometimes only women but sometimes both men and women, may gather in the house, to smoke, chew, gossip, play games, and generally take advantage of a moment of heightened excitement. In other societies the parturient woman is segregated with only one or two companions, separated from her husband and children, bidden to speak only in whispers, caught in a maze of supernatural and realistic anxieties. Sometimes anxiety, sometimes sociability, sometimes fear, is the ruling tone of the occasion. But no primitive society leaves the mother alone, nor does any leave her alone among strangers, although she may be left alone with only too well known but not loved or trusted in-laws. It remains for modern civilization, in the isolation of cities and suburbs, to leave a woman approaching childbirth all alone. Today, in an age that does not accord special privileges to women and whose women do not claim privilege because of sex, many girls think it part of the sturdy endurance demanded of them not to make a fuss. They put up with staying alone and taking the responsibility of calling a neighbor or a cab when they feel labor pains. This self-imposed heroism of questionable wisdom is then followed by isolation among strangers in the hospital. Even when people had neither the knowledge nor the skill to provide very much else, a warm human community sharing the same concern and the same interpretation of what was happening offered the woman a protection that often is lacking under modern conditions.

The relationship of the latest child to his older brothers and sisters has to be taken into account in every culture. The sense of competition between the displaced child, who will now become the knee baby while his mother holds the younger on her lap, is expressed in many ways. Very seldom is the older child isolated from the mother for long, although he may be banished from the delivery. The process of encouraging the older child to accept the younger takes many forms; sometimes people act as if the older child shared the mother's enthusiasm for the baby, making him a competitor for the new baby; sometimes outright enmity is allowed for; sometimes the older child is permitted theatrical forms of hostility toward strange and borrowed babies but forced to be wholly friendly to the newborn. But the whole situation is seldom complicated by the long absence characteristic of today, when the mother disappears abruptly from home and children and does not return until several days later, and then with a new baby in her arms. This situation, a by-product of hospitalization and fear of infection, has been somewhat modified today by fuller preparation of the older children, greater frankness about pregnancy and birth, care about who stays with the older children, and frequent use of the telephone.

Care of the new mother after the baby is born also has varied enormously. She may be allowed to rest for a whole month, sitting with the newborn baby on her lap, cooked for and cared for by her relatives. Or, her husband may come to lie down beside her to share the labor from which she is recuperating, and she may have to get up and start cooking while he stays in bed. But in most cases, whether the mother is allowed time to rest and get acquainted with her new baby or not, the baby is always near her, ready to be fed if he cries. When she walks about, she takes the baby with her, in a net bag, in a bark sling, in a basket, on a cradleboard, or swaddled as a protection against the cold. Mother and breast-fed infant are treated as a unity, although immediately after birth someone else may breast-feed the child, and later, when the child is several months old, he may often be left to the care and suckling of female relatives who have milk. The temporary separation immediately after birth that is characteristic of most western modern hospital systems did not occur in primitive societies. Baby and mother were kept close together, and the mother had a chance to adjust the baby's rhythm to her own, his hunger to her supply of milk. This custom was not, however, to be confused with self-demand feeding in the sense in which we speak of it today. Self-demand feeding is a very modern idea, based on our knowledge that infants differ among themselves and that each mother and baby, as a nursing couple, has a style of its own, plus the fact that we have writing and clocks. So today it is possible for a breast-feeding mother to keep track of the times at which an infant is spontaneously hungry and to be there to feed him. And she is able to establish, with the help of clock and record, a schedule that is regular and predictable but which is peculiar to her own baby. Primitive mothers, mothers in earlier times, had neither the concepts nor the necessary instruments with which to organize such a regime. Nevertheless, they did create cultural conditions that made it possible for enough breast-fed babies to survive. Babies who did not thrive on their mother's milk died, since a mother cannot respond with an adequate supply of milk if a baby is not nursing sufficiently. The development of reliable methods of bottle feeding has changed all this. Now infants who would never have thrived on their mothers' milk can be fed adequately. But in the course of developing bottle feeding, we acted as if bottle feeding were inherently superior to breast-feeding. Also, in order to deal with unlimited supplies of milk, we developed methods of measuring and weighing to artificially adjust the baby and the food. This adjustment had once been made naturally while baby and mother were adjusting to each other.

The interest in breast-feeding in the last quarter century has been stimulated partly by anthropological studies and partly by psychological studies of how infants grow and thrive. But it is important to realize that we are now able to make choices that were not open to mothers in other ages; we can find out whether or not a particular mother and a particular baby fit well together. If they do, the mother can breast-feed the baby; if they do not, we can feed the baby in other ways. The father can take part of the responsibility. The mother of today can be away from the baby without subjecting him to the hunger and anxiety that gnawed at yesterday's infant when his breast-feeding mother had to be away, in the fields or at the market, and there was no substitute for her milk.

The first few days after birth are crucial in the mother's acceptance of her baby. Having the baby near her is an important factor in achieving this acceptance, but so also is the presence of other women who can assist her in establishing breast-feeding, or making the choice not to breast-feed, and can reassure her when the baby, particularly the first baby, seems to be an overwhelming responsibility. In primitive societies, whether a girl has seen actual birth or not, she has cared for little babies all her life, and her own baby is just the last baby in a long series. She has learned how to hold a baby. She can tell how relatively weak or strong he is. She knows how to support the head, how to lull the baby with a firm, sure cradling, and the expected tone of voice. The characteristic lullaby (which to our unaccustomed ears may sound nothing at all like a lullaby) is ready on her tongue. Grandmother, aunts, older sisters sing the same song and in the same way.

All this natural-seeming support we have to provide artificially. Nurses and the other mothers in the hospital who have given birth that week become very important as models. Sometimes the fate of a whole series of mother-child relationships may be determined by one magnificent and competent mother who energizes all the others, but sometimes a dominating but destructive mother sets a model that injures the style of the others. And the hospital stay ends in an abrupt removal from the safe, highly competent, and knowledgeable environment, where someone knows how to meet every emergency, to a home where often there is no one but an inexperienced and anxious young husband to lean on through the baby's unnerving first attack of hiccups or colic. The trying experiences of early motherhood amply justify the attempt to reestablish some of the conditions of older societies. Women in their first pregnancies will be better off if they can spend time with other young women who have newborn babies. They can handle the new babies, bathe them, put them to sleep, and learn the skills that they would have learned as little girls had they grown up in a primitive village.

How the baby is to sleep, at home and when it is carried about, has always been a problem. If the mother were simply to carry the baby in her arms, she would get practically no work done. In societies more primitive than ours, some contrivance for fastening the baby on the back or under the breast was essential. On long trips, trekking across the desert or through jungle paths to the gardens, the mother had baggage or tools to carry and often needed her hands free to gather foods on the way, just as today she needs her hands free to get out change or tickets or grasp the stair railing or open and shut doors. Baby carriages are a recent invention and only suitable for certain kinds of living where mother and baby or nurse and baby go short distances on foot on paved roads. Under ancient conditions the baby had to be carried or fastened to the body of the rider or be slung from the saddle on a cradleboard. Today, when again the world is becoming unsuitable for baby carriages, various sorts of baskets and carriers, worn on the back or on the shoulder, have come into fashion.

We have found that the way in which a baby is cradled and carried makes a great deal of difference in his upbringing. If a baby is able to relax and to detach himself from the activity of his mother—as for example when he is carried in a cloth sling or firmly fastened in a shawl, and the mother is pounding rice—he will make one kind of adaptation, both to his mother and to other things in life. If the baby is required to grasp the mother around the neck or by the hair as he is carried on her shoulder, he learns much earlier to take charge of his own safety. Where the baby is fully swaddled, he learns the often painful discipline of confinement, and since his hands are not free to explore and grasp, he must depend more on his eyes. The manner in which a child is carried influences not only whether he will be active or passive, but what and how much of life he will see. He may ride peeking over the mother's shoulder and thus see what she is facing, or be carried facing away from the mother, so that while he may see a lot, he will not see what she sees. He may be carried facing in toward the mother's breast, shielded from other eyes, or set firmly down against the mother's breasts or on her arm, facing the world with her body supporting him and giving him confidence. In some parts of the United States, it is possible even within distances of a few miles to find differences in ways of carrying a baby in the presence of strangers.

Some peoples take their babies everywhere; they lay them down on dance floors to sleep just out of reach of the dancing feet, or else dance with the sleeping children on their backs; they do their work with children on their hips. Other peoples leave children at home, inside the tent or the house, in the charge of grandmothers. Some give the child of a few months almost entirely over to the care of little girl nurses, who must struggle all day long to carry and content the small charges who are almost too much for them. These differences in care again make a difference in the babies. Mothers are usually busy people able to give only part of their attention to their babies, and thus they convey to the children that while they are a part of life, once early infancy is passed they are only a part. Old grandmothers and nurses, on the other hand, may be able to give almost their entire time to the care of a baby, making him the center of their attention. Royalty and nobility and the wealthy have always had retainers or servants to care for children, and the distinctive behavior we think of as aristocratic has developed from the constant attentiveness of nurses. Sometimes the very poor almost reach the same position, in an inverse way; the mother who has nothing to do, no cloth to sew, hardly any house to clean, no food to cook beyond a snatched mouthful, may be able to give fuller attention to her child. The baby is really all she has.

Among primitive people life is often a periodic alternation. Busy days or weeks when the child receives minimum attention are followed by idle hours when mothers sit and enjoy their babies. Through the long afternoons after the harvest, groups of mothers, babies in arms, toddlers nearby, older children playing at a distance, gather together, doing light work such as shelling beans or preparing material for basketmaking. In contrast, the significant developments of modern living include contrivances we have invented for the baby—all the cribs, jumping chairs, swings, high chairs, baby carriages, playpens—which keep a child safe and reasonably content, within sight or at least within hearing of the mother, but not next to her body. Almost from birth we seem to put distance between us. We do not approve of babies' sleeping with their mothers, and even breast-fed babies are likely to be accorded a very limited patch of bare maternal skin. Our babies develop the senses of sight and hearing very early, but learn much less about touch and smell and the rhythm of their own hearts and breathing as this relates to the heartbeat and breathing of others. We have even invented an artificial soother, in the form of a steady sound tuned to the maternal heartbeat, to quiet little orphans or babies in hospitals who have no mother's heartbeat to attend to. Here again we have advanced a long way in making the world a safer place for babies; their own beds with their own sheets are easier to keep scrupulously clean; in their own beds they are in no danger of being overlaid by a mother lying in a too deep sleep; in a high crib or a playpen no dog or older child can get at them. Hung high in the kitchen doorway, they don't get under the refrigerator or close to the stove. Where a mother is all alone, sometimes with two or three quite small children, these aids are invaluable; she could not possibly do without them. But inasmuch as they substitute sound and sight for touch the child is subjected to a different kind of loneliness. He comes to fret at the walls of the playpen that fence him in, as he would not have fretted in his mother's arms.

Under these conditions separation carries an extra burden of emotion, and the partings when parents go out for an evening together leaving the children with a sitter are scenes that it would be hard to duplicate in many parts of the world. A mother who is always too busy to hold a child is also a mother for whom the child may cry noisily when she goes away. With all the gadgets for safety and circumscribed play, it becomes more nearly possible for a mother to be self-sufficient, to live without the help once provided by sisters and neighbors, grandmothers and older daughters, alone, just a small family, shut up in a small house with no hands free to soothe a child's fatigue or his growing pains. Children will wander safely within the circle of a group of women working near each other, but little brothers and sisters shut up together alone in a house may reach a point of dangerous quarreling or destructiveness. The presence of other women and older children to familiarize the child with different styles of behavior has been a safeguard through the ages, and is still worth cultivating.

The parts that fathers play in the care of children present some of the most dramatic contrasts. Among very primitive people the father hunts or fishes almost every day to keep the family alive. Once the hunt is over, these fathers have a lot of free time on their hands, and very little to do with it. They may spend a good many hours holding and playing with babies and small children, while the wives go about their more time-consuming tasks of preparing the food, gathering seeds and herbs, tanning skins, or making mats and baskets. Fathers seem to confine their attention to their own children, or sometimes to nephews and nieces, more than women do, and in such societies there is often closeness between fathers and babies. Where babies are entirely breast-fed, however, the tie between the mother and the child can never be replaced entirely by a father-child tie, and when the father-held baby cries, he is taken back to his mother.

As civilization became more complicated, and people lived not from hunting and food gathering but from crops they planted, harvested, and stored, there was division of labor, separating artisans from peasants, and the professions and governing classes developed. The more important men had nothing to do with small babies, or even with small children. And invariably as class divisions sharpened and men of high rank came to be surrounded with complicated retinues, the children were removed from the scene of adult business to the nursery, out of earshot. The fed and adorned child was brought into the parental presence very occasionally. While fathers of lesser rank might play with babies (even if they took little care of them), fathers of high rank had scant opportunity to enjoy children. Thick walls and the many female relatives and servants kept them apart. But today, for the first time in history, men of high rank and considerable wealth find themselves, in the modern household containing neither servants nor spare relatives, in the position of having to take a great deal of care of little babies. They sit up with them at night, feed them, bathe and change them, and perform all the small acts through which mothers traditionally have shaped children's responses to the world.

This change has had many repercussions. At first, in the United States after World War II, it was responsible in part for the large families that became so fashionable among the affluent, as fathers who had enjoyed one little baby found themselves eager for another. Now, with a more acute recognition of the need to limit the size of families, and with the invention of reliable contraceptives, new styles of family life are developing. Young parents may elect to have fewer children, perhaps only two, but during the time when the children are young, many young fathers are demanding, as one of the rewards they can ask from an affluent society, a way of life that permits them many daylight hours at home with their small children.

A share in the whole process of bringing a baby into the world, an active interest in the course of the pregnancy, shared instruction with the mother on the opportunities of parenthood, attendance at the birth, and a great deal of care of even the tiniest infants are new privileges of fatherhood. If this trend continues, then certain great changes are likely to occur in the character of men and women. Throughout history, both boys and girls have learned all the primary things about life from women. Girls sat back against their mothers' breasts and learned to be like them; boys were thrust away from their mothers' laps, told to be brave and strong and different. Boys developed an urge toward achievement, and society treated whatever men did as more important than what women did. Women learned from their mothers that being mothers was the most fulfilling activity in life, and society was organized to shape women's lives around their role of bearing and rearing children. In today's world, where families are small and fathers participate in day-to-day care, where many, many years remain to the parents after the children are grown, the central role of motherhood in the drama of a woman's entire life span will be diminished. It will be important for a baby girl to learn that she is an individual in her own right. The baby boy will have to learn that it is more important to be an individual than just to make certain that he behaves like a boy and not like a girl.

These very large issues of how men and women are to relate to each other and to their children, and of what kind of individuals we will be developing for the future, are thus subtly dependent upon the whole sequence of practices and policies surrounding pregnancy and gestation. Since obstetrics and pediatrics became separate professions and babies have been born in hospitals, the traditional relationships among members of a family and among members of the wider circle of relatives have been replaced by a series of professional relationships. A woman does not ask her mother or the old wise woman of the village if perhaps she is pregnant; instead, she takes a urine specimen to her doctor. Through the months of pregnancy mother-to-be and obstetrician or nurse in a prenatal clinic prepare for the birth. The expectant father is likely to be left pacing the hospital corridor. But shut out too are the grandmothers, the grandfathers, the aunts and uncles, and the older children. When the mother's eyes first fall on her baby, no loved arms hold it; she first sees her baby in the hands of a strange nurse. When she tries to get her baby to take the breast, a stranger, firm, efficient, often impersonal, helps her fit the baby's mouth to the nipple. Later, when she returns home, pediatrician replaces obstetrician, and the long months of anxious telephone consultation begin, often quite without the support of any relative or neighbor with whom she can share the small uncertainties that plague her inexperienced motherhood. Finally, as the children grow older, they have their own doctor, their pediatrician, who now is theirs and no longer mother's consultant, until, some fine day in their teens, they announce their budding adulthood by refusing to go to the physician of their childhood. Only too often they have ended up with no doctor at all, until the girl became pregnant, or the boy had an accident or became seriously ill.

Perhaps the most important lesson that can be learned from child care in other cultures and at other times is the importance of consistency. From watching old, slowly changing cultures we can learn how one practice reinforces another, and to what extent the care at birth anticipates the later stages of the child's life. We can see how the young mother is reinforced by her mother, and how the grandmother becomes a grandmother in response to grandchildren to whom she herself has given the first lessons in grandchild behavior. From studies of rapidly changing cultures, in developing countries where medicine and child care are just being introduced and where the behavior expected from young mothers differs drastically from the way in which their mothers treated them, from the practices they watched as children, and from the behavior the older women expect, we get an idea of what the conflicts are and what problems they present. In a country such as the United States we have the very rapid change in the habits of both the immigrant families from other countries and the migrant families from rural areas to the cities. And we have also experienced the whole set of rapid changes in obstetrical and pediatric practice. The impact of change is perhaps at its height. Each generation of young mothers has a new set of problems to face. While grandmothers, with visions of cuts and bleeding, still leap for the child who falls while carrying his bottle, young mothers know that the bottle is plastic and will not break. Neither the fears nor the precautions are in step. And yet it is very important that young mothers should not be so isolated that they have no one with whom to share the hundred small queries, uncertainties, and anxieties. The busy physician or the parents' encyclopedia is not enough.

When people are moving so often and selecting their homes with so little relation to other people, it seems important to build new institutions in which women who are having babies at about the same time may keep in touch with each other and with the newest precepts from the clinic and consulting room. Where such a group is composed of relatives, old friends, or neighbors who know each other well, it resembles the reassuring circle that characterizes primitive and village life. But where there is no such group, then clinics, churches, and physicians have to take the initiative in forming one. Groups that carry husbands and wives through a first pregnancy and into the early months of the children's postnatal lives can provide the doctor and nurse, as well as the parents, with valuable information. Brand-new practices can be tried out and criticized intelligently. Dealing with wholly shared problems, groups of this kind can make active contributions because each generation, reared at a different stage of knowledge and technology, has to find its own way to the kind of care its children need.

MARGARET MEAD, PH.D.

PART TWO

PREGNANCY

CHAPTER THREE

The Diagnosis of Pregnancy

SYMPTOMS

THE FIRST symptom that makes a woman wonder whether she is pregnant is delay in the menstrual period. Since the menstrual cycles of most women do not vary by more than three or four days, delay of a week or ten days suggests pregnancy. If the woman's periods normally vary by this amount, the delay has no significance. But by the time the second period has been skipped, there is usually very little doubt in her mind or in the mind of her physician.

Each month nature has prepared the way for a new pregnancy. This remarkable cyclic activity in women is under control of the tiny, hormone-producing pituitary gland, at the base of the brain. Hormones are internally secreted chemical substances that stimulate or repress the functioning of specific organs or tissues. The pituitary stimulates the development, or ripening, of eggs in the ovary. At the start of the monthly cycle, which usually has a period of twenty-eight days, some two or three dozen eggs begin to mature. By about the fourteenth day one egg has matured more than its fellows and is cast forth from the surface of the ovary. This process is called *ovulation*. The development of the other eggs halts at once. These others regress and are never used again.

Immediately after ovulation, the bed or follicle within the ovary where the egg had developed is transformed into a hormone-producing structure. Because the hormones are released directly into the blood-stream from the endocrine glands (ovary, thyroid, adrenal, and others), the reactions in distant parts of the body begin almost at once. After

[65]

ovulation the ovarian follicle assumes a yellow color; it is known as the *corpus luteum,* from the Latin for "yellow body." Its product, the hormone *progesterone,* has diverse effects on the female organism, one of the most important being to arrest the development of the other eggs that had begun to ripen prior to ovulation. If this ripening were not stopped, multiple ovulations and multiple pregnancies would be possible each cycle. For its ability to inhibit ovulation, progesterone is an ingredient of all birth control pills.

Progesterone raises the body temperature. By accurately recording your temperature day after day, you can tell when ovulation and the production of progesterone begin. Probably the most important action of progesterone is to prepare the lining of the womb for pregnancy. The lining must be receptive. If the egg does not become fertilized, the corpus luteum regresses in twelve to fourteen days. Production of progesterone ceases, and the built-up lining of the womb is cast off as the menstrual discharge. The whole process then starts all over again.

For a pregnancy to become established many events must occur at just the right time. The father must be able to supply adequate numbers of sperm cells, and the "adequate" numbers are truly astounding. Normal males have sperm counts in the neighborhood of fifty to one hundred million for each cubic centimeter of semen and produce two to three cubic centimeters at each ejaculation. If the sperm count is as low as twenty million for each cubic centimeter, it is difficult for most couples to have children. With counts of five million or less, sterility is usually complete and permanent.

Once in the birth canal, the sperm cells have to make their way up through the uterus and Fallopian tubes. We really do not know much about the mechanics of sperm migration and transportation, but time seems to be on their side. The sperm cell apparently is capable of fertilizing the egg even if two or three days have elapsed. After the journey up the uterus and Fallopian tubes, which lead from the body cavity to the uterus, the sperm has to locate the egg cell and join with it. This union is known as *fertilization.* Just how the sperm finds the egg is unknown. It is not known even where fertilization occurs. In most animals fertilization appears to occur in the outer portion of the tube, but in human beings there is much evidence that this happens in the general abdominal cavity. But regardless of where fertilization occurs, the egg must get from the ovary into the tube. While this is a short distance, less than an inch, the egg does not have its own means of locomotion; it must be buffeted or drawn into the tube in some manner as yet unknown. Pregnancies have occurred in women who by pelvic surgery have lost the ovary on one side and the tube on the other. On these rare occasions, the egg has to migrate several inches to get from the ovary into the tube.

While the sperm cells are viable, retaining their ability to fertilize the ovum for two or three days, the mature egg cast off at ovulation must meet and join with the male sperm cell within twelve hours, or twenty-four hours at the most. If not, it will degenerate. Pregnancy will then not be possible until the following cycle. When you think that there are only a few hours each month in which the female is capable of becoming pregnant, it is truly remarkable how easily most women conceive. The explanation is to be found in the fact that the sperm cells live so long. When a couple is having sexual relations two or three times a week, there are almost always sperm cells around, regardless of when ovulation occurs.

After the egg has become fertilized, it splits in half. The two cells so formed in turn divide, giving rise to a four-celled structure. Cell divisions continue, and the developing ovum assumes a spherical shape. It is wafted down the Fallopian tube by a gentle beating action of tiny hairlike projections on each of the cells lining the tube. The journey down the tube takes three or four days, and after the ovum reaches the cavity of the uterus, it waits another three or four days before becoming attached to the lining of the womb. This step is known as *implantation*, or *nidation*, and in humans it occurs roughly a week after ovulation.

You will recall that during this week the corpus luteum hormone, progesterone, has been preparing the lining of the womb for implantation. Once this process has occurred, the developing ovum produces a hormone of its own, called *chorionic gonadotropin*. Minute amounts of this hormone get into the mother's bloodstream and are carried to the ovary, where the hormone signals the corpus luteum to keep up the production of progesterone. If the corpus luteum falters at this time, as it does regularly in cycles where pregnancy does not occur, production of progesterone stops. If this should happen, the entire lining of the womb, including the implanted ovum, would be cast off. One can appreciate how sensitive the whole process is. If events do not occur at just the right moment, it may be difficult or impossible for a woman to conceive.

When this complicated process of conception has been successful, bodily change follows quickly. An early symptom of pregnancy is breast fullness and soreness. The nipples may be particularly sensitive. These changes are noted within a few days after the menses fails to materialize. Another of the very early symptoms is nausea. "Morning sickness" often occurs the very first thing in the morning on an empty stomach and is improved by eating almost anything. Some women, on the other hand, feel fine in the morning but have their nausea in the afternoon while preparing dinner. A few unfortunates have morning sickness all day long. Many do not become actually nauseated, but have a queasy feeling and develop sudden aversions to certain foods or tastes. Coffee and cigarettes are among the most common aversions. Morning sickness usually goes away after the third month of pregnancy. While the cause is unknown, it seems quite likely that hormones produced by the developing pregnancy are an important influence. These same hormones often cause nausea when given to nonpregnant women, as so many who are taking the birth control pills have discovered. There is little doubt that emotional factors are significant, especially when nausea and vomiting become prolonged and severe. There are numerous helpful and harmless drugs that the physician may prescribe. These often alleviate the condition.

By the time the period is a couple of weeks late, frequency of urination is noted; many women have to get up in the night to empty the bladder. Other common symptoms of pregnancy are constipation and fatigue.

DIAGNOSIS

The earliest a doctor can make the diagnosis of pregnancy is when the period is two or three weeks late; in other words, six to seven weeks from the previous menstruation period. By this time the uterus is appreciably enlarged and softened. Because of the increased blood supply to the uterus, its neck, the *cervix,* takes on a bluish coloration that is suggestive of early pregnancy.

Tests done on a sample of urine or blood are helpful in establishing the diagnosis of pregnancy. There is a good chance of getting a positive pregnancy test by the time the period is ten days late, and within another two or three weeks almost all women with normal pregnancies show positive results. Usually a test is done only when there is much urgency, either medical or social, for establishing the diagnosis of pregnancy; in a few days more the results of an internal examination will be conclusive. All pregnancy tests detect the presence of the hormone chorionic gonadotropin in the blood and urine. This hormone now is being elaborated by the placenta, which is one of the most important structures developed in pregnancy. (Its common name is the afterbirth.) The placenta is involved in both the nourishment of the fetus and the elimination of the fetal waste products. We shall have more to say about this organ later. (See page 114.)

The oldest of the biologic tests for pregnancy is still one of the most dependable. This is the Ascheim-Zondek or *AZ test*. Immature white rats are injected with a sample of blood serum or urine, and if chorionic gonadotropin is present, enlargement and redness of the ovaries are noted when the animals are sacrificed twenty-four hours later. The AZ test has the advantage of being very sensitive but the disadvantage of taking the longest to perform. In common with other biologic tests for pregnancy, the errors that arise are "false negatives." In these cases, the woman is actually pregnant but the result of the test is negative. "False positives" hardly ever occur. If the result comes back positive, it is most unlikely that the woman is not pregnant. Pregnancy tests of all kinds generally cost the patient from $5 to $10, depending on the local laboratory charge.

A more rapid pregnancy test uses a male frog. If chorionic gonadotropin is present, it will induce the appearance of sperm cells in the cloacal fluid. Since frogs are much easier to handle than white rats, the frog test is more convenient for the laboratory to perform and much quicker, taking only four to five hours.

The newest and fastest test is based upon an immunologic reaction involving the woman's urine, a serum taken from rabbits, and pure human chorionic gonadotropin. These immunologic tests can be done in minutes or a couple of hours at most and save the laboratory from having to maintain colonies of animals. While false positives have been somewhat more common than with other types of tests, the sensitivity, convenience, and rapidity make up for the errors. Most pregnancy tests done today are of this general type.

When the menstrual period is a few days late, some women not anxious to conceive ask the doctor for a pill or shot to "bring on the period." The administration of progesterone will induce vaginal bleeding in two or three days in nonpregnant women. This bleeding is similar to a menstrual period, but may not be of the usual amount or duration. If a woman is pregnant, nothing will happen and certainly no harm will come to the developing fetus from the progesterone. Progesterone will not cause an implanted ovum to abort. Indeed, this hormone is often given to women who are threatening to abort.

BODILY CHANGES IN PREGNANCY

Wonderful and dramatic things happen to a woman before, during, and after the birth of a child. She becomes a different person. She looks different, she feels different, she even thinks differently. Yet these changes develop so slowly and subtly that few wives (and even fewer husbands) realize what is going on. Many of these changes are mediated through the hormones produced by the placenta (see page 115). This remarkable structure becomes an efficient factory and by the end of pregnancy is producing large amounts of several different hormones. There is hardly any part of the body that is not involved in these changes. In the development of a new life the body must adjust to increased stress and strain, but so perfect is this adjustment that any woman free of serious health handicaps can go through repeated pregnancies with hardly any inconvenience or risk.

Circulatory System

The work performed by the heart increases in pregnancy by roughly one-fourth. Women with serious heart disease need strict medical supervision in pregnancy and must curtail other activities to prevent heart failure. Formerly abortions were sometimes performed on patients with serious heart disease, but modern medical care brings almost all these women through pregnancy safely. Obstetricians are seeing more and more women who have recovered from heart surgery. The experience with these patients has been gratifying. There are even a few who have undergone heart surgery in pregnancy. While this is possible, pregnancy is certainly not the ideal time for cardiac surgery, and unless it is a matter of life or death the cardiac surgery is best performed between pregnancies.

One of the most common changes in the circulatory system in pregnancy is the occurrence of varicose veins of the legs. Increased pressure in the veins of the lower extremity, a condition of pregnancy, is the cause. There does seem to be a strong heredity factor too. Any girl whose mother has had much trouble with varicose veins has two strikes against her when she becomes pregnant. Often the varicose veins are much worse on one side than on the other. This condition is due to the arrangement in the pelvis of the large arteries and veins that supply the legs. On one side the artery crosses over the veins, while on the other side it does not.

Respiratory System

A certain amount of nasal congestion goes with pregnancy. Often the ears feel plugged up. Women feel in summer that they have suddenly developed an allergy, and in winter they seem to have a cold that will not go away. Because of this congestion, nosebleeds are quite common. Women predisposed to sinus infections are likely in pregnancy to have acute flare-ups.

Many women notice breathlessness in the middle and latter parts of pregnancy. We are uncertain about the cause of this condition. In spite of the enlarged abdomen, pregnancy does not reduce the capacity of the lungs to perform the functions necessary to life.

Gastrointestinal Symptoms

Nausea, vomiting, and constipation in the early stages are such common changes in pregnancy that they have already been referred to as symptoms. In addition, the emptying time of the stomach is delayed in pregnancy; women with gastric ulcers frequently are relieved of their symptoms because food in the stomach keeps the ulcer quiet. In the middle and latter parts of pregnancy, many women have severe heartburn, which results from the pushing up of a nubbin of the stomach where the esophagus (the tube connecting the mouth and stomach) passes through the diaphragm. This condition is known as *hiatus hernia*. The discomfort is often worse at night or when lying flat. Sitting or sleeping with the head elevated gives relief. The condition goes away promptly with delivery. There is also a sluggishness in the flow of bile in pregnancy. As a consequence, gallstones develop more frequently in women who have had children. The change in bile flow accounts for the frequent indigestion that follows indulgence in rich or heavy foods.

Urinary System

The changes of most importance in the urinary system are dilation of the ureters and the kidney pelvis that convey the urine from the kidney to the bladder. This dilation predisposes to infections of the urinary tract, which are among the most common complications of pregnancy.

Musculoskeletal System

One of the hormones produced in pregnancy is thought to soften the joints that bind the pelvic bones together. While this softening does little to enlarge the capacity of the pelvis for childbirth, the resulting separation of bones can lead to backaches and pelvic discomfort in the latter part of pregnancy.

Skin

Even the skin undergoes changes in pregnancy. Most women will develop a darkening of pigment-bearing areas. The areola of the breast (the ring of color around the nipple) becomes darker, as do many moles and other nevi, the general name for congenital markings. You often hear that moles that become darker should be removed because of the possibility of cancer. In pregnancy you needn't worry. A blotchy discoloration of the cheeks and forehead is frequent. This *mask of pregnancy* is also known as *chloasma*. Changes in acne are not consistent. Some patients note that acne improves, others that it gets worse.

ARTHUR GORBACH, M.D.

CHAPTER FOUR

A Healthy Pregnancy

SEEING YOUR DOCTOR

O NCE YOU are reasonably certain that you have conceived, it is wise to make an appointment to see the doctor. There are several reasons for an examination early in pregnancy. Complications of a serious nature can occur at this time. An example is *ectopic* pregnancy, or pregnancy in the Fallopian tube. If this condition is discovered and treated early, the consequences are much less serious than if nature is allowed to run its course. Another reason for examination in early pregnancy is that at this time an accurate estimate of the duration of pregnancy can be made. Later on, accuracy is much more difficult. If it becomes necessary to terminate pregnancy, it is obviously of great importance to know how mature the baby is, and if the menstrual history is in doubt, the best criterion is the relative growth of the uterus from early pregnancy. Further, the prenatal examination is becoming more oriented toward preventive medicine. This is the only time many young women have a physical examination, and numerous abnormalities, from neglected teeth on down, are disclosed. Whether or not they have a direct bearing on the outcome of pregnancy, the sooner neglected disorders are attended to the better. Since the diagnosis of pregnancy is in some doubt until two or three weeks after the missed period, there is no point in seeing your physician earlier. You should call for an appointment with your doctor when your period is a couple of weeks overdue.

Our society is continually on the move. Many women find themselves pregnant in a strange city and are lost when it comes to picking out a doctor. Another doctor is one of the best sources of information. If you have had occasion to consult an internist or a pediatrician, you will almost certainly be able to get the name of an obstetrician from either of them. If you know you will be looking for a doctor as soon as you get settled, it is wise to ask for recommendations ahead of time, from your physician or from other doctors in the city where you have been well acquainted. Even though your doctor may not know anyone personally in the city you will be moving to, he has access to directories and lists of all types of specialists throughout the country. When you are completely at sea, the local hospital or medical society can furnish you with a list of qualified physicians. If there is a medical school in the area, someone there can supply the names of the members of the obstetrics staff. While there seems to be no letup in the increasing trend toward specialization, it is not essential to have a specialist in obstetrics. Many general physicians carry heavy obstetric loads and do practically everything that the obstetric specialist does. In large cities, hospitals have obstetric clinics where care of a generally high quality is given by the staff of resident physicians.

At your first visit, your doctor will take your regular medical history and find out what diseases or operations you have had. In the supervision of a pregnancy there is increasing emphasis nowadays on obtaining this sort of information. He will want to hear the details of any previous pregnancies, their duration, the length of labor, the weight of the baby, and any complications you might have had in pregnancy or labor. He will also ask you for details of your family history.

After taking the history, the doctor probably will do a complete physical examination, including an internal or pelvic examination. He will use an instrument called a speculum to separate the vaginal walls so that he can see the cervix, or neck of the womb. If he is going to do the *Pap smear* test he will do it at this time. As you may know, this test was designed to detect early cancers of the cervix. These may occur (but very rarely) in the course of pregnancy. When your doctor does the internal examination, he can determine whether the pregnancy is normal and whether the uterus is enlarging as it should at this stage. He will also evaluate the pelvic bones and get a fair idea whether small measurements are going to lead to mechanical difficulties in labor.

Some laboratory tests are also done early in pregnancy. The blood group and Rh type should be obtained, along with a blood count or hemoglobin determination to show whether anemia is present. Urinalysis is also done. Almost all states require a blood test for syphilis, because if an infected mother is not treated in pregnancy, this disease will be transmitted to the unborn child.

Before you are finished with your first appointment, your doctor will have discussed a number of matters with you. He will tell you the estimated due date; that is, the projected date for the birth of your baby. For women with regular monthly menstrual periods this calculation is done by adding a week to the date of the last menstrual period and counting back three months. For example, if the last menstrual period started on May 15, say, you would add a week, making May 22, and then count back three months, arriving at February 22 as the estimated delivery date. The great majority of patients (80 to 90 percent) will deliver within ten days, plus or minus, of the estimated due date.

There are do's and don'ts concerning pregnancy that your doctor will want to discuss with you, and he will tell you about such danger signals as pain or bleeding that should alert you to possible complications. You undoubtedly will have questions that he will be glad to answer. Either the doctor or his aide will tell you how he schedules his appointments and will make sure you know when and where you can call him between appointments, if necessary. Before you conclude this first visit, you may even want to make reservations in the hospital.

Before the twentieth century the doctor did not see the expectant mother until the onset of labor, unless she developed some sort of complication. Not until it became obvious that many problems could be dealt with properly if they were discovered early did the system of prenatal care as we know it today gradually evolve. In current practice, the pregnant woman usually sees her doctor at monthly intervals until the seventh month. After that the visits are more frequent. At each visit, the doctor examines the mother to see if the pregnancy is growing properly. By mid-pregnancy she should be able to feel the baby move. Women who have borne children previously and know the signs experience this quickening somewhat earlier than do those pregnant for the first time. This is an important landmark in pregnancy. Since the quickening occurs quite consistently at about four and one-half months, it helps the doctor to decide whether the estimated date of delivery is accurate. Two or three weeks after the mother has felt the baby kicking, the doctor will be able to hear the fetal heartbeat if conditions for examination are favorable.

Toward the end of pregnancy the doctor will be able to tell in what position the baby will be at birth. An internal examination in the last month of pregnancy will disclose the state of the neck of the womb. This information helps in guessing whether labor will be on time or a little early or late. It also is a good indicator of whether labor will be relatively short or long. Nevertheless, predictions on both the timing and duration of labor are no more than educated guesses. We all know women who, having been told that the baby would not come for two to three weeks, have delivered two or three days later. It will always be so, until we find out exactly what it is that makes labor begin.

At each of the prenatal visits the patient is weighed, the blood pressure taken, and the urine examined for protein. This precaution is taken to detect a condition known as *toxemia* or *preeclampsia*. The first symptom of toxemia is usually a retention of fluid in the body, reflected in a rapid weight gain. Later on, swelling of the hands, feet, and face develops, along with elevated blood pressure and protein in the urine. Early toxemia usually responds to the elimination of salt from the diet and rest in bed. If the toxemia becomes severe, it is sometimes necessary to terminate pregnancy prematurely. Fortunately, toxemia is seen less and less. Most cases today are found in patients who have had no prenatal care. Not all swelling is dangerous. Many women in the latter part of pregnancy will have a little swelling of the ankles at the end of the day, especially in summer.

The ideal weight gain in pregnancy might be set at two pounds a month, but many perfectly normal women do gain a little more. A gain of as much as five pounds or more in a month is abnormal and certainly calls for strict measures to reduce.

GENERAL INSTRUCTIONS FOR PREGNANCY

Pregnancy is a perfectly normal state of affairs. When you come right down to it, it is one of the most normal things a woman can do. Once a pregnancy gets started in the right direction, it is all but impossible to upset its development. Regardless of what the mother does, the pregnancy will continue to develop normally. But if things do not get started right within the first few days and the subsequent development of the pregnancy is faulty, then a miscarriage will almost certainly occur, in spite of all the patient and her doctor may do to prevent it. (See chapter 22, pages 412–16.)

Most young women look forward eagerly to having a baby and find that pregnancy is one of the best times of life. It is a disservice to tell a pregnant woman that because of her "delicate condition" she should drastically curtail her activities. The woman who is pregnant but does not want to be is not likely to heed advice to limit her activity, but somehow even she rarely seems to be lucky enough (in her view) to have a miscarriage. However, there is no question that pregnancy puts quite an added burden on the entire female organism. Most women find that at certain stages they tire easily and require more rest. It is wise to lead a normal life in pregnancy, but it is not prudent to get overly tired. If a rest in the middle of the day can be arranged, it will make life a good deal more enjoyable.

Birth and death—the ultimate events of our existence—have always stirred man's imagination. In every culture a large body of folklore about pregnancy has arisen to explain this phenomenal event and its complications. Our culture is no exception. The popular superstitions seem ridiculous to the sophisticated scientific community, but so firmly are some of these ideas established that many otherwise well-informed women accept them as fact. Not many people today believe that if you are frightened by a one-legged man your baby will be deformed, but many women are quite convinced that lifting heavy objects will produce a miscarriage, or that painting or inhaling paint fumes will be harmful to a mother with child. Lifting the hands above the head is supposed to wrap the cord around the baby's neck, while, on the blissful side of superstition, plenty of Bach and Beethoven is supposed to inculcate a love of good music in the baby from the very moment of birth. There is no truth to these beliefs.

COMMON QUESTIONS DURING PREGNANCY

There are a number of common questions that come up at some point during practically every pregnancy.

Weight Control and Diet

In the opinion of many (if not most) doctors, control of the weight through diet is the most important single aspect of prenatal care. Excessive weight gain in pregnancy can lead to complications and is dangerous. On the other hand, the mother and her unborn child obviously need proper nutrition. At first glance, those two statements may seem contradictory, but in fact they are not.

Everyone who has made a study of nutrition in relation to childbirth has concluded that, on the average, women who are well nourished have fewer complications in pregnancy than poorly nourished women, and produce healthier babies. After much investigation the consensus is that the ideal diet for pregnancy is one rich in protein. A good pregnancy diet will contain a serving of meat or of fish or fowl a couple of times a day, a glass or two of milk daily, and an egg at least three or four times a week, in addition to a variety of fruits and vegetables and some cereals. Meat, eggs, and dairy products are our main source of protein, but vegetables and cereals do contain it in some amount. The pregnant woman's serving of lean meat should be not less than three or four ounces at a meal. Liver is an excellent food for the expectant mother because in addition to its protein it has vitamins and minerals. If weight is a problem for her, seafood—because the fat content is relatively low—makes a good source of protein. The pregnant woman should not skimp on her meals. She should eat three times a day and should have enough at each meal to carry her over to the next. She should not be driven to snacking between meals. Foods prepared with oil should be kept to a minimum. There is a tendency in all pregnancies to retain sodium and water, and since excessive retention of fluid and sodium is in some way connected with toxemia of pregnancy, it is wise to cut down on salt.

While many persons (male and female, the nonpregnant along with the pregnant) do take vitamin supplements, there is no good evidence that extra vitamins will benefit women who are on a well-balanced diet. People who are well nourished do not suffer from vitamin deficiencies, and the only ailments vitamins can be expected to cure are vitamin deficiencies. Further, no study with adequate controls has proved that either mothers or their infants at birth do better with vitamin supplements if the diet has been a good one to start with. For those who do not have a well-balanced diet, vitamins may be necessary. The diets of busy, though well-to-do, women are not always much better than those of the poor. Most physicians will review the patient's diet and will then recommend on an individual basis.

The average woman will lose fifteen to twenty pounds in the first couple of weeks following delivery. Consequently, your weight gain in pregnancy should not exceed this amount. Moreover, any extra weight gained in pregnancy is likely to stay with you for the rest of your life. The gynecologist's world seems to be full of rotund ladies who wistfully tell him, "You wouldn't believe it, but I weighed 105 pounds when I was married."

While the ideal weight gain averages out to about half a pound per week, this rate does not remain constant in each of the nine months of pregnancy. In the last few months it will be greater, because the baby himself is gaining almost an ounce a day. Also, toward the end of pregnancy, there is more of a tendency to retain fluids.

To keep the weight gain in pregnancy under twenty pounds is a struggle for most women, but it is a necessary one. You should be continually conscious of your caloric intake. In spite of what a popular book asserted a few years back, calories definitely do count, but there is a large variation in the caloric requirements of different individuals. One person could lose weight on the same diet on which another gains. For pregnancy, nutritionists usually advise diets yielding 2500 to 3000 calories per day. Many women would gain excessively if they had a caloric intake that large. They have to restrict their calories to something like 2000 a day to keep from putting on too much weight. A few must go even lower. It is not wise to go below 1500 calories per day in pregnancy because it then becomes hard to prepare a balanced diet containing all the essential food.

For the many women who have trouble controlling their weight gain in pregnancy, here are a few bits of advice. Keep a count of the number of calories eaten each day. Most stores selling paperback books carry a little booklet that gives the exact number of calories in different foods. Try to skimp and save calories every way possible. Drink skim milk or buttermilk instead of homogenized milk; use vinegar or lemon juice on salads instead of mayonnaise. Make a sandwich with one slice of bread instead of two. With little tricks like these, you can easily save a couple of hundred calories a day. This skimping could make the difference of a pound or two a month, since a pound of fat is equivalent to about 4000 calories.

Many women struggling to control their weight will try to fill up on vegetables or fruits, since they are not satisfied with only a salad. Put some protein, like a hard-boiled egg, sliced chicken, or cheese, on the salad and it will stick with you a lot longer. Hot foods are more satisfying than cold ones. A cup of hot soup for lunch or supper does not contain many calories but will go a long way toward filling you up.

Many of the canned and dried soups, however, do contain a lot of salt, so it is better to make your own.

Cut out salt. Do not add any to the food when you are preparing it or at the table. Do not buy salty foods, such as ham or corned beef. It is not necessary to buy specially prepared salt-free foods, such as salt-free milk or bread. You may use a salt substitute if you wish. Monosodium glutamate, since it contains sodium, should not be used as a salt substitute. You can use simple spices freely (pepper, thyme, cloves, and the like), but most of the prepared condiments, such as soy sauce and Worcestershire sauce, contain a lot of salt.

Appetite-suppressing pills have very limited usefulness in the control of weight during pregnancy (or at any other time for that matter). If nothing more than a few pills were required to lose weight, those of us who are heavier than we want to be would have our problems solved. In practice, it will be found that pills do not suppress the appetite for very long unless administered in ever-increasing dosages. The jitters and sleeplessness are frequent side effects. Still, it cannot be denied that appetite-suppressing drugs have been prescribed to large numbers of pregnant women, and there is no evidence that they interfere in any way with the development of a perfectly normal baby, provided the nutritional requirements are met.

Pregnant women are usually advised to drink a quart of milk a day. Milk is an excellent food, but many mothers throughout the world go through pregnancy without any at all. If you are not particularly fond of milk, a couple of glasses a day will be enough. You may substitute other dairy products for milk, if you wish. Cottage cheese is a favorite substitute (in addition to being a great filler-upper and low in calories). A scoop of cottage cheese is a little low in calcium, but it will not do any good to try to correct this deficiency with calcium pills. Almost none of the calcium taken in this form is absorbed. You do not need great quantities of calcium, anyway. (Incidentally, you do not have to worry that your teeth and bones will become demineralized as a result of your carrying a child. They will not.) Other cheeses are good milk substitutes. A cube of cheese an inch and a quarter on each side is equivalent in calcium and protein to a glass of milk. Since many cheeses are quite salty, you will have to avoid them if retention of sodium and fluid is a problem.

Leafy and green and yellow vegetables should be eaten once or twice daily. Examples are peas, beans, broccoli, cabbage, spinach, peppers, carrots, and the like. Since cooking destroys some of the vitamins, it is good practice to eat a serving of raw vegetables each day in a salad. Frozen foods are as nutritious as fresh, but they have an appreciable salt content.

Starchy vegetables—potatoes, corn, eggplant, and squash among them—contain necessary minerals, but are more caloric than leafy ones. If weight gain gets to be a problem, go easy on them.

You should have a daily minimum of one serving of citrus fruit or some other fruit or vegetable rich in vitamin C. Examples are oranges, grapefruit, tomatoes, pineapple, and cantaloupe. Frozen or canned juices are as satisfactory as fresh ones.

Breads and starchy foods, such as rice and spaghetti, can ordinarily be eaten once or twice a day. They round out the diet and satisfy the appetite, but yield relatively little of nutritive value except calories. If you are gaining too rapidly and want to cut down on your caloric intake, here is one of the first places to begin.

The other food to cut down on is fats. A couple of pats of butter a day are prescribed for the usual diet in pregnancy, but this allowance can be eliminated if calories must be restricted. Nutritionally, margarine is the same as butter. Other ways to reduce fats in the diet are to drink skim milk (instead of homogenized) and to boil or broil meats instead of frying them. Avoid foods prepared with gravy, cream, or shortening. Pregnant women should drink a lot of fluid through the day. This intake will insure a larger volume of urine and thus help to prevent infections of the urinary tract. Try to get a couple of quarts of fluid each day. In pregnancy it is a good idea to eat for one and drink for two.

Iron Deficiency Anemia

There is good evidence that most women develop an iron deficiency anemia in pregnancy, and for this reason an iron preparation should be taken. An important side effect of iron administration, however, is gastrointestinal upset. Because morning sickness is often a part of early pregnancy, iron may contribute to the discomfort and therefore can be withheld until after the morning sickness has subsided.

A warning about iron pills (and all other medication) should be sounded. If a small child should swallow a large number of iron tablets, he might become seriously ill. Keep iron pills (and all other medication) well out of reach of young children.

Bathing

A daily tub bath or shower should be taken throughout pregnancy. Until recently many women avoided, or were advised to avoid, tub baths in the latter part of pregnancy in the erroneous belief that the bath water would get into the birth canal and lead to infection. No water enters the birth canal in the bathtub. It is perfectly harmless to take a tub bath right up to the day labor begins.

Douching

Douching is usually unnecessary in pregnancy. There are increased mucoid secretions from the neck of the womb, but these are not abnormal. If the secretions become bothersome, relief can be obtained by douching with plain tap water, or tap water and vinegar in the proportion of one quart of water to four tablespoons of household vinegar. Douching in pregnancy calls for certain precautions. In no circumstances should a syringe of the hand-bulb type be used. With this instrument there is the danger of introducing air into the uterine veins. For douching in pregnancy, you should lie on your back in the tub with the knees drawn up, the same position you assume when a physician examines you internally. Use a syringe of the fountain type and suspend it a foot or two above the level of the tub—the handle of the faucet is a convenient place. The douche nozzle should not be inserted full length. Only approximately one-half of it should be introduced into the vaginal canal. The douching solution should be allowed to run into and out of the birth canal. If the vaginal discharge is associated with itching and irritation, these are symptoms of an infection. Your doctor will prescribe appropriate treatment for the type of organism in the infection.

Breast Care

There are many different opinions about care of the nipples and breast prior to delivery, ranging from doing nothing at all to hand expression of colostrum several times daily for several months prior to delivery. Some suggest "twanging" nipples and applying creams. We have never been impressed that special care makes much difference. Particularly light-complexioned women with sensitive skin and especially those who have had difficulty with their nipples during previous lactations, may find "toughening" maneuvers to minimize nipple discomfort with onset of nursing useful. This is an individual matter to discuss with your physician or nurse.

Shoes and Clothes

Nowadays you can buy comfortable, stylish maternity clothes almost everywhere at reasonable prices. Early in pregnancy the breasts become heavier and larger and consequently require a larger brassiere for adequate support. There are numerous undergarments designed to support the enlarging uterus, but most women do not need a girdle or foundation garment. You can get a simple garter belt to hold up your stockings. This is much better than a garter around the leg, which constricts the circulation and favors the development of varicose veins and ankle swelling. Some women who have had several children or who have chronic backaches will be more comfortable in a maternity girdle. If you are going to buy one, do not skimp on price or quality. Inexpensive ones are almost always unsatisfactory. Many department stores do not carry maternity girdles, but you can purchase them at maternity shops. Although there is no real reason to stop wearing high-heeled shoes, most women find they are not too comfortable as pregnancy progresses. About the fourth or fifth month, you would be wise to buy a pair of comfortable shoes with a low or medium heel. If you get them as soon as you know you are pregnant, they might not fit at the end of pregnancy. The bones of the feet do not actually enlarge, but almost everyone has some fluid retention, which during the day tends to accumulate in the legs and feet. This swelling makes a larger shoe necessary.

Sexual Intercourse

There are various highly opinionated beliefs about sexual intercourse in pregnancy, but few are based on sound scientific observations. Many authorities state that couples should abstain from intercourse in early pregnancy because of the danger of precipitating a miscarriage. However, the majority of early miscarriages are due to defective development of the ovum. Abstaining from intercourse will not salvage them. If sexual intercourse in pregnancy caused miscarriages, the human race probably would have petered out many millions of years ago.

Just how long in pregnancy it is advisable to have intercourse is a moot point. Many women find the libido diminishes remarkably, and therefore the question never comes up. Others find intercourse uncomfortable and so stop having relations as pregnancy progresses. Most physicians tell their patients to stop sexual relations by the last month of pregnancy because of the danger of infection of the birth canal should labor ensue or the membranes rupture shortly after intercourse. However, several recent studies failed to confirm the danger of intercourse in the last few weeks of pregnancy.

Exercise and Sports

The woman who is having a normal pregnancy and has had an uncomplicated history in past pregnancies can participate in almost any sport. Violent activity that might result in a severe, direct blow to the abdomen should be avoided, of course, but tennis, golf, swimming, and sailing can be enjoyed. Good skiers have continued to ski in pregnancy without harm, perhaps because one does not often fall on one's stomach. On the other hand, because pregnant women lack the stamina and reserve of the nonpregnant, they are prone to become exhausted when engaging in competitive games. If you feel you must take part in competitive games in pregnancy, play for the joy of playing, not for the joy of winning.

Travel

Traveling does not cause complications of pregnancy. If you cared to, you could go around the world in perfect safety. But in the latter part of pregnancy, you are likely to find long trips by car or in planes uncomfortable. Having to sit all day (or all night) in one place will give almost every pregnant woman swelling of the legs. Muscular action, particularly in the legs, helps to drive interstitial fluid from the tissues back into the circulation. If you are just sitting, you lose this relief. Periodic breaks to exercise the leg muscles will improve the circulation and prevent swelling.

A question about pregnancy and travel that comes up with increasing frequency concerns car seat belts. In a collision what happens to the pregnant woman who is constrained around the middle with a safety belt? The consensus is that even in pregnancy you will be safer with a seat belt than without one. The ideal safety device in gestation is the shoulder harness (more commonly seen in Europe or in European cars), which does not exert pressure over the abdomen. The conventional lap belt should be arranged to exert pressure low over the pubic area, rather than higher up directly over the enlarged body of the uterus.

Airlines used to restrict travel in the latter part of pregnancy, but in this country, they no longer do so. The only possible danger in air travel specific to pregnancy would be lack of oxygen at altitudes over twelve thousand to fifteen thousand feet. Since commercial planes flying at these altitudes are all pressurized, the oxygen supply is no problem. It is barely possible that an unpressurized private plane would reach these altitudes. Severe oxygen deprivation could seriously damage the fetus, but this hazard in flying is mainly theoretical.

Since no one can predict accurately the date of delivery, it is wise to leave travel out of your plans for the last month of pregnancy. Avoid trips that would take you so far from your doctor and the hospital that you could not get back in an hour or two if labor should begin or if some complication should arise. Mothers who have a history of premature labor should apply this rule earlier than the last month. An untold number of women in labor have walked, crawled, ridden horseback, or driven cars over considerable distances for help, and come through unscathed. But why go out of your way to make things difficult? Play it safe is a good rule for the last month or so of pregnancy.

Working

A normal pregnancy is perfectly consistent with normal activity, and this includes most forms of employment. There is no reason for the pregnant woman to give up her job. But even when women want to work, many large companies have rules prohibiting employment in the latter half of pregnancy. Most employed women want to leave a few weeks before the baby is due; there is much preparing to be done before the baby is born, especially if it is the first one. Pregnant women tire easily and lack the stamina they formerly had. A good rule of thumb on working in pregnancy is this: work as long as you enjoy or need to work and do not get overly tired. In any case, be assured that working will not endanger the baby.

Dental Care

Pregnant women often ask whether it is all right to have dental care in pregnancy. Every woman having a baby should see her dentist at least once. There is nothing universal about the old saying, "You lose a tooth for every baby," but the age at which most people have their families coincides with the age when cavities are so common. If you put off dental care for the nine months of pregnancy and another three or four months after delivery, a whole year has gone by. Any dental work neglected this long can result in loss of a tooth, or worse. Dental work in pregnancy should be done under local anesthesia. Nitrous oxide should not be taken because administration of this so-called laughing gas might deprive the fetus of oxygen. If the dental work is so extensive that local anesthesia will not be sufficient, a general anesthetic is necessary, even at the cost of being hospitalized.

Many pregnant women have swollen, baggy gums that bleed easily when brushed. Not a few have undergone extensive oral surgery, known as *gingivectomy*, for this perfectly normal change, which regresses after delivery. This is not to say that a gingivectomy is never indicated in pregnancy, but if the procedure is contemplated you will be wise to seek the advice of an experienced oral surgeon who would certainly be familiar with the gum changes of pregnancy. The question of dental X rays in pregnancy often comes up. Completely routine films can and should be deferred until after delivery. Films your dentist seriously needs—for example, to help him decide whether or not you must lose a tooth—should be taken under proper precautions of shielding. Let your dentist know if you are pregnant. If there is any question about an X ray, he can always check with your doctor.

Alcohol and Tobacco

There is no reason to restrict alcohol in moderation during pregnancy. Many women find the occasional drink a pleasant persuasion to relax. But that before dinner cocktail, particularly if it is accompanied by a snack, can be the downfall of many who have trouble controlling their weight.

It has been shown that babies born of mothers who smoke tend to be several ounces lighter at birth than those whose mothers are non-smokers. These are statistically valid observations based on thousands of pregnancy records, but are completely valueless in predicting the birth weight in an individual pregnancy. One cannot tell the mother of a four-pound baby that she would have had a four-and-one-half-pound baby if she had not smoked. Although the babies of smoking mothers tend to be smaller, they are just as healthy as the babies of nonsmokers, and the infant survival rate is the same in both groups. There are much more compelling arguments against the use of tobacco in general. Cancer of the lung and other diseases of the heart and lungs are undoubtedly much more common in smokers than nonsmokers. If these facts are not sufficient to deter women from smoking, it is doubtful that the foregoing statistical observations on the size of babies will make additional converts.

Drugs

The administration of certain drugs to the mother in pregnancy may result in abnormalities in the offspring. This lesson was brought home dramatically to us all by the thalidomide tragedy. Fortunately the strict governmental controls here in the United States on the approval of new drugs prevented the distribution of thalidomide in America. Since the trouble with thalidomide, the controls have been tightened even more. Now even useful new drugs are withheld for many months on the very slightest suspicion. This is as it should be. In pregnancy particularly, most of the drugs taken are not lifesaving but are given for minor aches and pains. It is better to take nothing than to risk a drug that is under even the slightest suspicion. Actually, the number of drugs known to cause fetal abnormalities is very small. There is little to worry about. A good rule to follow is to take only the drugs that your doctor prescribes. Do not dose yourself with patent medicines or nonprescription items.

Radiation

The effect of radiation on living organisms is a complex subject, and a little background in genetics (see pages 436–37) is necessary to understand it. Genes are the hereditary factors present in cells and are responsible for the characteristics we inherit from our parents—the color of our hair, our blood type, and an almost infinite number of others. From time to time a change in the genes occurs, known as a mutation, and an individual is born with characteristics different from those of either of his parents.

For example, a mutation may occur in one parent's gene that determines vision. Even though both parents may have 20/20 vision, the child will not inherit the perfect eyesight of his parents but will have defective vision and will then pass this gene for defective vision on to his own children. It is by similar processes that genetic mutation goes on all the time. (This of course is not limited to undesirable traits.) The sum of these processes has been responsible for the gradual change that has taken place in the human race over the millions of years men have existed on the earth.

Geneticists tell us that exposure to radiation in any form, X ray, radium, even the cosmic background radiation with which we are all continually bombarded, increases the rate of genetic mutation. The greater the amount of radiation the higher the rate of genetic change. So there is really no dose of radiation that can be said to be perfectly safe. We can all see easily that while one pill is perfectly safe, three or four of the same would be harmful, but the concept that there is really no safe dose of radiation is harder to grasp.

The amount of radiation exposure in diagnostic X rays is extremely small and consequently results in an infinitesimal increase in the rate of genetic change. The information gained by diagnostic X rays can be very great. From a practical standpoint, there is nothing to worry about from one or even several diagnostic X rays in pregnancy, or at any other time, if they are necessary for the diagnosis or management of an injury or ailment. The amount of radiation exposure in X-ray or radium *treatments* is generally much greater than for diagnostic X-ray films. The effects of radiation are cumulative; that is, they build up year after year. For this reason, X-ray and radium treatments should not be given to children, male or female, or young adults unless absolutely necessary. Unfortunately, in the past many young people were treated with radiation for relatively minor conditions when some other form of therapy would have been just as good or better.

Extremely heavy exposure to radiation is fatal to the developing embryo. About the only time we see this in clinical practice is when cancer of the womb is found in early pregnancy. Sufficient radium treatment to destroy the tumor will invariably cause a miscarriage. Since cancer of the womb is so serious if untreated, we accept the loss of pregnancy as one of the unfortunate complications of complete cancer treatment.

DANGER SIGNALS

Vaginal Bleeding

Vaginal bleeding is probably the most important and frequent of the danger signals in pregnancy. Even so, bleeding does not always mean that some grave complication is in the offing. Frequently none is. But bleeding is never a good sign and cannot be ignored.

Many women have slight, painless bleeding at the time of the first missed period. This is not in the least dangerous to mother or developing baby. Its only practical significance is that it can throw the predicted date of delivery off by a month if it is interpreted as a normal period.

Bleeding in early pregnancy sometimes means a miscarriage is impending. It is also one of the symptoms of a tubal pregnancy in which the pregnancy develops not in the uterus but in a Fallopian tube. In the middle part of pregnancy bleeding that is no more than a slight brown show may indicate an *incompetent cervix,* requiring treatment. Minimal bleeding after sexual intercourse in pregnancy usually indicates the presence of a benign *cervical polyp* or merely a congested *cervical erosion.*

In the latter part of pregnancy bleeding can become dangerous to both the mother and child and should be reported at once. Heavy bleeding at this time indicates some abnormality in the attachment of the placenta. Either it is attached too close to the neck of the womb or part of its attachment comes loose before labor or delivery. At the onset of labor there is often a small amount of bleeding or "show." At the end of pregnancy the show is often found following internal examinations.

The foregoing are some of the commoner causes of bleeding in pregnancy. There are many others that are encountered less frequently. While bleeding in pregnancy is not always serious, let us stress again that it should always be reported to the doctor.

Abdominal Pain

If you called your doctor each time in pregnancy you had a twinge of abdominal pain, both you and he would spend a good deal of the nine months on the phone. On the other hand, severe and persistent abdominal pain often indicates a complication and should always be reported to your physician. When the neck of the womb opens, whether in miscarriage or labor, there are severe menstruallike cramps. Between cramps there is no discomfort. Pain that comes from the neck of the womb is felt in the midline, low in the abdomen or back, and even at times branching to the thighs.

There are many causes for abdominal pain in pregnancy. In early pregnancy many women experience a vague, poorly localized sense of lower abdominal cramp, which is of no significance. In both miscarriages and tubal pregnancies there usually will be moderate to severe pain and abnormal bleeding. When the uterus enlarges out of the pelvis (after the third month) , the ligaments holding it in place begin to stretch. Even a slight movement of the uterus, which can occur with a cough or sudden change in motion or sudden change in the mother's position, can cause a sharp twinge of pain low down in the groin, on one side or the other.

Pregnancy does not offer any protection against serious conditions that cause abdominal pain in women who are not pregnant. A good example is appendicitis (see pages 120–22), which requires prompt surgical treatment in pregnancy as at any other time. Sometimes the operation is delayed because the discomfort is thought to be one of the "aches and pains of pregnancy."

Toward the end of pregnancy one of the more frequent serious complications giving rise to abdominal pain is premature separation of the placenta. This condition is almost always associated with bleeding, which can be heavy at times but not necessarily so.

Labor pains are menstruallike cramps felt in the middle, either in front or in back. They gradually become more severe and the interval between them gradually decreases as the labor progresses. Patients often wonder how they can distinguish between true labor pains and a false alarm. Sometimes at the beginning of labor there is slight vaginal bleeding or "show." This showing does not occur with false labor. Physical activity sometimes will make false labor pains disappear. Get up and pace the floor for fifteen or twenty minutes. If the pains cease, it is not the real thing. Activity will often make true labor pains more frequent and intense.

Persistent and severe pain at any time in pregnancy should be reported to your physician.

Rupture of the Membranes

The bag of waters surrounding the baby breaks before the onset of labor in 10 to 15 percent of cases. Usually this happens at the end of pregnancy, and labor begins a short time later. If labor does begin, there is no danger. But if the onset of labor is long delayed, there is the possibility of an infection developing in the birth canal. An infection of this sort could be serious to both the mother and infant. Every once in a while a woman will come into the doctor's office and blithely report that the membranes have been ruptured for several days. Do not put yourself into this position. Report rupture of the membranes to your doctor when it occurs. If you are close to term, your doctor usually will induce labor if it does not start spontaneously within a few hours.

If it is a long time until your due date, your physician may not want to induce labor because the risk of prematurity will outweigh the risk of infection. In this situation it is important to check your temperature several times a day to pick up early evidence of developing infection and to avoid douching and sexual relations. Douching and sexual relations in pregnancy are harmless as long as the membranes are intact, but after the membranes have ruptured, there is always the possibility of introducing an infection. Many women will have a gush of fluid at the end of pregnancy but will not be sure whether it has come from the bladder or the vagina. When the membranes rupture, there is usually no great flood and often no more than several tablespoonsful. After the rupture, however, there is a continuous slight dribbling over which the patient has no control. While the dribble may not amount to much at any one time, it is enough to saturate a couple of sanitary napkins in the course of a morning or necessitate a change in underclothing three or four times in the same interval. If this occurs at any time during pregnancy, call your doctor. Even if you can't be sure, let him know. He will be able to tell by examination whether the bag of waters is broken or intact.

Symptoms of Pregnancy Toxemia

Anyone who develops any of the following symptoms in the latter part of pregnancy should notify her doctor without delay: sudden puffiness of the face, eyes, or fingers; sudden unremitting headaches; blurring of vision.

Loss of Fetal Activity

Pregnant women begin to feel their babies move at about four and a half months. Some babies are much more active than others, but even the inactive ones should be felt at least once every twenty-four hours. Once you have felt life, if a whole day goes by without your having felt the baby move at all, you should notify your doctor—something may have happened to the baby. Usually the doctor will be able to hear the baby's heartbeat and can reassure you that all is well. Occasionally, at a routine visit, he may have trouble locating the baby's heartbeat, but the mother has no trouble in feeling the baby move. This is nothing to worry about. The baby just happens to be in a position that makes heartbeat hard to find. If, however, the mother does not experience fetal movements and the doctor is unable to find the fetal heart, it almost always means that a stillbirth will occur. Stillbirths, fortunately, are uncommon. The most frequent cause in the past has been the Rh-negative problem, which now is almost always preventable (page 151). Other causes are premature separation of the placenta, high blood pressure, and diabetes. Knots and twists of the umbilical cord also can be responsible for a stillbirth, but considering how much fetal activity there is in pregnancy, it is truly remarkable how seldom this occurs.

Babies with congenital anomalies (birth defects), even severe ones, move around inside the womb just as normal ones do. These babies are almost always born alive and it is not until after delivery that the abnormality becomes evident.

ARTHUR GORBACH, M.D.

CHAPTER FIVE

Growth of the Fetus

*M*AN IS a beautifully complicated creature. From some simple organism of only a few cells, he has evolved, over millions of years, into the modern spaceman of our computerized, nuclear age. Remarkable as this evolution has been, it is no more so than the individual's development before birth. We all start life within our mother's abdomen, in the union of two microscopic flecks of matter. The development of these two cells into a new individual is the subject of human embryology.

Many pregnant women want to know what is going on inside them and repeatedly ask the doctor, "What does my baby look like now?" The answer to this question, incidentally, is easy. After the first couple of months the baby, not surprisingly, looks like a baby. To compile *all* the facts of a baby's development in chronological order in words would make even the fascinating story of embryology boring, except to the specialist. The hundreds of strange terms would soon discourage the reader unfamiliar with medicine. In acceptance of the adage that a picture is worth a thousand words, we have selected several pictures of human prenatal development, Figures 1–11. If you will study these pictures and go back to them repeatedly while you read the accompanying text, you should get a good idea of the progress from two-celled speck of matter to baby.

At the beginning of pregnancy the development is very rapid. While he is becoming longer and fatter and his organs more mature, nothing new is added.

PHOTOS BY LENNART NILSSON

First cell divisions

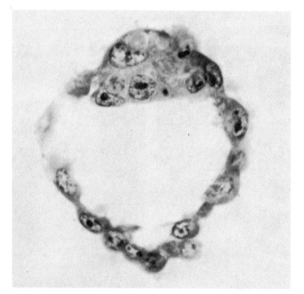

Blastocyst

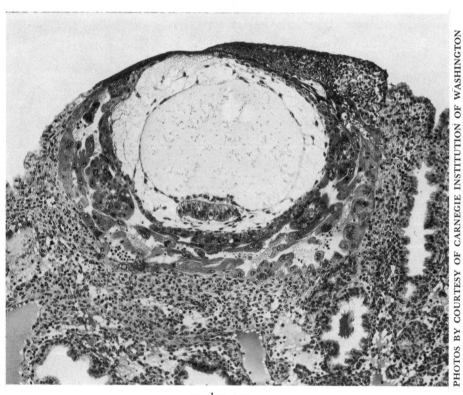

12-day ovum

PHOTOS BY COURTESY OF CARNEGIE INSTITUTION OF WASHINGTON

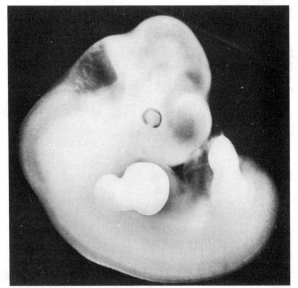

35-day embryo

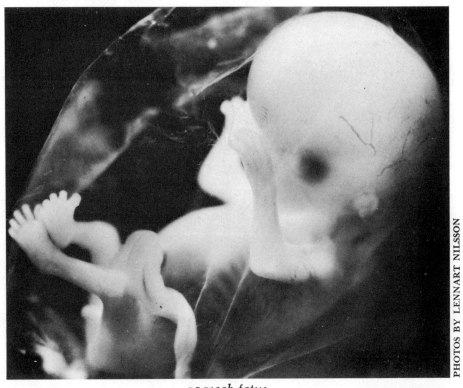

11-week fetus

PHOTOS BY LENNART NILSSON

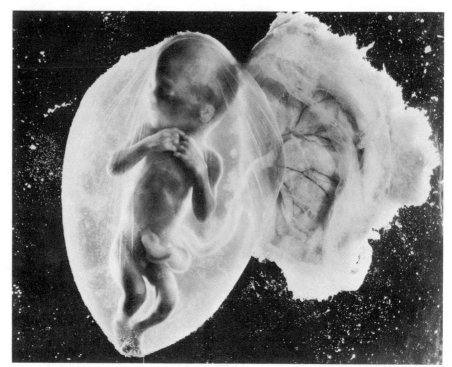

4-month fetus

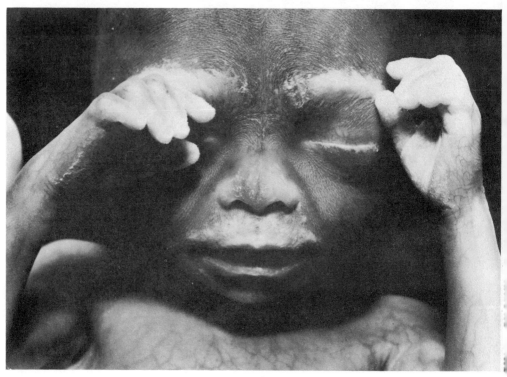

5½-month fetus

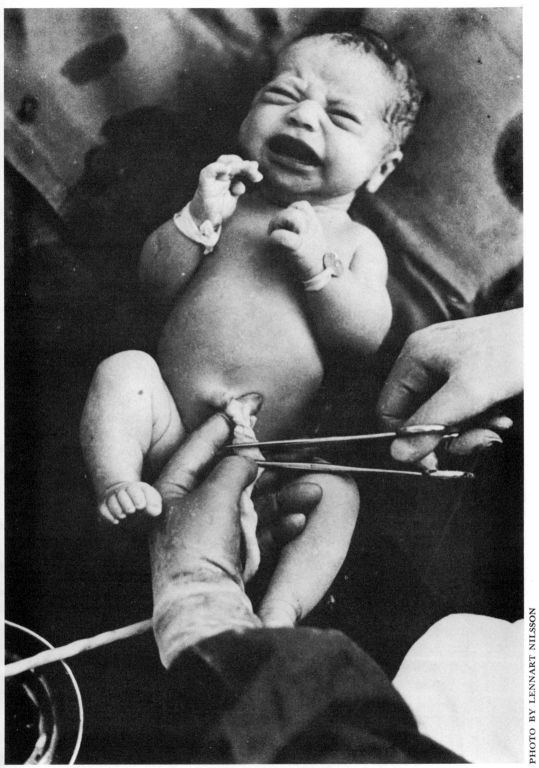

The newborn baby

PHOTO BY LENNART NILSSON

FERTILIZATION

At the time of fertilization, the male sperm cell joins the female ovum. Each has twenty-three chromosomes, and each chromosome contains thousands of genes. Genes are the bearers of hereditary traits such as hair color, blood type, and the almost infinite number of other features that distinguish us as individuals. The chromosomes from the male sperm become mixed with the chromosomes from the female ovum to produce a total of forty-six chromosomes, the constant and characteristic number for the human species.

The future sex of the baby is determined at this time. Of the twenty-three chromosomes in each male sperm cell and each female egg cell, twenty-two chromosomes are called the autosomes. The twenty-third chromosome is called the sex chromosome and it determines sex. Sex chromosomes are of two types, called X and Y. Females are capable of producing only X-type chromosomes. All female ova, at the time of fertilization, carry an X-type chromosome. The male, on the other hand, produces both types. One-half of the sperm cells have an X chromosome, the other half a Y chromosome. If an X-bearing sperm cell fertilizes the egg, a female child results, while a male child develops if the sperm bears the Y sex chromosome. So it is the father who determines the sex of the baby. The king who chopped off the queen's head because she could not produce a male heir was all wrong. He should have looked for a way to produce more Y-type sperm cells.

The X chromosome is larger and heavier than the Y chromosome and, therefore, X-type sperm cells are thought to travel more slowly in their journey up the uterus and Fallopian tube. Sperm cells of the X type are thought to live longer than the Y. From the theoretical standpoint, a couple should have a better chance of conceiving a boy by having sexual relations just before ovulation, and a better chance for a girl if the intercourse is a day or two sooner. From a practical standpoint, however, this information is of little help. We have no easy way to pinpoint the moment of ovulation. There are also great gaps in our knowledge of the fundamental biology of reproduction. Unknown factors in sperm transport and mobility are likely to be of more importance than the weights of the different types of sperm cells.

Just prior to the first cell division, which is illustrated in Figures 1 and 2, the forty-six chromosomes are lined up in a long broad band and split down the middle. Each of the two cells in Figure 2 received forty-six chromosomes, half of the genetic material coming from the father and the other half from the mother. You cannot make out the chromosomes in the photograph, but they are there, in the round central nucleus of each cell. This first cell division is the most important of the billions that are to follow before the baby is completely formed. If the initial splitting of the chromosomes is anything less than perfect, if even just a piece of one chromosome gets lost or fails to divide symmetrically, a fetal abnormality may result. A number of conditions are known to be due to chromosomal abnormality. More are being discovered each year. Fortunately, most occur very rarely. We also think many miscarriages result from these genetic accidents.

A few hours after the first cell division, each of the two cells splits into two, giving rise to a four-cell unit (Figure 3), then each of these cells in turn divides, and so on (Figure 4).

THE BLASTOCYST

A period of rapid cell division ensues giving rise to a hollow sphere, the *blastocyst*. Figure 5 shows the cross section of a human blastocyst four days of age, recovered free from the uterine cavity on the nineteenth day of the menstrual cycle. The large group of cells in the upper portion is known as the inner cell mass; it will form the embryo. The single layer of smaller cells comprising the outside of the sphere is the trophoblast, and will form the placenta. As the blastocyst is forming and enlarging, it is gradually being swept down the Fallopian tube; this journey is accomplished by the beating action of the hairlike cilia on each of the tubal lining cells. The trip down the tube takes about three days. If abnormalities of the tube prevent passage of the blastocyst, a tubal pregnancy can result.

After reaching the womb, the blastocyst continues to enlarge and, after another three or four days, attaches itself to the surface of the womb's lining. This event is called *nidation*. It occurs six or seven days after fertilization. Just how the egg attaches itself into the womb's lining, and why it chooses the particular time and place are not known. Attachment too close to the mouth of the womb can lead at the end of pregnancy to a complication known as *placenta previa*. You will recall that the corpus luteum hormone from the ovary has been preparing the lining of the womb for pregnancy since the time of ovulation, and transforms it into a special tissue known as the decidua.

SEVEN-DAY OVUM IMPLANTATION SITE

The blastocyst, now composed of several hundred cells, invades the decidua and gains a firm attachment to the mother. In the process, this sphere collapses, like a popover just out of the oven. The cells of the inner cell mass take on a somewhat different appearance. From this germinal disc the entire baby will form. The rest of the cells compose the invading *trophoblast*. This is the primitive placenta. The trophoblast is unique. It is the only tissue, outside of malignant tissue, which invades another. If we understood just how it operates and what forces can stop its invasion, we might be a long way toward solving the riddle of malignancy. In addition, the trophoblast is like a tissue graft. It is remarkable that this trophoblastic graft is not rejected. Ordinarily, a tissue from one part of an individual will grow if moved to a suitable site on the same person for grafting. If an attempt is made to graft from one individual to another, however, the graft almost always fails to grow unless the body's rejection mechanisms are greatly suppressed. Drugs to accomplish this are administered when organ transplants, such as heart or kidney, are attempted. In pregnancy the trophoblast is certainly a different tissue from the mother because half of the trophoblast is derived from the father. Yet, for some reason, it is not rejected. We wonder if some problems of sterility or habitual miscarriage do not arise from a complication involving rejection, but at this point, we have no definite proof.

TWO WEEKS

Once the blastocyst has become implanted, its trophoblast grows at an astounding rate, sending out fingerlike projections into the surrounding decidua, as can be seen in Figure 6. These projections become honeycombed, with walls and spaces. At about two weeks of embryonic age, maternal tissues are destroyed to such an extent that eroded maternal blood vessels allow maternal blood to rush into these trophoblastic spaces. Thus, the placental circulation is established, and the mother's blood begins to nourish the developing embryo.

At the time when the maternal blood vessels are eroded, when the maternal circulation to the placenta is "turned on" so to speak, there may be slight vaginal bleeding. This bleeding, called *implantation bleeding,* occurs at about two weeks of embryonic age and corresponds to the time of the first missed menstrual period. The trophoblast produces the chorionic gonadotropic hormone. It keeps the corpus luteum functioning. If the corpus luteum failed at this point, the entire lining of the womb would be cast off, including the developing blastocyst. It is the presence of chorionic gonadotropin in the mother's blood and urine, you will recall, which gives rise to the positive AZ test for pregnancy.

The embryonic disc, at this point, is a double-layer plate, like an empty sandwich. The upper outer layer is called the *ectoderm;* from it develop the skin, hair, nails, and the entire nervous system. The lower layer is the *endoderm;* it gives rise to the digestive tract, the respiratory system, and many of their accessory glands.

Between these two layers a third layer, the *mesoderm,* soon develops. The muscles and tissues lining the abdominal and pleural cavities derive from it. Scattered between these three germinal layers are loose cells called the *mesenchyme.* The mesenchyme does not belong to any one layer but acts as a sort of loose packing tissue between layers. The mesenchyme gives rise to the heart, blood vessels, and also bones and cartilage. All animals on earth form these three layers as the first step in their development. Each layer, regardless of species, forms the same type of organ. The ectoderm forms the skin in man, the scales in fish, and the feathers of a bird.

THREE WEEKS

Man's most important parts are the first formed. The more expendable portions of his anatomy can wait. His most indispensable organs are his brain and his heart. These start to develop in the third week.

The germinal disc rapidly changes its shape. At first oval, it soon becomes pear-shaped and finally resembles the body of a violin. It also bends in the middle, losing the flat shape. Down the middle of the ectodermal surface, which will be the baby's back when he finally acquires one, a couple of parallel ridges form. Between them is a groove or trench, known as the *neural groove*. This will form the central nervous system. The bottom of the groove becomes deeper and wider, while at the top the edges join and seal over, trapping a hollow tube of ectodermal cells beneath the surface. The front part of this tube will thicken and expand to form the brain, while the back part gives rise to the spinal cord. This *invagination* (or folding in) of surface cells is a common embryologic mechanism for forming hollow tubes. In the same manner nature develops the digestive tract and some of the tubes in the urogenital system.

In the third week of embryonic life the heart and blood vessels also begin to develop. Within the mesenchyme, groups of cells called the *blood islands* develop. As the central portions of these islands liquefy, cells at the center become detached. Thus are the first blood cells formed, the free detached cells becoming the first blood corpuscles. The edges of the islands will make blood vessels as the islands enlarge and join one another. In the head region the blood islands form a large single tube that acquires a thick muscular coat and becomes the heart. Before the complicated four-chamber human heart is complete, this simple tube will undergo many twists and turns. Nevertheless, it begins to contract almost at once, forcing blood through the germinal disc and primitive placenta.

FOUR WEEKS

From the twentieth to the thirtieth day the embryo is in the *somite* stage. This is characterized by the development of paired blocks of tissue (somite), which arise on either side of the neural groove. From these somites come the muscles and bones. The symmetric distribution of the somites is the first indication of the symmetric arrangement of bones and muscles in the two halves of the human form. As the embryo enlarges, more and more somites are added; eventually there are forty-four pairs of them.

Within the body of the embryo changes of great rapidity are taking place. Shortly after the laying of foundations for the nervous and circulatory system, the *gut* begins to form. This indelicate term, perfectly proper in embryologic circles, is used to describe the beginning digestive tract. By a process similar to the formation of the neural groove, the endoderm gives rise to the foregut in front and the hindgut in the tail region. The blind pouch in front pushes gradually forward and soon breaks through upon the undersurface of the head, forming the mouth.

By four weeks of age the kidneys have begun to form in the mesodermal layer. The kidneys differ from most other organs in their way of development. The usual mode is for a simple embryonic organ to arise, then to be modified more and more to meet the complexities of human existence. The kidneys, however, arrive at the end result by what appears to be a series of nature's experiments. In the last week of the first month of embryonic life a type of kidney, which is found only in a few very primitive fishes and eels, develops in the human embryo. This is the primitive *pronephros,* or first kidney. Within a few days it regresses, and a second, more complicated attempt at formation is made in the *mesonephros,* or middle kidney. This stage is no more successful than the first. Finally, a third and even more complex kidney is formed, the *metanephros.* This endures and develops into the human kidney. This hasty recapitulation, in the embryo, of the long history of evolution of the species is also seen when gill slits appear temporarily in the neck region of the human embryo.

At four weeks the embryo does not yet look like a baby. He has a head and a tail, which can be distinguished readily. The neural groove has sealed over completely, and formation of the brain is progressing rapidly. In the head, the beginnings of the eye and the ear can be seen. The mandibular process is beginning to form the face. The heart is now a large bulge on the underside of the embryo, already beating rhythmically.

Miraculous changes have occurred in the first month. Starting from the fertilized ovum, the embryo has enlarged an astonishing fifty times in size and eight thousand times in weight. Still it is only a quarter of an inch long. Yet, within this tiny month-old creature can be recognized the beginnings of almost all the organs that must serve man for his traditional three-score years and ten.

The first month is characterized by the organization within the body of the various parts that make it function. During the second month the external form takes shape. The most dramatic changes are seen in the face. The bulbous brain seems to bend the head end of the embryo

over, as if it were too heavy for the body. This large head comprises a
third of the embryo's length.

SIX WEEKS

In just two weeks the embryo takes on a much more human appearance. The brain is still the predominant feature, but now the eye is
forming (Figure 7). It is at the side of the head and looks out laterally,
like the eyes in those ancient Egyptian paintings. The eyes will gradually move around as the face takes form. The slit beneath the eye looks
as if it may be the mouth, but actually it is the ear. The unusual thing
about the ear is how low set it is. As you can see in Figure 7, it is almost
in the neck region. It appears that the embryo is listening to his own
heartbeat. The large swelling on the undersurface of the embryo, on
which the head rests, contains the heart and liver. At this point these
organs are too big for the body cavities.

Formation of the arms and legs has started (Figure 7). The flipper-
like appendages, at the sides of the embryo, are appropriately known as
the *limb buds*. For some reason, formation of the arm and hand at this
stage of the game is a little ahead of development of the foot and leg.
You can see that the hand is already like a flat paddle, while the foot is
still a nubbin. You can see also that four parallel grooves are forming in
the hand, marking off the five fingers. These grooves will deepen
gradually and cut through completely, setting off five distinct digits. It
was at this stage of the development that thalidomide had such devastating consequences. It arrested development of the limb buds. When
thalidomide was taken before formation of the limb buds began, or
after it was complete, no harm was done. If, however, the drug was
taken in the several weeks when the limbs were forming, development
stopped at the limb bud stage, and the infant was born with rudimentary arms and legs.

At six weeks the somites have set off what will become the backbone.
A little tail is present but does not grow and will soon be lost from view
as the buttocks develop.

The face now rests upon the bulge formed by the heart and liver. A
large gaping mouth was formed when the foregut broke through the
undersurface of the brain. Shallow nasal pits are present on the upper

edge of the mouth. Behind the eye on either side a series of slits, the gill slits or *branchial clefts,* develop. These are embryologic leftovers from another species; since we humans do not need gills, they are used for other purposes. Between the clefts are compact masses of tissue known as the *branchial arches.* The first pair of branchial arches joins together beneath the mouth to form the lower jaw. The second pair is used to form the ear. Islands of tissue at the angles of the jaw grow together above the mouth to form the upper jaw. It is at this time that abnormalities of development may lead to such conditions as harelip and cleft palate.

TWO MONTHS

By two months the baby has assumed a definite human form. He has eyes, ears, and a nose. His hands have fingers and his feet have toes (Figure 8). His head still looks too big for his body. He is potbellied because the liver is too large for the abdominal cavity. He is now slightly more than an inch long. Up to now he was referred to properly as an embryo, but henceforth he shall be called the fetus.

By the end of the second month, the face is formed and the eyes have moved to the front of the head. The ears have developed from the second set of branchial arches, but are still low set on the head. Bones begin to develop within the limbs and trunk in the latter part of the second month. For the most part, the body first forms bones from a cartilage model, or template, of the definitive bone. In the latter part of pregnancy, true calcified bone gradually replaces the cartilage model. This change follows a definite pattern. An X-ray picture of the baby in the last weeks of pregnancy will demonstrate how mature the baby is by showing which bones are calcified and which are not.

While these changes proceed, the complicated musculature of the body is developing beneath the skin. Flesh fills out the body contours of the fetus to give a more human form. Soon fetal movements will begin, but not until the fetus is about four and one-half months old will the movements become strong enough for most mothers to perceive them.

By the end of the second month the limbs are well formed. Arms and legs are well developed. The fingers and toes (Figure 8) are now almost completely shaped. Within the body the various organs are assuming more and more adult forms. The liver is relatively very large, comprising a tenth of the body weight and accounting, as we have said, for the potbellied appearance of the two-month fetus. The digestive tract enlarges, and its various parts shift to their adult positions. At this stage, even the appendix is formed. The diaphragm, that tough muscular sheet between the chest and abdominal cavities, closes over to separate these two compartments.

Now the sexual organs are beginning to form. Though the future sex of the individual is determined at the time of fertilization, it was impossible in the earlier stages of development to distinguish male from female. The gonad, or sexual gland, developing adjacent to the kidney may become either testes or ovary. In making the external sexual organs of all embryos, nature begins by forming a dual set of structures. By then emphasizing one set and allowing the other to degenerate, she fashions the completely different sexual organs that characterize the sexes. This bisexual nature of the embryo has its philosophic implications. It is said that every man, even the most patently masculine, has feminine traits. The opposite is supposed to be true of women. If this is so, is it because we were at one time both male and female within our mother's womb?

If the differentiation of the sexual organs is imperfect, a great number of abnormalities can result. It is possible for an individual to develop both male and female at the same time. The name for this condition is *hermaphrodism*. Hermaphrodites are a far cry from those individuals who in less sophisticated times used to stir the imagination of schoolboys. Posters depicting the half-man-half-woman were standard features of traveling "freak" shows. One side was complete with curls and bosom and a silver slipper, while the other half showed half a black moustache, bulging biceps, and a black boot with tassels.

Real hermaphrodism would not likely be quite so garish or geometric in its external appearance. Inspection of the genitals of a real hermaphrodite would disclose, most likely, a small, rudimentary penis overlying a shallow vaginal pouch.

THREE MONTHS

The human body is a wonderful machine, the various parts highly specialized to perform different functions for the individual. The third month is characterized by the beginnings of this specialization in many different organs of the body.

In the mouth, the first evidence of tooth formation appears. This is a series of ten tooth buds of both the upper and lower jaws that will form the "baby" or milk teeth. Although the teeth will not break through the gums until the baby is about five months old, they are beginning to form in the three-month fetus.

In the third month the cartilages making up the *larynx,* or voice box, form at the upper end of the *trachea,* or windpipe. The vocal cords compose the structure that actually produces the sounds. These are a pair of delicate bands tightly stretched across the top of the voice box, and they vibrate when air is forced past them. The vocal cords do not form until later; even at birth they are relatively thick and inflexible. It is not until the baby is six months old or so that the vocal cords are completely finished.

Changes in the digestive tract are in keeping with the greater degree of specialization that is occurring throughout the body. Although the child will have nothing to digest until he begins to eat after delivery, the stomach and liver cells that produce digestive juices are perfected at this early age. The liver, in addition, becomes an important site for manufacture of the red blood corpuscles. After birth the bone marrow performs this job, but during fetal life the liver is one of the important locations. In some conditions, such as the Rh-negative problem, there is destruction of fetal blood. The liver then becomes greatly enlarged because the demand for red blood cells, caused by the resulting anemia, is excessive.

Insulin is the hormone, manufactured in the *pancreas,* that controls the metabolism of sugar in the body. When insulin is lacking, diabetes develops. In keeping with the differentiation going on elsewhere, insulin-producing cells appear in the third month. These are found in groups known as the Islands of Langerhans, after the German pathologist who first described them. As might be deduced, the fetus of a diabetic mother often has larger and more numerous Islands of Langerhans. It seems as though the fetus intends to make up for the mother's lack of hormone.

In the third month, the third and final kidney stage forms and begins to function, but the finishing touches will not be added until after delivery. When the fetal kidneys first begin to function, there is a relatively large increase in the volume of amniotic fluid in which the baby is suspended. The fetal kidneys produce most of the amniotic fluid. It does not contain all the waste products of adult urine. It will be remembered that the waste products of fetal metabolism pass into the mother's blood, via the placenta, and are excreted largely by the maternal kidney. There is roughly a quart of amniotic fluid in full-term pregnancies. An excess or deficiency of fluid is caused sometimes by an abnormality in fetal development. As you might expect, there is too little amniotic fluid when the kidneys are congenitally absent or if there is an obstruction to the urinary passage. Excessive amounts of amniotic fluid sometimes are associated with an interference of the swallowing mechanism, caused either by an anomaly (defect) in the brain or an obstruction of the digestive tract.

The most dramatic changes of the third month are seen in the sexual organs, especially of males. Differentiation is more rapid in males than in females. The latter remain in that indifferent limbo for several weeks longer than males. By the end of the third month, close inspection of the fetus should reveal whether it is a little boy or a little girl.

In the two-month fetus the indifferent sexual gland was developing in the body cavity, beside the kidney. By the end of the third month, this gonad in males shows definite cords of cells, the forerunner of the sperm-producing *tubules* of the adult testes. An elaborate system of ducts now forms, which will someday convey the sperm cells produced in the testes to the outside of the body. You will recall that to start with we are bisexual. Embryos have two complete sets of ducts developing alongside the gonad. By emphasizing one set and allowing the other set to degenerate, nature fashions the entirely different sexual apparatus of the two sexes.

Alongside each indifferent gonad a tub forms. The upper end is open like a funnel; the lower end grows toward the bladder, where it joins its fellow from the other side. These are the *müllerian ducts*. They will be used to form most of the female reproductive tract. They do not persist in the male. When the middle kidney degenerates, its main duct and some of its tubules are taken over by the male as the main sexual duct. In the third month this duct persists in the male, and enlarges, becoming the *vas deferens*. It runs from the primitive testes toward the bladder, where it empties in a little mound called the genital tubercle.

The opening for the urinary and sexual systems is at the base of this genital tubercle, which will develop into a penis. During the third month the penis grows markedly longer. A long groove on the surface gradually closes from behind forward, only a small slit at the tip of the penis remaining open. Failure of this mechanism to proceed normally results in a condition called *hypospadias*, where the penile opening is on the undersurface, instead of at its tip. The tissues at the base of the penis become pouched out. This is the scrotal sac that will contain the testes. The testes do not enter the scrotal sac until near the end of fetal life, when they migrate into it from their original position close to the kidneys.

Even though the female sexual organs are not completed for several more weeks, their development can best be described here. The long tube or duct (known as the müllerian duct) developing beside the primitive ovary gives rise to the Fallopian tubes, the uterus, and most of the vagina. The duct of the middle kidney (which was used by the male as the vas deferens) degenerates. The müllerian ducts on either side grow together toward the midline. When they meet at the midline, they fuse. The upper halves remain separate as the paired Fallopian tubes. The lower halves join and acquire a thick muscular coat to become the uterus. Most of the vagina (or birth canal) is also derived from the lower end of the fused müllerian ducts. By the fifth month the vaginal opening breaks through to the outside, beneath the genital tubercle. This structure, you will recall, gave rise to the penis in the male. In the female the tubercle becomes the clitoris. The urethral groove, which in the male is closed along the undersurface of the penis, remains open in the female. It forms a vestibule into which both the bladder and vagina open. The scrotal swellings of the male become the paired *labia majora,* or major lips, of the vestibule in the female.

FOUR MONTHS

The changes occurring in the remainder of pregnancy are much more subtle than those up to this time. For the rest of pregnancy it is largely a matter of simple enlargement and maturation of the various organs. There are few new developments, but finishing touches are applied. The four-month fetus (Figure 9) looks like a little baby in every respect, although the head is still relatively large, and the legs relatively short. The skin is thin, red, and wrinkled. In later pregnancy, the skin will thicken and no longer transmit the color of the blood vessels coursing through it. The fetus will acquire a layer of fat beneath the skin and fill out the wrinkles. A fetus in the fourth month weighs about one-half pound and is some eight to ten inches in length from head to toe. If delivered at this time, the baby will move, its heart will beat, and there may even be feeble irregular respiratory movements, but, of course, the fetus is much too small and immature to survive. An X-ray picture of the mother's abdomen will show the beginnings of calcification in some of the fetal bones. An X ray is made in some problem cases where the diagnosis of pregnancy remains in doubt. By the end of the fourth month the doctor may be able to hear the baby's heartbeat if conditions are favorable.

Between the fourth and fifth months the mother feels the baby's movements. He has been moving earlier but not strongly enough for the mother to perceive the movements. This feeling of life is known as *the quickening*. It starts as no more than a vague fluttering sensation, but soon the baby's actions become unmistakable.

The age-old response to this dramatic event is evident throughout our culture. We speak of the quick and the dead, meaning the living and the dead. Many of our laws derived from the old English common law give certain rights to the unborn fetus, but only after the time of quickening. The fetus was not considered completely human until the mother was "quick with life." Even today, if the fetus is born before the time of quickening, it does not have to be recorded in the vital statistics. But if it is born just a few days after quickening, the delivery must be recorded as a birth and death, and the body must be disposed of by burial or cremation.

At the quickening the mother may feel the full impact of pregnancy for the first time. To many women the first months of pregnancy are unreal. They know they are pregnant, but until they feel the kick, they do not really believe that a baby is developing within them. If the feelings of the mother are unreal at the beginning of pregnancy, those of the father can best be described as somewhere between confusion and fantasy. But soon after the mother notes quickening, the father too can feel the baby's movements through the abdominal wall. Then, for the first time, he begins to feel that he really is a father.

SIX MONTHS TO BIRTH

Let us now jump forward a couple of months and see what the fetus is doing. He now weighs between one and one-half to two pounds and would stand slightly over a foot tall. If born at this stage, many fetuses live for several hours but very rarely does one survive. Even though the odds are all against him, the fetus nevertheless has a chance, for the first time, of living outside the maternal environment. For those who make the grade, the first two or three days are critical. It appears that the respiratory system is the most important single factor. If the lungs are mature enough to sustain the premature infant for the first two or three days, he stands an excellent chance of survival, even though he weighs less than two pounds and will have to be in the premature nursery for weeks to come. The baby's sex has some bearing on ability to survive. Premature girls have a somewhat higher survival rate than premature boys. Through the seventh and eighth months the baby's chances of survival go from practically zero to almost 100 percent. It is in this period that each day increases the baby's chances. Sometimes the difference between life and death is determined by the doctor's skill or luck in buying a few days of time to forestall delivery of a premature infant.

By six months of age specialized structures in the baby's skin are formed (Figure 10). There is a fine growth of hair on the head and sometimes over the back and shoulders. The color of this hair has little resemblance to the color of the hair the child eventually will have. Fingernails and toenails appear and grow slowly. At the time of birth they will project slightly at the tips of the fingers and will have to be trimmed in the first few days of life to keep the baby from scratching himself. Oil glands appear in the skin and manufacture a greasy, tenacious substance known as the *vernix caseosa,* which is like a salve or ointment. It coats the baby's skin and is thought to keep the skin from becoming macerated and waterlogged while in his fluid world of the womb. The amniotic fluid contains flecks of the vernix and skin cells of the baby that are continually cast off from the surface. It is possible to draw off some of the amniotic fluid (see Amniocentesis, p. 419) and by examining the skin cells to tell whether the baby is a boy or girl. Since this procedure carries a slight risk, it should not be done merely to satisfy the curiosity of the patient or her doctor. It should be done only of it is essential to know the sex of the baby before delivery. This comes up when dealing with some rare inherited diseases that are sex-linked. This means that they occur in offspring of only one sex. Babies of the other sex are unaffected. At this time, examination of the amniotic fluid is the only accurate method of determining the sex of the infant before delivery. The fetal heart rate is a totally unreliable indicator of sex.

During the sixth month the eyelids, which have been sealed shut, open. Eyebrows and eyelashes appear (Figure 10). The iris, which gives rise to eye color, is lacking in pigment; consequently, all babies when born have dark, bluish gray eyes. When pigment forms in the iris after birth, the characteristic eye color becomes manifest and remains for the rest of life.

At approximately seven months the fetus is fully developed. From now until term, it needs only to grow, in length, weight, and strength, in order to face the demands of the world outside the womb (Figure 11). Nor does the development of a child stop at birth, obviously. There is the general process of growth. Among the specific physical maturations that occur after delivery is enlargement of the head to accommodate brain growth. The bone structure must be able to expand or the brain would suffer from the confinement. The teeth mature slowly, the wisdom teeth not appearing until the second decade of life. Apart from the general growth, the most spectacular changes come at puberty, when the body begins to assume its adult appearance and the sexual organs start to function.

THE PLACENTA

One of the most important structures to develop in pregnancy is the *placenta* or afterbirth. This is a flat, pie-shaped structure, some seven or eight inches in diameter and about an inch in thickness, weighing roughly one pound. It is composed of millions of fronds, or fingerlike projections, called *chorionic villi*. These villi are part of the fetal blood vessel system and connect up with the rest of the baby's blood vessels via the large umbilical veins and artery in the umbilical cord. In the body of the placenta, the villi are suspended in maternal blood. While there is no actual mixing of the circulation between the mother and the fetus, only a thin layer of cells, the villi's covering, separates them, and it is across this layer that all the nutrients pass into the baby's circulation. The baby also has an active metabolism of its own; the waste products from the fetal metabolism must pass into the mother's circulation.

In structure the placenta can be likened to a giant tree (Figure 9). The trunk of the tree is analogous to the large umbilical cord, which contains the umbilical blood vessels. There is a continual branching of these blood vessels into progressively smaller ones, similar to the branches of a tree. The chorionic villi are like the leaves of a tree. Here the vessels are so small they are only thin-walled capillaries into which oxygen and other nutrients can diffuse with ease. This whole "tree," except for the trunk, is suspended upside down in a lake of maternal blood that surrounds each of the chorionic villi.

Around the rim of the pie-shaped placenta the membranes are attached. These are a thin, semitransparent sheet of tissue, something like a plastic bag forming a round dome. The baby, tethered at the end of the umbilical cord, is suspended throughout pregnancy in the amniotic fluid within this rounded dome (Figure 9). Because fluid surrounds the baby throughout pregnancy, it is practically impossible for the fetus to sustain injury from the outside. A severe direct blow on the abdomen in pregnancy could have severe consequences to the mother, but even a jolt of this kind would probably not injure the baby.

The placenta and the embryo are both derived from the fertilized ovum. By the time of nidation (implantation) into the womb's lining six to seven days after fertilization, it is possible to distinguish those cells that will form the fetus from those that will become the placenta. At this stage the placenta is much larger than the embryo. It is quite some time before the baby catches up.

The placenta acts something like a filter or sieve, in that it allows only particles of relatively small size to pass through from the mother to the baby. Particles of larger size, the proteins of greater molecular weight and some of the hormones, are held back in the maternal circulation. If any of these materials are needed for the development of the fetus, they must be manufactured by the fetal organs from those simpler, smaller compounds that can pass readily through the placenta.

In addition to furnishing the fetus with the necessary materials for its growth and development, the placenta must also supply oxygen for the active metabolism of the developing new individual. Carbon dioxide, which is formed in the fetus when oxygen is used up in the metabolic processes, must also be disposed of. In the placenta carbon dioxide passes from the fetal to the maternal circulation and is largely expired by the mother. Because of this ability to supply oxygen and carry away carbon dioxide, the placenta is sometimes referred to as the internal lung of the fetus.

Another important function of the placenta is the production of hormones. Pregnancy poses a unique strain on the entire maternal organism. The special requirements of pregnancy must be met by adaptations involving almost every organ system in the body. The uterus must increase tremendously in size, as must the breasts. The blood volume must increase. To some extent, the pelvic joint loosens. There is a host of other changes. These adaptations are brought about largely by the action of the placental hormones on the mother's womb, breasts, blood, and so forth. The placental hormones are also thought to be important in maintaining pregnancy. While no one knows what it is that makes labor begin, many investigators feel that a change in placental hormone production at the end of pregnancy initiates labor.

ARTHUR GORBACH, M.D.

CHAPTER SIX

Diseases and Conditions That Complicate Pregnancy

ANEMIA

TO SAY that a person is anemic is about as specific as saying that someone has "lung trouble." There are many causes of the condition we call *anemia*. The layman's term for anemia is "low blood," and this is perhaps as good a description as any. Anemia is a reduction in the number of red blood corpuscles or in the amount of hemoglobin (the oxygen-carrying chemical in the individual red blood cells) or both together. We can establish the existence of anemia by taking a blood sample and measuring the concentration of hemoglobin or of whole red blood cells in a standard unit of the sample.

The symptoms of anemia are pallor, weakness, and fatigue. If the anemia has come from destruction of the red blood cells (*hemolysis*), there may sometimes be jaundice too. But pallor and fatigue are the most noticeable symptoms. Now, general weariness, as we have noted earlier, is a common symptom of pregnancy, but this condition should not be confused with serious anemia. While it is true that most pregnant women are slightly anemic, their fatigue is due to the pregnancy rather than to the anemia.

By far the most common anemia in women is that due to iron deficiency. Blood, and hence iron, is lost in each of the monthly menstrual periods. This is a chronic drain on the female's supply of iron. When pregnancy intervenes, there is a large loss of iron in the formation of the baby and placenta and in the bleeding that inevitably accompanies childbirth. Most women simply do not get enough iron in their diets to make up for these losses and as a consequence have some degree of iron-deficiency anemia all the time. Women have in general lower hemoglobin concentrations in their blood than men have. They have to include iron supplements in their diets for several months if they are to approach the "normal male values."

Iron-deficiency anemia is the most common medical complication of pregnancy. Almost without exception, women should take iron throughout pregnancy. The physician will prescribe the dosage. Incidentally, iron is the only drug that needs to be taken routinely before childbirth. The vitamins and minerals usually given along with iron are costly and unnecessary for healthy persons on good diets. The concentration of hemoglobin or red blood corpuscles should be checked in pregnancy. If the count is unusually low and does not improve with iron supplements, some other explanation of the anemia should be sought. Iron preparations will occasionally cause gastrointestinal upsets. To give iron in the first few weeks of pregnancy on top of morning sickness can be something like adding insult to injury. If the stomach is upset from pregnancy, the iron supplement can wait until morning sickness subsides. Gastrointestinal upsets from iron supplements can be corrected by adjusting the dosage or changing to a different iron product.

One final word of caution is in order regarding iron pills. As was mentioned earlier, these are a common cause of poisoning in children. A large number of iron pills will make a small child seriously ill. Keep your iron pills, along with other drugs, well out of children's reach.

Other types of anemia also are encountered in pregnancy. One of the rarest is an anemia that is due to a deficiency of folic acid. This vitamin-like product (see page 78) is widely distributed in foodstuffs. The anemia of folic acid deficiency has many characteristics in common with pernicious anemia. The latter is a type of anemia found in older individuals. True pernicious anemia is almost unheard-of in pregnancy. Most of the reports of folic acid–deficiency anemia have come from England. It is unlikely that the disease is more common there. Probably our British colleagues are more meticulous in searching out these interesting cases.

Folic acid, though widely distributed in nature, is not stored in the body to any great extent. It is needed in the formation of all new cells and hence there is an increasing demand for it as pregnancy progresses. When diets are inadequate in this substance or if the body is unable to absorb or utilize it, then anemia will result. If this is the case a small daily supplement of folic acid will restore the blood picture to normal.

There are several types of hereditary anemia seen in pregnancy that at times cause serious complications. One is called *sickle-cell anemia* because of the shape of the red blood corpuscles. It is found almost exclusively in members of the Negro race. Individuals with sickle-cell anemia are chronically ill and have repeated "crises" when their blood cells are both destroyed and used up in the formation of clots that form at various organs of the body. These clots occur in the vessels supplying the bones, the lungs, and some abdominal organs. Fever and pain in the affected organs are prominent features of a sickle-cell crisis. If a vital organ loses all or part of its blood supply as a result of a crisis, serious complications ensue. The only form of treatment consistently effective is transfusion of nonsickling red blood cells. This is a temporary measure, as the life span of a normal red blood corpuscle is only somewhere in the neighborhood of three to four months.

Another of the hereditary anemias seen frequently is called *Mediterranean anemia* because it is found in the people native to the countries of the Mediterranean basin. It is also called Cooley's anemia and thalassemia. Persons with Mediterranean anemia are also chronically ill, with varying degrees of pallor and jaundice as a result of a destruction of red blood corpuscles. The red blood cells of patients with thalassemia are unusually fragile and as a result are easily destroyed within the vascular system. There is nothing specific about pregnancy that aggravates either sickle-cell anemia or thalassemia, but young women having these illnesses do become pregnant. The illnesses are serious in themselves without pregnancy, and management of them is always difficult. The added burden of carrying a child further complicates the picture.

Even though the mother may be anemic, whatever the cause, rarely is the baby similarly affected at birth. Because the density of oxygen is lower in the intrauterine environment than in the outside world, all babies are born with elevated blood counts and hemoglobin concentrations.

It is sometimes necessary to give mothers blood transfusions. The most frequent occasion is to replace blood lost in delivery if the loss is excessive. On rare occasions a woman who is suffering from severe anemia and not responding to treatment may be transfused before delivery in anticipation of the expected loss of blood when the baby is born.

ANENCEPHALY

This is a rare fetal anomaly characterized by marked impairment in the development of the brain and head. Although many anencephalic fetuses are born alive, it is impossible for them to survive for more than a few hours. No one knows why most of these abnormalities occur. Mothers who have had these babies rarely have a history of virus disease or exposure to harmful chemicals in pregnancy. Some genetic tendency may be at work, for there are occasional reports of the same accident happening in a subsequent pregnancy. Another puzzling feature is that the great majority of anencephalic babies are girls. This would seem to indicate that hormones in some way are involved.

When a mother carries an anencephalic baby, there is often the excessive accumulation of amniotic fluid called polyhydramnios (pages 147–48). Any condition interfering with the swallowing mechanism favors development of polyhydramnios. In anencephaly the centers in the brain that should control the swallowing apparatus are poorly developed. The doctor may order an X ray if he finds an excessive amount of fluid. The film will disclose the abnormality in the bones of the baby's head.

When a doctor diagnoses anencephaly, he will be under great pressure to terminate the pregnancy immediately. There are few emotional strains greater than those a woman must endure when she knows that she is carrying an abnormal baby. If the doctor can induce labor without complications, he certainly will, but it is often safer to await the onset of spontaneous labor rather than to attempt an induction before conditions are favorable.

APPENDICITIS

Appendicitis is the most important surgical complication of pregnancy. It is primarily a disease of young people and occurs with about the same frequency in pregnant women as in the total nonpregnant population.

Pregnancy makes the diagnosis of acute appendicitis more difficult. The nausea and abdominal pain characteristic of this disease may be confused with the aches and pains of pregnancy. Certainly, any persistent pain on the right side in pregnancy should arouse a suspicion of appendicitis. If the pain is accompanied by nausea and vomiting or by lack of appetite, the diagnosis is even more probable.

Some of the usual aids in the diagnosis of appendicitis are altered or lacking during pregnancy. The appendix, displaced by the enlarging uterus, may come to lie in a spot considerably removed from its usual position. Consequently, the location of pain may be quite different from the location in ordinary appendicitis. Muscle spasm, so characteristic of abdominal inflammation, may be almost completely absent in pregnancy. Even the white blood count, which is the most useful diagnostic laboratory test for this disease, is often of little help because in normal pregnancy there is usually an elevation in the number of circulating white blood cells.

The importance of early recognition of acute appendicitis and prompt surgical treatment is familiar to almost everyone. A ruptured appendix is a serious business at any time, but it is particularly dangerous in pregnancy. Therefore, it is more important than ever to establish the correct diagnosis.

In the latter half of pregnancy, the operation may be difficult technically because the enlargement of the pregnant uterus makes exposure of the appendix difficult. Often a larger incision is necessary. Mothers who have to undergo the operation in pregnancy worry about the effect of surgery and anesthesia on the unborn baby. The rare patient will go into labor after almost any type of abdominal surgery. When this happens, the surgery is presumed to be the cause of the accident. Of course, it is impossible to predict what would have happened if the operation had not been performed. There are cases on record in which premature labor has been blamed on surgery, only to have the patients deliver prematurely again in subsequent pregnancies without surgery. So, who can say?

Even in surgery lasting several hours, there should be no danger to the baby from anesthesia when the anesthetic is administered properly. It is important that the mother suffer no lack of oxygen during surgery; deprivation could damage the baby. A competent anesthesiologist will see that the oxygen supply is adequate. The anesthetic drugs given to the mother do get to the baby but are not damaging and are promptly eliminated once administration of the anesthesia is stopped. Women who must undergo surgery in the latter part of pregnancy wonder what might happen to the abdominal incision if labor should begin shortly after surgery. If labor should begin as soon as the operation was finished, even a large abdominal incision would be unaffected.

BACKACHE

One of the most common discomforts of pregnancy is backache. Almost every pregnant woman endures at least a touch of it. (Of course, a great many people who are not pregnant also complain of intermittent low backache.) The causes of backache, in or out of pregnancy, are to be found usually in the muscles and ligaments of the back. In pregnancy postural changes and a slight relaxation of some of the ligaments aggravate the condition. One of the hormones produced in pregnancy appears to be responsible for the loosening and relaxation of the pelvic joints, which suggests the possibility of a hormonal association with backache. Backaches in pregnancy seem to come and go without much rhyme or reason. Even without specific treatment, it is not unusual for a woman who has been having considerable pain and is all but disabled to be relieved within a week or two.

Rest is the best form of treatment for backache. If the pain is severe, about the only time the sufferer is comfortable is when she is lying flat on her back on a hard bed. Bed boards are certainly a good investment for anyone with much backache. Lifting, stooping, and bending aggravate a backache, but unless she is truly incapacitated, it is ridiculous to tell a woman with a couple of small children that she must not lift, stoop, or bend. A good girdle or similar support helps because it tends to keep the back from twisting. Heat in the form of a hot tub or heating pad will provide temporary relief.

As in so many conditions in medicine, prevention is better than cure. Persons subject to backache can do a great deal to prevent this affliction by systematically doing exercises to strengthen the back muscles and keep them supple. There is no reason why these exercises cannot be done in pregnancy. But it is important to stress that this exercising should not be attempted while the victim is in actual pain. If you have had some backache, wait until the pain and spasms subside before you gradually take up the exercising.

One of the best exercises for the back is to bend over and touch the toes with the tips of the fingers. It is permissible to bend the knees in order to get all the way down, but you should work toward being able to do the exercise with the knees straight. Sit-ups are also a good back exercise. Lie on your back and raise the upper part of the body to the sitting position while keeping your feet on the floor. "Bicycling" is another favorite. While lying on your back on the floor, draw up your knees and raise yourself until your weight rests upon your shoulders and upper back, with your elbows on the floor and your hands supporting the small of your back. Then pump your legs as if you were riding a bicycle upside down. Your doctor probably will have additional exercises to recommend.

Although the great majority of the backaches of pregnancy are rooted in orthopedic disorders, this is not true of all of them. Kidney infections will also cause aching in the back. While most women who have these infections will also have fever, pain, and burning on urination, the latter symptoms are not invariably present. Backache similar to that experienced before and during menstruation may be one of the first signs of labor or impending separation of the placenta. Your doctor will certainly want to hear from you if you have a pain of this type accompanied by even slight vaginal bleeding.

CANCER

As this disease (or, to be accurate, this group of diseases) occurs largely in the older age groups, it is unusual to see pregnant women who have or have had cancer. When this rare patient does appear, the question then arises, Should a woman with cancer have become pregnant in the first place? And is it wise to continue the pregnancy? Since the many types of cancer behave differently and may present unique problems in pregnancy, few generalizations can be made. It can be stated, however, that pregnancy does not influence the growth of most malignant tumors. Further, it also appears that, as in so many other complications of pregnancy, the best results are obtained when the usual treatment is applied to the underlying disease and the pregnancy is allowed to proceed normally.

The first exception to these generalizations is cancer of the breast. This is the malignancy encountered most frequently in pregnancy and one of the most serious. No one knows the cause of breast cancer. It is certainly not caused by pregnancy. Indeed, there is good evidence that pregnancy and especially lactation do something to prevent this condition. If, however, a breast cancer does appear in pregnancy, it often seems to grow more rapidly and to spread more quickly than if the patient were not pregnant. One explanation is that the diagnosis is often delayed. The lump is overlooked because the breast is enlarged and engorged due to pregnancy. The doctor usually examines the breasts at the time of the initial physical examination but he does not check them again. It is important to remind women that through the whole course of pregnancy they should call to the doctor's attention any lumps or abnormalities that appear in the breast.

If a localized tumor of the breast is discovered in pregnancy, surgical removal of the breast should be undertaken without delay. Therapeutic abortion in early pregnancy is often justified although it may not mean the difference between success and failure of treatment. Pregnancy does aggravate this disease.

Women who have had cancer of the breast and are apparently cured present a different problem. They may safely become pregnant after an interval. If four or five years have elapsed and the patient has been free of the disease, it seems reasonable to allow another pregnancy. But if she inadvertently should become pregnant before this, interruption of pregnancy should be seriously considered.

Cancer of the neck of the womb is the next most frequently encountered malignant tumor in pregnancy. Its growth does not appear to be stimulated by pregnancy. Evaluation for this condition presupposes taking a smear of the vaginal and cervical cells (Pap test) in all pregnant women, regardless of age.

In the evolution of cancer of the cervix (and many other sites as well) the initial stage is known as *cancer-in-situ* or *carcinoma-in-situ*. Cancer-in-situ of the cervix differs from true cancer in several important ways. It is confined to just a few layers of surface cells. Because it does not invade, it does not cause pain and bleeding. The diagnosis usually is made when abnormal cells are found on the vaginal smear test. In contrast to true cancer, no one ever dies of cancer-in-situ. Its only importance lies in its potential to become truly invasive. Cancer-in-situ may often be found at the edge of an invasive growth. Then it is imperative to investigate the possibility of true cancer underneath.

Nothing is done to cancer-in-situ of the cervix in pregnancy other than to exclude the possibility of an associated genuine malignant growth. Following delivery the treatment is undertaken. Local excision is performed in women desirous of more children. The entire womb is removed (hysterectomy) if the patient has completed her family.

Patients are occasionally encountered who have or have had cancers in other sites. Pregnancy leaves them largely uninfluenced. During pregnancy they do not present any unique difficulties of management.

DEAFNESS

One form of deafness is influenced by pregnancy. This is *otosclerosis,* one of the leading causes of loss of hearing. Otosclerosis is a disease of hereditary tendency affecting the spongy bone of the inner ear and is often accelerated by pregnancy. Many women will first become aware of deafness during or after a pregnancy. While pregnancy does frequently seem to aggravate otosclerosis, it does not appear to be the underlying cause. The person destined to have this type of hearing difficulty will eventually develop it regardless of pregnancy.

The surgical treatment of otosclerosis has made much progress in the last decade or two. Results are usually dramatic. Because the treatment is so satisfactory and the eventual outcome of the disease is the same regardless of pregnancy, there seems to be little reason to delay or forgo having a child because of this condition.

DENTAL CARIES

The old saw that you lose a tooth for every baby is not true. The time of life when cavities are so common just happens to coincide with the childbearing age. Unfortunately, drinking milk or taking calcium pills will do nothing to protect the teeth during pregnancy. Teeth do not become decalcified during gestation or at any other time of life. (See dental care in chapter 4, pages 86–87.)

DEPRESSION

So common are depressed feelings after birth of a baby that mothers who escape them almost wonder whether something is wrong. Everyone talks about the baby "blues." On the other hand, relatively few women realize how common periods of depression are before the delivery.

Depression can be manifest in many ways, and pregnant women may be depressed without knowing it. Crying spells with little or no provocation are a common and unmistakable symptom. During the depression the victim often will have difficulty sleeping. She usually can fall asleep without trouble, but wakes in the middle of the night and cannot get back to sleep again until morning. This is a favorite time to mull over and exaggerate the real and supposed troubles we all have. Pregnant women who are depressed are melancholy and discouraged. They just cannot see how they are going to cope with the new baby. In a depression everything seems to require a special effort. Depressed persons do not want to go places or do things. When the depression is severe, they do not feel like eating. They often lose their sexual desire as well.

A particularly sad or discouraging event can precipitate depression. Serious illness or death of a close member of the family is a good example. There would be something wrong with our relationships within the family if such events did not cause us to be melancholy. In many other instances, however, there is no particular event to point to as the cause of depression. Without knowing why, the woman just feels depressed and discouraged.

Fortunately, most depressions cure themselves. After a few days or weeks, the victim finds that problems that had seemed insurmountable are really not that bad after all. The future begins to look rosy again. The woman who had been unable to get herself to do more than a minimum now has the desire, the inspiration, and the energy to get things done.

Time is one of the best treatments for mild depressions. To rationalize or to "talk yourself out of" a depression is difficult, if not impossible, because depressions are not rational. To do so would be like picking yourself up by your bootstraps. A depressed person can look at herself and see that she has no reason to feel depressed, but recognition of the fact does not make the depression disappear.

Recent years have seen the introduction of a variety of new drugs for depression. Almost every month, some new agent is presented to the American physician in glowing terms. Artfully prepared brochures predict that this one will supplant all the previous competitors. There are few truisms in medicine that are more appropriate than this: whenever there is a large number of remedies for the same condition, none of them is very effective for the majority of cases.

At this stage, the development of drugs for the treatment of emotional and mental diseases is in its infancy; the next few years should see dramatic, even revolutionary, advances in this field. At present, however, most of these drugs are so new that they have not been evaluated thoroughly in pregnancy. It is therefore prudent to avoid them until thorough testing has established beyond question that they present no hazard in pregnancy.

The generalist or the obstetrician *can and should* handle most of the depressions that occur in pregnancy. They are usually mild and self-limited. If the depression is severe and prolonged, consultation with a psychiatrist is indicated.

DIABETES

This is a common *metabolic* disease of hereditary tendency, caused by improper balance between the sugar in the body and a hormone called *insulin*. This hormone, which is elaborated by the pancreatic gland, controls the *metabolism,* or processing, of sugar. When the body lacks insulin or is unable to make effective use of its insulin, excessive amounts of sugar accumulate in the blood and are excreted by the kidneys. Administration of insulin to a diabetic removes the excess sugar from the blood to the liver, where it is kept in reserve for future use by the body. The insulin also permits muscle and fat to utilize sugar in a normal manner.

Before the discovery of insulin, successful pregnancy in a diabetic was a medical curiosity. Today it is commonplace. The majority of diabetics can anticipate successful childbirth. The outlook in pregnancy is better when the diabetes is a mild case of short duration. When the diabetes has existed for many years, some of the inevitable complications will have commenced, and the outlook for pregnancy will be more guarded. But it is not at all unusual, in this day and age, to see successful pregnancies in women who have been diabetics since early childhood. Pregnancy causes many changes in the course of diabetes. Success in pregnancy can be achieved only by meticulous care on the part of both the patient and her physician.

The amount of insulin needed usually increases in pregnancy, sometimes changing almost daily. If the need is not met, acidosis can result. This is one of the gravest complications for both mother and fetus and should be avoided at all costs. Frequent checks of the blood and urine sugar levels should be made and the doctor seen each week or two. In addition, the diet must be adhered to scrupulously. Any infections, which notoriously increase insulin requirements, should be reported immediately.

Toxemia is a common complication of diabetic pregnancies. Salt restriction is even more important than in normal pregnancy.

Term babies of diabetic mothers (and some of those destined to develop diabetes in later years) are sometimes huge, weighing ten pounds or more. Any woman having a baby this large should be examined for diabetes. Babies of this size present many mechanical difficulties during pelvic delivery and sometimes sustain injury.

Unexplained stillbirth is another common complication of diabetes. Because of this possibility, most clinics advise delivery three or four weeks before term. Since conditions for induction of labor are often not favorable at this time, Caesarean sections are done in many instances.

Babies of diabetic mothers are often swollen with fluid. They are more likely to have respiratory complications in the newborn period, partly because they are prematurely delivered by Caesarean section (see Prematurity, page 334). It is essential that these babies get expert pediatric care.

DISPROPORTION

When the baby is too large for the mother's pelvis, *disproportion* exists. Usually the measurements of the bone structure are abnormally small, but disproportion can occur with normal measurements if the baby happens to be huge ("huge" for a baby, that is).

Nutrition has a great influence on bone development. A generation or two ago, rickets, which is due to a lack of vitamin D, was a common cause of pelvic deformity and led to much obstetric difficulty. As diets have improved, so too from an obstetric point of view has the pelvis. Doctors today have much less disproportion to deal with. Heredity is also very important. It stands to reason that a small girl would have a small pelvis. Many women five feet or less will have disproportion.

Disproportion is a relative term. Very few women have such small pelvic measurements that a normal delivery is impossible. Indeed, most of those with disproportion do deliver pelvically, although their labors are often longer than for women with large pelvic measurements. This prolongation of labor is by no means due solely to mechanical difficulties. Often there is an associated uterine inertia, the medical term for ineffective and inefficient muscular contractions of the uterus.

The doctor takes the pelvic measurements early in pregnancy and usually knows quite well whether there will be any disproportion during labor. If he anticipates this, he may want an X-ray picture of the pelvis late in pregnancy or in the early stages of labor. A new technique called ultra sound, based on the principle of radar, offers promise of giving even more accurate information about the size of the baby's head. While it is advisable to keep X-ray exposure to a minimum during pregnancy, the small amount of radiation required for a pelvic X-ray is perfectly allowable. By this technique, the different parts of the pelvis can be ascertained to within a few millimeters of their actual measurement. Naturally, this exact information can be of great help to the obstetrician. Lack of accurate information on the configuration of the pelvis can be a lot more dangerous to the mother and the baby than the small amount of radiation required for an X ray.

Women known to have disproportion are allowed to go into labor, which usually progresses slowly but surely, terminating in a relatively easy low-forceps delivery. Nowadays, of course, sedation and anesthesia are available if necessary during a prolonged or difficult labor and delivery. The mother may have a few extra stitches but is none the worse for the experience. A bit of a squeeze does not bother the baby either, although the head may become elongated or "molded" during labor. It then takes several days for the baby's head to round out.

A few women with disproportion will not make satisfactory progress in labor, but these cases usually have a combination of disproportion and inertia.

When progress is not satisfactory, Caesarean section becomes necessary to prevent prolonged labor. Very long labors are harmful to mothers and babies. It is hard to lay down any hard and fast rules, but in general it is not good to let the sun set twice on the same labor. With known disproportion the issue can usually be settled long before this. By the time the mother has been in labor for ten or twelve hours, it is usually obvious whether she is going to be able to deliver normally or will require a Caesarean section.

EDEMA (SWELLING)

In pregnancy all women retain some fluid. Part goes into the blood, causing the increase in blood volume characteristic of pregnancy.

Under the resulting greatly increased pressure in the veins of the legs, some fluid is forced from the veins into the tissue spaces. As long as the patient is erect, the fluid is trapped there. In the last weeks of pregnancy, most women at the end of the day will note some swelling of the ankles. This swelling is particularly evident in warm weather or after long periods of standing without much walking or muscular activity. Exercise tends to squeeze fluids from the tissue spaces back into the blood vessels.

There is some connection between retention of fluid and the complication of pregnancy known as toxemia. In pregnant women who develop toxemia, the first sign is a rapid and excessive weight gain, followed shortly by swelling of the feet, hands, and face. In its early stages toxemia is thought to be a reversible condition. If further fluid retention can be prevented or the retained fluid eliminated, the more serious signs of toxemia do not follow. If, however, retention of large amounts of salt and fluid continues unabated, the blood pressure eventually rises and protein appears in the urine. This is the full-blown picture of severe toxemia of pregnancy, with all its implications for both mother and infant. The possibility of toxemia is what the doctor has in mind when he has his patients weighed at each visit. He will be concerned if he finds excessive gain. The ideal weight gain is around two pounds a month. If more than five pounds a month are gained, there is some cause for concern.

The various tissues of the body contain chemicals that are in a most delicate state of balance with the blood's slight degree of salinity, or saltiness. This salinity of the blood is thought to hark back to the very beginnings of evolution, when life existed only in the sea. When salt is retained, the body must then retain water also to preserve this delicate balance. Since there is a tendency to retain salt in pregnancy, limiting the intake of salt to a large extent will control the tendency. The intake of other substances containing sodium, notably sodium bicarbonate (baking soda), should also be controlled carefully. Some women are careful about table salt but ingest large amounts of baking soda or Alka-Seltzer for heartburn.

A liberal intake of fluids is advisable in pregnancy. When eliminated by the kidneys, the fluid will carry away a certain amount of salt.

Swelling of the hands and tightening of rings on the fingers are definite indications of *edema,* the medical term for collection of fluid in tissues or body cavities. Most pregnant women will have retained more than just a little fluid before it shows up in swelling of the hands or face. While a little ankle swelling at the end of a hot day is not alarming, your doctor will want you to call him if you should develop edema of the hands or face. There are drugs that are both effective and safe for the treatment of excessive swelling in pregnancy. The doctor often prescribes them in the latter part of pregnancy if he thinks too much fluid is being retained.

FALSE PREGNANCY

False pregnancy is a condition that captures the imagination. So many references to it appear in novels and stories that you might suppose it is common. Actually, it is rare. There are many women who skip a period and wonder whether they are pregnant. If pregnancy does not materialize, they have merely skipped a period for some reason and are not examples of *pseudocyesis,* the medical term for false pregnancy.

In bona fide false pregnancy the woman will skip several periods and experience many of the symptoms of pregnancy. She may even swear that she can feel the baby kicking. She will often gain some weight and even look pregnant. The breasts may enlarge, and she may complain of minor discomforts characteristic of pregnancy. Nevertheless, repeated examination will disclose that the uterus is not growing. Persistently negative tests for pregnancy confirm the diagnosis. It is generally believed that false pregnancies are manifestations of emotional disturbance. For many of the women in this condition, pregnancy is either highly desired or greatly feared. Sometimes, when tests have proved that the woman is not pregnant, she will become very resentful of the doctor. It is not unusual, under these circumstances, to have a big blowup in the clinic or doctor's office. Finally convinced, some of these women begin to menstruate almost immediately.

FIBROID TUMORS

These are fleshy growths within or on the uterine wall. In pregnancy, fibroids are encountered somewhat more frequently in older mothers and in those of the Negro race. While there are many possibilities for complications in pregnancy and labor, the great majority of women with these common benign tumors go through delivery without incident. Most are unaware that they have tumors.

Fibroid tumors grow in pregnancy. This growth is due to the action of pregnancy hormones. (A similar growth, incidentally, is seen in the fibroid tumors of women taking birth control pills.) Some fibroids enlarge to such an extent that their limited blood supply is no longer able to sustain them. The tumor then undergoes degeneration. It is painful and tender and may be confused with other conditions of pregnancy causing abdominal pain and tenderness. In pregnancy it is not wise to remove a degenerating fibroid. After a few days the symptoms subside.

Fibroid tumors may obstruct labor. Delivery by Caesarean section then becomes mandatory. Fibroid tumors are usually not removed at the time of Caesarean section because most often they regress spontaneously after delivery.

GERMAN MEASLES
(See Virus Diseases)

HEADACHES

Headaches in pregnancy are common. There is usually no cause for alarm, especially in the early months. A headache may be one of the signs of the severe toxemia of pregnancy, but this condition rarely occurs before the last three months. When it does occur, there are usually other symptoms to reinforce the diagnosis. But if you should develop a severe, unremitting headache in the final three months of pregnancy, notify your doctor without delay.

Headaches in early pregnancy are often of the sinus type, in the frontal region over the eyes. Sinus headaches characteristically are aggravated by bending over, as you would to tie your shoe or pick up something. The nasal congestion common in pregnancy tends to prevent proper draining of the sinuses, and headaches are frequent. A hot moist Turkish towel applied over the forehead and eyes is one of the most effective remedies.

Another type of benign headache in pregnancy is the simple tension headache. These headaches radiate from the back of the neck into the back of the head. Rest and relaxation are the best cure. Aspirin can be taken without danger in pregnancy if ordinary doses are used. A couple of aspirin tablets two or three times a day are harmless. If the headaches are so severe or persistent that you need more aspirin than this, you should be in touch with your doctor. Migraine is one of the few conditions improved by pregnancy. It is the experience of the great majority of women who have been subject to migraine that they have fewer attacks in pregnancy, or none at all. If his patient complains of frequent migraine attacks in pregnancy, the doctor is inclined to wonder whether the diagnosis of migraine is correct.

HEARTBURN

Heartburn is a hard symptom to describe, but anyone who has experienced this discomfort beneath the breastbone needs no explanation. In pregnancy heartburn often occurs when a nubbin of the stomach is pushed up through the diaphragm. This can happen any time after the fourth month. Since position has a lot to do with heartburn, the discomfort is often worse at night or when you lie down to rest. Heartburn is not a symptom of serious disease. Though pregnant women may suffer much discomfort from it, they invariably are relieved within twenty-four to forty-eight hours after delivery. The expectant mother with heartburn should be on a bland diet. Foods that trigger it should be avoided. Coffee is a frequent offender. It is better to eat five or six small meals daily than three larger ones. It is wise to eat lightly in the evening. The antacid preparations often prescribed for ulcer patients can afford relief in many cases of heartburn in pregnancy. Avoid baking soda or Alka-Seltzer; these contain sodium. Elevation of the head of the bed or propping oneself up on pillows at night are other simple measures worth trying if heartburn is severe.

HEART DISEASE

A vivid example of the way time changes the practice of medicine can be seen in the approach to heart disease in pregnancy. For a book of this kind, the discussion not so many years ago would have been limited to rheumatic heart disease. That disease is not so common as it was twenty or thirty years ago, and there is every indication that it will continue to diminish. More or less concurrent with progress on this front, advances in cardiac surgery have made it possible for many girls with congenital heart disease to survive childhood and reach the childbearing years. We are now seeing an increasing number of such patients and are confronted with the special problems they present.

Women with heart disease often ask about the advisability of pregnancy. In general, if there is no history of heart failure and if it is not necessary to limit activity because of heart disease, there is no problem. The outlook is much less favorable in a patient whose heart has already failed, whether or not failure occurred under the stress of pregnancy. Other factors affecting the outlook adversely are age (thirty-five years or over) and the involvement of more than one heart valve in the disease process.

Even women with severe heart disease stand the strain of labor surprisingly well. It is neither necessary nor wise to perform a Caesarean section to avoid labor. However, the pushing and bearing down that go with the expulsive stage of labor can precipitate heart failure. Once the cervix has become completely dilated and the baby's head has reached the pelvic floor, the baby is delivered by forceps rather than by the mother's efforts.

Women who have undergone successful cardiac surgery should be evaluated individually before undertaking to have children. Some of them, though quite recovered from surgery, do not have normal cardiac function.

Successful cardiac surgery in pregnancy has been performed on numerous occasions. However, this is hardly the ideal time for these delicate operations. With rare exceptions, they should be performed either before or after pregnancy.

HEMORRHOIDS

In pregnancy there is increase in pressure (see pages 70–71) in the veins of the pelvis and leg. The superficial leg veins may become swollen and dilated and are then known as varicose veins. When the same kind of swelling occurs in the veins around the anal opening, the unpleasant result is called *hemorrhoids*. These begin as painless swellings just inside the anus. If forced outside by straining at stool or during a bout of diarrhea, the swollen tissue cannot retract back inside where it belongs. This condition is called a prolapsed hemorrhoid. The blood flow through the vein is impeded, and a clot forms within the swollen hemorrhoid. These are thrombosed external hemorrhoids. They bleed slightly and are exquisitely painful.

Since you want to avoid both diarrhea and the straining at stool that accompanies constipation, you will do well to pay attention to the bowels in pregnancy. A proper diet, plenty of liquids, and exercise will help avoid such complications. If a hemorrhoid should occur and prolapse, there are many remedies that afford some relief. A warm tub is one of the simplest. Some astringents are helpful. Cold witch hazel is a favorite. There are soothing ointments and suppositories your doctor may suggest. It is pointless to try to replace a prolapsed hemorrhoid as it will just pop back out again. Major rectal surgery for hemorrhoids should not be performed in pregnancy, but the thrombosed external hemorrhoid can be incised under local anesthesia in the doctor's office. Once the clot has been removed, the hemorrhoid will shrink down. The relief from this procedure is often dramatic. If hemorrhoids are pushed out during delivery, they may remain painful for the first few days in the hospital. But once the pressure of pregnancy is removed, the hemorrhoids shrink and therefore give little or no trouble.

IMMUNIZATIONS

We do not give vaccine made from living viruses (measles, mumps, rubella, yellow fever, smallpox, polio) to pregnant women because of our concern that the vaccine viruses may infect the fetus, causing fetal damage. Because German measles (rubella) infection during the first trimester is so dangerous, it is particularly important to check on the immunity of women prior to pregnancy so that they can be given the rubella vaccine if they are not immune. Killed vaccines like flu, tetanus, or diphtheria can be given during pregnancy if needed.

INJURY AND TRAUMA

It is hardly possible to go through the entire nine months of pregnancy without at least one good fall or bump. While external injury conceivably could disturb a normal pregnancy, complications are rare, even from severe accidents. Pregnancies have survived bad automobile collisions, where the victims have suffered broken legs and even broken pelvic bones. Suspended as he is in fluid, the baby is so well protected that only a severe direct blow on the abdomen may jeopardize him. Since there is a reflex tendency to double up if an accident is impending, this type of injury is rare. If any complication follows injury in pregnancy, it is usually separation of the placenta, and it almost always occurs immediately. There will be vaginal bleeding, abdominal pain, and maybe absence of fetal movement. If a couple of hours have gone by without any of these signs appearing, you can be quite certain that nothing has happened to the pregnancy because of the accident.

Contrary to a rather widespread impression, severe emotional trauma rarely, if ever, causes any complication of pregnancy. We have all heard a story of some woman or other who miscarried or went into labor prematurely after a fight with her husband or mother-in-law. Nevertheless, examination of the miscarriage would probably have disclosed that no fetus had formed, or the mother's obstetrical history would have shown that all her babies have been born a month early. Perhaps the question to ask is not whether emotional trauma will cause complications, but whether complications will cause emotional trauma. Now that it has become possible to analyze and study the amniotic fluid (see pages 154–55 and 419) without disturbing the pregnancy, we may begin to learn a great deal more about hitherto obscure relationships between the developmental progress of the fetus and the well-being of the mother.

INSOMNIA

As pregnancy advances, most women have trouble sleeping the entire night through. Some of the causes for this are purely physical. The uterus is so large by the end of pregnancy that no position of the body seems comfortable or relaxing for long. Because the uterus exerts pressure on the bladder, most women have to get up at least once a night to void. Emotional factors, too, often contribute to the insomnia of pregnancy, as we have said in the discussion of depressions (see pages 125–27).

No set number of hours of sleep is necessary in pregnancy or at any other time. It is surprising how well many people feel on five or six hours of sleep, especially if they can get a nap in the daytime. The simplest remedies for insomnia are often the best and most enjoyable ones. A bracing walk, a warm tub, and a glass of brandy or sherry at bedtime are often more effective than a sleeping pill. There are, however, many safe sleeping pills that your doctor can prescribe if he thinks one is indicated.

ITCHING

Generalized itching of the skin is common during pregnancy. It is most annoying at night and seems to be worse in hot weather. While the itching may cover the entire body, it is usually most annoying over the enlarged abdomen in the latter part of pregnancy. Sometimes a mild sedative at bedtime helps. Lotions and salves seem to be singularly ineffective. Itching is not a serious symptom and goes away promptly after delivery.

LATE DELIVERY

Very few mothers deliver exactly on their calculated due date. The great majority will deliver within a couple of weeks of their due date if menstrual periods before pregnancy were regular, coming at four-week intervals. Mothers with shorter menstrual cycles tend to deliver a few days early, and those with longer cycles are prone to be a few days late.

We define postmaturity (late delivery) as any gestational age beyond forty-two weeks, that is, forty-two weeks after the last menstrual period. (The gestational age of the full-term baby is between thirty-eight and forty-two weeks; the premature is any gestational age under thirty-seven weeks.) In most cases of postmaturity, when delivery and birth eventually do occur, the baby and placenta appear perfectly normal. In a few cases, however, the baby has failed to grow in the last few days of intrauterine life and may even have lost a little weight. At birth his skin is dry and wrinkled. We interpret these signs as indications that the placenta has not been operating at full efficiency. In many instances, therefore, when the mother is overdue the doctor will recommend induction of labor.

No one knows the cause of postmaturity. The most important single thing that obstetricians would like to know is what process it is that initiates labor. If this were known, we could do something to stop labor when it begins too early, or to start it when the onset is delayed.

LEG CRAMPS

The majority of women have leg cramps in pregnancy. These cramps occur in the calf muscles at night and if prolonged are followed by soreness and tenderness that may last for a day or two. For most pregnant women these cramps are infrequent and present no problem, but when the spasms occur almost every night, they become a great nuisance.

No one knows what causes these cramps. Many doctors believe that calcium metabolism has something to do with them. Some women who are heavy milk drinkers seem to be relieved if they cut down on milk intake. Large doses of thiamine, one of the B vitamins, are an effective remedy in many cases, but just why is not clear. Antacids and antihistamines also sometimes seem to relieve the cramps. The drug quinidine is most effective. As you can see, there is nothing specific about the treatment. Stretching the leg in bed often initiates the cramp and should be avoided. If the cramp begins, flex the foot or stand up. This activity will often check it.

There is no danger of premature labor after the use of quinidine, in spite of some opinion to the contrary. Even quinine, a closely related drug often tried in days gone by to induce labor, is harmless in this regard. Doctors in the deep South used to prescribe huge doses of quinine for malaria throughout pregnancy, and there is no literature to suggest that premature labor was an unusual problem among their patients.

MISCARRIAGE

(See chapter 22.)

MORNING SICKNESS

When morning sickness becomes protracted and severe, it is known by the awesome name *hyperemesis gravidarum*. Simple morning sickness can be most unpleasant and annoying, but it is not harmful to the mother or fetus. Severe hyperemesis gravidarum, on the contrary, is a serious complication because the repeated vomiting depletes the body of fluid and chemicals. The fundamental body processes can then become deranged. In the days when not so much was known about fluid balance and body chemistry, it was not unusual to see pregnant women critically ill from this condition. Nowadays, fortunately, proper supervision and treatment will avert these crises.

As long as the weight is maintained, dehydration is not severe. A loss of ten pounds or more is a sign of severe dehydration. In these circumstances it is usually advisable to hospitalize patients and restore the fluids and chemicals they have lost through the repeated vomiting. Furthermore, we have drugs for this condition. Simple sedatives are often effective. Several newer drugs appear to act directly on the vomiting center in the brain and suppress its activity.

No one knows the cause of hyperemesis gravidarum. It is much less of a problem now than it was a few years ago, partly because of our greater knowledge. Abnormalities can now be corrected rapidly and accurately before further trouble results.

MULTIPLE PREGNANCY

Rare is the pregnant woman who has not at some time half convinced herself that she is going to have twins. In actuality, twins occur only once in something like ninety births. The incidence of triplets is about one in nine thousand births. Multiple births of more than three babies are truly medical curiosities.

Mothers who are going to have twins will often have more severe symptoms of pregnancy than those having single births. Protracted and severe morning sickness is characteristic. If morning sickness has not been a problem in a woman's previous pregnancies, its appearance this time makes one suspicious of multiple pregnancy. So does excessive weight gain in a woman who is watching her diet carefully and is not taking too much salt or drugs containing sodium.

The symptom that usually tips the doctor off is the size of the uterus, which has become larger than it should be for that particular point in the pregnancy. When the doctor has an opportunity to make regular periodic examinations, he can tell whether the womb is enlarging too rapidly, but if he sees his patient only once in the latter part of pregnancy, he may easily miss the diagnosis. Contingencies of this sort point up the value of prenatal care. Twins are usually diagnosed in the last three months. To be able to spot twins earlier requires a high degree of clinical judgment. The probability of twins increases somewhat with the age of the mother and the number of her children.

Once the doctor suspects twins, he can confirm the diagnosis by finding two separate heartbeats, which can usually be detected with his stethoscope. Several sophisticated electronic devices capable of demonstrating twin pregnancies have been developed recently. It is possible as early as the fourth month to obtain fetal electrocardiograms from the electrical impulses generated in the babies' hearts. Twin pregnancies will show two distinct waves in the fetal electrocardiogram. There are also electronic stethoscopes and sensitive amplifiers that can magnify the sounds of the baby's heartbeat many times. While apparatus of this complexity is interesting and even exciting, it is mainly a research tool and at this stage of the game not essential to proper supervision of the usual multiple pregnancy. The doctor will often want to confirm the diagnosis of multiple pregnancy with an X-ray picture of the abdomen. While we try to keep X-ray exposure to a minimum in pregnancy, the importance of the diagnosis of multiple pregnancy is of such magnitude that it far outweighs the theoretic objections to X-ray exposure.

There are two types of twins, fraternal and identical. A close inspection of the placenta will disclose which is which. Fraternal twins come from two different fertilized ova and therefore may differ in sex, blood type, eye color, and any other genetically determined characteristic. They are three or four times more common than identical twins. They arise when two eggs are released and fertilized at the same time. Some women tend to ovulate more than one egg each month, and they are the ones who tend to have repeated multiple pregnancy. That multiple births occur in some families more frequently than statistically expected suggests an hereditary factor. These twins are usually of the fraternal type. You hear that twins "skip a generation," but there is nothing to this theory. The tendency to twinning is present in some families but does not seem to follow any distinct genetic pattern. Some studies have shown that there is almost as great a tendency for the twinning characteristic to be carried by the male as by the female. This might mean that some males produce sperm cells in a greater number or with greater ability to fertilize the ova.

Racial differences have been shown to exist in the distribution of fraternal twins. The chances of producing fraternal twins are somewhat greater for blacks than for whites and somewhat less for Orientals than for whites. There appears to be no racial difference in the incidence of identical twins.

There are certain relatively new drugs capable of inducing ovulation in women who are unable to ovulate spontaneously. This is a big advance in the treatment of infertility due to failure of ovulation. One complication of this type of therapy, however, is multiple pregnancy. There have been numerous incidents of twin pregnancy and a relatively large number of higher multiple births. The multiple births that occur are of the fraternal type because these drugs cause several eggs to be released from the ovary at the same time.

Identical twins derive from a single fertilized cell. Very early in embryonic life the developing ovum splits completely into two, and each half goes on to form a baby. This division probably occurs in the first week after fertilization. In rare instances the fertilized ovum does not split into two until after the *amnion,* or inner layer of the membranes, has begun to form. When this happens, both babies will develop in the same sac. This condition is dangerous because the babies may become entangled in each other's cords. Otherwise, twins, whether identical or fraternal, are always in separate sacs. They rarely get in each other's way, even during delivery. The placentas of identical twins are fused, and there is often a mixture of fetal blood supply between the two placentas. Occasionally, one twin will get a large majority of the blood. Its sibling will then be small and poorly developed. This deprivation can be severe enough to cause the death of one twin.

A very rare type of twins, called Siamese, are always identical. For some unknown reason, they are likely to be female. They usually are joined together in the region of the lower back (sacrum) and often share vital organs. Because vital structures are involved, surgical separation is rarely successful. With Siamese twins the separation of the developing embryo into two halves occurs later in embryonic life and the divison is incomplete.

Identical twins, having developed from the same fertilized ovum, have identical chromosome distribution and therefore identical characteristics such as sex, eye color, and blood type. As they grow up, there may be slight differences in appearance due to variations in height, weight, and so forth. Identical twins are the joy of scientists who are interested in learning whether a given condition is inherited or developmental in nature. If they can study a large enough number of identical twin pairs with the condition, they can usually find the answer.

There are several complications associated with twin pregnancies. The most important is premature delivery. It is uncommon for a mother with twins to carry the entire nine months of pregnancy. Most patients with twins will deliver about three weeks early and many much sooner. Twins have a mortality rate about four times greater than single births, but the difference is due largely to the frequency of premature birth. Because of the likelihood of premature delivery, mothers with twin pregnancies should rest more in the critical seventh and eighth months.

Twin babies are usually smaller than single infants at the same stage of gestation. If twins are carried to term, they weigh about a pound and a half less than single babies. Twins carried less than the full nine months are proportionally smaller. The relatively small size of twins is due to a relatively inefficient placenta. Doctors talk glibly about "placental insufficiency" or "placental dysfunction," which is found in a number of conditions other than twinning, mainly in overdue pregnancies. Yet little is known about placental insufficiency because we have so few tests of placental function. Those we have are time-consuming and expensive and are used mostly in investigative studies.

Another complication to watch for in a twin pregnancy is toxemia of pregnancy (see pages 157–61). The ultimate cause, as we have stressed several times, is not known, but toxemia does seem to be more frequent when there is reduction of uterine blood flow. It is presumed that the greatly distended uterus of twins has a relatively reduced blood flow and hence leads to development of toxemia of pregnancy in some twin gestations. Be that as it may, it certainly behooves the mother carrying twins to be extremely careful of her intake of salt and other forms of sodium. She should be meticulous in keeping her weight gain at no more than two pounds a month and should report swelling of the hands and feet or rapid changes in her weight. Many women carrying twins will develop an excessive amount of amniotic fluid in one of the sacs, an instance of hydramnios or polyhydramnios (see pages 147–48) . In single pregnancies polyhydramnios is often associated with congenital anomalies, but the association does not hold for the polyhydramnios seen in multiple births. In twin gestation polyhydramnios contributes to the overdistention of the uterus and may be responsible in part for the increased incidence of toxemia.

Labor may proceed normally with twins, but often the contractions are mild and relatively infrequent. As a result, progress in labor is delayed and prolonged. The best remedy is patience. Sometimes it will be necessary to give drugs to stimulate the uterus.

The choice of anesthesia depends on many considerations, the size and position of the babies being among the chief ones. The first baby born rarely presents any problem whether it comes head first or feet first. The second, too, will usually be born without difficulty within a few minutes. But with some frequency circumstances do arise after the birth of the first baby that make delivery of the second twin without delay desirable. If any manipulation within the uterus must be done to effect this, a complete ether anesthetic is easiest for the doctor and safest for the mother. It may not be ideal for the baby, however, especially if the second twin is very small. As in so many other aspects of obstetrics, no rule can be laid down. The doctor has to decide in each individual case which anesthetic will be the safest for the mother and babies.

NOSEBLEEDS

Nasal congestion to a greater or lesser degree is present in almost all pregnancies. In winter this annoyance leads women to believe they have colds that hang on indefinitely, and in summer to think they have developed an allergy. This nasal congestion is responsible for nosebleeds, which are common and harmless complications of pregnancy. Fullness of the ears is another symptom that accompanies nasal congestion.

OBESITY

Obesity is a hard term to define. Most of us seem to think we are too heavy, especially when we compare our own weights to those "ideal" charts compiled by life insurance companies. Even though you may not quite fit into the insurance company tables, pregnancy represents no hazard in respect to your weight.

There are a few unfortunate individuals, however, who are truly and unmistakably obese. Usually they have been markedly overweight children and adolescents. In spite of pills, diets, and good intentions, most of these unfortunates are destined to continue in this condition for the rest of their days. It is a grim prognosis, but for most of these persons obesity is an incurable disease. When they become pregnant, and have to watch calorie intake, they respond much better to sympathy and understanding than they do to attempts to browbeat them into submission. Actually, most of them do not gain excessively during pregnancy, and when it is all over they weigh about what they did when they conceived. In going over their charts at the hospital, one gets the impression that in the course of their pregnancies these women have heard a good bit about their weight, but the warnings and scoldings rarely seem to have been effective.

Obese women can safely be put on rigid diets during pregnancy. If motivated enough, it is possible for them to lose fifteen or twenty pounds. These individuals, like other women, will lose an additional fifteen or twenty pounds after delivery. Their babies are healthy and of normal size. Unfortunately, few women are willing to submit themselves to semistarvation. Even sadder is the outcome for many of those who do submit. Within the first year after delivery they will gain back all they had lost. For a permanent cure the "crash" diet approach to obesity is no more successful in pregnancy than it is at any other time.

When a woman is markedly overweight, the diagnosis of pregnancy becomes difficult and sometimes impossible. It may be weeks before the uterus can be palpated through the thick abdominal wall. Later on in pregnancy, twins and abnormal positions can easily be missed because the fetal parts cannot be felt. In women with irregular menstrual cycles, progressive increase in size of the uterus is the best yardstick to measure the duration of pregnancy. With marked obesity, it may be impossible to guess when the patient is actually due. Marked obesity can also make it difficult or impossible to locate the baby's heartbeat. Luckily, most obese women do not have mechanical difficulties during delivery because of the obesity per se, although there may be, of course, other complicating factors.

OVARIAN CYSTS AND TUMORS

There are literally dozens of different kinds of ovarian cysts and tumors that may complicate pregnancy. To describe them all is beyond the scope of a book like this.

Surgery is not performed for all ovarian cysts during pregnancy. While no generalizations can be made, most small, soft, and freely movable ovarian cysts are not removed. Larger growths are usually taken out.

PIGMENTATION: THE MASK OF PREGNANCY

The skin becomes pigmented in pregnancy. This condition is undoubtedly due to hormone changes. The same skin change happens to non-pregnant women who take similar hormones in birth control pills. After pregnancy the pigmentation gradually fades until eventually little or none is noticeable. The *mask of pregnancy* is a very light brown, blotchy discoloration of the skin over the forehead and cheekbones. Other pigmented areas of the body become darker. The skin around the nipple (*areola* of the breast) becomes darker. The *linea alba,* that little line down the middle of the abdomen, becomes darkened and is then known as the *linea nigra*. Pigmented moles become darker. This change is not cause for concern and does not make removal of the moles necessary. No treatment is effective or necessary for this pigmentation. If unsightly, the pigmented areas can be covered up with cosmetics.

PLACENTA PREVIA

In *placenta previa* the placenta is implanted too close to the neck of the womb. Ordinarily the placenta implants high up in the uterine body.

No one knows why or how the ovum first decides on a particular place to attach itself, but if this point is close to the cervix, a placenta previa results at the end of pregnancy. This is not a common complication. It occurs in only about one of every hundred deliveries. It is a good deal more common in women who have had several children than in those pregnant for the first time. It is uncommon (although not unheard-of) for a woman to have placenta previa in more than one pregnancy.

As pregnancy draws to a close, the neck of the womb gradually thins out and dilates in anticipation of the changes that will occur when labor ensues. If the placenta lies too close to the uterine cervix (neck of the womb), the attachment of the placenta to the womb's lining is disturbed. Bleeding to a lesser or greater degree follows, depending on how much of the placenta is detached. The bleeding is painless and, in the usual case, intermittent. After the initial episode, which often produces no more than a few teaspoonsful, days or even weeks may pass before another occurrence. The recurrent incidents of bleeding are more profuse, and if these warning symptoms are ignored, in some cases a truly alarming hemorrhage can result.

There are several methods for locating the site of the placenta. The placenta can often be seen in an X-ray picture, but this method is far from accurate. In another method, radioactively tagged albumin is injected into the mother's bloodstream. It collects in the placenta and can then be detected by sensitive counters. This method is more accurate than the X-ray picture and, surprisingly, subjects the infant to considerably less radiation than he would get from a standard X-ray exposure. There are also accurate ultrasound techniques.

When the placenta is implanted in the lower part of the uterus, it prevents the baby's head from entering the pelvis. Consequently, the fetus often assumes a transverse or oblique orientation in relation to the axis of the birth canal. Such abnormal positions are a common accompaniment of placenta previa.

With rare exceptions, significant bleeding in the latter part of pregnancy is due either to placenta previa or premature separation of the normally implanted placenta. Both of these are serious conditions that can endanger the mother and the infant. When bleeding occurs in the final month of pregnancy, diagnosis and proper treatment should be undertaken without delay if the condition of the baby and mother is good. At this time the infant will be mature enough to do well. Procrastination may result in more serious hemorrhage. Prior to the last month, it may be wise to withhold treatment in hope that a more mature infant will be delivered. Selection of the proper time to institute treatment requires expert critical judgment depending on many factors.

In spite of the several diagnostic tools available, the differential diagnosis between placenta previa and premature separation of the placenta must be made by internal examination. If the physician can feel the placenta at the opening of the womb, the patient has a placenta previa. If not, he can safely assume that the bleeding comes from a separated placenta. This examination is best conducted in the operating room under anesthesia with preparations made for immediate Caesarean section. The operation must sometimes be done with a minimum of delay if a placenta previa is discovered. Most women with placenta previa will require Caesarean section, but most of those with premature separation of the placenta can safely be delivered vaginally.

POLYHYDRAMNIOS

Excessive accumulation of the amniotic fluid is called *hydramnios* or *polyhydramnios*. Normally there is about a quart of this fluid, but in a severe case of hydramnios there may be four or five quarts. This fluid is continually manufactured and absorbed, the process proceeding so rapidly that in a few hours the entire volume has been turned over. The fetus swallows amniotic fluid and excretes it through the fetal kidney.

When polyhydramnios develops there is often (but by no means always) an associated congenital anomaly of the baby. The usual anomalies encountered are such that they interfere with the swallowing mechanism. Obstructions of the fetal esophagus and upper digestive tract are common causes of polyhydramnios. A fetal brain anomaly that interferes with the swallowing reflex can cause this complication. In many cases of twins there is an excessive amount of fluid even though the babies are perfectly normal. The same situation can exist in diabetes. Rh-negative mothers often have polyhydramnios, but then it is usually a sign that the baby is getting into trouble from erythroblastosis. (See page 151.) There are also many mothers who have an excessive amount of fluid with normal babies, and no cause of the polyhydramnios is ever found.

The doctor suspects polyhydramnios when the uterus is larger than it should be for the length of pregnancy. In rare instances, the polyhydramnios develops in just a few days. If the abdomen suddenly becomes huge, tense, and tender, the diagnosis is unmistakable. An X-ray picture is often helpful in diagnosing polyhydramnios. The extra fluid gives a hazy shadow. The baby's extremities are seen extended, rather than folded compactly against the body, as in normal pregnancies.

In most cases of polyhydramnios no treatment is necessary, but when the fluid accumulates rapidly, the mother is miserable and may even have respiratory difficulty due to her enlarged abdomen. The excessive fluid can be removed safely by tapping the amniotic sac with a small bore needle. Unfortunately, excess fluid often forms again; repeated taps may be necessary. Many mothers with polyhydramnios go into premature labor.

Since there is an increased incidence of toxemia of pregnancy associated with polyhydramnios, mothers with this condition should have extra rest and be particularly careful about limiting their salt intake.

PREMATURE SEPARATION OF THE PLACENTA

This serious complication in the latter part of pregnancy is associated with vaginal bleeding. The placenta, or afterbirth, becomes partly or entirely detached from the lining of the womb before the baby is born. The separation usually occurs suddenly, hence, the name *abruptio placentae* (abruption of the placenta), which is descriptive of the onset of symptoms. The British refer to it as accidental hemorrhage, pointing up the fact that it comes on unexpectedly. Premature separation of the placenta occurs in something like one case in 125 deliveries. In most cases the separation is not complete and the outlook for both the mother and baby is excellent. When as much as one-third or one-half of the placenta becomes detached, it is often fatal to the baby because he is deprived of the life-sustaining oxygen supplied by the placenta. Major degrees of placental separation are dangerous to the mother too, because severe hemorrhage may ensue.

A rare complication of premature separation of the placenta occurs when fibrinogen, an element in the formation of blood clots, is depleted from the blood. When this happens, fibrinogen must be administered to the mother to prevent the development of a hemorrhagic tendency.

In addition to their vaginal bleeding, many (but not all) women with separations will have pain in either the abdomen or back. The pains are like labor pains because they arise in the womb. With major separations the abdomen is hard and tender to the touch, the pain severe and unremitting. The pain in lesser degrees of separation may be no worse than a generalized backache, such as sometimes accompanies menstruation. Some women will have high blood pressure or protein in the urine or both, but a majority will not. One occasionally comes on a patient with separation who has separated the placenta in a previous pregnancy. No one knows the cause of this condition, but recent work from England suggests it may be associated with the failure in some individuals to absorb or to utilize folic acid, a vitaminlike substance needed in the formation of all cells. During the active metabolism of pregnancy, there is an increased need for folic acid.

Women with premature separation have to be hospitalized. A number of laboratory tests are usually in order to determine the blood count and so forth. One of the difficult things for the doctor to determine is whether the bleeding is due to a premature separation of the placenta or the condition known as *placenta previa* (see pages 145–47). In the latter complication the placenta is attached too close to the neck of the womb. There are tests that help in locating the position of the placenta. Often an internal examination is done under anesthesia so that immediate Caesarean section can be performed if a placenta previa is encountered. Most patients with premature separation of the placenta can be delivered safely through the vagina, and therefore labor is induced and allowed to proceed normally. When labor does not progress satisfactorily in a premature separation, a Caesarean section will be done if there are signs of fetal distress or continuance of the separation.

RESPIRATORY INFECTIONS

Common colds are no more frequent in pregnancy than at any other time. There is no evidence that colds, although apparently due to a virus, affect the outcome of pregnancy adversely. Colds do seem to "hang on" longer in pregnancy. The nasal congestion accompanying pregnancy (see page 143) contributes here. It is also responsible for the flare-ups of sinus disease in pregnancy following a respiratory infection. At this writing, there is no cure for the common cold. They say a cold lasts for two weeks if you treat it and a fortnight if you do not. The aspirin and simple cough syrups commonly administered to relieve the symptoms of a cold certainly appear to have no ill effect on the developing fetus.

Severe respiratory infections can be serious complications of pregnancy. Women carrying a child do not seem to tolerate pneumonia as well as their nonpregnant sisters. In the disastrous flu epidemic after World War I, recovery was the exception rather than the rule when this disease struck in pregnancy, but the flu of recent years has been much milder than in that first great epidemic. Pneumonia occurring in pregnancy often runs a more protracted course. It sometimes takes weeks before patients are completely recovered.

RETROVERSION OF THE UTERUS

Usually the body of the uterus bends forward, toward the bladder. When it bends backward into the cavity of the pelvis, toward the rectum, it is said to be retroverted. In years gone by, most of the ills to which female flesh, pregnant or not, was heir were blamed on retroversion of the uterus. It is now believed that this condition rarely causes any trouble.

In early pregnancy retroversions are common. As the uterus enlarges and gets heavier, it naturally tends to flop backward. This shift does not cause any trouble. After the third month the uterus becomes so large it grows up out of the pelvis; hence, it is impossible to have a retroverted uterus in the middle and latter part of pregnancy.

Adhesions from some previous disease in the pelvis may bind the uterus down in a backward position, but this is a rare condition. In these cases there may be cramps or even vaginal bleeding as the body of the uterus enlarges. If the uterine body can be brought forward, it can sometimes be held in position with a vaginal pessary or ring. After the third month it is no longer possible for the uterus to get back into the pelvic cavity; the pessary can then be removed.

THE RH-NEGATIVE PROBLEM

A more appropriate heading would be the "former Rh-negative problem." For all but a very small percentage of mothers and infants, the Rh problem is a matter of historical interest now that prevention is a reality. Mothers who are Rh negative will continue to relate to the problem, but in terms of prevention only, and rarely treatment.

The Rh factor was discovered in 1940 by Dr. Karl Lundsteiner and Dr. A. S. Wiener. They injected the blood of rhesus (Rh) monkeys into guinea pigs, which responded (as expected) by producing a substance called an antibody. When a sample of the monkey's blood and the antibody were mixed, the red blood corpuscles agglutinated or stuck together. Again, this was the result expected. But when the antibody was tested against human red blood cells, the investigators were surprised. Although agglutination occurred in most of the samples tested, in a few it did not appear. What was different about the few? Some factor responsible for agglutination must be present in most cells but missing from the cells of those few. This factor or substance was named the Rh factor in honor of the monkeys of the original experiment.

Subsequent study showed that 85 percent of the white U.S. population possessed this Rh factor while the remaining 15 percent lacked it. The latter were said to be *Rh negative*. Studies showed also that at least 95 percent of all Negroes and 99 percent of Orientals were Rh positive. A review of the obstetric histories of Rh-negative women showed that a few had had repeated deliveries of children afflicted with *erythroblastosis*, until this time a disease of unknown cause. A whole new field of investigation opened up. These differences of blood type have turned out to be useful to anthropologists in their search for the origins of races.

When a mother carries a child whose blood type is different from her own, the baby may develop the disease known as *erythroblastosis fetalis*. The baby's blood cells are destroyed by an *antibody* manufactured in the mother. (We will describe antibodies shortly.) In the effort to make up for these lost blood cells, numerous immature red blood corpuscles called *erythroblasts* are pushed prematurely into the baby's circulation from its own blood-forming organs.

Since difference of blood type underlies this disease and since there are numerous blood types, there are many possible kinds of erythroblastosis. Some are too rare for discussion in a book of this kind. From a practical standpoint we can think of erythroblastosis as occurring when an Rh-negative mother carries an Rh-positive baby or when the baby of a type-O mother is either type A or type B.

The body makes the protective substances called *antibodies* whenever it is exposed to certain foreign substances. The production of antibodies is usually beneficial, one of the main protections against infectious disease, but not always. While the antibodies in erythroblastosis are not beneficial, the mechanism of their formation is the same as it is for a number of better-known diseases. If a person has typhoid fever, for instance, the typhoid germs will induce the body to form specific antityphoid antibodies. These antibodies surround individual typhoid germs to mark or tag them for destruction (when the process is successful) in time to effect a cure of typhoid fever. If this person is ever exposed to typhoid germs again, the specific antibodies are on hand to tag the typhoid bacilli, and a second attack of typhoid fever is less likely and milder, if it occurs. To immunize a person so that he will not get typhoid fever in the first place, we inject killed typhoid germs. Since the germs are dead, they are innocuous as far as causing the disease, but they do lead to formation of antityphoid antibodies, just as living typhoid germs would. To induce this formation of antibodies is the purpose of the typhoid "shot."

In erythroblastosis a similar process goes on. If an Rh-negative mother carries an Rh-positive child, it is possible under some conditions for some of the baby's red blood corpuscles to pass through the placenta into the mother's circulation. These Rh-positive red blood cells, acting as an *antigen,* stimulate the formation of specific antibodies that are capable of destroying Rh-positive cells. The antibodies are of such small size they have no difficulty in diffusing through the placenta back into the baby's circulation. Once there, they surround and attach to the baby's own red blood corpuscles, causing their early removal and leading to the condition known as erythroblastosis fetalis.

The fact that a mother is Rh negative is not in itself cause for alarm. Though one mother of six in this country is Rh negative, erythroblastosis due to the Rh factor was an uncommon disease in babies even before prevention was available. Even then only 10 percent of Rh-negative mothers had any difficulty, mild or severe, and 90 percent, the overwhelming majority, had none. Even then, Rh-negative mothers had less to worry about than was popularly thought. Only about one baby in 150 births was affected. Most cases were relatively mild, and the baby recovered completely. Erythroblastosis occurs only when the mother has the specific Rh-positive antibodies in her blood. She is then said to be "sensitized" to the Rh-positive cells. This is one important reason for careful typing and cross matching of all individuals before blood transfusions. If an Rh-negative person who has become sensitized to Rh-positive cells should receive a blood transfusion of Rh-positive cells, the cells would all be destroyed and a serious transfusion reaction would occur. Once a person has become sensitized, he remains so for life. The sensitization does not wear off in time. Rh-positive mothers who carry Rh-negative children have nothing to worry about. If any Rh-negative cells do get into the circulation, they do not cause the formation of antibodies.

The surest way for an Rh-negative person to become sensitized is to receive a transfusion of Rh-positive blood. Another way for an Rh-negative woman to become sensitized is to carry an Rh-positive child. Sensitization occurs infrequently. Why it is not more common is really unknown, but there are several plausible theories. That any of the baby's blood cells should find their way into the mother's circulation in the first place presupposes an imperfection in the placenta. The maternal and fetal circulations pass side by side in the placenta, but there should be no actual mixture of blood between the baby and mother. Small leaks do occur, however. Also, individuals must vary in their ability to produce antibodies. Some seem to make many more than others. Strangely enough, a mother's chances of becoming sensitized from the Rh-positive factor are influenced by her blood groups (ABO system). If the baby is "compatible" with the mother in the ABO system, she is much more likely to develop Rh antibodies than if he is not compatible. It appears that when incompatibilities exist in the major blood groups, any fetal red cells reaching the maternal circulation are destroyed before they have an opportunity to stimulate the formation of anti-Rh antibodies. Recent research has made it possible to prevent sensitization in most Rh-negative mothers by giving them Rh-positive antibodies at the time of delivery or shortly thereafter. These will destroy any Rh-positive cells gaining entrance into the mothers' circulations. It is becoming increasingly evident that if any of the baby's red blood cells are going to get into the mother they do so mainly at the time of labor and delivery rather than earlier in pregnancy. This is why Rh-sensitization was almost never a problem of the first baby. About 1 percent of Rh-negative mothers carrying Rh-positive babies are sensitized prior to delivery, excluding those who have been sensitized to the Rh-positive factor by transfusion prior to the first pregnancy. For this few, giving antibodies at delivery is too late. Once sensitization has occurred, there is no known way at present to reverse it. With the new techniques it is possible to prevent sensitization of the mother and hence erythroblastosis in all but this small number.

Sensitization can be determined by measuring the antibodies in the mother's blood. If the mother is sensitized and carries an Rh-positive child, the baby, as we have seen, will have erythroblastosis. In general, the higher the antibody level, the more severe the erythroblastosis will be. Since the antibodies do not decline with time but tend to build up in the carrying of successive Rh-positive babies, erythroblastosis tends to be more severe with each pregnancy of the sensitized mother. It takes at least one pregnancy to develop sensitization.

While now largely past history, it is worthwhile to detail the problem, which is now preventable. Stillbirth (death of the baby in the womb) is the major problem of Rh-negative mothers who are sensitized. In severe erythroblastosis, the infant may succumb to the disease prior to delivery. If the baby can be delivered alive, there is a good chance of survival with exchange transfusions, even when the erythroblastosis is severe. To prevent stillbirths, sensitized Rh-negative mothers were often delivered prematurely. The remaining sensitized Rh-negative mothers whose childbearing preceded preventive measures still are. Just how prematurely depends on the histories of the previous pregnancies and the indicated severity of the erythroblastosis. The baby cannot be delivered too early, however, because he then would have to cope with the effects of prematurity in addition to erythroblastosis. In the past, testing the level of Rh-positive antibodies was about the only method we had of predicting the severity of erythroblastosis. This method left something to be desired, for it gave only a rough index of the severity of erythroblastosis.

An important advance was the examination of the amniotic fluid prior to delivery to predict the severity of erythroblastosis. Dr. A. William Liley of New Zealand deserves most of the credit for this method, which entails the insertion of a hypodermic needle through the abdominal and uterine walls into the amniotic cavity to draw a sample of the fluid. The procedure is called *amniocentesis*. The sample so obtained contains a chemical (see Bilirubin, page 382) reflecting the severity of erythroblastosis with a high degree of accuracy.

When an erythroblastotic baby is born he faces two dangers. One is anemia, or lack of blood cells. If severe, this can lead to heart failure. The other is *jaundice* (see pages 382–85) . The latter is due to the destruction of large numbers of the baby's own red blood cells. If prolonged and severe, it can lead to permanent brain damage. The degree of jaundice can be measured accurately by determining the level of the pigment *bilirubin* in the blood (see pages 382–83) .

The red blood cells tagged with antibodies are removed by a special system of the fetus (known as the reticuloendothelial system) and destroyed. To keep up with this process of destruction, the baby must produce red cells at a higher than normal rate. In most situations the infant can increase red cell production to keep up with the losses. If the process is greatly accelerated, however, the destruction may exceed the baby's capacity to manufacture red cells. The number of red cells will be reduced, and the baby will go into the state we call *anemia*. The more severe this process is, the harder the baby's hematopoietic (blood-cell-forming) system must work, and, just as the biceps of the arm enlarges under training at weight lifting, so does the baby's hematopoietic system enlarge under this extra load. In the fetus, major sites of blood-forming and -removing tissue are the liver and spleen. Hence, babies who have undergone excessive destruction of red cells are likely to have enlarged livers and spleens. In the section on jaundice (see pages 382–83) we follow the sequence in which hemoglobin from the destroyed red cells is liberated and processed into bilirubin, which enters the fetal blood stream. As long as the baby is in utero the placenta constitutes an escape hatch for removal of the excess bilirubin, which the mother's liver can handle. After birth, the excess bilirubin of the infant becomes a medical problem.

If anemia or jaundice is dangerous to the baby, an exchange transfusion of Rh-negative cells is given. In this procedure a certain amount of the baby's blood is removed and replaced with blood from a donor. The bilirubin level in the blood is reduced, eliminating the danger of neurological damage. Also the new red cells correct anemia, and the exchange removes unattached antibodies, thus decreasing the potential for further red cell tagging and removal. Naturally the exchange transfusion is carried out before the blood bilirubin reaches a dangerous level. After exchange transfusion, 75 to 85 percent of the baby's blood cells will be Rh negative. The rest are Rh positive. Since Rh-negative cells are unaffected by Rh-positive antibodies, the transfused cells will not be destroyed but will survive for the cells' usual life span, which is two or three months. By that time the baby will be mature enough to get by on his own and will not be receiving any more of the dangerous Rh-positive antibody from the mother.

Another exciting chapter in the story of the Rh-negative problem is the perfection of the technique for intrauterine blood transfusion. In severe cases of erythroblastosis, stillbirths occur long before it is possible to deliver a living baby with any hope of survival. It is now possible in some instances to transfuse Rh-negative red blood cells into the baby weeks before delivery. In this way, intrauterine life is prolonged until the baby reaches a state of maturity that will enable him to survive outside the womb. These babies are usually delivered by Caesarean section prematurely, weighing the risks of progressive erythroblastosis against those of prematurity itself. (See Prematurity, p. 330). There are still many failures with this type of treatment, but there is every reason to expect better results as we gain experience. It is ironical that as techniques of treatment have been perfected, prevention in the new generation of Rh-negative mothers will reduce the need for such treatment. For the very few who despite availability of prevention will become sensitized, the improved methods of treatment should be reassuring.

Erythroblastosis due to incompatibilities of the ABO system is, in general, less severe than erythroblastosis due to incompatibilities of the Rh-positive factor. Stillbirths are rare, but jaundice occurs and if allowed to become severe could be a source of danger to the baby. Elsewhere in the book (see pages 369–72) we discuss at greater length all these topics related to blood incompatibility.

SEPARATION OF THE SYMPHYSIS

The bones making up the pelvis are bound to each other and to the spinal column by tough joints of fibrous tissue and cartilage. Hormone changes in pregnancy make these joints somewhat softer and more pliable. An X-ray picture in pregnancy sometimes will show a separation, by as much as an inch, of the two halves of the *pubic symphysis bone* in front. While this spreading of the pelvic bones does not do much to increase the capacity of the pelvis for childbirth, it occasionally leads to a great deal of pain and discomfort in the region of the pelvic joints. Motion of the pelvis in walking and especially in climbing stairs can cause much discomfort. Pressure over the pubic bone is distinctly uncomfortable. A firm support around the hips will help greatly to relieve the symptoms of separation of the symphysis. A broad canvas belt, which can be applied tightly, is available for this purpose.

SKIN DISEASES

There are several rare skin diseases encountered only in pregnancy, but in general most of these disorders occur with about the same frequency in both pregnant and nonpregnant individuals. Pregnancy appears to have a variable effect on established skin diseases. Such conditions as acne and psoriasis appear to improve in some individuals and to grow worse in others.

Vascular spiders are tiny bright red dots that may appear at various places on the skin, but mainly on the arms, neck, and chest. They are quite common and often become more numerous in pregnancy. They are not a skin disease but, as the name suggests, collections of very small blood vessels, which blanch when you press on them. If picked open or otherwise torn, they may bleed copiously.

Another skin change common in, but not confined to, pregnancy is reddening of the palms of the hands.

SPONTANEOUS ABORTION
(See chapter 22.)

TOXEMIA OF PREGNANCY

This disease occurs only in the course of pregnancy. It is characterized by the development of high blood pressure, protein in the urine, and generalized retention of fluid. Nonpregnant women may have the same symptoms with some forms of kidney disease, but even so the two conditions are not the same. Termination of pregnancy usually results in prompt disappearance of the symptoms of toxemia. In untreated cases (or if treatment is not successful) the symptoms get progressively more severe as pregnancy progresses. It then becomes necessary to terminate pregnancy prematurely or convulsions will supervene. When convulsions occur in the course of toxemia, the condition is known as *eclampsia*. This is one of the gravest complications of pregnancy. Some 5 to 10 percent of mothers who have eclampsia (and 30 percent of their babies) will die. Our whole system of prenatal care is an outgrowth of the systematic search for the cause and means of control of toxemia. By frequent observation in the latter part of pregnancy, the mild and early cases of toxemia can be identified. If the disease progresses, pregnancy can be terminated before eclampsia develops. Two synonyms for toxemia, *preeclampsia* and *eclamptogenic toxemia,* are probably better terms for this condition as they are descriptive of the course of this disease.

In spite of decades of research, the cause of toxemia remains obscure. It seems that a true *toxin* causing the symptoms characteristic of the disease must be elaborated by the body, yet no such toxin has ever been isolated. The known facts in toxemia are like the pieces of a jigsaw puzzle. We know they belong in the picture, but we cannot figure out just where they fit.

Toxemia varies widely in incidence in different parts of the world and even in our own country. In any large metropolitan area there will be found neighborhoods that seem to have an unusually high incidence of toxemia. Diet apparently is an influence. People who live on diets low in protein or high in salt, or both, are likely to have a relatively high incidence of toxemia. Socioeconomic factors are undoubtedly important. By and large, although there are many exceptions, toxemia is a disease of poor people. Some animals have diseases with some similarities, but no animal has true toxemia of pregnancy nor can the disease be induced artificially. Some workers in this field believe that toxemia of pregnancy is a price the human race has had to pay in evolving from a four-footed creature to a two-footed one.

Toxemia of pregnancy is almost exclusively a disease of the last few months of pregnancy, but there is one very rare complication of pregnancy, the *hydatidiform mole,* which sometimes causes toxemia much earlier. In this bizarre condition, there is an overgrowth of the placental elements, but no embryo is present. It proves that the cause of toxemia resides in the placenta. No fetus is required for this condition to develop.

Toxemia of pregnancy is more common in first pregnancies, especially if the mother is very young. It is a particular hazard of illegitimate pregnancies since many of these mothers are young and do not get adequate prenatal care. Conditions associated with overdistention of the uterus predispose to toxemia: twins, polyhydramnios, and hydatidiform mole.

Diseases of the blood vessels and the kidneys present before pregnancy markedly predispose the expectant mother to the development of toxemia in gestation. About a third of patients with essential hypertension (high blood pressure), chronic nephritis (kidney disease), and diabetes will develop a superimposed toxemia while they are carrying their infants. It is obvious that from the onset of pregnancy such persons should be under the strictest medical observation.

Perhaps the most perplexing observation of all is that on rare occasions the toxemia is not manifest until several hours or even days after delivery of the baby and the placenta. It seems impossible to reconcile postpartum toxemia with almost any of our theories of the cause of this condition.

In toxemia, as in so many other conditions, an ounce of prevention is worth a pound of cure. Restriction of salt in the diet appears to prevent many cases of toxemia and cures many others in the incipient stage. An excessive and unexplained gain in weight is usually the first sign of impending toxemia. It is due to generalized fluid retention and precedes by several weeks the development of visible swelling. The average woman has to retain eight to ten pounds of fluid before it begins to show. The fluid then accumulates in the feet and ankles when she is up and about. During the time she is recumbent, it gravitates to the hands and face, which are likely to be puffy when she gets out of bed in the morning.

Simple bed rest is one of the most effective remedies in the prevention of toxemia. When a person is recumbent, the fluid that has been trapped in the extremities is picked up again in the general circulation. The kidneys then are able to excrete the excessive salt and water. Pregnant women in this condition will often be several pounds lighter after going to bed for a day.

If restriction of salt and bed rest do not eliminate the excessive fluid, the doctor will often prescribe a diuretic to help the body eliminate sodium via the kidneys. Once you start taking these diuretics, it is a little like having a tiger by the tail. It is hard to stop. If you do, you are likely to retain several pounds of fluid almost immediately. When doctors warn their patients about retaining fluids, some think the most direct approach is to eliminate fluids from their diets. Don't. Your body needs a large volume of fluid to function properly. If you eat nothing salty along with the fluid, the water will pass right through you and wash out some sodium along with it.

Women with mild toxemia often have labor induced in the last two or three weeks. By this time the baby is mature, and there is no question that it will do well. The induction is done because the doctor is never sure when mild toxemia may progress to the severe stage. All obstetricians, on rare occasions, have seen this happen in the course of a few days. Once the baby is mature enough to do well, there is no point in waiting around for complications to arise.

When toxemia becomes severe, patients have to be hospitalized. The blood pressure is now elevated; there is protein in the urine. Mild toxemia causes little discomfort. It is often difficult for the doctor to convince his patient that her condition is potentially serious. On the other hand, women with severe toxemia are sick. They are likely to complain of headache and visual difficulties. There is a suppression of the volume of urine. Often the mind becomes dull. A particularly ominous sign is a severe, steady, boring pain in the upper abdomen. This symptom often precedes the onset of convulsions.

In addition to the measures employed for mild toxemia, the medication for patients with severe toxemia includes sedatives and drugs to bring down the blood pressure, which rises in rough proportion to the severity of the condition.

In severe toxemia, once the elevated blood pressure and other symptoms have been controlled, some thought must be given to the best way of terminating pregnancy. Except in rare cases, this should be done, regardless of the degree of maturity of the baby. Even though the symptoms of toxemia may be controlled, the disease progresses. Many doctors feel that prolonged episodes of severe toxemia are permanently damaging to the maternal vascular system. There is little point in prolonging the pregnancy, to wait for the baby to "grow up." With severe toxemia, babies literally do not grow and are small in proportion to the length of gestation. They wither on the vine, so to speak. There is a real danger of intrauterine death if the pregnancy is not interrupted. Although smaller than the premature baby of an otherwise healthy mother, the premature baby of a mother with severe toxemia stands a better chance in the nursery than he would remaining in the womb.

Since women with severe toxemia are sick, the easiest method of delivery is best for them. When possible, labor is induced. Many of these women, however, are several weeks from term; for them safe induction of labor is out of the question. Caesarean section becomes necessary as the only alternative method of delivery.

Mothers who have had one experience with toxemia wonder what will happen in future pregnancies. Paradoxically, the more severe the toxemia, the less likely it is to recur in subsequent pregnancies. The young girl who has normal blood vessels and kidneys but nevertheless develops severe toxemia in her first pregnancy rarely has any trouble with later babies. If she goes to a different doctor the second time, she will think him miraculous. In her first pregnancy she almost died but in her second she had no trouble at all. In reality, all he will have done is to insist on a low salt diet, restriction of weight gain, and an additional amount of rest. It is not difficult, incidentally, to convince women of the value of these measures once they have been through severe toxemia.

Women who have mild toxemia, in contrast, are more likely to have the disease recur in subsequent pregnancies. Many of them have slight underlying disease of the kidneys and of blood vessels that may become manifest only under the strain of pregnancy. Women with a history of even mild recurrent toxemia, like those who have had the more severe disease, should restrict their intake of sodium and keep weight gain to a minimum.

TUBAL PREGNANCY

There are a number of sites outside the uterus where a fertilized egg can attach and a pregnancy begin to develop. These are called *ectopic* (misplaced) pregnancies. In the commonest form the pregnancy begins to develop in the tube between ovary and uterus. Symptoms usually arise two to four weeks after the first missed period. Because the symptoms can be so varied, correct diagnosis is most important. The consequences of a ruptured tubal pregnancy are serious.

Women with tubal pregnancies often have a history of decreased fertility or pelvic inflammatory disease. After skipping a period, they may exhibit mild symptoms of pregnancy but rarely the marked nausea and vomiting that sometimes characterize normal pregnancies. Within a short time, they complain of one-sided pelvic pain and usually of some slight vaginal bleeding. A pelvic examination will disclose a tender swelling on one side and pain on motion of the cervix. While all this sounds perfectly straightforward, in practice it is rarely ever so.

When ectopic pregnancy is suspected, the patient must be hospitalized. The examination usually requires anesthesia. Sometimes it is possible to inspect the tubes visually through an instrument called the culdoscope. This procedure requires only a minor operation, and if no tubal pregnancy is found, the patient can go home the next day. If there is a tubal pregnancy, an operation is necessary. Usually the involved tube is removed. If the opposite tube is damaged or abnormal, it may be possible to remove the pregnancy and reconstruct the remaining tube, in order to make possible future pregnancies. Most gynecologists prefer abdominal surgery in these operations, although a few perform them through the vagina.

URINARY TRACT INFECTIONS

Infections of the female urinary tract are common. Bacteria easily gain entrance to the bladder through the urethra, the short passageway for emptying the bladder. Once established in the bladder, the infection may ascend to the upper urinary tract.

Pregnant women are especially prone to urinary infections. There is a certain amount of stretching and dilation of the upper urinary tract. The enlarging uterus often tends to impede the free flow of urine from the kidneys to the bladder. The resultant sluggish movement of urine along the tract favors the development of infection. A large daily volume of urine will do a great deal to prevent these infections, and a liberal intake of fluid will provide the volume. Pregnant women *need a lot of fluid.* (In the latter part of pregnancy, when swelling of the ankles is so common, the doctor will often remark that his patient is retaining fluid. Some women take those words as a cue to cut down drastically on their fluid intake. As we said before, to do so would be neither wise nor effective [see pages 81 and 130]. Salt is usually the offending substance; once the intake of salt [or sodium] is reduced, the swelling disappears.)

For the pregnant woman infections of the urinary tract are of special significance. It is believed that some cases of kidney disease and high blood pressure in later years have their origin in improperly treated urinary tract infections of pregnancy. It is also believed that there may be a connection between low grade urinary tract infections in pregnancy and premature delivery.

Urinary tract infections cause pain and burning on urination. Frequency of urination and having to get up at night to void, while they would be important symptoms outside of pregnancy, are of little help in diagnosis of urinary tract infection during gestation because so many pregnant women have these symptoms. The urine is often cloudy, but this cloudiness is in itself no help in diagnosis—it often occurs normally. But with more severe infections of the bladder, it is not unusual for the urine to be bloody. Pain in the back is a common symptom. Chills and fever often accompany kidney infection. Temperature of 101° or 102° is not unusual; with severe kidney infections there may be sudden rises of temperature to 104° or even 105°.

Microscopic examination of the urine will disclose a large number of white blood cells. A culture will show that in at least three-fourths of the cases a single organism, the *Escherichia coli,* is responsible. Sulfa-type drugs are usually prescribed and are almost always effective. The symptoms should be much improved within forty-eight hours after a course of these drugs has been started. If the symptoms do not respond, the organism is probably not sensitive to the particular drug, and a different one should be tried. The first step in finding an effective drug is to obtain a culture of the urine and isolate the offending bacteria. The sample can then be tested with various antibiotics in the laboratory until a suitable drug is found. There is a growing feeling that the treatment of urinary infections in pregnancy should be more intense and prolonged than it has been in the past. In some stubborn cases, treatment is advisable throughout most of the pregnancy.

In severe or recurrent cases such complications as kidney stones or partial obstruction of the urinary tract by kinks and displaced blood vessels should be suspected. If such complications are found, consultation with a urologist is advisable. While it is not often necessary to correct these obstructions in pregnancy, surgical relief may be imperative if the infection becomes severe.

We are paying increasing attention to silent, or asymptomatic, urinary tract infections in pregnancy detectable by urine culture because they may predict future urinary problems and may predispose to premature delivery.

UTERINE ANOMALIES

In embryonic life, fusion of the paired müllerian ducts (see page 110) forms the uterus. If this fusion is incomplete, some degree of a double uterus results. In the most severe form there are two separate uterine horns, each attached to a tube and each having a cervical opening. There may even be a vaginal *septum* (dividing wall), which creates a double-barreled vagina. Most often the reduplication of the uterus is incomplete. There is only a partial septum at the top of the uterine body. The normally pear-shaped uterus then becomes heart-shaped.

Uterine anomalies are fairly common. Many women go through life without ever having the anomaly detected. While many of these women may have normal pregnancies, on occasion uterine anomalies do give rise to complications. Some women with uterine anomalies have repeated miscarriages or premature deliveries. In early pregnancy they often have slight bleeding that subsides without treatment. Breech positions and other abnormal presentations are more common in women with a double uterus. Sometimes a doctor may think his patient has a fibroid or other pelvic tumor when actually the mass the doctor feels is the other half of the uterus. As pregnancy progresses, there is often a non-symmetric bulge, and the patient may remark (with acute intuition) that she "seems to be carrying the baby on one side."

For most patients with uterine anomalies no treatment is necessary. In rare instances, when there have been repeated pregnancy losses due to this condition, it is possible to reconstruct the uterus surgically. There are good chances of success in pregnancy following this operation.

VAGINITIS (VAGINAL INFECTION)

The symptoms of vaginitis are discharge, itching, and irritation. The organisms causing vaginitis are, like death and taxes, always with us. The action of vaginal acids and competition with other organisms (among other things) ordinarily hold the offending organisms in check. But if anything happens to change the status quo, the intruders will often grow and multiply with a resulting vaginal infection. Hence, recurrence is common.

The most frequent type of vaginitis encountered in pregnancy is due to a yeast- or funguslike organism called *Monilia*. It causes a thick white discharge, which may be expelled in small clumps. There is more external irritation with this type than with many of the other varieties. Often the labia are red and swollen. Husbands will sometimes complain of slight penile irritation at the same time. Some patients experience pain and burning on urination.

The other common type of vaginitis is caused by the *Trichomonas vaginalis* organism. A thin malodorous yellow discharge is associated with this type of infection. The itching seems more internal than external.

Vaginal infections are not dangerous in pregnancy (or at any other time) but can be very annoying. Some pediatricians think that *thrush,* a funguslike infection of infants' mouths, is related to *Monilia vaginitis*. Mothers with severe Monilia infections, however, usually have un-affected babies, and babies with thrush are often born of mothers exhibiting no evidence of vaginal infection.

Your doctor will prescribe a proper treatment depending on the type of organism involved. Some doctors advise douching for vaginal infections. Douching is not dangerous in pregnancy, provided the douche nozzle is not introduced all the way into the vagina and precautions are taken to prevent excessive pressure (see page 82). While it is usually possible to cure the acute attack, recurrence is common, and more than one course of treatment may be necessary.

VENEREAL DISEASE

Venereal disease can be transmitted from mother to baby in pregnancy, but proper treatment can prevent the devastating consequences in childhood. Almost all the states have laws requiring a blood test in pregnancy for syphilis. Prophylactic treatment of the newborn's eyes is mandatory to prevent infection by the gonorrheal organism, which formerly was the leading cause of blindness in childhood. In most hospitals silver nitrate drops are used. Since this compound sometimes causes a transient irritation of the baby's eyes, newer drugs have been tried. None has stood the test of time as well as silver nitrate, and use of this agent continues.

Venereal disease in pregnancy is rarely seen among population groups with stable marriages. It is (or has been) a fact that those who are disadvantaged economically and socially have a higher rate of venereal disease. Poverty breeds many woes that lean upon each other. In poverty stability of marriage is more difficult. The incidence of venereal disease goes up as the number of stable marriages goes down. Another group with a higher risk of venereal disease in pregnancy are the unwed mothers. Some girls are unfortunate enough to become pregnant and contract venereal disease at the same time.

The treatment of venereal disease in pregnancy is entirely satisfactory, and if given in time, assures the birth of a normal baby. The only danger is that if the mother does not come in for early prenatal care, diagnosis and proper treatment may be delayed. Unwed mothers and those who live in poverty areas, the very ones having a high incidence of venereal disease in pregnancy, have in the past been known to seek little or no prenatal care.

VIRUS DISEASES

Viruses are the cause of many contagious diseases. Measles, mumps, and chicken pox are all virus diseases that most of us have had as children. Viruses are much smaller than even the microscopic bacteria. In distinction to bacteria, which grow and multiply readily in broth and a number of other simple media, viruses usually thrive only inside living cells. Because of their properties, viruses have special significance in pregnancy. They are so small they pass through the placenta with ease and can then invade the cells of the developing fetus. The congenital anomalies seen after German measles in early pregnancy are well-known to all. There are also less familiar virus diseases that have important implications in pregnancy. However, the effects of most of these diseases are usually mild. While these viruses may be more familiar to the pediatrician than to the obstetrician, they nevertheless do afflict women of the childbearing age.

German Measles (Rubella)

Doctors in Australia noted in 1942 that severe congenital anomalies of the eyes, ears, and heart occurred in many infants whose mothers had

German measles in early pregnancy. Then doctors all over the world rapidly confirmed the observations. Until recently, diagnosis had to rest solely on the character of the vague and fleeting rash and associated symptoms. In addition to the rash, patients with German measles sometimes have enlargement and tenderness of the lymph nodes in the back of the neck and may have mild joint pains. However, many pregnant women infected with rubella virus showed few or no symptoms at all, making diagnosis on clinical grounds alone very unreliable. The need for an accurate diagnosis is imperative since therapeutic abortion sometimes is to be considered. Nowadays, accurate tests can be performed in many laboratories to measure specific rubella antibodies in the mother's serum and establish the diagnosis beyond doubt. Development of the successful vaccine for rubella can be expected to change the whole picture, but until its use is extended we will still have to be on the alert for German measles in the first three months of pregnancy.

The difficulties in deciding whether therapeutic abortion should be done after German measles are compounded by vague and ambiguous medical and legal opinion. As this was being written, a group of physicians in one state was brought before the court because they performed therapeutic abortions. At the same time, another physician, three thousand miles removed, had legal action pending against him because he had not recommended therapeutic abortion for an expectant mother who had German measles and who subsequently gave birth to a malformed baby.

It is obvious that the risk to the baby should be considered carefully if the doctor is to give wise advice about therapeutic abortion. The reported incidence of malformed children born after German measles in the first third of pregnancy varies from as little as 5 percent to more than 50. As with most things, the truth probably lies somewhere between. From a practical standpoint, all that is really known is that the risk of a malformed baby is appreciable and that many of the malformations are not amenable to surgical correction (see chapter 22, Abortion, page 420) . If German measles occurs after the third month, the risk of congenital anomalies is no greater than for any uncomplicated pregnancy.

Nowadays, the emphasis is on determining whether a woman is immune to rubella before pregnancy. Immunity is presumed only if she has received the rubella vaccine. Doctors do not rely on a history of having had rubella, since such histories are not always reliable. As part of the marital examination, along with a test for syphilis, or at a regular check-up when the woman is known not to be pregnant, her blood is checked for antibodies to rubella, the only certain proof of immunity. If she is immune, the fact is noted and nothing more is done. If she is not immune, she is given the vaccine if, and only if, she is on a predictably safe form of birth control for the next two months. (The vaccine virus can also attack the fetus and make a therapeutic abortion necessary.)

Once pregnant it is too late to give the vaccine and the most important thing for a non-immune woman to do if exposed to German measles is to have a serological test to determine whether or not infection has occurred (see therapeutic abortion, page 417).

Coxsackie Virus

This virus causes a mild contagious disease characterized by fever and sore throat. There may be abdominal pain and vomiting. It is possible to isolate the virus from the stool, but most laboratories are not equipped to make this analysis, which usually is done only in research projects. The importance of Coxsackie virus infections in pregnancy is that they can occasionally be transmitted to the baby.

Herpes Simplex

This is the medical term for fever blisters or cold sores, which most of us from time to time have had on our lips. The same virus is thought to cause a vaginal infection in rare cases. Until recently herpes simplex was not considered an important disease, and most newborn infants were thought to be immune by virtue of the transplacental passage of antibodies (see pages 373–74). There have been recent scattered reports, however, of severe disease of newborn infants from the virus of herpes simplex if the mother has had the vaginal infection with this virus. Both the obstetrician and pediatrician should be alerted if the mother has had a fever blister within a short time of delivery.

Measles, Mumps, Chicken Pox

The course of the common virus diseases—measles, mumps, and chicken pox—is not altered by pregnancy. These diseases, unlike German measles (see pages 166–67) , are not considered to be causes of congenital anomalies, although there is some evidence that the rate of spontaneous abortion is increased when the diseases occur in early pregnancy. A team of doctors studying young children with a rare type of heart disease called *endocardial fibroelastosis* reports many of them have positive skin tests for mumps. This finding certainly raises the possibility of an intrauterine infection. As yet, the exact significance of this observation is unknown. These diseases are rare in pregnancy because most mothers are immune from prior exposure or immunization (see page 166) .

ARTHUR GORBACH, M.D.
RICHARD I. FEINBLOOM, M.D.

PART THREE

BIRTH

CHAPTER SEVEN

Labor and Delivery

*I*N THE last month or so of the first pregnancy most women start to wonder how they will know when labor begins and whether they will get to the hospital in time. They have visions of the baby appearing suddenly without warning, and of the father having to tie the cord with a shoestring. Don't worry—you'll get there. The first baby usually takes ten to twelve hours. Even if labor should be only half that long, you will still make it, and with plenty of time to spare. Over the years of his practice the obstetrician usually can count on the fingers of one hand the patients who did not get to the hospital on time. Some women think it is smart to arrive at the hospital at the last moment; they don't want to wait around there all day long. But since there is a variety of things that could happen to you or your baby during labor, you certainly should be hospitalized once labor has started. If you are not in labor, you are better off at home.

PREPARATIONS

At some point in the last few weeks, it is a good idea to pack a bag with a few things you will need in the hospital. If you wait until the last minute you will forget half of what you want to take. You will need a housecoat and some slippers. It is a good idea to take along a couple of nightgowns because the hospital gowns are not especially comfortable. You will need toilet articles and cosmetics, possibly a pen and some writing paper. Your husband can bring in some of the clumsier things, such as books or a radio, after you get settled. Do not bring along a lot of cash or your valuable jewels. Most hospitals will lock money and valuables in the safe, but it is much simpler to leave them at home. Bring a dollar or so in change to buy newspapers or a magazine.

Your doctor will instruct you about calling him when the time comes. He will have good advice about arrangements for the care of the baby after delivery. If your doctor is a generalist, he probably will take care of the baby too. If he is an obstetrician, ask him to recommend a pediatrician. It is a good idea to select a pediatrician in your own neighborhood to make office visits easy for you. Call the pediatrician beforehand and ask him to see the baby right after birth while you are still in the hospital. If you can arrange an interview with the pediatrician before delivery (see pages 269–76), by all means do so. It may seem strange to see the pediatrician before the baby's birth, but more and more parents are doing it. It gives you an opportunity to get acquainted, and there are important matters, such as the type of feeding, frequency of checkups, and familial diseases, that you and he will want to discuss.

INDUCTION OF LABOR

Toward the end of your pregnancy, your doctor may suggest induction of labor. By this he will mean the procedure of artificially rupturing your membranes to stimulate the onset of labor ahead of nature's timetable. Induction of labor is a fairly common practice, and the women who have it done can be divided into two groups. For the smaller group there are medical reasons; the woman being induced has high blood pressure or is past term or has an Rh-negative problem, for example. No one argues about the propriety of these medical inductions. The larger group comprises the so-called elective inductions done merely for the convenience of the doctor or the patient or both.

A number of heated critical articles about elective inductions have appeared in the general press. Most of the steam has been generated in the magazines for women. But you should know that some highly respected obstetricians also condemn this procedure. The arguments against elective induction are formidable. Induction is meddlesome obstetrics. If you wait, labor will start on its own. Any large series of inductions will show a small number of premature babies, and premature babies do not do as well as full-term babies. It is a rare accident, but on occasion when the membranes are ruptured, the umbilical cord slips down into a place where it is squeezed, and the baby's circulation is compromised. Then a Caesarean section usually must be done to save the baby. Finally, if the membranes are ruptured but labor does not ensue in twenty-four to thirty-six hours, both the mother and baby are exposed to the risk of infection.

With such good arguments against them, are elective inductions ever justifiable? Yes, they are. The elective makes the obstetrical delivery a planned procedure, more like a scheduled surgical operation. Both the mother and the doctor are at the hospital at a stated time, and the mother can be prepared properly for anesthesia. In the hurly-burly of modern living, in the large urban centers, coordinated punctuality can be a serious problem. For the woman who lives in the suburbs or out in the country but wants to have her baby at the big medical center in the city, elective induction can offer definite advantages. If her doctor has been able to supervise her pregnancy closely, he should not find himself in the position of having to deliver a baby prematurely, and with all the facilities of a great hospital at hand he can deal promptly with any emergency. Inductions have acquired a bad name in some places because they have been performed before the mothers have been really ready for labor. Because elective inductions are purely a matter of convenience, it behooves the doctor to lean over backward in selecting the patients he plans to induce.

To be a fit candidate for induction the mother must be near her due date and have a history of regular menstrual periods, or the doctor must have followed her throughout pregnancy and be in no doubt about the infant's maturity. The baby should be of good size. His head should be in the pelvis, and the pelvis should be large enough. The neck of the womb should be thinned out and partly dilated. Since mothers having a first baby rarely have difficulty getting to the hospital in plenty of time, there is less reason for induction, but many good obstetricians do advise elective inductions even with first babies. Finally, the mother should want to be induced. No woman should be pressured into an elective induction.

If the doctor is careful in selecting the patients for induction, it is a safe procedure and highly satisfactory for the doctor and the mother. Induction is especially convenient for the mother with other children at home. If she can arrange for their care for a couple of days ahead of time, her departure for the hospital will be much more organized. From the physician's standpoint inductions also have advantages. Induction can be arranged when he is not having office hours or occupied elsewhere. The obstetrician may find, however, that he can induce only a few of his patients. The rest either start labor spontaneously before the physician is thoroughly convinced they are ready, or they do not want to be induced. Pregnant women who are up on such matters have heard stories about doctors who induce "all their patients" or "half their practice." There is reason to believe that doctors who induce 50 percent of their patients are not strict enough in selecting their cases and sooner or later will run into complications.

The procedure of rupturing the bag of waters takes only a minute and is not painful. For most women who are at term, labor will then start within a few hours. To shorten the interval between rupture of the membranes and the onset of labor, or to bring on contractions if labor fails to ensue, a drug called *pitocin* is given. This is a hormone produced by the posterior part of the pituitary gland in the brain. Even in minute amounts, it produces labor contractions. A synthetic counterpart also may be used. Since these drugs are also capable of producing contractions that are too strong and too long to be good for the baby, women receiving them must be watched carefully and the dosage reduced if labor contractions become excessive. Pitocin can be given before the membranes are ruptured, but when administered at this time, it is not as effective in dilating the neck of the womb.

Once induced labor begins, it is like any other labor. It is sometimes quite rapid. This rapidity is not from the induction itself but from the condition of the woman who is being induced. Her pelvis is ample and her cervix already is soft and partly dilated. In these circumstances women often deliver rapidly after rupture of the membranes, whether the rupture occurs artificially or spontaneously.

ONSET OF LABOR

When labor begins, the contractions are usually far apart—at intervals of fifteen to thirty minutes. They are like menstrual cramps. The discomfort is either in front or in back but always in the middle, not at one side or the other. In the beginning the contractions last fifteen to twenty seconds, and during this time the abdomen firms and tenses. The contraction does not start suddenly but builds up gradually and eases off.

Many women have episodes of false labor in the last weeks of pregnancy and not a few get to the hospital only to have everything peter out. No harm is done from these false alarms, but everyone's face is a little red. There are several clues that help to distinguish a false alarm from real labor. False labor often starts at night. If the pains begin then, get up and walk around. If the pains go away, obviously you are not in labor. Once true labor begins, nothing stops it until the baby is born. At the onset of real labor there is often slight vaginal staining, the so-called show. It is possible to be in early labor without show and it is possible to have the show even several days before labor begins. But if you have both the show and the contractions, you can be sure you mean business and belong in the hospital. Sometimes a mild sedative will make false labor go away. If you do not have a sedative, a glass of sherry (or something similar) will sometimes do the trick.

Once you begin to have contractions, keep track of the intervals between them. In real labor the intervals between contractions become shorter and shorter while the contractions last longer and longer. False labor pains are more erratic. A good rule of thumb is to wait until the contractions are coming every ten minutes before calling your doctor. If you wait this long, you can be quite sure that they are the real thing and that you can still get to the hospital in plenty of time.

What has been described in the preceding paragraphs is the average onset of labor. Not all labors will start this way. Sometimes the pains are further apart, sometimes closer together, right from the start. If you are not sure what is going on, call your doctor.

Sometimes the membranes rupture before labor begins. Often there is not the gush of water that many women anticipate. There may be no more than several tablespoonsful. Once the membranes have ruptured, there is a dribbling that cannot be controlled. While the dribble may not amount to much at any one time, it is enough to saturate two or three sanitary napkins in the course of the morning or make a change of underclothing necessary four or five times in the same interval. Labor usually begins within a few hours. If your membranes should rupture, let your doctor know. Because there is always the slight risk of infection after rupture of the membranes, he may want to induce labor if it does not start spontaneously.

Sometimes when the membranes rupture prematurely, the baby is too small. The doctor may then do nothing to initiate labor—the risk of prematurity is much greater than the risk of infection. He will hope that labor is postponed until the baby has more time to mature. Unfortunately, this is seldom the case. Labor usually starts within a few days even when the mother is weeks from term.

Once your labor pains have begun or the membranes have ruptured, you should not eat or drink anything. Your stomach should be empty when it comes time to administer an anesthetic. Remember, even if you have planned on little or no anesthesia, something may come up in the course of labor to change your plans.

Routines of hospital admission vary so much that no description we could give here would fit in every particular the conditions you will encounter when your time comes. Often the doctor notifies the hospital that his patient is on the way, and he leaves orders for her. In some places the woman herself is expected to call the hospital before leaving home. Once you get to the hospital, you will go through the usual admission procedure. After you are in bed the nurse will take your *vital signs* (pulse, blood pressure, and temperature) and time your labor contractions. It is a good idea to remind her about any drugs to which you are allergic. Tell her when you last ate. When it comes to choosing the anesthetic, this information is important. The nurse will notify your doctor that you have arrived and will report your condition. He will probably order a shave of the pubic region and an enema to cleanse the lower bowel.

LABOR ROOM

The ideal physical arrangement for an obstetric unit provides individual labor rooms. A special nurse should be with each patient during her entire labor. Due to the costs and a shortage of nurses, few hospitals have such facilities. In most you will have to share the labor room and the obstetric labor room nurse with one or more mothers. You will be watched carefully during labor, but you may not have individual attention. A busy obstetric service often has several patients in active labor at the same time. You can well imagine why the labor room may not have the quiet, serene atmosphere most conducive to relaxation. It is not that the doctors and nurses are hardened or insensitive to the feelings of their patients. At this point, many hospitals, sad to say, cannot afford anything better.

STAGES OF LABOR

Labor is divided into three stages. The first stage is the longest and the hardest. This is the travail of labor. It is the dilating stage. The first stage lasts from the onset of labor until the cervix, or neck of the womb, is completely dilated. It takes eight to ten hours for most women having the first baby, but in subsequent pregnancies it is often much shorter and easier. The first stage of labor, especially with the first baby, may be greatly drawn out. The cervix does not dilate at a constant rate. Early in labor dilation is slow. At the end of the first stage it usually speeds up.

Early in the first stage the contractions come every ten to fifteen minutes and last twenty to thirty seconds. They do not hurt much—many girls have menstrual cramps that are far worse. As labor progresses, the contractions come closer together, last longer, and are more severe. At the end of the first stage the contractions are coming every two to three minutes and lasting forty to fifty seconds. If you have no medication at all, these contractions will curl your toes a bit, but you do get a respite in the intervals between them—when you are relaxed and perfectly comfortable. Once you get to this stage, you have the satisfaction of knowing that delivery is not far off. This stage is the hardest part of the whole process (see prepared childbirth, page 189) .

PROGRESS IN LABOR

Progress in labor is determined by following the dilation of the cervix and the descent of the baby's head in the birth canal. This is done by internal examination, either rectal or vaginal. As labor progresses, most women will find that they want some relief from the discomfort and will receive shots or pills. This analgesia, if given early in labor, may slow the contractions temporarily, but nothing stops labor once it has begun. Slow progress in the first stage can be very discouraging. Some hospitals are set up to allow husbands to be with their wives during labor at this stage; if things are not moving along as rapidly as you would like, your husband can be worth his weight in Demerol. Periodically the nurse or attendant will check the frequency and duration of contractions and listen to the baby's heart to make sure everything is all right. You may feel the baby moving around the same as always, but at this stage the baby is often relatively inactive (see prepared childbirth, page 189).

STIMULATION OF LABOR

If the doctor feels you are not making the proper progress, he may do something to stimulate labor. Breaking the bag of waters, if this has not happened already, may make the contractions a good deal more effective in dilating the cervix. Breaking the bag, as we have said, takes just a minute and is not painful. Sometimes the contractions are relatively mild and infrequent and as a consequence progress in labor is arrested. In some situations the hormone pitocin is given to stimulate labor. This will often do the trick and often produces better labor. Not everyone, however, is a suitable candidate for this drug. If the pelvis is small or if the baby is in an abnormal position, it is not prudent to administer pitocin. Every once in a while labor will be prolonged to such an extent that it is safer for both the mother and the baby to deliver the baby by Caesarean section. The adage "Don't let the sun set twice on the same labor" is a good one, although there are exceptions. Some people think that a Caesarean section cannot be performed after labor has begun. This is not so. In some respects a few hours of labor make the operation easier.

DELIVERY

The second stage of labor is the *expulsion* or *transition* stage. This extends from the full dilation of the cervix to the actual birth. With first babies this stage lasts an hour or two. In labors after the first it is often much shorter and may take only a few contractions. When the baby's head gets to the floor of the pelvis and starts to distend the vaginal opening, the mother gets the urge to "bear down" or push. With this urge comes some relief of the discomfort although the contractions are still hard and frequent.

Complete dilation of the cervix is the signal to move the laboring mother to the delivery room. The baby's head will gradually descend to the floor of the pelvis. When the baby's head begins to separate the vaginal opening, preparations are made for delivery. The mother, unless completely anesthetized, will have the uncontrollable urge to push with each contraction. If spinal or general anesthesia is to be used, it is given at this time. The mother is then positioned for delivery, lying on her back. The knees are flexed and legs supported at the sides of the delivery table in stirrups. The entire genital area is washed with an antiseptic solution. Local anesthesia, if it is to be used, is administered next. An internal examination is performed to determine the position of the baby.

Babies are born most easily when the *occiput,* or back of the baby's head, is *anterior* (up) and the baby's face is *posterior* (down). The baby should be looking down when he is born. The first objects he would see (if he could see) would be the doctor's feet. If the baby is not in this position, the doctor will usually turn him before proceeding with the delivery. He manages this turning either with manual manipulations or with the obstetric forceps. The baby's head is then gradually delivered either by the mother's efforts or by gentle, intermittent traction on the forceps. Episiotomy, or incision, is usually made to increase the size of the vaginal opening as the vaginal tissues begin to stretch. The baby's head is the largest part; after it emerges, the rest is easy. If the baby is huge, the shoulders sometimes present a problem, but after the shoulders have emerged, the rest of the infant just slips out.

Most people think that the delivery of a baby is difficult and requires much skill on the part of the doctor. Actually, the delivery is the easiest part. Once the neck of the womb is completely dilated and the baby's head rests at the vaginal opening, all it takes is a few pushes, or the doctor can lift the baby's head out with forceps. All that will be needed in most cases is a little local anesthetic, or a few whiffs of gas, perhaps no anesthesia whatever. The hard part of having a baby is getting up to this point.

As soon as the baby is delivered, the mucus in his nose and throat is removed to open the air passages. The doctor holds him upside down by his feet so that the mucus will drain out of the respiratory passages.

The baby will usually begin to breathe and cry within a minute. In most cases it is not necessary to spank him to make him breathe. If respiration is delayed, oxygen is given to sustain the baby until he begins to breathe on his own. The cord is then tied off. Now he is separated from his mother and henceforth must depend on his own organs to keep him going. An identification tag or bracelet is placed on the baby and an identical one on the mother to make sure that no babies get mixed up in the nursery. Most states have laws requiring the dropping of silver nitrate solution into the eyes of the newborn infants. This is done to prevent eye infections from the germ that causes gonorrhea. If the mother has this disease, the baby may pick it up on his passage down the birth canal. Eye infections from this germ were formerly the leading cause of blindness in infants, but now, thanks to these laws, blindness from this cause is almost unheard-of (see prepared childbirth, page 189) .

THIRD STAGE

The third stage of labor lasts from the birth of the baby until the delivery of the afterbirth, or placenta. The expulsion takes only ten to fifteen minutes and during this time there is usually minimal discomfort. After the baby has been examined and attended to, the doctor will inspect the afterbirth for abnormalities. If the placenta is not expelled normally by the mother, the doctor may have to take steps to remove it. Sometimes the appearance of the placenta offers a clue to disease in the infant.

With the infant taken care of, stitching of the mother's episiotomy or incision (if stitching is required) comes next. This entire procedure in the delivery room may take the better part of an hour. At the conclusion the mother goes to the recovery room or the postpartum floor, depending on the system of the particular hospital. In many hospitals, the mother will spend an hour or two in the recovery room for close observation. The attendants will be looking for changes in pulse or blood pressure or excessive bleeding, all of which in combination could be the first signs of an impending complication. These signs are also watched on the postpartum floor, but it is not necessary to make the observations so frequently after the first hour or two.

FORCEPS

Obstetrical forceps have been known for centuries, but until the modern era they were used only for difficult deliveries that could not be accomplished in any other way. Often the doctor turned to the forceps as a means of last resort. It was only natural for both doctors and laymen to associate obstetrical forceps with many woes. But since the early 1900s American obstetricians have come to use forceps for most of their deliveries, even the uncomplicated ones. Obstetrical forceps are specialized tongs, made from bands of surgical steel molded to fit the curvature of a baby's head. With this instrument the doctor can exercise better control over the movement of the baby's head. He can make the baby's head emerge more quickly or more slowly to fit the individual situation. Forceps are used also to shorten the second stage of labor. A prolonged interval between full dilation of the cervix and delivery is thought to be dangerous for the baby and is exhausting to the mother.

Some patients still have the idea that forceps are dangerous for the baby. Actually, they prevent squeezing and so protect the baby's head. For full-term babies this protection is not so important, but it may be for a tiny premature infant. Prematures have a better chance of survival if delivered by forceps. On the other hand, forceps used improperly can be dangerous. They are not applied until the cervix has opened completely and the baby's head is completely in the pelvis.

The routine use of forceps in uncomplicated cases has been one of the chief differences in the delivery of babies in this country, compared with European practice. In many European clinics forceps even now are used infrequently and only for the most difficult deliveries. Several years ago a new obstetric instrument, called the vacuum extractor, was developed in Sweden. This is a suction cup that strongly resembles the business end of that tool known as the plumber's friend. When the cup is applied to the baby's scalp, a firm pull can be exerted to assist the descent and delivery of the head. There has been great enthusiasm for this instrument in Europe. Here in America it has been tried but is not used to any great extent. European obstetricians have found use of the instrument advantageous in shortening the second stage of labor. It is not wise to apply the instrument before the cervix is fully dilated. In actuality American obstetricians, for several decades, have been putting their forceps to the same use (see prepared childbirth, page 195).

EPISIOTOMY

In most deliveries an incision, called the *episiotomy,* is necessary to enlarge the vaginal opening. This operation is done mainly to preserve the proper functioning of the pelvic tissue. It sounds paradoxical that you must cut something to save it, but this is really what happens. The vagina is like a hollow cylinder. It is surrounded by a dense, tough layer of supporting tissue known as the *endopelvic fascia.* In the normal course of delivery, the vagina must stretch tremendously. The vaginal lining has many folds, something like an accordion, so it dilates readily. The endopelvic fascia, however, has no such arrangement and so becomes greatly strained. If it subsequently becomes ineffective in supporting the vagina, the bladder and rectum will bulge into the vaginal canal. When this happens, the doctor explains to his patient that the "bladder has dropped" or the "bladder has fallen." In the episiotomy the endopelvic fascia is cut to enable it to spread to the side as the baby is delivered.

An episiotomy is also done because without episiotomy many mothers, especially in the first delivery, would sustain lacerations at the vaginal opening. The episiotomy is easier to repair than a tear, and leads to less discomfort in the postpartum period. The episiotomy is made between the vaginal and rectal opening. If there is not enough room here, the incision is carried off to one side. This is a sensitive area, and for the first few days after delivery and repair, the stitches will be a little uncomfortable. In almost all cases a mild sedative and local application of heat are effective in relieving the discomfort.

ANALGESIA

As applied to obstetrics, analgesia is pain relief prior to delivery. Shortly after the turn of the century, German obstetricians began using a combination of morphine and a drug called *scopolamine* for analgesia. Scopolamine is related to atropine, which the eye doctor uses to dilate your pupils when you are examined for glasses. Scopolamine has no sedative action on its own, but in combination with narcotics or sedatives it produces a state of slumber and amnesia. Combined with morphine, it was known as twilight sleep, which was thought at first to be the answer to pain relief in childbirth. But it soon became evident that morphine depressed the onset of respiration in some babies, and so the twilight sleep combination is no longer used. Today, scopolamine is often given with barbiturates and tranquilizers for analgesia. In the doses used, these drugs do not depress the baby's respiration. Some people are afraid the drugs will harm the baby. You need not worry. There has been enough experience with them that your doctor knows what the safe and reasonable doses are. Regardless of what you may ask for, he will not give you more than the safe dose. These drugs do get through the placenta and into the baby in small amounts. They can make the baby a little sleepy for a few hours after birth, but this drowsiness is not harmful. What *is* bad for a baby is lack of oxygen. Your baby is getting as much oxygen when he is sleeping as he does when he is awake. If your baby should need an operation in the first few days of his life, he could receive large doses of anesthetic drugs without harm as long as he got enough oxygen during surgery.

Like everything else, these drugs do have their drawbacks, particularly scopolamine. Some women under scopolamine get very restless during contractions. The effect of the drug prevents these patients from cooperating fully. They have to be restrained, or they could fall out of bed. Being under sedation, the mother does not mind, but when scopolamine is given, the labor room may not be as quiet and relaxing as one would like. In spite of the drawbacks, however, most women find the combination of scopolamine, barbiturates, and tranquilizers very satisfactory. It is possible to be knocked out for the hardest part yet wake up almost as soon as the delivery is over (see prepared childbirth, page 189) .

ANESTHESIA

Anesthesia for childbirth is not essential. No one has yet figured out how to remove your appendix or lung without anesthesia, but women for centuries have been having babies without anesthesia. Serious anesthetic accidents are great rarities, but they have occurred in delivery. An anesthetic accident then is a double tragedy. Most often the patient could have delivered without anything.

Then why give an anesthetic? Anesthesia is part of modern obstetrics along with antibiotics, blood transfusions, forceps, and episiotomy. The great benefits of modern obstetrics are reflected in the dramatic reduction of the maternal and infant mortality that has taken place in the last fifty years. Modern techniques of anesthesia have certainly contributed to these gains. From a purely practical standpoint, anesthesia is wedded to obstetrics. When complications of delivery, such as an abnormal presentation or disproportion, arise, anesthesia enables the physician to handle the situation safely for mother and child.

Fortunately, anesthetic complications are very rare. Literally thousands of anesthetics are given for each complication. The complications, when they do occur, often have serious consequences unless treated immediately. Therefore, the person giving the anesthetic should have undergone thorough specialized training.

Properly used, all the anesthetic agents of modern obstetrics are good. This is not to say that in all situations the different agents can be used interchangeably. A general anesthetic given properly to a patient who is properly prepared and selected is perfectly safe for both the mother and child. The same can be said of spinal and local anesthesia. No obstetric anesthetic is dangerous if given with care and consideration for the patient's condition.

General anesthesia for obstetrics implies the inhalation of ether or some similar gas in quantities sufficient to produce unconsciousness. Ether is a very satisfactory agent for mature babies and uncomplicated obstetric situations. It is also a safer agent than any other in some complications associated with hemorrhage. The big disadvantage of ether is that it can induce vomiting. The aspiration (inhaling) of vomitus is one of the most serious anesthetic accidents. This hazard explains why you should not eat or drink anything once your labor has begun. Even though your labor lasts for hours, there may be food in your stomach when you are ready for delivery.

Spinal anesthesia, along with caudal and epidural anesthesia, is referred to as a regional anesthetic because an entire region, the lower part of the body, is anesthetized. Spinal anesthesia is very satisfactory for delivery. It makes you numb, without feeling, from the waist down, but you can be perfectly conscious. It has no depressing effect whatever on the baby, and it is therefore of great advantage in a large number of obstetric complications. The name spinal anesthesia has a bad connotation in some places, and you will hear the technique referred to as "saddle block." Some people are apprehensive about spinal anesthesia because they fear a spinal headache. This complication used to happen with unpleasant frequency until it was learned that the headache is due to the size of the needle used for the spinal tap.

It takes just a minute to give a spinal anesthetic. Usually you are curled up in a ball on your side when it is given. All you feel is a tiny stick as the needle is put through the skin. The effects of spinal anesthesia are immediate and last an hour or so. It is usually given just prior to delivery although it can be given a little sooner if precautions are taken to assure that labor will continue.

Caudal and epidural anesthesia are very similar, differing only in the location selected for the needle puncture. An epidural anesthetic is given at the same spot in the back where a spinal is given, while the caudal is introduced at the very tip of the spine. These two are particularly well suited to obstetrics because they can be given several hours prior to delivery. A tiny plastic tube is inserted until its tip touches upon the tough dural membrane enclosing the spinal cord—hence the name epidural. The plastic tube can be left in place for hours without discomfort or risk to the mother. One of the newer novocainelike local anesthetic drugs when introduced into the plastic tube will block the nerves where they leave the spinal cord. This block results in a numbness similar to spinal anesthesia. As the drug is gradually used up, more can be added from time to time and the anesthesia continued. It takes a while to get epidural or caudal anesthesia going. If labor is progressing too rapidly, the baby is born before the anesthetic takes effect. Because of anatomic variations the numbing effect can be spotty. The patient may experience discomfort on one side and be perfectly comfortable on the other. While nothing stops labor, an epidural or caudal can slow its progress if given too soon. Therefore, this anesthetic is not given until the woman is in active labor. In any type of anesthesia it is essential to follow the patient's general condition carefully, and, since this anesthetic is so prolonged, it requires more technical supervision and physical facilities than most hospitals can afford. Therefore, not all hospitals provide epidural or caudal anesthesia.

One of the most satisfactory anesthesias for obstetrics is local anesthesia, using novocaine or one of the newer counterparts, but successful use calls for a special kind of patient. She has to be relaxed, cooperative, and confident. It may also take a special kind of doctor. Some doctors use a great deal of local anesthesia with excellent results, but others are not so successful.

There are two types of local anesthesia used in obstetrics. One is called the *paracervical block*. The anesthetic agent is injected into either side of the cervix (neck of the womb) before it becomes completely dilated. The agent blocks the nerve impulses leaving the uterus and abolishes the sensations of labor pains. The procedure is very easy, and internal examination is all that is required. While most patients find dramatic relief from discomfort, a few note no benefit at all. This difference or reaction must be due to anatomic variation in the location of the nerves. The chief drawback of the paracervical block is its relatively brief action. It lasts only a hour or so. If, however, it is given at the proper time, just an hour or so before delivery, the results are very satisfactory.

Local anesthesia given for the actual delivery is called the *pudendal block*. The novocaine is injected into the vagina or through the skin on either side of the vaginal opening. The pudendal nerve that supplies the vagina and the adjacent skin is blocked. Even when forceps are used and an episiotomy is performed, the pudendal block is sufficient for most deliveries (see prepared childbirth, page 189) .

ARTHUR GORBACH, M.D.

CHAPTER EIGHT

Natural Childbirth

FOR THOUSANDS of years women gave birth without analgesia, anesthesia, or forceps. In many parts of the world they still
do. If it were not for the risk of complications of one sort or another
(including infections and difficult presentations) , any healthy, normal
woman carrying a normal baby could go through labor and delivery
without medical intervention. This is not to say that any woman would
want to be alone in her labor or that every woman could count on childbirth free of all discomfort. Because of the basic facts of human anatomy, no human society is known in which childbirth is consistently
free of discomfort or pain. The obstetrical techniques described in the
preceding chapter were devised in large part to be an answer to woman's
age-old cry for support in labor and relief from the pain of childbirth.
Yet more and more women and men today are expressing dissatisfac-
tion with this accepted medical approach. They want a different method
in which the use of drugs will be kept to a minimum and from which,
because of their participation, they can expect to achieve a greater
emotional fulfillment. Most of all, these women want to be conscious
and aware of what is happening when the baby is born.

Several systems aimed at achieving these goals have been developed
in the last few decades, and although they may differ quite a bit in their
specifics, it is customary to group them all in the category of *natural
childbirth.* Some authorities prefer the term *psychoprophylaxis* (signifying psychological preparation to prevent pain) and others *prepared
childbirth* or *education for childbirth,* but all the schools of thought

have the same underlying theory: childbirth is a natural, healthy process, not a disease, and there must be some natural, healthful method of preparing for it in order to reduce or eliminate pain and the dread of pain.

The British obstetrician Grantly Dick-Read* is regarded by many as the founding father of natural childbirth. He found it hard to reconcile the obvious naturalness of childbirth with the sufferings he witnessed in his patients. Like everyone else, he knew that women accumulate myth and misinformation about childbirth pain and hand down the lore from generation to generation. And there was, of course, the Bible to cite for final authority on the predestined agony of the female. But why should this be? No other healthy natural process was accompanied by pain. Why childbirth? He asked himself two questions.

1. Is labor easy because a woman is calm, or is she calm because her labor is easy?

2. Is a woman pained and frightened because her labor is difficult, or is her labor difficult because she is pained and frightened?

The conclusion Dick-Read drew was that fear in some way was the main agent for producing pain in a labor that in every other respect was a perfectly natural process. According to his theory, fear overstimulated the sympathetic nervous system, and this overstimulation gave excessive muscle tone, which in turn compressed nerve endings and thereby caused pain. It was a vicious circle. Fear caused pain; pain increased fear. Get rid of the fear, he proposed, and the pain, if not eliminated altogether, would at least be reduced and the labor eased.

In the years since Dick-Read made his first proposals concerning natural childbirth, it has become a commonplace in obstetrics to speak of the "pain-fear-tension syndrome" of labor. As long as the art (and science) of obstetrics has existed, good obstetricians have worked to build up the knowledge and confidence of their patients and so to reduce fear and eliminate tensions, but it was not until the concept of *natural childbirth* was formalized that attempts were made to devise a system of training and education for pregnant women.

The Russians, drawing on the work of their great physiologist Ivan Pavlov (1849–1936), went into training for childbirth on a big scale. Pavlov, you perhaps will remember, established the existence of the *conditioned reflex*. A reflex is an automatic response of the body to some specific stimulus. For example, when your doctor taps your leg just under the kneecap with his rubber hammer, your leg kicks out; you cannot keep it from kicking. What Pavlov proved was that by a program of training to set up a competing or distracting stimulus, he could alter the natural response to a painful stimulus like that of labor. A woman could be conditioned to the new contrived stimulus, which would lessen the painful one. A way of breathing in quick pants to offset the discomfort of the contractions and a system of exercise to promote relaxation figured prominently in the program (see page 196).

The Russian ideas were picked up in France and developed by Dr. Fernand Lamaze, and as the *Lamaze method* they have spread through Europe and come to the United States. Though interest in programs of preparation for childbirth is certainly growing in the United States, we seem to lag behind the Europeans in making it an integral part of the medical establishment. State clinics for this training have existed for years in the Soviet Union. And the London Hospital, for another example, has such a clinic. While attendance at the London clinic is not required of all pregnant patients, a large percent of them are said to make use of the training it offers. Here in the United States the work is being fostered to a great extent by enlightened and dedicated nursing groups, who can speak with the authority of their many years of accumulated experience in the labor and delivery rooms of some of our largest and most highly regarded hospitals. Childbirth education programs are springing up in most major cities in response to the growing awareness of young parents that they can better prepare themselves for all aspects of parenthood.

If you live in a large American city, you will be able to find a class in childbirth education. Many smaller communities now have them too. Your doctor or nurse or the local hospital can give you information or refer you to suitable sources. Lacking a local source of information, you may inquire of the International Childbirth Education Association.† This organization will have suggestions about starting a class if there is none in your community. They can also provide a list of books and pamphlets on all aspects of childbirth.‡

The need for this kind of education has developed in a most interesting way. In the "old days," say sixty or seventy years ago, most babies were born at home. Rather early in life girls had personal observation of human labor and perhaps even of delivery. Furthermore, in those days proportionally more people lived in rural areas much closer to animals than we do now and, except for a sheltered minority in the cities, probably had a more down-to-earth attitude toward the process of birth in general. If labor had unpleasant aspects (as it always has) , at least those aspects were known and on that account, so it would seem, less frightening.

Around the turn of the century, women in this country began to have their babies in hospitals, which until then were dreaded institutions for the poor and terminally ill. Advances in obstetrical technique, including asepsis, anesthesia, and blood banks, may have been the constructive force behind the trend but the Ford Model-T auto, improved roads, and the convenience of the family physician were contributory influences. The trend accelerated, and today the person who would by choice have her baby at home might be looked upon as a bit odd. Only among the extremely disadvantaged or the upper class would a woman be likely to give birth at home today without professional attendants, except, of course, in the rare emergency of premature or precipitous delivery.

Without question, the transfer of childbirth from home to hospital has resulted in dramatic improvements in the treatment of the complications of pregnancy. Death in childbirth, which in the 1600s in London, England, claimed one woman out of every forty, has become a rarity. In the hospital the mother has a clean if not sterile environment where the risk of infection is minimized. A trained staff with intricate equipment is on duty to monitor for the earliest sign of abnormality. Fresh blood is on hand to replace losses in delivery or surgery, and in complicated labors or emergencies, surgery (Caesarean section) can be carried out when needed. A variety of medications for analgesia (deadening of pain) and anesthesia (elimination of pain) has been developed to relieve the discomforts of the laboring mother.

One consequence of this shift from home to hospital is that the young person is now denied an invaluable experience. Until she has a child of her own, the woman who is not a nurse or a doctor has no opportunity to witness labor, let alone delivery. And the man, excluded as he is from the female grapevine's lore concerning pregnancy and birth, is left out altogether. Also, in this impressive setting of highly trained men and women working with specialized techniques and drugs, one element that has always been important to women in labor is often missing. This is the element of close psychological support from a friend or relative.

If the woman has her own obstetrician and has been under his care for the duration of her pregnancy, she has him to turn to, but otherwise she may be in the midst of strangers. Moreover, though labor and delivery do not recognize and honor the time clock, nursing staffs do.

When a shift ends, one staff leaves and another comes on duty. These nurses, in addition to being highly trained, are sensitive and compassionate, but they cannot replace the familiar and trusted sisters, mothers, aunts, and close neighbors who in times past have been the chief supports of the laboring woman. Close human relationship has always been important to women in labor. This psychological support is the missing element when technology has been emphasized at the expense of human concerns.

In the move into the hospital and the parallel development of safe and more effective analgesia and anesthesia, it was taken for granted that these advances would offset any new anxieties that might be occasioned by the strangeness of the hospital scene. Now for the first time, the physician and his staff could take a therapeutic stand between the laboring woman and the vagaries of nature. He could guide and control the progress of labor and delivery to an extent not imaginable in the past. Anesthesia allowed him to intervene surgically at any stage of the process while sparing the woman all or most of the discomforts. Analgesia could control pain of labor. Other medicines known as amnestics (scopolamine is a prime example) could dull the senses and memory so that what was regarded as an unpleasant experience could be blotted out altogether. Many mothers required several days to realize that they had actually had their babies and often had a feeling of unease and unreality about "the missing days" of their lives.

With the use of the pain-killers, including general or spinal anesthetics, and analgesics, and amnestics, women lost the ability to deliver the baby by bearing down or pushing in the second stage of labor. There was a technical answer to this consequence too. As a substitute for the mother's bearing down with her chest and abdominal muscles, the physician extracted the baby with forceps. Relaxation of the *perineum* (the area between the vulva and anus) by the anesthetic agents assisted this elective use of the forceps. Obstetrical technique thus overcame even this loss of the mother's natural ability to expel her baby, but as generally practiced, it meant that the mother might be unconscious when the baby was born, and in no way responsible for the actual birth process.

As the pace of all these changes quickened, the attitude toward women about to give birth changed too. Hospitals are places for sick people called *patients,* who take anesthesia and have surgery performed on them while unconscious. Gradually, almost imperceptibly, the pregnant woman came to be thought of as a "patient" who in due course would go to the hospital to have her "problem" taken care of. Pregnancy, labor, and delivery came to be thought of and written about in the terms used to discuss disease. One went to the hospital to be cured of pregnancy, as another might go to be cured of appendicitis or pneumonia. Just get there on time, and the doctor and staff would take over. There was nothing to worry about. The doctor would eliminate the pain, blot out the memory, extract the baby, deal with any complications. The woman did not have much to do with any of it beyond submitting herself to the "treatment." At some hospitals, in fact, she might not be sure that she had had a chance to say whether she did or did not want to breast-feed her baby. Breast-feeding was not in harmony with such a view of labor and delivery and more often than not was actively discouraged. Until finally discharged and sent home, the mother was dealt with and acted upon but had little to do herself and not much to say about how it should be done.

It is important to see that there has been a relationship among all these diverse elements in the development of obstetrical practice in the past one hundred years: the first-time mothers' and fathers' lack of experience, the transfer of labor and delivery to the hospital, the impersonal atmosphere of the hospital, the use of drugs to diminish pain and dull memory, the use of forceps to extract the baby because the mother cannot push with her abdominal muscles, the subtle change of attitude toward childbirth, the availability of milk formulas for infant feeding, rigid feeding schedules, and lastly, the firm conviction that women in labor, like other sick people, need to be in hospitals under intensive care. That these attitudes and practices have done wonders for pregnant women with severe complications is proven beyond argument by medical statistics from all the advanced nations of the world. But what about the other 95 percent who could have had their babies successfully with or without this highly technical medical attention?

In recent years, many women have rised questions about the purely technical approach to labor and delivery. They resent the passive quality of the woman's role in the process and want their husbands to share in the experience. They do not want to "be delivered"—they want to deliver. They regard bearing a child as one of the great milestones, if not the ultimate personal experience, in the development of a mature woman—the culmination of her biological destiny. Today they reject the attitude, "right" for its time, that sees pregnancy in the light of disease. Far from wanting the experience blotted out by drugs, to them the birth of a child is a normal process that they want to live and exploit to the full.

Unlike some of the early converts to natural childbirth, today's advocates do not rigidly oppose all medical intervention or reject the modern accompaniments of forceps, analgesia, and anesthesia. What they seek is to have these aids placed in a different perspective, available when needed, but only then. For the normal woman having a normal pregnancy, labor, and delivery, the emphasis, in their view, should be on the psychological and emotional preparation for childbirth and parenthood.

Whether one accepts the position of the advocates of natural childbirth or disagrees, it is important for women of childbearing age to know that a choice does exist and that they can profit from attending classes in education for childbirth even if in the end they elect (or their doctors advise them) to follow standard medical approaches. The pregnant woman has nothing to lose and everything to gain from having her husband participate directly in the events immediately preceding birth, and she is almost bound to benefit emotionally from the atmosphere in which the classes are held, as well as from the instruction itself.

As might be expected, the emphasis and the instructional details vary from course to course, but certain main themes are fairly standard. Usually, the woman joins a class about two months before the expected date of her delivery, and the class meets weekly. Groups are kept small to enable the enrolled couples to get to know each other as well as the instructors and advisers. There is an element of "group therapy" in the procedures. When the enrolled couples begin to warm to each other, they share their questions and worries about the impending events. Learning that others have the same concerns and worries you have and are learning to deal with them always tends to reinforce your confidence and enable you to face the future with greater equanimity. "Graduates" of the course who have recently given birth return to describe their experiences and answer questions. Often hospital visits are arranged to acquaint the group with the practices that will be encountered.

The instruction in the physiology of labor and delivery is given with films, tape recordings, video tape, charts, diagrams, still pictures, and anatomical models, as well as written material. Much attention is paid to the nature and rhythm of the uterine contractions in the various stages of labor (see pages 179–83). The idea is to educate the pregnant woman to recognize the characteristics of her labor at any point in order that she may have an idea of what comes next and how soon.

In the transition stage, for example, just prior to the full dilation of the cervix (see pages 180–81) , the discomfort approaches the maximum. This is the time when the laboring woman might be expected to ask for anesthesia. But if she has been trained to recognize that only a few more contractions will carry her out of this stage and to the beginning of expulsion of the baby, she likely will be able to summon enough resolution to go on to deliver herself. The mother who has had the training offered in these courses will know immediately what the physician means when she hears him say that the cervix is five centimeters dilated and 80 percent effaced and will be able to gauge from this information her capacity to continue without getting demoralized and giving up. Mothers are taught when to accept support from the "team" as they deal with the most intense contractions in transition. Fortunately, transition passes quickly, and the more active pushing of the second stage, leading soon to the delivery of the baby, is a welcome change.

Physical fitness is emphasized in these courses. Peak muscle tone, according to advocates of natural childbirth, assists the mother in meeting the strenuous demands of labor and in the final stage enables her to bear down strongly without tiring. In order to help the mother conserve her strength and preserve her calmness in the intervals between contractions, the courses also teach techniques of general muscle relaxation.

A more specific element of the training is the psychoprophylactic conditioning. As we said earlier, its essence, which stems from the Russian physiologist Pavlov, is to set up a distracting stimulus to take the mind off labor. In the language of behavioral psychology, the mother is deconditioned to the pain of uterine contractions by conditioning her to another stimulus, in this case a system of breathing. One strong stimulus thus is led to counteract another.

In the Lamaze system the rate of breathing is regulated according to the intensity and duration of the uterine contractions. The mother's inhalations and exhalations are slow and deep in the early stage of labor. As the frequency and intensity of her contractions increase, she switches to shallow, rapid panting. The rate of breathing is timed to the contraction. In the final stage another rhythm of breathing helps her to either bear down or relax and so gives her some measure of control over the speed of the delivery. Certain techniques of massage or effleurage are also taught, which help both during and between contractions. The husband can render invaluable support in this way.

The attitude in these courses toward control of pain is not heroic but realistic. It is accepted that analgesics, in judiciously small doses, and sometimes paracervical or other local anesthesia (see pages 187–88) may be given without violating the concepts of natural childbirth, and it is assumed that general or spinal anesthesia will be used if in the physician's opinion some complication requires it. The immediate availability of anesthesia, should it be needed, is one of the reassuring facts about modern natural childbirth. The mother can proceed with the psychoprophylactic approach in complete confidence because she knows that the full apparatus of modern obstetrics—anesthesia, surgery, fresh blood—is there for her rescue if some complication should arise. In practice, the majority of mothers in natural childbirth may not require anesthesia, but each is expected to do what is most comfortable and best for her.

Some obstetricians supplement the formal courses with review sessions late in pregnancy to tie together all that the parents have learned and bring it into focus with the actual "team" that will be involved in the delivery. This can be an invaluable aid to the confident management of labor and delivery with "awake and aware" mothers and fathers.

As pointed out elsewhere in this book (see page 185), however, the effects of analgesics and amnestics are not confined to the mother. These medications pass through the placenta into the baby's circulation. The old idea that the placenta constitutes an all but impenetrable barrier between fetus and outside world is no longer tenable. In addition to deadening pain, the effective analgesics also depress the functioning of the nervous system, and they have a greater depressant effect upon the baby than upon the mother. Babies whose mothers have received heavy medication rid themselves of the analgesia slowly and remain sleepy, at times even too sleepy to eat for several days. Not only may they not feed as well, but this sleepiness may cause needless worry for their mothers. Such worry, while undesirable for all mothers, is particularly deleterious to mothers who wish to breast-feed because of the sensitivity of milk production and ejection to emotions (see pages 300). A baby born with some problem, a respiratory difficulty for example, would be especially sensitive to the extra burden of depression from medication. The precarious condition of the youngest prematures (see pages 330–34) calls for avoidance of analgesia whenever possible to stave off even the smallest degree of depression of the respiration, which tends to be borderline at best. Appreciation of the effects of analgesia on the newborn has given rise to a much more critical assessment of analgesic agents for all labors, psychoprophylactic or otherwise. The less the better is the modern idea, which fits in, of course, with the basic philosophy of natural childbirth.

The proponents of natural childbirth also point out that certain discomforts are attendant upon use of the anesthetics and should not be overlooked. For example, the spinal, while unquestionably an effective relief from pain, does bring on temporary paralysis of the legs. This condition clears in hours but is nonetheless an annoyance. The spinal may also leave the mother with a mild to severe headache that will keep her in bed for twenty-four hours or longer. After spinals some women have difficulty voiding and pain in their backs at the site of needle puncture. The point here is not whether anesthetics are effective but that the issue of discomfort and pain cannot arbitrarily be confined to the labor and delivery. In an honest assessment, one set of discomforts has to be weighed against another.

The nursing groups who promote the Lamaze method (and remember, they are professionals with much experience in these matters) say that mothers who deliver without anesthetics bounce back quickly after childbirth. They come through the experience exhilarated and are out of their beds in short order. They seldom look bent and stiff, and they are back in the swing of things before the mothers who have had general or spinal anesthesia.

In the original plan of organization each couple in a childbirth education course was encouraged to form a close relationship with one of the nurses or one of the trained lay persons. This nurse, the *monatrice,* or trained lay person would act as coach for the pregnant wife and see her through labor and delivery at the hospital. The great popularity of the courses has made this personal attention an impossible luxury, and the emphasis now is on teaching the husband to do the same job. He supervises the preparatory exercises and, where permitted, accompanies his wife into the delivery room. There is nothing staged or artificial about his participation, and this drawing together of husband and wife at a pivotal event in their lives tends to cement their dedication to each other and gives them a stronger approach to parenthood.

Doctors and hospitals reflect the tastes and interests of the communities they serve. By and large, a physician's ability to make drastic changes in existing standards is limited; he must give his patients more or less what they demand. Until quite recently, the great majority of pregnant American women wanted amnesia and an anesthetized delivery with the least possible preparation and participation. After all, it was partially in response to this feeling, which represented the best thinking of those times, that modern obstetrics developed along the lines it has followed. But now times are different and many physicians are showing an interest in the psychoprophylactic or other preparatory techniques. Prepared childbirth has challenged the physician's way of thinking and acting. Instead of "delivering" the baby, he is now asked to be available if needed, a valued supporting player, but not the star in the drama of childbirth. More physicians these days will be supportive and sympathetic for couples who want to give natural childbirth a try, while at the same time not pushing this approach upon their patients. This trend among the doctors is in line with a somewhat parallel trend in the hospitals. An effort is being made to provide a comfortable atmosphere for natural deliveries and for rooming-in arrangements for the mother and her new baby (see pages 31–32 and 218–19) , as well as relaxed arrangements for the father's visiting. Breast-feeding tends to be fostered, is greatly aided by livelier nonmedicated babies, and may often begin on the delivery table minutes after birth.

There is now even a reawakening of interest in home deliveries. In normal uncomplicated pregnancies with adequate medical supervision and childbirth education and hospital facilities nearby, such as in Holland and England, excellent results are achieved. To what extent this experience can be transferred to the United States remains to be seen.

Whatever your thoughts about "natural childbirth" or "prepared childbirth" actually are, you would do well to remember that most proponents of these approaches do so from an honest conviction that it is better for the mother and father to know what is happening and to prepare for it together, from an equally honest conviction that it is better for the newborn baby to have had less medication, and from a very firm and honest conviction that the couple that achieves this kind of experience has accomplished something that will make them better and more understanding persons, better mates, and better parents. The whole phenomenon can be looked upon as a complex social, medical, and personal experience that draws upon the accumulated experiences of psychologists, psychiatrists, obstetricians, and parents themselves. In the newness of these approaches there is excitement and promise; in the familiarity of the context, human reproduction assumes a fulfillment and stature that is gratifying to participate in for the parents, the physician, and nurse, and in the long run, the child, who is the focal point of it all.

RICHARD I. FEINBLOOM, M.D.

* Grantly Dick-Read, *Childbirth Without Fear*, 2nd ed. (New York: Harper and Brothers, 1959).

† International Childbirth Education Association, Post Office Box 5852, Milwaukee, Wisconsin 53220.

‡ Two paperback books that might be read with profit: Irwin Chabon, M.D., *Awake and Aware* (New York: Dell, 1966). Elizabeth Bing, *Six Practical Lessons for an Easier Childbirth* (New York: Bantam Books, 1967).

CHAPTER NINE

Complications of Labor and Delivery

PREMATURE RUPTURE OF THE MEMBRANES

*M*UCH GREATER attention is being paid these days to high-risk pregnancies. For example, regional obstetrical centers which specialize in complicated labor and delivery are being established. Among other aspects of the care of high-risk pregnancy is much closer monitoring of the baby's heart rate and labor contractions by means of electrodes (as in an electrocardiogram) placed on the mother's abdomen.

The delicate fetal membranes (*the amniotic sac*) are like a plastic bag attached around the rim of the placenta. Inside, the baby is suspended in the amniotic fluid. These membranes protect the baby from bacterial infection. Cultures taken from the vagina throughout pregnancy invariably yield numerous bacteria. Most of these are perfectly harmless in the numbers in which they exist. In contrast, cultures taken from the amniotic fluid before rupture of the membranes or the onset of labor are sterile; that is, no bacteria are found. But once the membranes have ruptured or the patient has been in labor for several hours, the possibility of intrauterine infection arises. The vaginal bacteria then can invade the uterine cavity and multiply. In general, the longer the membranes have been ruptured or the longer labor has lasted, the greater are the chances of an infection in the uterine cavity.

The membranes rupture spontaneously in about 10 percent of cases before the onset of labor. Since labor usually begins within a few hours, there is no problem of infection. If labor does not ensue, however, there is always the possibility of an infection. Fortunately, infection is the exception rather than the rule, even though the membranes may have been ruptured for days. When intrauterine infections do occur, however, there may be serious consequences for both the baby and the mother.

It would seem logical to put mothers with premature rupture of the membranes on antibiotics to prevent infection. Experience has shown, however, that the prophylactic use of antibiotics in this condition is worthless.

The doctor will often induce labor when premature rupture of the membranes has occurred. This is usually accomplished by a dilute intravenous infusion of pitocin (see page 176) or its synthetic counterpart. He will probably induce when the pregnancy is close to term, but if he feels the baby is premature he may prefer to wait. If labor is not induced, the patient should refrain from sexual relations and douching as both might introduce potentially harmful bacteria into the vagina. While these bacteria present no problem as long as the membranes are intact, once the membranes have ruptured it may be a different story. In addition, the patient should take her temperature several times during the day and notify her doctor of even a slight elevation of temperature, as this may be of significance.

When the membranes rupture before the onset of labor, the ensuing labor is sometimes referred to as a "dry birth." Such a delivery is popularly believed to be more difficult, but this is not so. Nor is it so "dry," either. The amniotic fluid continues to be produced in large quantities even after the membranes have ruptured.

In the latter weeks of pregnancy the pregnant woman may experience a little gush of fluid and not know whether it has come from rupture of the membranes or from the bladder. If the membranes have ruptured, there will be an uncontrollable continuous dribbling of fluid. If the fluid comes from the bladder, the flow or dribbling will not continue. Since the bladder does get pushed around a bit toward the end of pregnancy, control may be more difficult, especially when a full bladder is subjected to the pressure of coughing or sneezing. Women have reported that when their membranes ruptured they have felt, almost heard, a little "pop." Like many other things in life, it is hard to describe, but the sensation apparently is unmistakable. The ultimate in perception in this regard was exhibited by the wife of a physician. As she was soaking in the tub she suddenly called out to her husband, "What should I do? I've just ruptured my membranes."

PREMATURE DELIVERY

By all odds, the most important complication of pregnancy is premature delivery (see pages 330–41). Throughout the United States some 5 to 15 percent of all babies are born prematurely. Hospitals with a large proportion of charity cases may have an incidence of almost twice that percentage. It is obvious that socioeconomic factors figure in the statistics of premature delivery.

Although we know a great deal about the mechanism of labor, we still do not know what makes labor begin. Until we can learn how labor is initiated, there is little hope for any real breakthrough in the problem of prematurity. If we are to make progress, instead of concentrating on care of the infant who is too immature to survive outside his mother's womb, we must find some way of preventing early delivery.

Although we do not know the ultimate cause of premature labor, we do know a number of conditions associated with it. Sometimes a woman is delivered prematurely on purpose. If the doctor feels the baby is large enough to survive complications like diabetes or the Rh-negative problem, he may deliver the infant prematurely to forestall stillbirth in the last few weeks of pregnancy. There are other occasions for delivery before term. The mother may have a serious complication that threatens her safety if pregnancy is allowed to continue. Examples are toxemia of pregnancy and bleeding of late pregnancy. Here the pregnancy is ended prematurely in the best interest of the mother.

Women with twin pregnancy usually deliver early; so do many who have anomalies of the uterus. For the great majority of early deliveries, however, no cause can be found. If a woman has had one premature baby, she has roughly a 30 percent chance of having a second baby early. If she has had two premature babies in a row, her chances of having a third are very great.

Because of the importance of prematurity, a great deal of research is going on. Most authorities agree that progesterone, one of the main placental hormones, inhibits the activity of uterine muscle. Nothing will stop labor once it has actually begun, but many doctors believe that progesterone may forestall the onset of premature labor. There are times in pregnancy when even a few days are important. At the beginning of the seventh month (twenty-eight weeks) a baby's chances of survival are very small. By the end of the eighth month (thirty-six weeks) his chances are virtually the same as for a full-term baby. It follows that during the seventh and eighth months each extra week means a great deal as far as the baby's outlook is concerned. Anything that you can do that might add a week or two to the length of gestation is certainly worthwhile. This is why doctors may give progesterone even though they know it is not the entire answer to the problem of premature labor.

THE VARIOUS PRESENTATIONS

The baby usually comes through the birth canal headfirst with his chin bent down on his chest. This is the position that takes the least room. If you have ever tried to put a tight sweater on a small child, you know that the garment goes on most easily when he has his chin down on his chest and you can start the sweater over the back of his head. Not all babies at birth are so accommodating, however, and there is a special vocabulary to describe the various positions in which they prepare to make their entrances into our world.

The part of the baby that the physician's examining finger would touch first through the mother's cervix is called *the presentation*. When the baby in delivery is looking straight ahead, instead of having his chin down on his chest, the head is said to be *extended*. A little more uplift of the chin gives rise to a *brow presentation*. A *face presentation* comes about when the neck is extended as much as possible. It is as if the baby were looking up at the sky. In the *breech presentation* the baby's buttocks come first.

While these positions of the baby may impede the progress of labor, the mother will usually be able to deliver normally. If progress is arrested during labor and further labor might jeopardize either the mother or baby, a Caesarean section can be performed.

In a *transverse presentation* the baby is lying crosswise in the mother's abdomen. The baby's head is at one side and its feet at the other, with the consequence that either the back or abdomen is over the pelvis. Often there is some obstruction preventing the baby's head from entering the pelvis: the placenta may be implanted low down over the cervix, or there may be a fibroid or ovarian tumor. Sometimes the obstruction is due simply to small pelvic measurements. Not all women with transverse presentations have these obstructions. The positions may be encountered when the pregnancy is in every other respect perfectly normal.

Vaginal delivery is impossible for a full-term living baby in the transverse presentation; a Caesarean section becomes necessary once labor has become established. Frequently the transverse presentation in late pregnancy will convert to another presentation once labor begins. When the obstetrician discovers a transverse presentation close to term, he is alerted to the possibility of an obstruction of the pelvic inlet. If none is found, he ordinarily will let labor begin, hoping that the baby then will come either headfirst or feetfirst. If he is disappointed, a Caesarean section is in order.

When the baby is turned around and the buttocks appear first, the delivery is said to be a *breech presentation,* or breech birth. There are several varieties of breech presentation. The most common is the so-called *frank breech presentation.* Here the thighs are flexed on the infant's abdomen but the knees are not bent so that the baby's feet are up around his ears. This jackknife position seems most unusual, but it is surprising how easily labor progresses in most of these cases. Sometimes one knee or both will be bent. Then the feet come first and we have a *single-* or *double-footling presentation.*

A full breech is the same as a double footling. The knees are bent and thighs flexed against the abdomen. It is the same position a child is in when he jumps off a diving board for what we used to call "the cannonball."

Breech births occur in 3 to 4 percent of all deliveries. Any condition that tends to prevent the baby's head from entering the pelvis in the last few weeks of pregnancy favors the development of a breech presentation. If the pelvis is too small, the baby is likely to come feetfirst. He also may arrive in this position if the placenta or a tumor of the uterus or ovary encroaches on the pelvic inlet. Breech births are more common among premature infants. It seems as if labor begins before the final headfirst position has had time to establish itself.

A breech delivery is often a little more difficult for the mother, the baby, and the doctor, who would be happy if none of his patients ever had a breech birth. By external manipulation it is sometimes possible to turn the baby around so that he comes headfirst. This procedure is called an external version. Many doctors will try to perform an external version in the office in the last few weeks of pregnancy, if a breech presentation has been discovered. There are other doctors who do not try to turn the baby. They argue that if the version is successful the baby would have turned anyway. This is something impossible to prove in the individual case. It is not a bit unusual, however, to follow a patient with a breech presentation throughout the latter weeks of pregnancy and find that the baby has turned of his own accord within a week or two of delivery.

The largest part of a baby is the head. When the pelvis is known to be small, the doctor usually will allow the mother to go into labor if the baby is coming headfirst. Then if the forces of labor are not sufficient to push the head through the pelvis, he can always perform a Caesarean section. But when the baby comes feetfirst, the situation is not so simple. The doctor must have made up his mind ahead of time whether there is disproportion between the size of the baby's head and the mother's pelvis. The pelvis may be large enough for the trunk and extremities but not for the baby's head. If the doctor should get the baby's legs and trunk delivered but be unable to deliver the head, it would be too late for Caesarean section. When the doctor questions whether the pelvis has room for a safe delivery, he will perform a Caesarean before labor begins or shortly after the onset.

For his estimate of the capacity of the pelvis the doctor relies on internal examination and, possibly, X-ray pictures. Of course, if the mother has had a good-sized child or children previously the capacity of the pelvis obviously is adequate for a baby of average size.

As far as the mother is concerned, the usual breech delivery is about the same as if the baby came headfirst. She may have a few more stitches after it is all over. The labor contractions do not feel any different. Once the breech begins to distend the floor of the pelvis the urge to push is all but irresistible, just as when the baby comes headfirst.

Some doctors prefer one form of anesthesia for a breech, while others may prefer a different type. It is certainly possible to deliver a breech with little or no anesthetic. Sometimes in the course of labor, however, it may become necessary for the doctor to perform intrauterine manipulations. This procedure is known as "breaking up the breech" and consists of bringing down the feet in a frank breech presentation. The anesthetic that makes this maneuver easiest and therefore safest is ether. For this reason it is especially important that the mother should not eat or drink anything once labor has begun. Though the doctor may not usually use a general anesthetic for breech deliveries, circumstances may arise in labor that may make breaking up the breech mandatory.

UTERINE INERTIA

In active labor the uterus contracts firmly every two or three minutes. The contraction begins at the top of the uterus and spreads downward like a wave. But with uterine inertia the contractions are irregular in interval, intensity, and duration. Studies have shown that the contraction wave in uterine inertia does not begin at the top of the uterus but more in the middle and spreads both ways. This behavior has led to the term *incoordinate uterine action,* which is more descriptive than uterine inertia. While these contractions may be just as painful to the woman in labor, they are ineffective in dilating the cervix. Women with uterine inertia, therefore, are prone to have prolonged labor, and with all the disadvantages to both the mother and the baby that come about as a consequence.

Uterine inertia commonly is associated with disproportion between the size of the baby and the size of the pelvis. It can, however, happen even when the pelvic measurements are large. In those cases it is almost always in the first pregnancy. Though these labors may be like an endurance contest the first time, in subsequent deliveries labors are often rapid and easy.

There are two methods of treating uterine inertia. We know from long observation that the uterine contractions sometimes become more effective after the laboring woman has had several hours of rest. In consequence, one school of thought on uterine inertia believes in giving a narcotic or sedative to allow the patient several hours of sleep. The more active philosophy of treatment dictates that the uterus needs to be stimulated. There are several drugs capable of evoking strong uterine contractions. The one whose action is most predictable is the hormone *pitocin,* and it is the drug commonly given for uterine inertia.

There are very few women with uterine inertia who do not respond to either resting or stimulation. But if unproductive labor does go on hour after hour, eventually a Caesarean section must be done.

CAESAREAN SECTION

Caesarean section is the delivery of the fetus through a surgical incision in the uterine wall. It is a popular belief that Julius Caesar was born in this manner. (He was not.) No living child was born by Caesarean section until long after Caesar's time.

Caesarean sections used to have a high mortality rate and consequently the operation was selected only as a last resort when all other methods of delivery had failed. A high Caesarean section rate was thought to be synonymous with substandard obstetrical practice; hospitals in those days prided themselves on the low number of Caesarean births. This picture has changed completely. Caesarean section has become one of the safest methods of delivery. Over the last few decades, while there has been a dramatic drop in the maternal and fetal mortality rate, there has been an equally dramatic rise in the number of Caesarean births.

At present, the operation is performed in most hospitals in about 5 percent of the cases. The rate of some of the leading obstetric clinics, which receive a large number of referred complicated cases, may be almost twice as high.

The main drawback of Caesarean section is that the operation has become too easy and too safe. There is the natural tendency to turn to Caesarean section whenever any complication of pregnancy arises. Vaginal delivery is still the safest and best method of delivery for the overwhelming number of mothers, including many with serious complications.

There are several types of Caesarean operations. The usual type of abdominal incision is the midline approach beneath the navel. The incision is about six inches in length. It is possible to perform the operation through a transverse incision in the abdominal wall but this procedure is a good deal more time-consuming. Some obstetricians using the transverse incision cite "compelling cosmetic reasons" for their preference.

Originally the uterine incision was made through the thick muscular portion of the womb. This type of Caesarean section is known as the classical type. Infection used to be one of the most dreaded complications of Caesarean section, and to prevent infection operations were devised for the section to be made instead through the thin *lower segment* of the uterus. In this technique a thin flap of the delicate peritoneal membrane covers the uterine incision to confine any infection that might occur. While uterine infections are much less common and serious than formerly, the lower segment type of operation has supplanted the classical type because healing is better and there are fewer complications than with the classical incision. The great majority of Caesarean sections done today are of the lower segment type.

Caesarean sections are done for many reasons. The most common is that the mother has had this operation in a previous pregnancy. There are more "repeat" Caesarean sections than any other kind. Once a Caesarean, always a Caesarean, many doctors believe. They think that the scarred uterine wall may be weak in a small number of cases and might give way under the force of labor. Should this rupture occur, it would certainly become a serious complication for both the mother and the infant. Unfortunately, there is really no practical way of spotting beforehand the few uterine scars that are defective. There are a few iconoclasts in America (and a good many more in Europe) who argue against the "once a Caesarean, always a Caesarean" rule. If the scar is defective it may give way before labor begins, they argue, so the whole problem of uterine rupture cannot be solved by doing Caesarean sections at full term. In practice, repeat sections usually are scheduled a couple of weeks before the due date. When this practice is followed, any large series of cases will include a small number of babies delivered prematurely who do not do well.

Aside from the requirements of repeat sections, the most common reason for performing a Caesarean section is that the pelvis is too small to accommodate the baby. This is called *cephalopelvic disproportion* to make it sound complicated, which it really is not. The majority of mothers with small pelvises need not be delivered by Caesarean section. When they go into labor they will usually deliver normally although labor often is slow. Only a very few women have pelvises so small that normal delivery is impossible. Usually, ineffective contractions and an unfavorable position of the baby are involved also when a Caesarean is deemed necessary for disproportion. Since no one can predict beforehand how effective the labor contractions will be, or what position the baby will assume during labor, the woman known to have a small pelvis is allowed to go into labor spontaneously. This procedure is known as the *test of labor*. If labor progresses normally, a Caesarean section is not necessary. If the progress is not satisfactory, the operation is performed after the patient has been in labor several hours. Some women have the idea that Caesarean sections should not be done after labor is started. No so. In many respects the operation is easier to perform after several hours of labor, since the lower segment of the uterus enlarges.

It is necessary to perform Caesarean sections at times if the baby is in an abnormal position. The position with the baby lying crosswise is known as a *transverse lie*. Since a normal birth is impossible when the baby is in a transverse lie during labor, the Caesarean section is done for this complication. But if the baby is found to be in a transverse lie before the onset of labor, the Caesarean is not always necessary. In most cases, once the labor is begun the baby will come into the pelvis either head first or as a breech.

In breech presentations the incidence of Caesarean section is higher than normal. Women with this complication are not allowed a test of labor when the pelvis is too small but are delivered by Caesarean section before the onset of labor. Even if the pelvic measurement is normal there is a growing tendency to deliver by Caesarean section when the first baby of a woman thirty-five or over is found to be in a breech position.

Caesarean sections will be found necessary in a certain number of face and brow presentations, but not all. The operation is performed only when the progress in labor is not satisfactory.

Caesarean sections may be done if the doctor has reason to believe that the baby will not survive labor. *Fetal distress* is the condition in which there is interference with the blood supply to the baby, who suffers from lack of oxygen *(anoxia)*. Changes in the baby's heart rate during labor and discoloration of the amniotic fluid reflect this condition. If fetal distress develops at the end of labor, the doctor will usually hasten the delivery all he can, but he can safely speed things along just so much. If fetal distress occurs early in the course of labor, when there are several hours more to go, Caesarean section may be the only choice. In severe fetal distress, time is of the essence. Surgery then is a response to emergency. Distress is due to twists or knots in the cord. Sometimes the cord prolapses into the vagina ahead of the baby and gets pinched off. In many cases, as the operation proceeds, no cause for the fetal distress will be evident. The doctor may feel somewhat chagrined, but he should not. It is certainly better to do a Caesarean section than to take a chance on losing a baby in labor. There are few greater disappointments to a mother than to lose the baby she has carried for the whole nine months of pregnancy.

There are a number of complications of pregnancy associated with high stillbirth rates when pregnancy has been allowed to go to term. Examples are diabetes, some types of kidney disease, and severe Rh-negative complications. When the mother has these complications, the optimum time for delivery for the well-being of the baby may be three, four, or even five weeks before term. Many of these women have to be delivered by Caesarean section since at this stage of pregnancy it is often not safe or possible to induce labor.

Sometimes pregnancy has to be terminated before term not so much because of the baby but because of the mother. The best example is severe toxemia of pregnancy. This condition does not improve until the uterus is empty. Since these patients are medically ill, pelvic delivery would be far preferable but it is often not possible to induce labor. A Caesarean section, therefore, becomes the only way to effect delivery.

These are the main occasions for performing Caesarean sections. Naturally, there are others, but they are too technical for a book of this kind.

There is no "best" form of anesthesia for Caesarean sections. Either a general or regional type may be used. Often the complication that makes the operation necessary will determine the choice of anesthesia. Many women have Caesarean sections under regional anesthesia and are wide awake through the whole procedure. They do not get to see much of the actual surgery, however, as they are well covered up with surgical drapes.

After any abdominal surgery (and Caesarean section is no exception) there is a certain amount of abdominal pain and discomfort for the first two or three days. Patients are also likely to experience discomfort in one or both shoulders; a certain amount of blood and air collects under the diaphragm and irritates it. (Although it is the diaphragm that is affronted, you feel pain in the shoulder.) But the discomfort following Caesarean section is not so severe that it cannot be relieved by sedatives. Each day should see a marked improvement. By about the third day the intestinal tract, whose activity is always greatly diminished after surgery, begins to function normally again, and most patients then experience some sharp gas pains. This discomfort can be distressing to the patient for a short while, but it is good news to the surgeon. If gas is being moved normally down the intestinal tract, he knows that no infection is causing the intestine to become paralyzed. A conservative practice, which may be old-fashioned, is to keep patients hospitalized for seven or eight days after Caesarean section, but some surgeons do not insist on so long a stay. There is no set time a woman must wait after a Caesarean before she ventures on another pregnancy. Plenty of women have conceived again three or four months after a Caesarean and experienced no complication in the subsequent pregnancy.

UMBILICAL CORD ACCIDENTS

The umbilical cord is usually about two feet long. Sometimes it is much shorter or longer. No one knows what determines the length of the cord.

When you think how much the baby moves around in the nine months of pregnancy, it is truly remarkable how seldom serious knots and twists of the cord occur. Sometimes the cord is so short the circulation through it is impeded. This constriction is especially likely in labor as the baby moves down the birth canal and stretches the cord.

Many babies are born with the cord around the neck, but in ninety-nine cases out of one hundred this is not serious to the baby. On rare occasions, tight knots or entanglement about the baby may compromise circulation in the cord, especially when the cord is excessively long. If the circulation is completely shut off for even a few minutes, a stillbirth will result. When this accident happens anywhere except in the hospital, there is nothing anyone can do. During labor in the hospital if there are signs of fetal distress, delivery can be hastened, or a Caesarean section may be performed to save the baby.

After rupture of the membranes, the circulation in the cord might be compromised if the cord should slip into the vagina ahead of the baby. It could be pinched between the baby and the sides of the birth canal. This condition is called *prolapse* of the cord and requires the same treatment as knots or entanglement of the cord. Any condition where the round baby's head does not fill the round pelvic cavity predisposes to prolapse of the cord. This complication consequently is more common in breech positions and transverse lies. Prematurity favors prolapse of the cord because the baby is tiny. So do obstructions of the pelvis, which prevent the head from entering. If the membranes are ruptured before the baby's head is in the pelvis, prolapse becomes a hazard in induced labor.

INJURY AT BIRTH

It is possible for the baby to sustain an injury in delivery, but in this day serious injury is a great rarity. It was not always so. Before Caesarean section became such a safe and frequent operation, birth injuries were common. Not even the wealthy or privileged were spared. Kaiser Wilhelm II, who was the last emperor of Germany and a grandchild of Britain's Queen Victoria, had an Erb's palsy (see page 214) from birth injury. Paralysis of the arm is characteristic of this condition. Wilhelm's withered left arm caused him acute mental anguish and undoubtedly accounted in part for his overbearing personality, which made him unpopular among his royal relatives and contributed to the events leading up to World War I. This is one well-documented instance in which we can link childhood trauma to a subsequent social catastrophe.

When birth injuries do happen, the baby is usually either very large or very small. It is easy to understand that a very large infant can be injured at birth, but you would not expect the same kind of accident could happen to a very small one. The explanation is that the head of a very premature baby is so soft it can be injured merely by the squeezing in passage through the birth canal. For this reason, premature babies are delivered with forceps. Any pressure from the maternal tissues is exerted against the forceps and not against the baby's head. A liberal incision at the vaginal opening (*episiotomy*) is made for the same reason. Many a mother of a premature baby has been dismayed to find that she has just as many stitches as the woman in the next bed who has had a baby twice the size.

The most serious injuries at birth are due to hemorrhages within the brain, and result from difficult labors and deliveries. The increased incidence of Caesarean section when pelvic measurements are too small has all but eliminated this cause of birth injury. Many of the babies who do sustain a cerebral hemorrhage at birth will recover completely. Not all are so fortunate. If the hemorrhage is a large one, or in a vital spot, it usually will be fatal within the first two or three days of life. If less severe, the baby will survive but may have some permanent neurological damage. It is germane here to point out, however, that the great majority of babies with cerebral palsy and related neurological diseases are not victims of mechanically difficult deliveries or fractured skulls. Indeed, this is the riddle of cerebral palsy. A review of the obstetrical record in cases of cerebral palsy will often fail to disclose any obstetric complication at all.

In most deliveries, the baby's head is the largest and most difficult part. Once this has been delivered it may, however, be very difficult to deliver the shoulders. In situations like this, fractures of the clavicle (collarbone)) are not uncommon. This is not a serious fracture and heals promptly when a splint is applied. The obstetrician may even fracture the clavical on purpose to cause the shoulder girdle to collapse and make the delivery easier. Tugging on the baby's head and neck when the shoulders cannot be delivered might tear some of the nerves leading to the hand and arm muscles. If this should happen, the arm is partially paralyzed and remains so for life. This is the condition called Erb's palsy.

Bones other than the clavicle can be fractured in birth, but an accident of this sort is now very rare. When it does happen, the baby is usually premature and in addition is in some abnormal position. The doctor has to perform intrauterine manipulation to effect delivery, and he works with the mother under local or spinal anesthesia. Since these agents do not relax the uterus, undue force may be needed to carry out the intended procedure. No doctor likes to give a deep ether anesthesia in the face of prematurity, but when intrauterine manipulations must be done, it is probably the lesser of two evils.

Mothers often ask about certain markings left after delivery. These conditions can hardly be classified as birth injuries. Forcep marks are likely to be present after all but the easiest deliveries. The baby, especially if fair skinned, will have a red mark or abrasion of the skin in front of the ear and look bothered for the first day or two, even though the delivery has been quite uneventful. When really difficult forceps deliveries are performed, the facial nerve may be compressed by the forceps in front of the ear. A temporary weakness of the facial muscles on the affected side may result. For a day or two a slight lack of symmetry of the mouth when the baby cries may be noticeable. Permanent injury to the facial nerve by forceps is almost unheard of. Another innocuous condition resulting from birth is the *cephalohematoma.* This is a prominent rounded bulge, very soft and fluctuant to the touch, on the side of the baby's head. Most of these bulges are an inch or so in diameter. The parents should be assured that the condition is harmless and requires no treatment. The cephalohematoma is a collection of blood between the scalp and skull bone. It results when a small scalp vein is torn, usually during forceps rotation of a posterior or transverse position prior to delivery. The blood collects under the scalp resulting in the cephalohematoma. It is gradually absorbed, the process usually taking two or three weeks.

ARTHUR GORBACH, M.D.

CHAPTER TEN

Postpartum Care

*I*N PREGNANCY, as we have seen, striking changes occur to prepare women for motherhood. Deliver sets in motion another series of events no less dramatic. The changes of pregnancy have come on so gradually they have seemed at times almost imperceptible, but the impact of delivery is sudden. One moment a woman is childless—the next she is a mother!

Much of the postpartum change is physical. The physical changes of pregnancy occurred largely through the action of the placental hormones. By the end of pregnancy the amounts of female hormones produced by the placenta have increased, and the mother's body has become accustomed to them. When the afterbirth is cast off, the maternal organism is suddenly deprived. Among other immediate changes, the blood volume drops rapidly. The generalized retention of fluid ceases, and in the first day or two an excessive volume of urine results. Usually the new mother loses four to five pounds. Thus, including the weight of baby and placenta, there is, within just a couple of days, an immediate weight loss of twelve to fifteen pounds. Another two to ten pounds will go in the next week, depending on the amount of fluid that was retained in pregnancy. Almost at once, a certain amount of the swelling and fullness of the face characteristic of pregnancy disappears. The difference in the looks of the new mother in the first few days postpartum is striking.

Following the delivery of the placenta, there is some bleeding from the place of its attachment to the uterus, the placental site. This vaginal bleeding, called the *lochia,* persists until the placenta site is healed, which takes the better part of a month. In the first few days the bleeding is heavy, about like the first day or two of a menstrual period. Sanitary napkins have to be changed a couple of times in the morning and again in the afternoon. The lochia gradually gets lighter in color and less in amount until, in four or five weeks, it ceases altogether.

Immediately after delivery, there is a heavy flow. Large uterine blood vessels course through the thick interlacing bundles of muscle that make up the uterine wall. The blood supply to the uterus at term is tremendous. It receives one-fourth to one-fifth of the entire cardiac output. Following delivery of the placenta, these vessels are wide open. The uterine muscles clamp down and squeeze off the blood vessels going through them, thereby preventing excessive blood loss at delivery and for the first few days postpartum. Drugs that cause hard contractions of uterine muscle, pitocin and ergonovine, are given at the time of delivery to make sure that no relaxation of the uterine muscle occurs.

When the uterine muscles contract, a woman experiences a cramp, like a menstrual cramp or labor pain. Following placental delivery, these cramps are known as *afterpains.* They may continue for three or four days, but a couple of aspirins combined with something like codeine will relieve the discomfort. Afterpains are generally somewhat more troublesome following the second or third delivery than after the first. By the second or third baby the uterus is a little more stretched and relaxed than after the first, and consequently has to contract more to get back to normal. Mothers who breast-feed their children are likely to have more afterpains. This is not an argument against breast-feeding. It is thought that the uterus gets back to normal more quickly in mothers who breast-feed than in those who do not—hence the afterpains. Since there is no nerve connecting the breast to the uterus, the uterine contractions associated with breast-feeding are thought to be brought about by a hormone. When the infant suckles, the pituitary gland in the brain releases a hormone into the blood stream that induces strong uterine contractions. When this hormone reaches the uterus a powerful contraction ensues and the mother experiences an afterpain. In time, anything the mother associates with breast-feeding may produce an afterpain. For example, the mother may get an afterpain by merely hearing her baby cry. This is called a conditioned reflex.

In addition to the afterpains, a certain amount of discomfort in the postpartum period comes from the stitches. The episiotomy incision has been made in a sensitive area; it is not surprising that the result is uncomfortable. The type of episiotomy has some bearing on the amount of discomfort experienced. Naturally, a large incision is more painful than a small one. If the incision is in the midline, it is more comfortable than when the incision is off to one side. The pain is far from severe, and may be largely relieved by any one of a number of drugs that can be taken by mouth. Heat, in the form of a hot shower or heating lamp, will also help a great deal. Sometimes local anesthetic sprays or salves are ordered by the doctor. The episiotomy incision, like any other surgical incision, heals in two to three weeks. If absorbable sutures are used (which is generally the case), there is no need to remove the stitches.

Among the lesser postpartum developments is one that can be rather dismaying. Some women whose ankles have remained more or less normal all through pregnancy will begin swelling after the delivery. This swelling of the ankles disappears in a few days and is nothing to worry about. It is not necessary to restrict salt.

A doctor of long experience once remarked, with a twinkle in his eye, that in all his years of practice he had never heard a patient complain about a "small" hemorrhoid. The dilated veins around the anus may become swollen and tender during delivery and will feel anything but small for the first few days. The same measures that are effective in relieving the discomfort of the episiotomy are used also in treating hemorrhoids in the postpartum period.

In the first few days after delivery quite a few patients experience a mild postpartum depression. The "baby blues" have had so much publicity that many mothers expect them automatically. This certainly is not the case. The obstetrician sees almost as many depressions before the baby is born as after delivery. Most postpartum depressions are mild and of short duration. No treatment is necessary. When they are more prolonged, patients should certainly be under the care of a physician. In severe cases the help of a psychiatrist would be appreciated by both the patient and the physician who is trying to cope with this difficult problem.

There is no set time for the new mother's stay in the hospital after delivery. The only generalization possible is that many mothers do not stay in the hospital as long as they should. Besides the wish to get home to the family, the main reason, of course, is that hospitalization costs too much. Economic factors should not determine the way patients are treated. The sorry fact, however, in this, the world's richest country, is that as the cost of hospitalization goes up, the length of stay after delivery goes down. In some places a mother is hospitalized only two or three days following delivery. This must be close to the irreducible minimum. In almost every other country in the world mothers do not go home until the baby is a week or ten days old.

Mothers always say how much more rest they can get at home than in the hospital with its rigid routine. Yet the commonest complaint the obstetrician hears at the six weeks exam is that the mother is utterly exhausted. Many wish they had stayed longer. While rest is important, there are other reasons for staying in the hospital after delivery. If mothers are breast-feeding, it is not the best idea to send them home before the baby begins to gain. Usually, this doesn't happen until the baby is four or five days old. Then, for both the mother and the baby there are sometimes certain complications in the first few days after delivery. If these are picked up early and properly treated, no harm is done, but if diagnosis and therapy are delayed the results can be altogether different.

ROOMING-IN

Some hospitals are set up to have the baby stay in the room with the mother, rather than in a large nursery with many other newborns. This arrangement is called rooming-in. It has certain advantages, especially for women having their first child. While you are learning to care for all the baby's needs, it helps to be in the cloistered atmosphere of the hospital. Also, there should be less chance of cross infection between babies if they are in separate rooms rather than in a common nursery. One would think that rooming-in should take some of the load off the overworked nursing staff, but most nurses do not seem to agree.

Rooming-in also has certain disadvantages. The chief one is that some mothers do not get all the rest they should. This is a serious drawback, because rest is the main thing that the hospital has to offer the mother after delivery. If the baby is fussy and cries a great deal, the new mother cannot possibly get enough rest. A modified rooming-in arrangement has been tried in some hospitals and may prove to be a sensible solution (see pages 31–32).

It has always seemed to me that the very mothers who would benefit most from rooming-in are the ones who are afraid to try it. These are the young and inexperienced women who have never had the responsibility of caring for a newborn. Even though they see the baby several times a day in the hospital, they do not really learn to take full care of him. Being presented with the total care of this demanding creature at the age of four or five days can be a shattering experience if you are not particularly self-reliant and confident of your ability to rise to the occasion. On the other hand, if you have taken care of your baby in the hospital, you are less likely to lie awake the first couple of nights at home wondering whether your baby is still breathing.

DISCHARGE FROM THE HOSPITAL

When you leave the hospital, your doctor will answer any questions you have and will tell you a number of things to do and not to do. Naturally, different doctors will give different advice. The opinions that follow will probably vary a good deal from those you get from your own doctor. By all means follow his advice. All that can be claimed for the following instructions is that they have worked over the years.

The most important thing when you go home is to get plenty of rest. This is especially important these days when mothers leave the hospital so soon after delivery. For the first couple of weeks you should certainly get off your feet for a while in the morning and again in the afternoon. Get to bed early at night. You will probably be up in the small hours feeding the baby for at least the first two or three weeks. In the beginning, do not have a lot of friends and relatives in to see you. They can run you ragged, in addition to exposing your household to a host of germs. If visitors are going to be a problem, just tell everybody your doctor says you cannot see any outsiders for a couple of weeks. Then you will not hurt anyone's feelings.

There is no reason why you should not go outdoors, even in cold weather. You have to expose yourself to the elements merely to get home. The same thing goes for the baby. He is a good deal tougher than you think. People did manage to raise large families in log cabins and covered wagons back in the good old days. If you walk through a cemetery, which dates from Colonial times, you will be shocked to see how many died in childhood, but those deaths were from infections like diphtheria and diarrhea, not from lack of central heating.

There is no reason not to climb stairs when you go home. If you go up and down stairs a few dozen times a day, you are not getting all the rest you should, but there is nothing specifically harmful about climbing the stairs. To save yourself steps, plan your activities so that once you are upstairs you stay for a while.

A daily tub bath is preferable to a shower. You do not have to worry about water getting up into the birth canal any more than you did during pregnancy. A warm soak is relaxing and will relieve any discomfort you may have from stitches or hemorrhoids.

Exercising after delivery will help to restore your youthful figure, but do not feel guilty if for some reason you do not get around to it. A few people enjoy exercising and a few are motivated to do it, but for most of us push-ups at 7 A.M. are sheer boredom. If you have been up at 5 A.M. feeding the baby, you will feel even less like calisthenics. To do any good, exercise must be done regularly. You have to exercise religiously every day for two or three months to accomplish anything noticeable. Going through the motions for a week or two is not worth the effort. In any case, if you are one of those stalwart souls who plan to exercise, wait until your baby is three or four weeks old. Your usual activities are enough exercise until then.

Since the abdominal and back muscles complement each other, exercises using these muscles are the ones you want to do. Bending down to touch your toes is a good one. Sit-ups are excellent. If you are really interested, there are several systems of exercises that have you working a little more each day, and you will find them both taxing and worthwhile.

Mothers about to go home from the hospital often ask whether it is all right to pick up their older children. Without specific medical advice to the contrary, there is no reason not to. It would not be good for you to go home and move the piano, but it will not hurt you to pick up your child. If you have a baby a couple of years old, the first thing he will want is to be picked up. He is going to be mighty glad to see you, so don't treat him as if he had smallpox. You must show him that you are still as much interested in him as you are in the new baby.

If you drive a car, it is quite all right to run short errands as soon as you are out of the hospital. You ought to be able to sit in a car as well as you can sit on a sofa. Wait three or four weeks before you plan any long trips. Traveling is exhausting, and you will not be up to it before then. Little babies are great travelers, especially if they are breast-fed. On a long trip, breast-feeding is infinitely more convenient than getting involved with formulas and bottles.

Your diet in the postpartum period should be similar to the one you were on in pregnancy. It should be well balanced and rich in protein. It is not necessary to restrict salt, as you did in pregnancy.

After childbirth wives usually want to know when it will be safe to resume sexual relations. You should wait until the vaginal flow (lochia) has ceased completely and the stitches are all healed. This usually takes four or five weeks. Many doctors advise their patients to wait until the postpartum exam, which usually is scheduled for six weeks after delivery. Because of the stitches, intercourse may be a little uncomfortable at first. This discomfort should not last long unless a very large incision was necessary at the time of delivery. Your chances of conceiving immediately after delivery are slight. If you are breast-feeding, these odds hold for the first two or three months. Nevertheless, it is possible to become pregnant even before the first period, because ovulation normally precedes menstruation by two weeks. Even though you are unlikely to become pregnant again at this time, you should certainly be taking precautions to prevent pregnancy. Most women find a new pregnancy and a new baby incompatible.

Mothers will sometimes ask how far apart they should space their children. There are so many factors involved that it is impossible to make any generalizations. Spacing of one and one-half to two and one-half years works out well for many families. Many mothers feel that if their children are close together they will be more companionable. There is at least some reason to believe, however, that more children suffer from being too close together than they do from being too far apart. Women who conceive again soon after delivery do not seem to suffer any ill effects in the subsequent pregnancy and delivery, but they will find that taking care of several young babies is much more taxing than producing them has been.

Most doctors want to examine their patients about six weeks after delivery to make sure everything is back to normal. By this time, the flow of lochia has ceased, and in many mothers who are not breast-feeding the first menstrual period after delivery will have occurred. The time of return of menses varies considerably. As a general rule, the first period comes four to six weeks after delivery and a little less than this after lactation has stopped. In perfectly normal women it is not unusual for the return to take twice as long. Many lactating mothers will begin to menstruate regularly after two or three months and will continue even though they nurse their babies for a number of months. The first menstrual period is likely to be considerably heavier and may last longer than usual; unless the flow gets heavier than twice normal, there is no cause for alarm.

At the time of the postpartum examination, it may be necessary for the doctor to cauterize the neck of the womb. This will be done if the cervix does not heal completely after delivery. Cauterization is usually done with an electric needle. It is not painful, but often the patient will feel a cramp as it is done. Following cauterization there is usually a heavy mucous discharge for ten to fourteen days.

The postpartum exam is an excellent time for you to discuss birth control measures with your doctor. If you need further assistance, call or write the Planned Parenthood center nearest you, or the Planned Parenthood Federation of America, 515 Madison Avenue, New York, New York 10022, which will refer you to a local clinic or specialist. If your doctor finds that everything has returned to normal, he will probably not have to see you again soon. It is an excellent idea, regardless of your age, to plan to see him every year for an internal examination and Pap test.

ARTHUR GORBACH, M.D.

CHAPTER ELEVEN

The Psychological Impact of New Parenthood

T HE INTENSE feelings early spring may arouse are evoked not only by the opening buds and the warming sunshine, but also by a bittersweet awareness that these pleasures are connected with the passage of time. So it is with the experience of becoming a mother for the first time. While offering possibilities of future gratification and emotional growth, the experience also reawakens barely conscious memories of the new parent's total life history. The stereotyped picture of the joyful mother with her first newborn does not begin to suggest the full range of the feelings and responses, both negative and positive, that are an integral part of this process. A one-dimensional view of new parenthood, displaying only the emotional fulfillment and the pleasures, may be superficially pleasing, but it will ignore or deny the complexity of feelings so characteristic of all profound human experiences.

We have become accustomed to thinking of certain periods in the life cycle of a person, for example adolescence, as developmental phases. We recognize these periods by the biological and psychological changes that mark them. The individual has reached a new step in maturation and must shift his life style to accommodate to a new level of functioning. Some of the emotional painfulness of adolescence, for instance, arises from the impact of these changes, which are only slowly resolved as the young person moves on to adulthood. Therese Benedek and others have pointed out that the process of becoming a parent is a developmental phase in the life history of the adult. It is a time of disequilibrium at all levels of experience. The man, once himself the dependent boy, is now for the first time the father. The woman, who has moved through many struggles with her own mother, is now herself a mother. If we accept the continuity of our past with the present, then the rich complexity of these changes can more readily be imagined.

The birth of a first baby begins an experience that is new to the parents both as individuals and as a marital pair. At the same time, it is continuous with all that has gone before in their individual and marital lives. Becoming a parent, therefore, involves more than meeting the needs of the newborn. Parenthood entails a life change experience for the parent. To adjust to this new reality, the parent must refocus his or her view of both the external world and also of the inner, psychic world. The parents already have had one major experience with adjustment of this sort when they shifted from being single persons to becoming marital partners. The simple act of signing one's name "Mrs. John J. Smith," for example, does not begin to suggest the levels of change through which a single woman must move to become a wife. Certain events are irreversible turning points in a life history. Parenthood is one such event. It demands significant change on many levels of one's life, and simultaneously holds out the promise of continued emotional growth.

In recent years, much attention has been given to the needs of the newborn, and somewhat less to the feelings and needs of the new mother. While the new mother must be viewed in relationship to her baby, as is done throughout much of this volume, she deserves to be understood as a woman undergoing the first impact of a major life change. As in most life experiences of significance, parenthood combines pleasure and fulfillment with anxiety and tension. If the various sources for such feelings are to be revealed, the experience of becoming a mother for the first time must be examined closely. What sometimes escapes notice is that not all of the mother's anxiety is related solely to her concerns about her baby. Women have personal aspirations and needs that are unrelated to motherhood and that may seem (and rightly so) to be threatened initially by the demands of the new baby.

Women come to motherhood with an infinite variety of prior emotional commitments. A woman may be deeply involved in her relationship with her husband, in the achievement of intellectual goals and professional status, in pursuing community activity, in the maintenance of personal beauty, in the development of a particular talent. Simultaneously, she may strongly wish to be a good mother to a longed-for baby. A woman who intends to maintain her career, for example, will face many new issues at the birth of a first child. While previously she enjoyed almost unlimited freedom to make commitments of her time and energy, she now deals with a drastically altered life situation. While pursuing her career, she must simultaneously meet the needs of her baby, satisfy her own desires to mother, and provide substitute care for when she is out of the home. While this can certainly be managed by many women, the changes involved may generate new problems and tensions.

The inevitable conflict between personal needs and the demands of mothering can be experienced with considerable intensity. One new mother, feeling the anxiety of this conflict, may intuitively tell herself that she will slowly work out a realignment of her commitments. Until she is ready to consider a long-range approach to safeguard her personal interests, she may settle for temporary activities that conflict least with the new tasks of mothering. As she becomes more familiar with the demands of mothering and with her own related feelings and needs, she will be more ready to consider the directions in which she might want to move. Another woman, feeling puzzled and guilty over her conflicted feelings, may begin to question her adequacy as a mother. Some women choose to deny the existence of any conflict and turn themselves toward their infants with a sense of total commitment. Other interests and involvements are not modified but relinquished. The danger in such a solution is that it may eventually lead to a lessening of the mother's gratifications as a human being.

In our culture the early days of motherhood are projected as idyllically happy ones in which all the mother's feelings are directed toward the baby. Psychiatry stresses that the early mother-infant relationship is vital to future mental health. This observation has been frequently misunderstood and misapplied. It does not mean that a good mother experiences neither ambivalence nor anxiety about mothering. There is a great deal of clinical evidence to the contrary. Many mothers who subsequently do a fine job of mothering have been preoccupied initially not only with concerns about their babies but also with concern about themselves. A woman quickly senses with her first baby that a totally new burden has entered her life. She may experience the baby as a threat to her own personal needs and desires and find that her very love for him intensifies this distressing feeling. She rightly senses conflict between her own aspirations as a person and the demands of motherhood. Some women, for example, may find that the curtailment of physical activity during hospitalization feels like an upsetting loss of personal freedom. Each woman brings a varied personal history and present life situation to bear on the process of becoming a mother. There are many pulls, stresses, and strains that arise out of the very complexity of womanhood. As Dr. Helene Deutsch says in *Psychology of Women,* "At least in our civilization, with its regulated births, woman has wide opportunities for making compromises between motherhood and her other, more personal needs, drives, and interests. As a result, there are as many variations in the psychology of motherhood as there are mothers."

Although we accept that spring must precede the full bloom of summer, we are frequently less responsive to the natural pace of human affairs. Women are sometimes profoundly disappointed because of their unrealistic expectations of how they will feel toward their newborn. One woman may anticipate motherhood with happy dreams of the intensity this love will have. Another may be aware of no special feeling during pregnancy and assume that love will arrive in full force along with the baby. What needs to be known is that maternal love—that altruistic, tender, highly personalized love of a mother for her child—does not arrive in full bloom. Maternal love develops slowly out of the feelings of concern that characterize the first weeks of being a mother. Our psychiatric emphasis on the early mother-infant relationship has made many young women highly aware of their first reactions to their babies. This somewhat artificial sensitivity has often opened the door to misconception or distortion.

There is great variation in how mothers initially feel about their newborns. As Helene Deutsch says in *Psychology of Women,* "Joy and pride on the one hand, disappointment on the other, are in conflict, and many motherly women admit later that they felt the child as alien and repulsive, and were conscious that their feelings were a mixture of joy, fear, and sometimes even a curious indifference." There is ample clinical evidence that a mother's feelings and responses to her infant shift and deepen. The sources for these changes are not only in the mother herself, but also in the gradual social responsiveness of the baby. As John Bowlby remarks in *Attachment and Loss,* there are "electrifying effects on a mother of seeing her baby's first social smile, and it seems to make her henceforth altogether more responsive to him. When she is tired and irritated with her infant, his smile disarms her; when she is feeding or otherwise caring for him, his smile is a reward and encouragement to her."

The fear of being inadequate to the tasks of mothering arises from the wellspring of a woman's feelings. A young woman who will go on to do a fine job of raising her baby often is troubled by considerable anxiety about her ability to be a good mother. This anxiety, touching two vital centers as it does, seems to be part of the psychic process of becoming a mother. She is anxious not only for the sake of her newborn, but for her own sake as well. For instance, a new mother faces many moments of uncertainty about how to decipher the crying of her newborn. If she can find or imagine any causes for the crying—the baby is hungry, wet, soiled, needing to be bubbled—then she can try to meet his needs. By involving herself in caring for him, she anticipates that she can make him comfortable. His crying, which is distressing to her, will then presumably stop. What happens, however, when the baby—as most newborns do—seems to be crying for no apparent reason at all? Some degree of anxiety is likely to be the mother's response. Not only does she feel that the well-being of her infant is momentarily in doubt, but she may also feel that her own longing to experience herself as a good mother is threatened. Although neither of these fears is justified by what is actually happening, they nevertheless do occur. Mothers have to tolerate such feelings and learn to master them gradually. If a woman is going to demand of herself that she exhibit total confidence in her mothering ability from the instant of birth on, she may end up being less able than others to tolerate this almost inevitable anxiety. Sometimes a woman interprets the presence of anxiety as a sign of her own inadequacy; instead, she should recognize it as part of the psychic experience of becoming and being a mother.

For most women motherhood becomes a development in counterpoint on two themes—the need to give and the need to be given to. Although these are familiar and continuous feelings in almost every adult life, there is a heightened interplay between them in the first weeks following childbirth. Most new mothers are intensely aware of an urge to give to their infants—to give time, attention, and love. The utter helplessness of the newborn and the woman's own maternal feelings combine to sustain the flow of giving. What is less obvious and frequently neglected is the mother's own need to be given to—to be given love, emotional support, and comfort. During the weeks following childbirth the new mother, whose body is recovering from the enormous physiological tasks of pregnancy and delivery, is indeed more physically dependent. The resulting fatigue in itself accounts for an increased need to be given to. There is also a psychic counterpart that arises as Therese Benedek says, because, "The mother . . . relives with her infant the pleasures and pain of infancy." It is as if the kettle that had been simmering on the back of the stove has now begun to boil. The early weeks of motherhood may loosen dim, half-forgotten memories of having *been* mothered. The mixture of feelings accompanying these memories is as varied as life itself, and the new mother may find the feelings simultaneously comforting and distressing. She may also experience a new longing to be closer to her own mother, whether or not such a reconciliation would be possible or even desirable for her. Frequently, old memories of past anger and resentment toward one's own mother are reawakened with this longing. The new mother may find herself struggling to form a new relationship with her own mother that is less conflicted and ambivalent. She may experience many such psychological tugs, as indeed she will throughout her lifetime, which are connected with old as well as new issues of giving and receiving. Only slowly does she work out for herself a balance between her needs and the needs of her infant and family. In the interim, she may have to tolerate (as she will many times again as a mother) some sense of uncertainty.

Researchers have found that many new mothers feel guilty about their increased sense of need—they equate this feeling with being an inadequate mother. Our emphasis on childbirth and infancy as natural processes has been misunderstood to mean that because they are natural they should therefore be free of conflict and difficulty. Our nuclear family system, in which each couple lives separately from the extended family of older parents and other relatives, makes it difficult in fact for the new mother to receive help. Very often the close relatives on both sides will be living in different sections of the country. Apart from chance assistance from neighbors, a young couple may have no one to count on but themselves and the professional advice they pay for. What often happens is that many new mothers turn to their husbands for greatly increased physical and emotional support.

A wife, caught up in the new demands of mothering her infant, may not recognize that her husband is dealing with problems related specifically to fatherhood. The earliest mother-infant relationship of holding and feeding (and especially breast-feeding) creates a physical unit from which the new father is excluded. For the time being the husband must step aside to some extent while the wife's interests focus on nurturing the baby. Not only does the mother have little energy with which to relate to her husband as she did before, but she simultaneously turns to him for increased help and understanding. Sometimes a wife, aware of her husband's isolation from physical intimacy with her and their newborn, may find ways of asking for help that minimize his exclusion. At the time he is receiving the least care and attention from his wife, the husband is called upon to be more giving and generous toward her. Under the thrust of these demands even the most loving husband may experience anxiety, anger, and ambivalence. The father, like the mother, experiences anxiety and conflict that arise, not directly from his concern for his wife and baby, but from his own need to take on for himself the new responsibility of being a father.

A marital relationship undergoes irreversible change with the arrival of a first baby. Sometimes both parents, busy with the new activities generated by the needs of the newborn, remain unaware of the profound changes occurring in their own marital relationship. Enriching and gratifying as parenthood is, it also takes a toll on the previous intimacy between husband and wife. No longer is there the exclusively one-to-one relationship between husband and wife, with all the possibilities of unlimited energy for intimacy, companionship, and shared activities. For both husband and wife this necessary change represents a real diminution of some aspects of the relationship that existed between them before the birth of the baby. Even with the gratifications of parenthood, both husband and wife, each in his own way, may experience a sense of considerable loss and deprivation.

Numerous parallels exist between the growth of a woman into a mother and the growth of a man into a father. Each has to expand his inner world to include a new dimension of relating, that of parent and child. The prototype of this relationship exists in each partner's past ties to his own parents. Each partner must slowly fuse his past with his current life situation, with all its strengths and weaknesses, in order to arrive at a sense of his own parenthood. The sweetheart and wife must also become a mother; the lover and husband must also become a father. There is continuity with the past, but there is also the disquieting pull of irreversible change. The directions of these fundamental changes are not always immediately apparent, and parents must slowly search out for themselves the appropriate clues within their own lives. The process of searching and learning that begins for a parent with his first child continues with many variations over a lifetime. That there will be some measure of anxiety, uncertainty, and pain is as inevitable in parenthood as in other aspects of living. There is also the promise of continued personal growth and profound gratification.

SHIRLEY STENDIG EHRLICH, M.S.W.

CHAPTER TWELVE

Parents Have Pasts

THE DESIRES and expectations of parents for their children are usually greater than they realize. These hopes are rooted in the parents' own experiences—in their joys and frustrations, their losses and deprivations, their beliefs and biases. It is self-evident that every parent has a history of this sort, but the extent to which that history will influence or perhaps govern the approach to parenthood is not so obvious. Often we have to do some digging to uncover the roots of these influences, and even then we may have trouble recognizing them.

But, some will ask, why bring up the past in our dealings with children, who represent the future? Why is it important to remind ourselves that the past is ever present?

It is important for a number of reasons. First, and perhaps most obvious, one should always try to be aware of *why* he is doing something. This is not to say that knowing why will always affect action, but if often helps. This is particularly true in our dealings with our children. A baby is experienced by his mother as part of her, as a unit, a oneness with her. The separation from the mother at delivery demonstrates that the new child is a separate physical being. Yet emotionally he is still often perceived as an extension of her, as though he is only *physically* on his own. Therefore, all the expectations of achievements and goals that the mother wishes for herself are assumed to be equally important for her child. And this is also true of the father. Much parental effort is aimed directly or indirectly at making the child continue in the life and spirit of his parents. Only slowly, and sometimes never, is the child seen as an individual in his own right.

Many of these expectations are revealed in the way parents react at the time of birth. There is usually at least some degree of joy or disappointment in regard to the sex of the baby. Next the parents decide whom the baby most resembles. Generally, these resemblances reflect the parents' wishes more accurately than they do the child's actual features.

Selection of the child's name offers the opportunity for a family to fulfill cherished dreams or to satisfy family obligations. Often a child is named for someone the parents would like to have been. A mother may have been clumsy as a child, turning to dreams about becoming a ballerina. She may name her child after a celebrated ballerina, hoping the child will have the grace that the mother felt she lacked. Children are frequently named after idealized family members to whom the parents wish to give new life. One father lost an uncle who had been a special friend to him during his childhood. The two had spent long hours doing scientific experiments. The birth of his first son gave him a chance to pay tribute to his uncle.

When a child is named for someone in the parents' past or present, feelings about the original person are bound to influence the parents' feelings toward the child. In naming his son after his favorite uncle, this particular father expressed the hope that his son would, in some way, fill the emptiness left by the loss. He wanted to do many of the same things with his son that his uncle did with him. Since the uncle was no longer alive, the father's memory of him gradually became distorted. His shortcomings were forgotten. Since the father's expectations for the son's performance in science were based on an idealized image of the lost uncle, they were impossible for the boy to meet. Both father and son became intensely frustrated. The father found himself unable to replace his lost uncle. The son was unable to please his father.

Finally, a new child is often made part of a religious tradition and is subjected to rituals with various meanings for the parents. There may be tensions and disagreements as well as pleasant associations surrounding these rituals. Raised in a religious family, a Jewish woman had always felt that she had been a disappointment to her parents by having been born a girl. She attempted to handle her feelings by dreaming of the day when she could present her parents with a grandson to be raised in the Jewish tradition. Her husband, also raised in a religious Jewish family, resented what he felt were pointless rituals. When this couple had a son there was friction over the ritual circumcision. Although the husband agreed to the religious ceremony, he felt afterward that the boy belonged to his wife, not to him. In his father's eyes, this child came to represent submission to his wife's pressures as well as his lifelong resentment toward his own parents for forcing their customs upon him. One can imagine the impact on a boy of being seen by his father as the embodiment of old wounds. With all of these factors coming into play so early in his life, there was little room left for the child's own individuality.

A vast variety of experiences contribute to the development of an individual's personality and shape him for parenthood. Critical among these experiences are the death of, or separation from, a loved one, frustrations of old ambitions, or changes in critical love relationships. A common statement by parents is, "I want my child to have all the things I never had." Thus, the newborn child gives new hope to old losses. The child's behavior, appearance, or mood may be seen by the parents in terms of the losses or deprivations that the parents wish to erase.

Long before parenthood, everyone makes private vows about how he will raise his children. Sometimes these vows represent a desire to treat the child the way the parents were treated. A parent may remember the generosity of his father who gladly responded to any reasonable request for money or material gifts. Now, when his own son asks for a new toy, the parent may feel very comfortable about simply giving it to him but may feel troubled if he is unable to meet the request.

On the other hand, there are *negative* vows, in which a parent is determined that he will *never* be like his own parent in a particular way. He has promised not to treat his children as he was treated. This kind of vow is often much more difficult to fulfill. Although he knows what he does not want to do, he has trouble knowing what to do instead. This is particularly true when it comes to handling angry feelings. For example, a father may swear he will never be ill-tempered like his own father. Even when his anger is justified, he may force himself to be unduly reasonable. It would be more natural for him to explode just as his father did. Often, despite good intentions, he finds himself losing his temper, doing just what was done to him. His anger may be appropriate, but it still troubles him. Sometimes his anger is truly out of proportion. At those times some of the resentment that he felt toward his temperamental father may be directed against his son, causing the boy to suffer in much the same way as he once did. The father senses that his anger is exaggerated and feels guilty and remorseful. The child is left feeling confused and angry when his well-meaning, ever-patient father becomes unpredictably aggressive.

Such psychological relics from the past make parents less flexible than they otherwise might be. Any form of rigidity that comes from un-settled conflicts is an obstacle to the enjoyment of parenthood. It prevents the parent from being tolerant or firm according to his mature judgment and intuitive understanding of his child.

Every parent has a system of values. One of life's more difficult goals is to try to pattern our everyday behavior as closely as possible to our principles and ideals. This struggle intensifies as we raise our children. For example, a parent may feel that honesty is a critical virtue. There are many aspects of his upbringing that might have led him to glorify honesty among human virtues. Perhaps as a child someone close to him had been dishonest and he was ashamed of it. As an adult he may be displeased by his own trouble in controlling the impulse to lie.

The child may suffer when a parent is displeased with him, when he feels that the child is not meeting his own standards. The father who values honesty above all else may not be able to resist the impulse to cheat the parking meter. When his child is not perfectly honest, he may unleash upon him this anger that he feels toward himself for his own lack of control. Whenever this child is honest, especially in a difficult situation, the parent will not accept it simply as expected behavior but will be extremely proud. On the other hand, he may be very harsh when his child lies. Innocent boasts and harmless fabrications, quite normal for a young child, may be seen by such a father as evidence that the child is becoming a malicious liar. He may respond without any humor to the child's exaggerations.

In another case, a woman had learned to embellish the truth because her exaggerations amused her parents. Because she has some problem with being truthful now, she may feel she has no business disciplining her daughter for lying. She may suppress her disapproval. The child is then confronted by a parent who seems displeased about something, but will not say what. This parent may take out her displeasure by punishing the child for some indiscretion other than lying. Let us say the mother is very punctual. She may not reprimand the child about lying but will be very harsh about any small lapse in the child's getting home on time.

In neither of the above examples does the child learn to deal constructively with the impulse to lie. The second child may fail to distinguish between wishful thinking and contrived lying. In the end she may lie like her mother; the conflict about honesty will have been transmitted from one generation to the next. The child is very likely to repeat the conflict in attempting to deal with her own children when *she* becomes a parent. How much better it would have been if the parent could have recognized her problem and simply admitted to the child that both of them have trouble being honest. The parent might even tell the child her own story about dishonesty—that she does lie occasionally and is bothered by it and that it is a problem they must both work on. Children have an uncanny sense about their parents' weaknesses. They are able to tolerate them far more easily when they are admitted openly; they recognize and loathe hypocrisy. For a parent to assume a "holier than thou" attitude almost always results in clouding over the real issues and stirring up resentment in the child.

Naturally it is not always easy to know when our past history is affecting current family life. Often our only clue is when we find ourselves repeatedly at loggerheads with a child on the same issue. It is upon such issues that unresolved conflicts from the past are likely to play.

All parents are anxious about their parental duties. Usually they are most anxious about those matters that were troublesome in their own childhoods. These anxieties may be related to specific issues, such as feeding, toilet training, separation, or self-control. One mother had endured strict toilet training as a child. She then found herself feeling panicky when her infant made a messy bowel movement or ate in a messy way. Her fears were conveyed to the child, who at first used messing as a weapon against his mother and later developed fears about messing similar to mother's.

Parents may experience more general anxiety about their parental roles. A mother who is still closely tied to her own mother will be eager to please her. In order to do so, the mother may find that she will have to do things in a way that conflicts with her own intuition or with her husband's wishes. In such a situation the child may find himself with divided loyalties.

There are instances in which a parent never had adequate parenting upon which to base her own behavior. It will be difficult for her to imagine how a parent might handle various situations since she has either no model or a poor one from her own childhood. She has the added burden of dealing with her feelings about what was lacking in her own childhood. For example, a woman who was orphaned at an early age was moved from foster home to foster home several times before she was ten. She had a sequence of foster mothers who did little beyond keeping her clothed and fed. When she became a mother, she had little trouble keeping an orderly house. Clothing was bought and cleaned. Meals were varied. However, in most instances when her daughter called upon her for sympathy or advice, the mother became frightened and angry. She had had no model on which to base this kind of mothering. When she did provide loving attention, she was occasionally struck with a feeling of jealousy for her daughter. She would think, "She's getting more than I ever did."

A parent's insecurity may be reflected in rigidly high standards for himself and his child. Priding himself on always doing things the "right way," such a parent may actually be very anxious about how he rates as a parent. Since children do not mature overnight, the perfectionist parent will find himself constantly frustrated by the difficulties in achieving his standards. He may blame himself, the child, or both for any failures or shortcomings. Anxiety about his role can also create in the parent a need to keep things under careful control. He may try to act big and strong to cover up his doubts about his own adequacy. The fact that there are several alternative ways of doing something may compound his doubts. He may be convinced things must be done one way—his way—if he is to cope with the situation. The child is likely to feel helpless in face of such inflexibility.

Most children are reared by two parents, but rarely do both parents' values and beliefs about children coincide completely. Sometimes such differences are resolved within the marriage so that a balance is achieved. Each parent can respect, or at least learn to tolerate, the partner's peculiarities. In this instance, the growing child can benefit from the differences; he will discover that there is more than one way to think or behave. Frequently, however, value conflicts arise that have not been or cannot be easily worked through. If the parents are able to observe and discuss the more troublesome differences, they may be able to prevent them from becoming destructive or confusing to the child. He should not feel torn between two warring parents.

Too often, however, differences in parental values are not dealt with openly. Even if the parents finally come to realize that they see things differently, they may be unwilling or unable to express their disagreement. They may think that it is important for them to avoid acknowledging differences in certain basic values, perhaps fearing that discussion will threaten the balance of power in the marriage.

Differences occur frequently in what each partner thinks is man's work and woman's work. Husbands and wives do not necessarily agree. For example, one couple disagreed about mealtime chores. When the wife was a child, all members of the family shared mealtime tasks.

Therefore she expected that her husband would help out as a matter of course. Her husband, however, was raised in a family that considered it demeaning for a man to be involved in domestic chores. He, therefore, saw his wife's wish to share chores as threatening to his masculinity, and found various ways to avoid doing household tasks. His wife was left feeling overburdened and resentful. Since the parents were unable to deal directly with their different views of the division of labor, their children became the focus of intense conflict. The wife, in exasperation, demanded that her son fill in for his father in helping around the house. The father in turn chided his son for being a sissy whenever he helped his mother with the dishes. It was not until the couple could bring themselves to discuss with each other how they came to their opinions that this potentially destructive tangle was unraveled.

Husband and wife may each depend upon the constant approval of the other. They may feel that any sharp disagreement represents a dangerous threat to the marriage. They strain to prevent or reduce friction. The inevitable annoyances that develop as their values or styles conflict are then often deflected onto the child. A wife fails to balance the checkbook accurately, the husband suppresses his annoyance and says, "It could happen to anyone." But when his third grader brings home a careless arithmetic paper, the father then reacts with sharp impatience. Their son becomes ashamed and guilty over his foolish mistakes—particularly if he feels both his parents are good at math. However, he may know about the checkbook and be very resentful because his mother is not punished for her carelessness.

Children make very convenient excuses. By their very existence they demand changes and adjustments in the life style of their parents. When a husband asks his wife to do something, she may not always want to do it. Her easiest way out may be to claim that she must do something for the child. A husband approaches his wife for sexual relations. Disinterested, she declines, saying that she has to prepare the baby's formula. If her husband is annoyed, he may feel angry at the child rather than at his wife. Why do mothers often use their children this way? It is an easy way to get out of something, and a mother may feel that no one will be the worse for it. But there are two frequent consequences: the father may either dislike the child for demanding the mother's attention, or he may resent his wife for electing to care for the child's needs rather than his needs. This resentment is often heightened if he typically took second place to a brother or sister in his own mother's attentions.

In reading about the subtle and often unconscious influences of parental history on child rearing, one may get the idea that the child is constantly subjected to the dangerous consequences of unreasonable child-rearing practices. None of the examples we have discussed would, in itself, be likely to do permanent harm to a child's development. In any case, there is much a parent is helpless to alter even if he does understand what is going on. A parent cannot always expect, in the intensity of the moment, to be aware of the historical influences in his treatment of his child. Some of these influences may never even rise to a level of consciousness. However, when he does know the root of his dilemma, he can use his own childhood experiences to help him raise his own children, and bring them closer to him rather than divide them from him.

Most of us have used the cliché, "When I was a child, we didn't . . ." We may also remember that if we complained of walking a mile to school, our parents replied they had walked five miles in rain, sleet, and snow. One-upmanship only serves to isolate the parent from his child. It is not a helpful kind of sharing.

There are ways a parent might usefully share with his child. Empathetic communication takes place when a parent lets his child know that "something like that once happened to me." He tells the child about an experience in his own life that gave him some of the same feelings that he sees the child attempting to handle. For instance, a mother may be aware that her older child is very competitive with his younger sister; she recalls that he deeply resented the new baby's arrival. She may remember that she also resented the birth of her own younger sister. Telling the child of these memories may help him to discover that he is not the only one who has ever had these feelings. Perhaps there is nothing so "bad" about them after all. He also learns that one can survive such feelings. He may even see that his mother and aunt are now good friends. Often when a parent shares with a child the way in which he handled the conflict, he provides a model that the child may elect to use in the current situation.

Another way to share one's life experience with a child is by acknowledging one's responsibility in creating the misunderstanding between himself and the child. A father buys his son a baseball glove. His son says it is not the right kind. Father blows up. Later, as he thinks about the issue, he realizes what was really at stake and decides to explain it to the boy. He had never done well at sports. He was uncoordinated. He never felt sure of himself about anything having to do with athletics—he was afraid the glove would not be right. Such honesty in a parent gets the child off the hook, and at the same time teaches him a more constructive way of handling criticism. The child will be freer to acknowledge his own errors and will feel less helpless in the face of people in authority. The parent is also helped to feel less guilty by having allowed the issue that really troubled him to come to the surface. The alternative is to allow these feelings of conflict to remain underground and to continue their destructive effect.

Certainly no adult ever resolves all his conflicts, nor is it necessary for him to do so in order to raise happy, healthy children. Human development is too complex and varied to pretend that there is any one right way to answer all of its problems. Looking to the past in the hope of finding answers for the present is only one among many skills a parent will need to employ. To hope that an adult could resolve all of his past history would be as unrealistic as the expectation that the child's life should be totally happy and without pain.

MARCIA H. CHASIN, ED.D.
RICHARD CHASIN, M.D.

PART FOUR

THE NEWBORN BABY

CHAPTER THIRTEEN

Heredity or Environment?

*A*T SOME point in her pregnancy every woman wonders what her child will be like. Will it be a boy or girl? Will it resemble either of its parents? How will it behave? Did the pregnancy leave any harmful effects? Will its behavior in early infancy be any indication of what it is to become?

Most of these questions go back to an age-old controversy about the influence of heredity and environment on the developing child. Primitive peoples who pondered the same questions tried to answer them in their mythologies. Universal concerns about the effects of the environment are also reflected in the superstitions and folkways by which parents try to protect the unborn child against harmful influences. As late as the last century many persons still believed that a woman who had seen a rabbit (hare) in pregnancy might produce a child with a cleft (hare) lip. Even today one sees pregnant women in rural America and Western Europe who wear amulets to ward off the evil eye or other malign influences.

In the sixteenth century some philosophers advanced elaborate arguments to establish at what precise moment the soul enters the human fetus. One school of physiology pictured the fetus as a tiny but completely formed human being (the *homunculus*) who entered the mother's womb in the male sperm and there simply marked time until it reached sufficient size to be born. This naïve explanation of fetal growth and development did not stand up against the systematic study of anatomy and physiology any better than the environmentalist view, but in its essence the philosophy of predeterminism survived well into the nineteenth century as a psychological doctrine that assumed that the child is ready-made and complete in all its faculties before it is born.

Advocates of either the extreme environmentalist or preformist positions have lost ground, yet the controversy goes on. Is environment or is heredity the major influence on the traits of the offspring? One might expect that by now the vast apparatus of modern science would have found the answers. Yet when we get down to the all-important details, the same debate still engages students of behavior. How completely determined at birth is the future course of development? To what extent are intelligence, temperament, appearance, and personality already fixed at birth? How much influence does the environment exert to bring about radical changes in young babies? It turns out that no collection of facts can resolve this issue because environment and heredity are only arbitrary distinctions about a single unitary developmental process.

To attempt here an explanation of all that is known or surmised about the genetic (inherited) influences on development would take us far afield, but we can sketch certain crude facts (necessarily oversimplified) to give some perspective. We know that forty-six microscopically visible, rod-shaped structures called *chromosomes* are to be found in each one of the millions of cells in the human body. These chromosomes carry the *genes,* which are the basic material for the transmission of inherited traits. In the past ten years, we have learned a great deal about the complex protein chemistry of these genes, but the ultimate meaning of these discoveries tends to fade when we try to apply our current knowledge to those aspects of human behavior with which parents are primarily concerned. Can we say that the genes have *caused* this or that specific trait in the fully formed infant? Usually not. On rare occasions we can say that a specific deviation from the expected norm in structure or behavior—that is, a variation from the pattern we see in the great majority of infants—is genetic in origin. However, it makes no sense to discuss genetic factors as if they alone were responsible for the enormously complicated patterns of structure and behavior that in sum compose an individual personality.

Some persons have blue eyes, others brown. In the last hundred years (see page 428), scientists have found a simple and quite consistent mathematical relation between the color of the eyes of married couples and the color of the eyes of their descendants. When a blue-eyed man and a brown-eyed woman have children, it is possible to predict on a statistical basis how many of their grandchildren (but not which ones) will have blue eyes and how many will have brown. The further along the line of descent we go the more involved the mathematics becomes, but the principle holds, or so we believe. Our observations on the transmission of eye color in families have been so consistent that we feel justified in regarding this physical characteristic as an inherited trait that follows a precise genetic law.

Our certainty about the genetic basis of eye color comes from a combination of facts. Eye color is a well-defined, clearly visible, and limited difference between individuals. We have no trouble separating the blue-eyed from the brown-eyed members of a family, and we can count how many are in each set. We have *numbers* to deal with when we talk about eye color, and numbers are the language of science. With somewhat less assurance we can assert a genetic basis for some other physical differences among individuals, the color of skin or hair, say, but the less specific the trait is the more complex the genetic relationship becomes, and the more difficult the task of deciphering the mechanisms of inheritance. It is also possible to speak of inheriting particular diseases such as phenylketonuria (PKU) or hemophilia. In certain instances it is even possible to demonstrate that a single gene is responsible for the transmission of a disease from parent to offspring. But how do we account for the fact that all normal babies are born with two arms, two legs, and one head? Is the "genetic determination" of those "traits" the same sort of process as the "genetic determination" of PKU or blue eyes? The formation of arms on the human embryo depends on much more than a single gene or a single set of genes, and it is impossible to identify a particular gene or set of genes as being responsible, since a host of interrelated factors, perhaps an uncountable number of them, must be involved. Some of these will have to do with specific genetic properties of particular chromosomes but these do not "cause" the formation of arms or legs. They interact with many other factors as parts of a more inclusive plan, one that establishes the properties of all living systems and fixes the direction and the boundaries of growth as well as limiting the uses to be made of experience.

For most of the attributes that make the human baby what it is we cannot point to any single gene and say, "This is responsible." The gene does not operate in splendid isolation. Generally, a gene produces its effect in relation to other genes on the same chromosome and genes on other chromosomes. Even in the cell, the fundamental building block of a human being, it is impossible to make a clear separation between heredity and environment. The cytoplasm (intracellular tissue) surrounding the nucleus is not associated primarily with genetic functions, but it does contain substances that influence the direction of development by mechanisms similar to the functions of the nuclear genes. Each cell in turn is surrounded by other cells that are part of that cell's environment and influence its functions. Groups of cells compose an organ, and the organ itself is influenced by other organs. The embryo made up of many interrelated organs is embedded in the wall of the mother's uterus and derives all its nutrient from the mother's bloodstream. Throughout the pregnancy, therefore, the survival of the fetus depends on the adequacy of the physiological environment. From the moment of conception to the moment of birth, heredity and environment contribute to development as inseparable factors. Although the distinction between heredity and environment may still be useful for some technical discussions, it is an artificial abstraction that has no direct reference to actual developmental processes.

Identical twins are often considered to be nature's experiment for demonstrating the pure effects of heredity, because both organisms by definition have the same chromosomal or genetic constitution. Yet even identical twins may be very different in appearance and behavior at birth.

Identical twins may, in fact, differ considerably in their birth weights; and such differences appear to be associated, at least in a statistical sense, with differences in the course of their respective psychological developments. Although we have no clear idea at present why birth weight should make any difference in the course of psychological development, we can be reasonably certain it is not due to differences in genetic makeup. When the single egg from which the twins come divides to make two separate organisms, the two embryos will be embedded in different regions of the uterus and their cords attached to different parts of the placenta. Hence, the twins will have different access to nutriment in the womb; in other words, they will be inhabiting different environments. At the moment of birth, one or the other of the twins must be born first, and it will prepare the way for its twin. Although it may experience difficulty during the birth process while widening the birth canal, its twin may be suffering some lack of oxygen while awaiting its turn. So despite their same genetic endowment, identical twins do undergo distinct experiences before, during, and after birth; and even in the earliest stages of development these different experiences help to make them into distinct individuals.

So it makes no sense to speak of *the* environment as if it were some well-defined feature that is sharply distinguishable from inheritance and remains constant throughout the individual's developmental life. But it is useful to make a first rough distinction between the *pre*natal and *post*natal environments of the infant. Let us think of the influence of the parental environment as limited to the provision of chemicals, nutriment, and oxygen to the cells and mechanical protection to the fetus—in other words, to maintenance of the minimal conditions necessary for the physiological growth and development of an embryo into a recognizable member of the human species. In the nine months of pregnancy the organism is not required to make delicate adjustments to the constant changes of our everyday physical world, but only to exist and grow in conformity to a built-in blueprint.

Immediately after birth the baby is bombarded with an infinite variety of novelties. This stimulating, specific new environment gives rise to the sensory impressions from which it will develop its knowledge of the world. To be sure, even in the mother's womb the fetus is not altogether isolated from the environment as we usually think of it. If the mother has been exposed to German measles in the first three months of pregnancy, if she has taken certain drugs or not been nourished adequately, the baby's development will be influenced, usually in a harmful direction. But the effects are almost always nonspecific and make themselves known only by their interference with normal development. As long as the prenatal environment remains relatively generous and neutral, the fetus will develop in a direction that is uniform for the species. Any individual differences noted at birth usually will be the expression of differences in genetic makeup collaborating with differences in the intrauterine environment.

Isolated experiments have suggested that babies can be "conditioned" before birth, more or less according to the methods outlined by the Russian physiologist Ivan Pavlov, who trained dogs to salivate in response to the ringing of a bell. For example, recent experimenters have reported using similar techniques to teach unborn infants to kick whenever they hear a particular sound through the walls of the mothers' abdomens. If these experiments could be corroborated more generally, we might have to modify our ideas about whether or not the prenatal environment can have a specific influence upon the unborn baby. In the same vein, there has been inconclusive speculation about the effects that the mother's emotional state can have on the unborn child. We know, for instance, that emotion can influence the hormone output of the mother's endocrine glands. We know also that major changes in the hormonal environment of the embryo can have a profound influence on the infant's behavior in later life. Since the mother's hormones can pass through the placenta to become part of the fetal environment, it is not unreasonable to speculate that they might have an indirect but specific effect on the behavior of the fetus. But in comparison to the radical changes that occur the instant a baby leaves the womb, these influences on the unborn are, as far as we know, of relatively minor importance—except, of course, in pathological situations.

From the state of comparative weightlessness provided by the amniotic fluid, the baby at birth passes almost instantaneously to a state where it must maintain its position against gravity. Now it must start breathing on its own and suck in order to feed. It is no longer protected against cold, or against noise and the painful knocks of the outside world. It must accommodate to constant change, which can at times be overwhelming. It is true that from the moment of conception the baby is subject to the effects of environment, but the process of birth represents an abrupt shift from a comparatively neutral environment to one making continual, and continually increasing, demands on it. How well equipped is it at birth to cope with this relentless external world?

Methodical observation of babies on a scientific scale to find out how they actually behave is a relatively recent undertaking. The first American to insist upon this approach to psychology was Dr. John B. Watson, founder of the Behaviorist school, who began his work at Johns Hopkins University around the time of World War I. He took the extreme position of picturing all human behavior as not much more than a mechanical response to external stimuli. Not many modern psychologists would accept this simple view, but Watson's influence has nevertheless been long lasting.

Until twenty years ago the prevailing picture of the baby (greatly influenced by Watson's original work) was an amorphous, vegetative creature able to suck, cry, sleep, urinate, and defecate and exhibiting a few isolated reflexes, but otherwise unstructured and for the most part indifferent to everything except those events that relieved his immediate bodily tensions. This view implied that the baby was not much more than an empty receptacle, whose development would depend almost entirely on the stimulus it received from its environment. In this scheme of things every act of a parent involving the baby was of vital importance because it was thought that parental actions and influences were filling the empty receptacle and thereby establishing the character and personality of the child.

Nowadays, our picture of the infant is quite different. The theoretical inferences that Sigmund Freud drew from his studies of adult psychiatric patients gave us a new conception of the psychology of the young organism. Anna Freud's clinical observations and the work of others along the same lines altered our view of the emotional development of young children. And from the meticulous studies of the Swiss biologist and psychologist Jean Piaget we have received a new interpretation of children's intellectual development. Empirical studies of the last two decades have taught us that the infant is remarkably well organized at birth, and not merely with respect to the reflexes required for maintaining posture, eating, eliminating, sleeping, and withdrawing from a painful stimulation.

We now recognize that the baby is not a passive being, haphazardly registering whatever sense impressions the environment may offer. It is an active organism that selectively takes in and processes those environmental events that have meaning for it. In other words, the baby participates in its own development, and to some extent guides its course.

A mother feeding her baby for the first time will discover that it "roots"; that is, it turns its head to the side where its cheek or lip is touched, and moves with considerable accuracy toward the touching nipple or finger. She may also notice that her baby grasps a finger when its palm is pressed. From the first day infants can fix on a light and follow it with their head and eyes when it is moved in their field of vision. They will turn to a source of a sound when it is presented at the right or the left side but not when it is presented above or below the head. Whether a newborn infant responds in different ways to different word-sounds remains a matter of debate, but babies do seem to react with greater interest to such complex noises as the human voice than they do to pure tones. Likewise, infants stare longer at some visual patterns than others; if the duration of gaze is a criterion of interest, then infants seem to "prefer" relatively complex visual patterns to simple figures.

The perceptual capacities of the newborn are probably far greater than we have dared to believe. We can infer much from our studies of animals. For instance, although the eyes of a newborn kitten are closed, the animal is born with a very detailed network of neural connections that link particular cells in the retina (the receptor region of the eye) with the various brain centers, including the visual cortex. When the kitten opens its eyes for the first time, this complex visual apparatus is capable of analyzing geometric shapes into particular brain patterns. We can only conclude that kittens are born with the capacity for pattern recognition. By inference, it is reasonable to assume that the human infant is similarly capable of pattern recognition long before it can show us that it has learned to discriminate forms.

It is far from settled how many of the older child's capacities are learned, or how many of those capacities have been there all the time as latent abilities, awaiting only the appropriate environmental conditions to show themselves. The recognition of "size constancy" is an example of such latent abilities. This is the ability to perceive that two identical objects are of the same size even when they are presented at different distances from the eye. Though the closer object projects a larger image on the retina, we still know that the objects are of the same size. If our knowledge of the real world depended purely on sense impressions, we would always see the nearer of two identical objects as being larger than the more distant one. Because of our capacity for "size constancy" we are able to make the appropriate adjustments that take distance into account when judging size. Whether size constancy can be taught at any age is questionable. Certainly, it is difficult to imagine how a child learns it in the first several weeks—yet we know from experiment that normal infants have acquired size constancy by the end of the first month.

Linguists have pointed out that the capacity to learn a language cannot be taught, yet with very little in the way of specific instruction the child manages to learn at least the rudiments of the particular language of its environment. In consequence, linguists assume that the infant is born with latent capacities to decode and abstract some general features of the language from samples of speech it hears, and that from this very limited information it can put together new sentences of its own, which are grammatically correct. Whether the rules of language can be taught at an early age or not, at least the child exhibits a feeling for grammar long before anyone has ever taught it grammar.

On the strength of current observations, it is likely that the patterns of crying in the infant—the pitch, the intensity, the duration of the sound—vary with the provoking cause. We have no proof that the infant *intends* to vary its cries and no way at present of finding out what the baby does intend. Yet it can send out different kinds of vocal signals depending on its different discomforts. Among lower animals such systems of vocal communications are far better developed, and although their sounds are not a true language in the human sense, they nevertheless constitute a complex system of vocal communication. The human infant's signals are not so differentiated or specific.

Whether the human newborn does or does not smile is a question that resolves itself into an argument over definitions. Certainly, the grimace we call a smile appears in the newborn; indeed, it can be seen in premature infants born ten weeks before term. Moreover, the newborn's smile is not just a sign of "gas," as many persons (including some pediatricians) contend, since we can get the infant to smile more or less on order by making certain sounds. We cannot say whether the infant is "happy" when it smiles, for we have some reason to assume that the smile is at first not a signal of social recognition at all but the reflex response to certain stimulations. But to accept this limitation is not to deny that the mechanism for smiling is present at birth.

As we saw earlier in this chapter, babies can be "conditioned" even before birth. Further experiments have shown that newborn infants can "learn," that is, that they can be trained to respond consistently to signals when the signals are accompanied by "reinforcement." By certain modification of Pavlov's classic conditioning methods, young infants can be trained to turn their heads to the right side when they hear a pure tone or to the left side when they see a flashing light. They can also be trained to make refined visual discriminations. Such experiments make it clear that the newborn infant can indeed "learn" in a limited sense.

At the same time, we must remember that the range of response to which the infant can be conditioned is probably quite limited. Almost certainly, the psychologist's methods of conditioning are qualitatively different from the intellectual processes required for acquisition of language, formation of symbols, and mathematical abstraction. While the baby does "learn" through conditioning, it would be meaningless and mischievous to assert that with these techniques one can train the baby to do almost anything as long as the teaching materials are properly programmed, or to argue that the acquisition of intellectual skills is determined by the same "laws" of learning that have been found so successful in teaching rats to run mazes or seals to jump through hoops. The human baby is neither a black box nor a rat but a well-structured organism with its own ground plan, its own timetable of development, and its own style of acquiring knowledge about the real world.

A comprehensive list of things that babies can do on their own at birth, or can be made to do by environmental controls, would be much longer than the foregoing discussion suggests. The picture that emerges from even these few examples is a far cry from the concept of the helpless, amorphous organism that vegetates in blissful indifference to the world around it. Despite its apparent helplessness, the infant is actively engaged with its surroundings. It takes in sights, sounds, smells, and other sensations and organizes them into experiences with meanings; moreover, it sends out social signals that exert some control over the people who are biologically "programmed" or psychologically willing to respond.

Nevertheless, there are obviously many things that the young baby cannot do for itself. In many ways it is truly helpless, so that a generous and compliant environment must always be available if it is to survive. It is particularly helpless when it comes to changing the physical environment by its own motor action, and it of course must be nurtured for months and years before it can fend for itself. To be fed and kept clean and warm are its most immediate needs requiring outside attention. Since it is acutely sensitive to the novelties of the environment, it must also be protected against excessive stimulation. Yet it appears to thrive better when it is regularly exposed to a moderate amount of patterned stimulation. Keeping it too long in total isolation from the normal environment (as may sometimes happen in the sterile surroundings of a nursery or orphanage) may retard its development. The evidence on this point is fragmentary, and should not precipitate us into a hysterical program of overstimulating young babies. Our current impressions in this matter have been influenced by observations of premature infants who for good medical reasons were isolated from human contact for long periods of time. Premature infants were found to become more active and to gain weight faster when they were picked up and handled as often as possible and as early as good medical practice would permit.

Another source of evidence leading to the view that children need stimulation, particularly human stimulation, comes from clinical observations on institutionalized children and more recently from reports about children growing up in the hopeless circumstances of unrelieved poverty and social disorganization. Orphans, for instance, may receive the best physical care, but if it is given under sterile conditions where human contact is kept to a minimum, the children are much more susceptible to illness and infection. They gain weight more slowly and may even die from the effects of social isolation. In contrast, infants in the same institution who are picked up regularly by caretakers and exposed to the usual amount of human contact will develop normally. Certainly thriving or not thriving does not depend on a mysterious love substance that flows between mother and infant, and the critical factors can probably be rationalized in scientific terms. The fact remains that infants (and probably newborn infants) fare better when they are in close proximity to a caretaking person, who in most cases will be the mother. Up to six months or even beyond, it does not seem to matter very much whether this person is always the same individual. One caretaker can replace another without doing the infant great harm.

The experiences of the children brought up in the communal setting of the kibbutzim in Israel suggest that the constant presence of a single mothering figure (the ideal of our conception of the nuclear family) is not as essential to healthy development of the child as we have been led to believe. Within the well-defined social organization of the group nursery designed especially for the life of the kibbutz, children do prosper, even though they spend most of the day apart from their parents. Nevertheless, we should not draw unwarranted conclusions from these special conditions. Success in the case of the kibbutzim probably rests on the fact that the social context of the nursery is an integral part of the kibbutz society as a whole, not an idiosyncratic pattern of child rearing adopted by some individual families. The experience with children of the kibbutz cannot simply be lifted out of its context and applied in other, alien circumstances. In our society here in the United States, for instance, prolonged separation from her infant may be psychologically harmful for a mother because it may interfere with the development of her maternal intimacy with the child. As the person designated by our society to be the child's primary caretaker, she needs this sense of intimacy in its fullest development. Physical contact in the early months is just as important for the mother as for the child, because it helps to seal the bond that establishes the two as a mother-infant couple.

Many mothers wonder whether the newborn infant's individual characteristics will set the course for later development. Will the easygoing baby boy become an easygoing man? Must the very sensitive infant inevitably grow into an irritable adult? And will the infant who peers intently at everything crossing its visual field remain alert and inquisitive?

This question of the relationship between the traits of infancy and the traits of adulthood has goaded child psychologists to pursue the study of individual differences among babies. Their great hope, of course, is that one day they will be able to predict the future development of a child from its behavior in the early weeks of life. But if we exclude from consideration babies with major congenital malformations or birth injuries and infants who are unique in some other significant way, all the questions about the persistence of individual differences become extremely complex. No two infants have precisely the same experiences in the early years, and even if they did, the experiences would not have the same meaning for both children. Unless the children are siblings, they are not likely to be exposed to similar parents. We all know that siblings and even twins provoke consistently different reactions from their parents and hence will experience a different social feedback from the same parents. At every turn some new complication prevents us from predicting what course the adult personality will take. Usually we cannot hold one factor in the child's development constant while we study the effects of another factor in shaping the course of development. The outcome is always a mixture of the infant's initial condition (including its genetic endowment) , and the experience it undergoes in relation to a particular set of parents, in a particular social environment, at a particular time in history.

At present, we know too little about the processes of human change to be able to trace this or that trait of the adult back through a direct chain of cause and effect to the infant. Where we do find some simple correlations or parallel differences at birth and at five or twenty years, these similarities are usually quite superficial and, even then, may not represent direct developmental lines.

It is important to remember that the baby is not just a miniature edition of the adult. To say, "The child is father to the man," is really quite misleading, because development is more than a simple increase in weight, height, size, physical skills, and intellectual sophistication. A baby is just as much an organism in its own right as the adult, and in psychological terms the young infant is not *quantitatively inferior,* but qualitatively different from the adult. Some functions may be superficially similar in infancy and maturity, but they will surely be different in terms of the significance they have for the child and in terms of the way they fit together as parts of the total organism.

For an exaggerated example of the changes that biological organisms may undergo in their life cycles, consider the butterfly. In its early stages this organism is a caterpillar, which must crawl because it has no wings. Nothing about its shape or color or behavior suggests that the lowly caterpillar will one day become the butterfly. Yet caterpillar and butterfly are the same creature even though there probably is very little of the physical substance of the caterpillar that remains in the butterfly, and even less of its behavior. Still, we correctly insist upon regarding them biologically as only different forms of the same organism. In what sense, then, is "the child the father of the man"? No outward change as drastic as the metamorphosis of the caterpillar separates the baby from the child or the child from the adult, but less obvious changes of equal or greater magnitude occur in psychological development. Just as we cannot regard the baby as merely an adult in miniature, so conversely we cannot infer from the superficial similarities of infantile and adult behavior that the "immature" adult is merely a child. Child and man are distinct and qualitatively different organizations.

This is by no means to deny the possibility of consistent individual differences in the behavior of infant and adult. It is just that we have not yet found the proper level at which to specify such similarities. Experienced parents and professionals who observe babies in clinical practice often agree that very soon after birth babies seem to take on personalities that persist throughout life. There are studies also that seem to point to the persistence of certain differences among children into adolescence. At the lowest denominator it seems certain that female babies are feminine and boys are masculine long before they are aware of themselves or of the differences between the sexes. Some children seem to be born with what in an adult would be called a sense of humor; they are sly or coy, or they laugh a lot and seem to retain a happy disposition throughout childhood. Some from the start are outgoing and aggressive; others give the impression of being serious, even reflective. At present our methods are inadequate to prove or disprove the constancy of traits of personality, but we have no reason to doubt that temperamental differences may persist over time. It is important, however, to keep in mind that constancies or inconstancies in development do not depend on the child alone. The child's personality does not develop in a vacuum. The original source of a child's restlessness and hypersensitivity may be traced to genetic differences, stresses of birth, poor diet, or too much excitement, but the restless baby does not grow into an irritable child just because it was born that way. Its peculiarities have influenced its parents' response to it, and this response may well have aggravated its peculiarities. Under more soothing parents, the same baby might have become a quieter child, more tolerant of its environment.

Some traits that distinguish babies are probably so fixed in life that they are irreversible and relatively beyond reach of experience. Others are merely transitory phenomena that will drop away, no matter what happens to the child. Still other characteristics go through complex transformations and may even swing around into their opposites before they take on definitive forms. From the little we know about psychological development, it is impossible to say which traits will remain unchanged, which are transitory, which go through radical transformation, and which are most susceptible to change by parental intervention. Clearly the child does not travel a fixed path—it grows up in the context of its family, which will influence it as much as it influences them. Its personality at birth determines how its parents react to it; their reaction to it in turn influences it either to continue on the original path or to take a new direction. In order to predict successfully the outcome of any individual's development, we would have to separate and examine one by one all the complicated factors contributing to its personality, and then study how these factors interact; the gene in relation to the cell, the cell in relation to the organs, the organs in relation to the other organ systems, and finally the young infant in relation to its parents, its siblings, its society, and its time.

PETER WOLFF, M.D.

CHAPTER FOURTEEN

Examining the
Infant after Birth

*H*OW IS my baby? Is he OK?" This is the new parent's first question. For the majority of babies the answer is an unqualified yes. But how does the doctor arrive at this judgment so early? What exactly does he look for? How can he tell that the baby really is normal and in good health?

The medical assessment of a newborn begins with the history of the pregnancy. How the doctor will interpret his examination of the baby depends to some extent on what he knows about events that preceded the birth. He will want to know about previous pregnancies and deliveries. Were they normal, or was there some problem—excessive jaundice, miscarriage, or prematurity? What about the mother's health before conception and during pregnancy? Was she taking some special medication? Her blood type will be of interest to the doctor, and so will the gestational age of the baby—that is, the time between conception and birth. Did the baby arrive before or after the expected date of delivery?

The course of the pregnancy and the details of labor will be taken into account. Was there an unusual medical problem, such as eclampsia (see page 158) or preeclampsia? Was there bleeding at any point in the pregnancy? How long did labor last and what anesthesia, if any, did the mother receive? Did the baby come headfirst or was it a breech presentation (buttocks first) ? Were forceps used? How quickly did the baby take his first breath and cry? Was resuscitation necessary? The answers to all these questions provide instructive background for the doctor's interpretation of what he finds in his physical examination of the new baby.

The experienced observer can learn a great deal about the newborn simply by watching him "from the foot of the bed," as doctors say. He can form an impression of the newborn's degree of maturity. Immature babies characteristically are smaller and weigh less, have thinner skin with less underlying fat. During the first day or two many babies have bluish (cyanotic) fingers and toes from sluggish circulation. This is quite normal. The rest of the body will be pink and in a few days the fingers and toes will take on the same coloration.

The baby's breathing tells us quite a bit about him. The breathing pattern in newborns is peculiar. Normal babies may breathe as rapidly as sixty to seventy times a minute and then slow down to twenty or thirty times per minute, all within the space of two or three minutes. We would be hard pressed to say exactly how fast a baby should breathe. An important point is that the breathing should not be labored or require hard work. A quality of struggle characterizes the breathing of babies with pulmonary difficulties that is different from the normal rapid breathing. We listen for the vigor and quality of the baby's cry, which gives information about the infant's airway, vocal cords, and general strength. When stirred up, the baby is apt to move all four of his limbs and thus give the doctor an excellent opportunity to detect any impairments of motion. Crying brings the facial muscles into play, and gives us a chance to see if these move normally. When a baby cries vigorously, his color usually changes from pale pink to a beet red. When we pick him up, we get some impression of his general muscle tone, whether it is normal, increased, or decreased.

Many of the visible and audible signs and responses of the newborn undergo change over the first few days. Having been through the trying experience of birth, babies characteristically are somewhat "exhausted" for the next twenty-four to forty-eight hours. In many respects, they seem a bit disorganized. We expect to find them slightly off form in various aspects of behavior. The mother may find that her baby does not suck well and has only minimal interest in eating. The cry may be hushed and the general body tone a bit droopy. Medication taken by the mother in labor and delivery can affect the baby's appearance and behavior. The infant whose mother had anesthesia by gas may be sleepy, as are the babies whose mothers needed more than the usual amount of analgesic (pain-relieving) medication during labor. Pain-relieving medicines pass to the unborn baby by way of the placenta and exert the same sedative side effect on the infant as on the mother. The effects of the medicines often show in a general slowing of the baby's bodily function. Conversely, the less medicine the mother receives in labor the more likely the baby will be vigorous and alert, even in the first few days. Though this "sleepiness" of infants whose mothers have received analgesic medication has little long-run significance, there is no question that infant behavior, in the first few days at least, is affected.

At birth the skin is covered with a greasy coating known as *vernix.* Most comes off in the first bath given to the baby in the delivery room or nursery, but occasionally bits of the vernix remain behind the ears and in the folds of the buttocks. The skin of the normal newborn is coated with long hair known as *lanugo,* which characteristically disappears over the first few weeks. If some interference with the normal placental function has occurred, the baby may be undernourished and show some of the hallmarks of so-called dysmaturity (see page 341). Dysmatures have decreased body fat, absence of lanugo, dry cracked skin (often described as parchmentlike), long nails, and sometimes yellow green staining of the nails and the skin too. The nails may be long enough for a baby to scratch himself, even to the point of bleeding.

Forceps used in delivery may leave marks on the skin of the face and head, but these fade within several days. Small yellow or white spots are present on many babies' noses, cheeks, or chins. These are trapped collections of sebum, the secretion of the sebaceous glands of the skin. They disappear in a matter of weeks and need no attention.

Small faint red spots or blotches are often seen on the upper eyelids, at the nape of the neck, and in a diamond shape over the bridge of the nose and the forehead. Clusters of microscopic blood vessels (or capillaries) present in the immediate newborn period and early infancy account for these markings. Why they occur is a mystery. In the old days marks at the bottom of the neck were often called "stork bites." (The back of the neck was the part of the anatomy grasped by the beak of the mythical stork in transporting the infant to his new home.) "Stork bites" tend to blush and become darker when the baby cries. They disappear in time. The diamond-shaped spot on the forehead fades but may remain for life, barely visible except during emotional upsets, when it may flush.

The common *strawberry nevus,* discussed elsewhere (see page 354), often is not present in the newborn and does not show up until after the baby is home. Sometimes in the hospital we detect small bright red spots on the baby's skin that we can predict will blossom forth into a nevus upon leaving the hospital. A newborn's skin is likely to be very reactive. When a baby is excited by hunger or stimulated by the poking fingers of doctor or nurse, large red blotches or mottling may appear over the body, sometimes more prominently in one part than another. Curiously enough, the blotching may involve precisely one leg, one arm, and one-half of the trunk with a clear line of demarcation from the unaffected side. This interesting phenomenon goes under the name of the "harlequin (clown) sign" because of its resemblance to the traditional costume of the clown. We do not know exactly why babies are susceptible to this blotching or mottling when excited, but we think it has to do with immature regulation of flow of blood to the skin. The irregularities of coloration have no medical significance. In several months the exaggerated responses of the skin will usually disappear.

A very common rash seen after the first day or two and for the next several weeks is *erythematoxicum*. The characteristic spot of this rash (whose exact cause no one really knows) is a red blotch with a small white raised center. The rash appears more on the face, neck, and trunk than on the arms and legs and may come and go right before your eyes. Neither the cause nor the treatment of erythematoxicum is known. The condition is so transient and harmless that it has not stimulated much investigation. The rash of erythematoxicum somewhat resembles prickly heat, or heat rash.

Prickly heat is caused by trapped sweat that accumulates deep in the skin and sets up an inflammation. Heat rash can afflict all ages but is more common in babies. Heat rash manifests itself in small, often pinpoint, red blotches with slightly raised whitish centers. The rash characteristically comes and goes with great rapidity, present in the morning and gone by noon. It is one of the conditions best left alone. Putting powders and creams on the affected skin only aggravates the plugging of the sweat ducts and if anything tends to make the condition worse. Keeping the baby in a relatively cool environment will reduce heat rash but may not eliminate it altogether. Why a baby's skin should be more prone to plugging of the sweat ducts is not clear. There seems to be little that can be done for prevention, and parents have to learn to live with heat rash. Fortunately, the babies seem to be less troubled than the parents.

Jaundice, which is a complex topic (discussed in detail on pages 382–86), is a yellowish coloration of the skin and whites of the eyes. It is a common condition among the newborn and requires no treatment unless it appears in excessive degree.

The head of the newborn often shows the effects of passage through the birth canal. A certain amount of molding occurs, and the result may be a transient lopsidedness. Fortunately, the bones of the baby's skull are not tightly knit together as they are in adults, and the head can adapt without injury to the squeezing of the birth process. The separations of the bone (or sutures) can be felt by running the finger over the head. You will have the distinct impression of a small groove separating one bone from the other. In the middle of the head toward the front is the major (anterior) fontanel or soft spot. The covering is very tough, and you can press on it without fear of damage. As the baby grows older, the bone structure comes together to cover the space completely. For most infants this closure is accomplished somewhere between six months and one and one-half years. In the quiet baby, particularly when he is held in a sitting position, the soft spot appears slightly depressed. When the baby cries, the soft spot tends to tense up. If you look carefully, you may see the fontanel pulsate in rhythm with the pulse. This pulsing results from changes in the pressure of the cerebral spinal fluid, the liquid that surrounds the brain and spinal cord. Most babies also have a soft spot toward the back of the head, the posterior fontanel. It is much smaller than the major (or *anterior*) fontanel and closes rapidly after birth. In many infants it is barely detectable. The veins of the baby's head are prominent because they are closer to the surface in the newborn and because babies have less hair to cover them.

Swellings of the skin of the head are common during the first few days. The most usual kind results from constricting pressure on the scalp when the head passed through the birth canal. Recall that the baby's head does not pass instantaneously through the cervix; usually passage through the progressively dilating cervix extends over a period of hours. The considerable pressure on the skin may interfere with normal blood flow and cause swelling. This swelling of the scalp, known as *caput succedaneum,* persists for twenty-four to forty-eight hours. It has no special significance to the baby and is usually gone by the time he leaves the hospital. Occasionally, under the pressure of birth, a small blood vessel in the inner tissue lining next to the skull itself (*periosteum*) will burst, resulting in hemorrhage. A fluctuant swelling appears at the side of the head, known as cephalohematoma. A swelling due to hemorrhage may persist for several weeks following discharge from the hospital. It is occasionally accompanied by a small crack in the underlying skull. While the very thought of a hemorrhage on the head is a bit awesome, in actuality bleeding there has little more significance than a bruise anywhere else on the body.

The eyes of the newborn are fully formed at birth. In most nurseries they are bathed with antiseptic drops designed to kill any bacteria that might have been picked up in the passage through the birth canal. These drops cause the lids to swell. Irritation from the drops may bring a discharge from the eyes. This swelling, plus the natural resistance of babies to having their eyes poked at, makes complete examination of the eye in the first several days well-nigh impossible. But after the initial swelling subsides, we usually can get a fairly good glimpse of the eye if we move carefully. A trick of the trade is to catch the infant while he is sucking on a pacifier or bottle. Gentle pressure then can open the eyelids. In the newborn the white of the eye (*sclera*) often has small reddish blotches representing small hemorrhages produced by the pressure on the head in delivery. These hemorrhages clear in a week or so and have no significance. The color of the eye (more specifically of the *iris*) in the newborn is almost always blue. If there is to be a change of color it usually comes gradually. If possible, we try to examine the baby with an ophthalmoscope (a special adaptation of a flashlight with a peephole and magnifying lenses) in order to check the lens of the eye for opacity (*cataract*). We then try to inspect the *retina* (the sensing part of the eye), which lines the back of the globe. Often we are unable to see this in any great detail because rapid shifting of the baby's eyes frustrates our efforts to focus in. However, even a fleeting impression of a red color in the back of the globe (the *red reflex*) is a reassuring finding that the retina is probably OK.

Infants see much more than we used to think. An infant can fix on a red or soft yellow object dangled before his eyes and follow it. Shining a bright light in his eyes causes tight shutting of the lids. If we pick a baby up and hold him under his shoulders and spin about with him, his head will turn reflexively in the direction of the spin, and his eyes, in a rhythmical series of alternating fast and slow movements known as *nystagmus,* will try to keep up with the spin. On stopping short, the baby's eyes will continue the quick, rhythmical movements in the direction of spin for several seconds. These reactions depend on the complex system in ear and brain for sensing position. If we pull a baby up to a sitting position, his eyes tend to open much as the weighted eyes on the old china dolls. This response is called the "doll's eye" reflex.

We inspect the ears to see whether they are properly formed and whether the canals are in their proper place. Often vernix in a canal blocks inspection of an eardrum. As a result, we do not routinely look at the eardrums at the examination in the hospital. As for hearing, fully awake infants usually respond with a startle to a sudden loud noise.

Immediate repetition of the noise usually elicits no reaction. The infant seems able to "shut out" the painful stimulus as a kind of self-protection.

When checking the nose, we of course look at its general shape and configuration. Dust or powder causes sneezing just as in adults. We want to be sure the baby can breathe through both nostrils. There is a relatively unusual condition of blockage of the (nonvisible) back of the nostril known as *choanal atresia* (see pages 351–52). If both nasal passageways are affected, the baby can breathe only through his mouth and has no end of trouble when his mouth is plugged, say with a pacifier or a nipple. If this condition is suspected, we pass a small plastic or rubber tube into the nose in order to find any obstruction.

We always examine the mouth of a newborn. We check the lips, inspect the gums and palate for defects (see pages 355–56). Occasionally babies are born with teeth, which usually will be "extras" in addition to the standard primary and secondary teeth. If these teeth interfere with nursing or are loose and in danger of being aspirated, we remove them. Despite a rich folklore that has grown up about them, these teeth have no special meaning for the baby. While checking the mouth, we look at the tongue. The tip is joined to the floor of the mouth by a little band known as the *frenulum*. Sometimes the frenulum is quite short. In the past short frenula gave rise to the concept of being "tongue-tied," and accordingly the frenula of many babies were clipped. We pay much less attention to this phenomenon nowadays because we find that babies with short frenula rarely have problems with sucking or, later, with speaking.

The tongue of the newborn may develop a whitish coating that is the symptom of thrush (see page 165), but usually not before the third or fourth day of life. We try to examine the baby's throat but not always with success; babies simply will not stick out their tongues and say, "Ah."

We inspect the neck for lumps or masses. There are several kinds of congenital cysts, some of which may have sinuses or small openings in the skin. These are not serious problems but occasionally one does require surgical attention. We look at the sternocleidomastoid muscle for swelling that might suggest development of torticollis (see page 398). These muscles (one on each side) run from the mastoid bone of the skull just behind the ear down to the inner third of each collarbone; they come into play when we bend our heads forward and turn them to the side. Bruises of this muscle, possibly occurring in birth or even in utero, may produce a swelling and later a scarring and tightening, the condition known as torticollis. While looking at the neck, we inspect the position of the windpipe or trachea. Ordinarily this is in the middle of the neck, but in certain abnormalities of the lungs it may be tugged to one side. While inspecting the trachea, we also gain some impression of the size and position of the thyroid gland, at the lower part of the front of the neck.

In checking the chest we look for symmetry of movement. Unequal expansion and contraction of the two sides of the chest would suggest need for further investigation. Attached to the lowest point of the breastbone there is a separate, distinct little bone known as the *xiphoid process,* which may be particularly prominent and slightly pointed in the newborn. Parents sometimes wonder about prominent xiphoids. They have no special significance. We listen to the chest with a stethoscope to check on the movement of air in and out of the lungs and on the normality of the lungs themselves.

With the stethoscope we also listen to the heart. We note the rhythm and rate of the heartbeat, and listen to each of the heart sounds. We listen for any extra sounds, like murmurs, which are common in newborns. Evaluating murmurs at this age is tricky. We may hear a murmur at one examination and find it gone the next. Fifty percent or more of the murmurs heard in newborns are normal and do not signify heart disease. The explanation of these rapid fluctuations in the newborn's heart sounds is to be found in the radical reorganization of the blood circulation that occurs shortly after birth. In utero, blood almost completely bypasses the lungs, whereas with the newborn's first breath blood begins to circulate through them. This reversal of blood flow is accompanied by opening and closing of various channels within the heart and large blood vessels. The process of reorganization may not be complete for a few days. Blood flowing through partially opened or closed channels generates the noise that we call a murmur.

In checking a baby's circulation, we try to feel the pulses in the groins (called *femoral* pulses). The presence of these pulses, one on each side, reassures us that there are no constrictions of the major artery leading from the heart to the body, the *aorta.* Sometimes these pulses are difficult to feel in the newborn but can be detected later at the baby's first examination in the doctor's office. A generally pink appearance is evidence of proper oxygenation of the blood and normal heart performance.

A dusky color (*cyanosis*) alerts us to the possibility that the flow of blood within the heart may not be proceeding as it should be and that a further look is in order. We have already mentioned that a dusky coloration of the fingers and toes for the first day or two after birth is normal. Concern develops if the duskiness persists beyond this time, particularly if blueness is widespread, appearing not only on the hands and feet but on other parts of the body as well. In general, if a baby's heart is functioning normally at discharge from the hospital, chances are great that no problem will show up later. The babies who exhibit no clue as newborns but later show up with heart problems compose a small minority. In general, a clean bill of health for the heart at birth is very reassuring about the probability of heart disease in the future.

We always check the baby's abdomen. The stump of the umbilical cord is prominent and firmly attached to the umbilicus. The stump, which is shiny and moist for the first day or so, gradually shrivels up and falls off in about ten to twenty days. We gently feel (*palpate*) the belly. We ascertain the size and shape of the abdominal organs, the liver, spleen, kidneys. Unless enlarged, these organs are difficult to feel in the grown-up but in the newborn are readily felt. We check for abnormal masses, such as a kidney dilated and stretched because of a congenital obstruction. The bladder of the newborn baby can be felt when full of urine. It normally rises up much higher in the abdomen than in the adult. As the pelvis grows, the bladder remains low down and can no longer be felt in the abdomen. We always inspect the anus, but if stools are being passed normally we ordinarily do no more than just look at it.

We carefully examine the genitalia. We check the boy's penis and scrotum. The skin of the scrotum reflects the maturity of the baby. The normal rough appearance develops only in babies whose gestation was close to term. In prematures (see page 331) the scrotal skin is likely to be smooth and shiny. We check for the presence of the testes (see *undescended testes,* pages 392–94) . We look for hernias and hydroceles (see pages 362, 363, and 366) . We check the opening of the urethra, the thin inner tube that runs the length of the penis. The urethra should open at the tip of the penis. If the infant has not been circumcised, the foreskin may hide the urethral opening (or *meatus*) . To see a jet of urine when the baby voids reassures us that there is no obstruction. In the female we inspect both labia. In the first few days a discharge from the vagina with mucus or even tinges of blood is quite common and represents the effect of hormones transmitted from the mother prior to delivery.

The legs of the newborn are normally bowed from the curled-up position in the womb. The bowing persists until the child starts to walk, thus demonstrating the principle that the shape of a bone depends largely on the forces it sustains. Until the weight of walking is put on them, the legs remain bowed because nothing has stimulated them to change. The same point can be made about the infant's feet, which are likely to be turned inward as they were in utero. In-toeing is most often due to bowing of the legs and to temporary tightness of the muscles that turn the thighs inward. Walking and growth reverse these conditions, and the feet then tend to become properly aligned. The legs and feet of breech babies may show the special effects of their uterine position. The legs are likely to turn outward, with the kneecaps meeting. The feet may also turn outward. In time these positions revert to normal.

In our "foot of the bed" observation of the baby we notice any unusual position, weakness, or limitation of movement of the extremities. Any restriction of motion or malpositioning prompts us to examine the affected part more closely. We pay particular attention to the hips, looking for dislocation, partial or complete (see pages 364–66). Dislocation of the hip is a progressive condition, and success in treatment depends mainly on early recognition. We take careful note of the hip at all examinations in early infancy.

Examination of the baby's nervous system begins with observation of his general behavior, his movements while crying, the quality of his cry, the muscle tone present at rest and when supported, and his general responsiveness. The newborn is endowed with certain coordinated patterns of behavior known as reflexes, which operate from circuits within the so-called lower centers of the brain and have nothing to do with the processes of rational thought. The so-called higher brain centers, which are involved in intellectual activity, do not begin to manifest themselves for several weeks.

Appropriate stimulation will automatically elicit these reflex responses. The baby's automatic responses to bright light (see page 260) and loud noise (see pages 260–61) have been mentioned. If the cheek of a newborn is stroked he will (if sufficiently awake and hungry) turn his mouth toward the stroking object, be it a finger or, as nature intended, the nipple of his mother's breast. This reflex is known as the *rooting response*. It is completely automatic and serves to zero the baby in on his source of nutrition before he "knows" where food comes from. Sucking occurs by reflex if something touches the lips, the mucous membranes of the mouth, or the soft palate.

If the newborn is startled by a loud noise or sudden change of position, particularly one with an element of falling, his arms and legs respond in a characteristic way. They move symmetrically, first outward, then upward, and then inward. The hands first open and then clench tightly into a fist, as though the infant were trying to grasp a branch of a tree to prevent a fall. The legs go through a similar sequence of movements although less consistently. In addition the baby's head bends down and forward. This reflex is known as the startle or scare response and is named the *Moro reflex* after the neurologist who first wrote about it. (This response no doubt reflects our primate ancestry.)

If pressure is applied by a finger to the palms of the baby's hands or to the balls of his feet, the fingers and toes will curl in to "grasp" the pressing object. The hand grasp is often so strong that the infant can be lifted off the crib. This automatic response of hands and feet is known as the *grasp reflex*. If the soles of the feet are stroked, the foot will pull up, the toes fan out, and the large toe elevate. This response is known as the *Babinski reflex* (again for the neurologist who first described it) .

If you support a baby by holding him under the arms and move him across a tabletop with his feet just touching the surface, his legs will make movements that are very similar to walking. This response to movement and pressure of the feet is reflexive and not to be confused with early walking. When a baby so supported is moved to bring the upper part of his foot in contact with a horizontal bar, he will lift the foot up and over the obstacle. If his feet touch the surface of a tabletop, he may extend his legs as if trying to support himself in the standing position. If placed prone, the baby will make crawling movements and lift his head off the table or mattress. He may even lift himself up on his arms.

There is a group of hand-mouth reflexes that can be elicited by stroking the cheek or the palm of the hand. The baby roots toward the stroking finger. His arm flexes and he brings his hand to his mouth. He opens his mouth, puts in the fist, and begins to suck. Stimulating the baby at either end of the line, cheek or hand, leads to the same complex series of movements. (No doubt this reflex is a precursor of thumb sucking. Even in the newborn, nature has endowed the infant with a way to handle tension.)

Place a cloth across the nose of a baby and he will first attempt to mouth it. When this fails, he will twist his head and flail with both hands in an effort to remove it. (This reflex makes it all but impossible for a baby to smother in his bedding.) If one leg is stroked, the other leg will by reflex move over to push the stroking finger away. If the upper part of the body of the baby is stroked, the opposite hand comes over to push the stroking finger away. By reflex, babies withdraw from such painful stimuli as pinches or pinpricks.

If a baby's head is slowly turned to one side when he is lying either prone or supine, the body predictably will assume the attitude of a fencer. The arm on the side toward which the head was turned will be extended; the other arm will bend at the elbow; the legs will move in exactly the reverse pattern, one bent, the other extended. This response of the extremities to head turning is known as the *tonic neck reflex*. If the baby is suspended in air by his feet (not harmful or bothersome to the infant), he will first assume the fetal position, flexing both arms and legs and curling into an upside-down ball. Then he will extend his legs and arms outward and arch his back, like an athlete in a swan dive. A sudden temperature change in the environment (cooling) causes the baby to pull his arms and legs in to conserve heat before he begins to shiver. When he is pulled into a sitting position, the head does not just bob about. Even at birth some tone is evident, and there is an effort to control the position of the head. The newborn, however, is unable to sustain his head for any length of time and it soon flops to one side or the other.

These reflexes and others are part of the baby's equipment at birth. In a sense, they are forerunners of the voluntary act and demonstrate that the "circuits" for complex movements such as walking are laid down before actual walking begins. The reflexes persist until voluntary control develops to the point of taking over. Thus, when, at three months or so, a baby begins to reach and grasp objects, the grasp reflex disappears. When the baby becomes aware of his surroundings and visually searches out his bottle or his mother's breast, the rooting reflex vanishes. In the newborn, reflexes give us a clue concerning the normality of a baby's nervous system. These responses, however, like so many other aspects of the baby's behavior, may be somewhat sluggish for the first day or two after delivery.

We can also find clues concerning an infant's personality. For example, we see differences in behavior. One changes from sleep to wakefulness with a startled jump and cry, while another awakens gradually and begins quietly searching his environment. These subtle clues may help in anticipating or predicting the kind of child he will be. We should caution, however, that the art of predicting personality is itself in infancy, and the best we can hope for would be fleeting impressions. As far as being able to predict intelligence on the basis of the first examination in the hospital, we do not have much to offer in our present state of knowledge. We can say neither that a baby will be a genius nor that he will be a slow learner.

Most, but not all, congenital defects are apparent in the first few days. Some do not show up until after leaving the hospital. We have already mentioned that a small number of heart problems undoubtedly present at birth cannot be detected until later. A similar possibility applies to other systems of the body, for example, the urinary tract and the central nervous system. Even though the condition existed at birth, its presence was not accompanied by abnormalities detectable in the physical examination at that moment. But with the passage of time the defect makes its appearance known. Developmental aspects of behavior, such as talking and reasoning, obviously cannot be checked in the newborn because their appearance depends on growth and the process of maturing. We stress these limitations of the "first exam" not to suggest that a report of normal can mask serious problems, but rather to indicate that repeated examination throughout infancy is necessary.

RICHARD I. FEINBLOOM, M.D.

CHAPTER FIFTEEN

Your Baby's Doctor

*W*HILE IT is certainly true that untold millions of infants have grown to healthy manhood and womanhood without being seen by doctors except in sickness, nevertheless, the only way to be absolutely sure that your baby is thriving in his early years is to have him checked regularly. For these checks you can take the baby to a public well-baby clinic or to a physician of your own choosing, either a family doctor or a pediatrician. Pediatricians are doctors who have undergone specialized training in the care of children.

The usual practice is to take the baby for a check once a month in the early months and then at intervals of three months through the second year. At these regular visits the baby will be weighed and measured and thoroughly inspected for all the signs that indicate normal development. He will receive a series of inoculations (see pages 285–88) according to a schedule based on worldwide experience in the protection of children from communicable diseases. In a small minority of cases the examination will reveal some abnormality, either of development or disease. The doctor will prescribe treatment or make recommendations regarding further investigation of the condition. Both he and the nurse will answer the mother's questions, not just about medical matters, but about all the day-to-day problems of caring for an infant.

One great benefit from these regular visits is the security they can give to a young mother. When the doctor pronounces the infant to be in good health, he is at the same time relieving those groundless anxieties that trouble so many inexperienced parents. If the mother will ask questions, the regular visit can also be a source of education for her.

She should never be hesitant for fear of sounding ignorant or stupid. The doctor and his nurse will have heard almost all of the questions before and nine times out of ten will be understanding and sympathetic in their answers.

Finding a doctor to look after the baby may take some time but it should not be difficult. There is no problem, of course, if the family doctor attended the mother through pregnancy and delivery—he probably will undertake supervision of the baby's health too. Or the mother's obstetrician can recommend a pediatrician. The names of pediatricians can also be obtained at hospitals, from the local medical society, or from a medical school if there happens to be one in the community. In prepaid health care plans such as Kaiser, parents have the choice among the physicians on the staff.

Information about well-baby clinics or child health centers can be obtained at the hospital where the baby was delivered, from city or county health departments, or from the Visiting Nurse Association. The various social service agencies listed in telephone directories would either have information on such matters or would be able to refer you to a responsible source. A person living in a remote rural area could write to the state health department for information about visiting nurses, baby clinics, and health centers of various kinds.

Nowadays it is not unusual for an obstetrician to suggest that his pregnant patient pay a *prenatal* visit to the pediatrician or general practitioner she has in mind for her baby. This is not yet a general practice or perhaps even a common one, but in some sections of the United States more and more parents are taking advantage of the idea. Some weeks before the expected arrival of the baby, they telephone the pediatrician to introduce themselves and ask whether he will be able to take on the care of the baby, beginning while the mother and child are still at the hospital. If the pediatrician is one who encourages this approach, he will probably suggest a get-acquainted visit at his office. He will want to see not just the mother alone, but both parents.

Considering how important this professional relationship will be, it is unfortunate if not enough thought is given to the selection of a pediatrician. If the parents are newcomers in a town or city or even in a big city neighborhood, they often have little or no information to go on. The new mother may still be groggy from the delivery room when she is called upon to make the decision. Obviously, it would be better for all concerned if the parents could have a little time to study the decision, free of pressure, and in a relatively relaxed condition.

However highly recommended he may be, a pediatrician whom the parents do not know will be no more than a name to them. The needs and wishes of every family are different, and if they are not in large part satisfied in this important relationship, someone is going to be disappointed. Some parents want a doctor who has definite ideas about child rearing and is very strict in his dealings with parents. Others may be looking for more permissive supervision, which will give the parents alternatives to choose from. Doctors of both schools, the strict and the permissive, can be equally competent, but each extreme will call forth a different doctor-patient relationship. The parent who is comfortable with the strict doctor will squirm in frustration with a permissive one. It is important that parents feel at ease and be able to communicate their needs to the doctor, and they should be aware that they have the right to look for the one who seems to fit their family ways.

The prenatal get-acquainted visit is a good idea, if both parties recognize its exploratory nature. It will establish a solid working relationship between parents and pediatrician. It is important that the prospective father be present, if he agrees. Though his concerns are just as crucial, he too often is left out. If he can be put at ease and his anxieties moderately allayed, then the mother will have a staunch ally after the baby is born.

The father's questions may be quite different from the mother's but not necessarily of less importance. For instance, he may want to know about the doctor's fees. To parents soberly beginning to realize the extent of the responsibilities they are assuming, this is an important question. If the father's job requires him to be away from home a good deal, he may be concerned about the doctor's policy regarding home visits. Some fathers will wonder about their own role and need encouragement in providing strength and support for their wives. These are genuine and important questions.

For the parents, the purpose of this visit is to transform a mere name into a human being to whom they can communicate any question, no matter how ridiculous they may think it sounds. They want to know that the pediatrician will hear them out with respect for their dignity. And, of course, they want to know that their doctor is able and informed. On his part, the pediatrician is trying to sense the parents' greatest concerns. What is it that makes them most anxious? In what areas are they well informed; in what areas will the pediatrician need to add to their knowledge? What are their sources of strength? What past or future crises should the doctor reckon with?

Most important, the prenatal meeting takes place in the quiet, confidential privacy of the doctor's office. Most mothers will be obliged to share the hospital room with as many as three other women. No woman wants to expose the extent or the nature of her concerns in the hearing of her peers unless she knows them well, and even then only to a limited degree. A prenatal visit in the confines of a doctor's office is a more likely place than the open ward for the truly significant question to be raised or the important observation to be made.

What are some of the questions that parents *do* ask? And what, in turn, will the pediatrician ask the parents? A brief look at some typical questions and topics will illustrate the sort of concerns that are discussed between parents and pediatricians.

1. Will the baby be healthy?

Everyone expects that he will be—99 percent are! But in the minds of most mothers there is always an element of doubt. The sooner the mother's worries can be brought into the open the better. Discussing fear in a professional setting helps greatly to dissipate it.

2. What is the pediatrician's role at the hospital?

Generally he will check the baby on the first and next-to-last day. He will probably visit the mother sometime in the first twenty-four hours. Someone in the family (often the father) will of course have to notify the pediatrician of the baby's birth.

3. How does the pediatrician know that the baby is normal?

Parents often wonder what kind of tests (see page 255) the pediatrician does. They ask whether he checks for "retardation," for defective vision, or hearing. It is well-known, or should be, that many things babies do seem strange and yet are completely normal. Some babies exhibit jittery arm movements or quivering of the chin. Others may protrude the tongue now and then or even drool a great deal. Some babies may seem quite passive. Some may be slow in sitting or walking, while others may not speak for a long time. These are just a few examples of how a baby destined in fact to do well may at first seem slow.

It obviously will be helpful to the doctor to find out whether the possibility of retardation is a serious concern for the parents. In such cases, the doctor can be very reassuring if the parents are misinterpreting their child's seemingly slow development.

4. How often will the pediatrician see the baby?

The frequency of visits will vary from doctor to doctor, but the pediatrician usually wants to see a baby once a month for at least the first four to six months.

5. What is the charge for the pediatrician's care?

Parents are too timid in asking about fees. They have every right to ask. Impressed by the apparent affluence of a few physicians, they may be somewhat misinformed about the nature of fees, the extent of office overhead. They may compare fees between physicians, even though the time or type of service provided may be entirely different. One doctor may charge primarily for the examination; another may have higher fees for immunization. Parents should ask why one doctor prescribes drugs by trade name, another by the apparently cheaper generic or chemical name.

Parents may wish to disclose the nature of the father's occupation and the family's current stresses, financial or otherwise. A physician in private practice cannot have a different fee schedule for every family. Nevertheless, how a family functions financially is information that parents should be able to feel they can disclose to a physician in a confidential way. His dealings with them will be more realistic and therefore more effective if he sees the whole picture. Ways of paying the doctor are changing. More and more families will have health insurance to cover office visits. Others will be members of prepaid health care plans, such as Kaiser, and will not pay for each visit separately.

6. Will the pediatrician make house calls?

There is no rule to keep parents from asking whether or not a doctor makes home visits when they seem indicated by virtue of weather, absence of transportation, or a child's condition. In addition many ask, and should ask, Who covers for the pediatrician in his absence? Where should we go in case of an emergency?

7. How does the pediatrician feel about breast-feeding?

Parents rarely ask these days, at least not by the time they get to the pediatrician. By then the mother usually has made up her mind, with or without the support of the obstetrician. Nowadays, many pediatricians, perhaps most, do not feel it is for them to decide. It should be a personal decision on the part of the mother, unhampered by doctor, dogma, or well-meaning friend or relative. Yet it is the pediatrician's responsibility to present the facts, put the myths to rest, and having determined what the mother clearly wants to do, to support her completely in her intention. The subject obviously is worthy of discussion and encouragement, but not under the pressure of persuasion or the menace of guilt.

The argument on this subject of feeding focuses too often on the baby's needs. The modern belief has been that physically the infant will do just as well on the bottle as on the breast. From the mother's point of view, however, it must be pointed out that the capacity to breast-feed indisputably is inborn, and is potentially a source of great satisfaction to the mother—if she desires to do it.

If the mother decides upon bottle feeding, she may wish at this time to ask the doctor whether he has any choice of formula, what kinds of bottles he may recommend, how he feels about sterilization. When to begin giving solid food is another common question. Since there are a number of different views (see page 326–27), this question is best left to the individual situation. The astute physician would do well to at least hear out the mother's views. In some areas of medicine there cannot be room for compromise, but infant feeding is not one of these.

8. What is the family's health history?

Deserving of separate consideration is the question of the family's health. It stands out in the minds of many doctors as being one of the foremost concerns of new parents. They worry that their own real or supposed predispositions, ailments, or abnormalities may be passed on to the baby. In this connection allergies worry parents. If the doctor is aware of the parent's concern, if he can anticipate the anxiety, he may be able either to prevent the problem or at least to keep the parent from being overwhelmed. He can certainly discourage the notion that the mother is in any way responsible for the baby's discomfort. Many parents tend to interpret each transient problem of a new baby (a rash, for example) as reflecting some "family weakness." A physician who is tuned in to the family may be able to point out the normality, the transient nature of the problem, and be able to support the parents through a period of excessive worry.

Parents see so many defects in their own histories. They bring up asthma, colic, foot disorders, weak kidneys, stuttering, and so forth. The lists are long. Suffice to say, almost all of these problems can occur transiently in any child. Yet if any of the problems has been an important issue in a parent's own development (when he or she was young), the parent may overreact to signs or symptoms in the child. But if the issues can be raised ahead of time, doctor and parents may be able to deal with the problems more appropriately when they do occur.

What has been said about the parents' health history applies equally to information about their relatives. Pediatricians make it a point to ask about the health of a couple's parents, about siblings, and about other relatives.

The health of previous children, if the parents have any, is of striking importance. A few points are worth stressing. Parents are particularly sensitive in respect to the successes or failures of their management of health issues in previous children. It is true that the second time around is a good deal easier, but certain crises are hard to forget and parents fear to stumble again. A full review of past pregnancies will be very useful in preparing for subsequent crises. What was the delivery like? How did the baby seem at birth? Were there any problems in the newborn period?

It may be useful also to review the record of diseases, illnesses, or early deaths in the family. In regard to the infant these are rarely of any realistic concern. Yet insofar as parents are aware of them, they may be responsible for some degree of anxiety, which can be relieved by discussion. It cannot be emphasized too strongly that the specter of familial ill-health or apparent defects probably account for more unnecessary anxiety than the realistic health crises that a child faces.

9. What is the mother's current health status?

The mother may have some immediate, fairly crucial health problems. The pediatrician should know about them if he is to anticipate certain problems after the baby is born.

For example, what is the mother's blood type? (See page 151.) Is she Rh negative? If she has previous children, have they appeared jaundiced (see page 382) or yellow in color soon after birth? Did they require transfusion? Did the mother ever have a transfusion? These problems deserve consideration before the baby is born. The information is even more important today when we know how to prevent almost all the difficulties associated with the Rh problem.

Or, has the mother a tendency to diabetes? (See page 127.) This condition might require medication during her pregnancy, perhaps even an earlier delivery date. The infants of such mothers may be premature or require special attention. The pediatrician may be able to give wise counsel about these matters.

Has the mother other types of special health problems—some form of thyroid disease or asthma, for example, which may or may not require some type of medication? Is her history of previous pregnancy or birth passage such that she will require a Caesarean section?

While almost all deliveries are routine and undramatic, it is the duty of the physician to anticipate the unexpected and deal with it appropriately. The foresight of the pediatrician and the insights he may derive from the prenatal visit should together provide the kind of information that builds confidence in the ability of all concerned to cope with these problems if they should occur.

10. Will nursing help be necessary?

During the prenatal visit the doctor may suggest that the parents consider hiring a nurse at home after the baby is born. Sometimes such professional assistance is a great help in getting new mothers off to a good start. The new parents may need some indoctrination on how to get along with nurses, whose methods are occasionally hard to understand. (Needless to say, many a new mother has done well on her own, with the assistance of her husband or at least with his indulgence for a temporarily sloppy household or a cold hamburger.) Occasionally, the Visiting Nurse Association may be helpful. Grandparents may or may not be. The main point here is that the possibility of needing help should be considered ahead of time.

11. Does the mother desire rooming-in?

Rooming-in at the hospital might be discussed at the prenatal visit. Under this arrangement the baby stays with the mother, in her hospital room, and she does most of the caring for him and all the feeding. Some hospitals have *modified rooming-in;* the baby spends much of the time with the mother but is taken back to the nursery at intervals to give the mother a period of complete rest. This choice is best left to the parents with the advice of the obstetrician.

12. What are the parents' attitudes toward pregnancy?

At some time in the prenatal visit the pediatrician may find it important to deal with unrealistic attitudes about the pregnancy. Many pregnancies are unplanned, or at least seem so. The pregnancy may upset plans; it may alter young parents' hopes for more schooling; it may have occurred before they felt secure financially; the onset of pregnancy may have antedated marriage. These or similar circumstances may engender ill feeling between the parents or even direct ill feeling toward the unborn child. While such resentment is very regrettable, it is also understandable. Unexpressed resentment may possibly result in a pattern of abuse or overcompensation that is good for neither child nor parent. If such feelings can be discussed openly, the parents will be better able to view the situation objectively and, with as little guilt as possible, balance their own plans and ambitions with their baby's needs and healthy development.

13. What is the parents' background and family situation?

Besides the usual questions about the ages of the parents, their schooling, their former or present occupations, it helps to know, for instance, whether a mother was a former nurse. Her previous experience might make her too anxious or not anxious enough in the illnesses of her child. A teacher of the mentally retarded might be too sensitive to minor "slowness" in her baby's development. The whereabouts of grandparents may be relevant. Their presence may be supportive after the new baby is born. On the other hand, if they are in ill health or troubled, they may be a source of worry to the new parents, and the concern may interfere with smooth adjustment to life with the new baby.

14. What is the doctor's training and experience?

This is also the ideal time to question the doctor about his professional background, his degrees, training, and so forth. Parents might also ask at which hospitals he has admitting privileges. How does he feel about questions over the telephone? Does he keep a telephone answering hour during which he can always be reached? The prenatal visit is also a good time to meet the nurse in the office and to inquire about her role. Nurses are becoming more and more involved in child care, and we can expect this trend to accelerate in the future.

After the prenatal visit is over, the prospective parents should ask themselves whether they feel comfortable discussing their most urgent concerns with this particular doctor. Since many of the above problems have no one simple answer, the most important factor is the parents' relationship with the pediatrician. Is he willing to listen, and yet be firm and clear in his replies? Is he too dogmatic, or does he allow parents to choose between alternatives if they have a logical preference? The main issue is not whether to use Evenflo bottles or Playtex, but whether you are able to *raise the question*. A prenatal visit with the pediatrician not only enables parents to learn whether they will feel secure and satisfied with this doctor in the years ahead, but also gives them practice in the all-important skill of asking the right questions.

HOWARD S. KING, M.D.

CHAPTER SIXTEEN

Early Care

THE BABY'S EYES

*W*HEN WILL my baby see? This is one of the most frequent questions the pediatrician hears. Newborns react to
light, following it with their eyes, and in the second month babies
notice, or seem to notice, movement of objects (see pages 247 and 260).
But these are probably not the answers parents really are seeking. What
they want to know is, when will he see *me* and all the love I want to give
him?

This dawning of love, the perceptible change from helpless infant to
human baby, has to wait for maturation of the visual system. The baby
must develop binocular vision, the process of fusing the separate images
from two eyes into a single image, and acquire the ability to focus
according to the distance between the object and his eyes. Only when
he begins to see you, in the adult's sense of seeing, will you be able to
count on the look of recognition and the pleased smile of greeting.
Your baby will then become a person and begin to develop a real
personality. Apart from the clinical fact that his eyes follow a spot of
light, we have no way of knowing what the newborn or very young
infant actually sees, but once he has learned to focus, the change in his
relationship with his parents is quite remarkable. This process takes
time, perhaps as short as three months or as long as six or more.

Though she has carried her child within her for nine months, a
mother may find herself unable to relate fully to the baby or even to
make his acquaintance. She should not feel guilty or frustrated. The
infant must respond before the parent can feel satisfied that her messages are getting across to him, and this response comes in full only

when baby and mother can look into each other's eyes knowing, somehow, that the other is seeing too. This period of early development may be even harder for fathers. Though he may help his wife by feeding, changing, and dressing the baby from time to time, the young father probably has to push himself a bit to produce a continual overflow of warm affection for a creature that does no more than eat, eliminate, sleep, and cry. All this will change at the first smile of recognition.

In a way, it may be somewhat of a blessing that the baby does not "see" for the first several months. This is the period of often agonized trial and error, of experimentation with sleeping schedules, formulas, and so forth. The baby is totally oblivious to our harried, even on occasion hostile, looks. His powers of perception, if we can call them that, are concentrated in his mouth. We have a period of grace in which to adapt to this new responsibility.

The eyes of the newborn sometimes show certain mild and temporary symptoms which can be of concern to parents:

1. From 30 to 50 percent of newborns exhibit a tiny spot of bleeding on the white of the eye. This will disappear in two to three weeks and has no significance.

2. Medication required by law to prevent infection (primarily gonorrheal infection) may cause considerable swelling around the eyes, sometimes enough to hide them entirely, and also a temporary discharge, which disappears by the fifth day. The silver nitrate of the medication causes the discharge.

3. A temporary plugging of a tear duct at the corner of the eye may cause an intermittent discharge. Your doctor will tell you how to deal with this condition, but usually no special attention is called for. Nevertheless, it is always a good idea to inform your doctor of any eye discharge, however minor.

4. While he is learning to focus, your baby may give the appearance of being cross-eyed. His lack of muscular coordination and control, together with the configuration of his features are responsible. Up to the age of five months this occasional crossing of the eyes has no significance.

In spite of all the crying he will do, your baby is not likely to produce tears before his fourth or fifth week of life; and since the majority of babies are born with "blue eyes," it may be months before you can be sure whether he will have mother's brown eyes or father's blue eyes (or, of course, vice versa) .

THE HEAD

Some distortion of the shape of the baby's head at birth is not at all unusual. In delivery the skull accommodates to the passage through the birth canal, and often the head emerges looking more like a football than a sphere. This distortion (or *molding*) is not cause for alarm. In from one to three weeks the head will regain its normal shape.

Curiously, though mothers are said to talk a good bit among themselves about distortions of the head, it is a subject they rarely bring up in their conversations with doctors. They do show concern about the *fontanel* and about the localized collections of blood that may form at the time of birth between the skull and scalp. These blood clots, known as *cephalohematomas,* are common and quite harmless. The clots may linger for three to four months but always disappear. They go away in the course of an intermediate process of hardening (or *calcification*), which may produce a bony lump standing out in prominent silhouette against the natural contour of the skull. In three to four months the lump blends in with the normal skull.

It should be emphasized that neither the distortion of head shape nor the collections of blood come about through anything either the mother or doctor has done. Nor do they in any way affect the infant's brain. You should not regard them as "damage." They have no significance for the infant's future.

The fontanel (see page 259) may remain open for a year. The time varies considerably from baby to baby. This soft spot is a source of worry to many parents, who think the head is vulnerable to injury until the skull is completely closed. Some parents are almost afraid to shampoo the baby's hair. Those fears are groundless. The "soft" spot is in fact an extremely tough fibrous covering.

The fontanel will be an area of special interest to your doctor if your baby should become ill, particularly when there is high fever. In the presence of infection the doctor will want to know whether the fontanel seems "full" or "tense." You have no need to worry about the doctor's routine interest in the fontanel at periodic examinations, but by all means *ask* if your concern has not been completely quieted.

The newborn's earlobes may be slightly folded down at birth, a minor and inconsequential deviation that comes from the position of the fetus in the womb. You can expect that by one or two months of age they will have returned to normal. The nose may be pushed to one side in the birth process, but with extremely rare exceptions, it will resume its proper place within a week or two.

CARE OF THE NAVEL

The skin at the base of the navel should be normal in color, not red. No discharge should come from the navel. If redness or discharge develop, let your doctor or nurse know. Inflammation around the navel signals infection, which, of course, should be reported at once to the doctor. Sometimes in the first three weeks (usually in the first) the stump of the umbilical cord falls off. A common practice is to dab the cord stump gently three or four times a day with cotton balls soaked with 70 percent alcohol. Whether such treatment is useful is not clear and we tend to recommend no special care other than keeping the area dry. Sponge bathe until the cord falls off, avoiding the stump. After the cord detaches, baths are in order. After bathing wipe the navel dry with sterile cotton and see that the top of the diaper is kept below the raw spot. A harmless small raw polyp within the navel after the cord has fallen off may be the cause of some bleeding, and the doctor may elect to cauterize it. After the cord has been detached, it used to be the practice to bind the baby's midriff tightly with a bellyband or (later on) to tape the navel with adhesive. This binding is no longer considered necessary or desirable.

In intrauterine life the abdominal wall is open below the navel. In most infants closure occurs prior to birth. In some, the opening persists and an umbilical hernia is said to be present. The defect closes in most cases by one year and almost certainly by age four or five. No treatment is necessary. (In the old days, people used to bind the navel with a band to flatten the sac.) Only rarely, in the largest defects that show no sign of closure, is surgery performed. The baby's strainings may push a small section of intestine through the opening. This protrusion causes the navel to puff outward like a small balloon. As the infant relaxes, the loop of intestine slips back into the abdomen and the sac of skin decompresses, like a balloon relieved of air. Even at its tensest, the sac will not break. Nor is it painful when distended. The sac usually bulges because a baby is crying, not because he is in pain. (Crying increases pressure in the abdominal cavity, thereby squeezing a loop of intestine through the wall defect into the sac.)

In the first few months of life the entire abdominal wall may appear quite protuberant. The distended abdomen is further evidence of the laxity of the wall at this stage. If the child is feeding with vigor, having regular bowel movements, and not regurgitating excessively, and if he seems alert and comfortable, the protuberant abdomen should cause no particular concern, assuming, of course, that he is undergoing the usual periodic examinations by a doctor. On the other hand, any sudden swelling in the groin or scrotum should be reported to the doctor immediately.

SKIN CARE

The newborn's skin tends to be dry and scaly. Since he has just come from spending nine months in a brine solution, this condition is not to be wondered at. But even if it should receive no special care beyond sponge bathing, this rough skin under natural conditions will soon become as smooth as . . . well, as smooth as a baby's bottom, to use a popular comparison. With one preventive exception aimed at diaper rash (of which most babies sooner or later have at least a touch), the newborn's epidermis can get along very well without special unguents, lotions, powders, or oils. This is not to say that infants do not enjoy being laved with oils and sprinkled with powder, only that oils and powders are not medical necessities. In fact, caking a baby with oil and powder may bring on or aggravate heat rash instead of preventing it or soothing it.

Until the cord falls off and the navel heals (that is, for the first couple of weeks), washing is usually confined to sponge bathing, with soap used only on the baby's bottom. A mild soap or cleansing lotion is satisfactory. Stronger soaps may be irritating and for normal skin they are not necessary.

Cradle cap, which looks like crusted, scaly skin, is not dried skin at all but dried oil from numerous tiny glands on the scalp. It is very common in infancy. The recommended treatment is vigorous massage, combing, and brushing, not soap and water. If the cradle cap does not clear up in a few weeks under this treatment, consult your doctor.

In the absence of cradle cap your initial washings of the scalp will be done with just warm water and a soft cloth. Later, say at three weeks, you can use soap on the scalp once or twice a week. Any of the baby shampoos that do not sting the eyes will do. For rinsing, wipe the scalp with the soft cloth and plain warm water two or three times. There is no need to soap the face. A transient rash from excessive sweating appears on the faces of many babies between a month and three months old. It almost always goes away by three months. When this rash is present, cleanse the face after a feeding by wiping very gently with cotton balls soaked in clear water.

In our society the almost universal skin problem of babies is, of course, diaper rash. Many remedies are offered, but it is useful to remember that the less we apply to a baby's skin the better off he is likely to be. In primitive tropical societies where few clothes if any are worn by small children, diaper rash is said to be nonexistent. Indeed, the very name of the affliction would suggest this possibility, and the quickest cure for it, weather and other circumstances permitting, is to let the baby go naked, his bottom exposed at all times to the air.

Since the conventions and conditions of our society demand the diaper, the best we can do is to try to prevent and to ameliorate its rash. To that end, we admit the one exception to our objections against application of nonspecific ointments in general. We suggest zinc oxide ointment (purchasable without prescription) applied to the buttocks and anal region at diaper changes to spread a protective, chemically inert blanket between the baby's skin and his urine and stools. (Zinc oxide is the main ingredient of a number of commercial preparations for baby's bottom.) The combination of two or three washings of the region every day and application of the zinc oxide is about as far as the mother can go in defending against diaper rash. Even with the best of care, the baby can have diaper rash, and it will take at least three or four days to heal. The mother can take consolation in knowing that diaper rash happens to everyone and is not a reflection on the quality of her care.

The rough redness of the skin in diaper rash is easy to recognize and there may be scattered pimples. If the pimples become pustules (that is, show whiteheads) or if the rash becomes quite angry looking, you should call the doctor. A medicated cream may be needed.

Rubber pants, because they hold in heat and shut out air, undoubtedly aggravate rashes, but most mothers find them all but essential. It probably is wise to avoid using rubber pants in the first three or four weeks of life. If the infant's skin is particularly susceptible to rash, use such pants only when absolutely necessary.

BREATHING

The noisy breathing of small babies frequently alarms parents. The infant's respiration in sleep may be loud enough to awaken a person in the same room. If he is thrashing about, he may pant like a fifty-year-old office worker running for a bus. At times he may sound as if he were in the throes of asthma. He may sneeze often and vigorously.

The parent frightened by these noises overlooks the fact that the nasal passages of a small baby are very narrow. A mere speck of dust can trigger a sneeze. Sucking in the necessary volume of air through the small openings sets up noise. The loudness of the baby's breathing is usually quite normal.

The asthmatic sound, which is extremely disquieting to a parent with a history of asthma, is usually heard after the infant has been feeding. This particular noise comes from the temporary lack of firm cartilage in the voice box and will be heard until the airway matures, perhaps as late as a year of age. Some doctors call it the "floppy epiglottis syndrome." The best analogy to explain this wheezinglike sound is that longtime favorite at New Year's Eve celebrations, the rolled-up paper pipe you blow on. The epiglottis is a thin structure, somewhat like a valve, that covers the opening to the larynx to keep out food or fluid. Fully developed, it is firm with cartilage, but in some quite normal babies it rolls up and flaps like the paper pipe, making a similar noise.

Feeding, bubbling, drooling, or a cold may accentuate this syndrome, but they do not cause it. Noisy breathing does not signify asthma or ill health, nor does it represent an inherited condition. It will pass.

SLEEPING POSITION

A number of orthopedists have suggested that minor foot problems of infancy can be prevented by controlling, to some extent, the baby's sleeping position. There is evidence that the occasional baby who is fretful unless he can spend most of the day and all the night on his stomach is rather more likely than others to become either pigeon-toed or flat-footed as he grows older.

The issue of sleeping position hardly seems a vital one, and there unquestionably are babies who appear to be able to sleep comfortably in only one position, usually on the stomach. If you have not had much success in switching the baby's sleeping position, you should not worry. If later on he develops some minor foot problem, who is to say that it would not have occurred anyway? Besides, a variety of simple ortho-pedic measures can be taken to correct problems of this sort. In the waking hours, however, it would make sense to place the baby for a while each day in the position opposite to his accustomed one.

The infant who is given to a single position may wake up and cry if he rolls over in his sleep. Parents can be drawn into a continuing situa-tion in which they get out of bed several times a night to turn the infant back into his usual position. If you should find yourself being awakened more than two or three times a night, try waiting a while be-fore you go to the rescue. Unless he is very hungry, the baby in time usually will fall asleep again in his new position.

Parents often ask whether there is any danger to the baby's back or legs from reclining in an infant seat in the early months or, later, from standing or stretching the legs or jouncing up and down while being held by the hands. The answer is no. The seat will not give him curva-ture of the spine, nor will the stretching exercises bow his legs if he is ready for them. If he seems happy in the seat and if his smiles and gurgles urge you on to help him in the standing and jouncing, he is ready.

CIRCUMCISION

A question that parents have to settle early is whether to have a baby boy circumcised. It is customary to perform this simple surgery while the newborn is still at the hospital, usually on his last day before going home. When circumcision is done as a ritual of the Jewish faith, it is performed on the eighth day of life.

In the natural state, the head of the penis is covered by a retractable sleeve of skin, called the *foreskin*. Circumcision is a surgical procedure in which this sleeve of skin is cut away. From start to finish, with the baby held frog-legged or strapped to a board, the operation takes about five minutes. The baby cries when the actual cutting is being done but shows no sign of discomfort afterward. Bleeding is easily controlled. For a dressing nothing more is needed than a Vaseline-impregnated gauze applied to the raw surface of the cut. If the diaper rubs against the cut, a few drops of blood may be left, but the cut heals rapidly. Nothing in the baby's behavior would suggest that the operation has been a trauma.

At the time of a boy's birth or before, it is advisable to be completely sure in your mind about whether or not to circumcise, since the operation when done later on in the child's life can be psychologically harmful. This is a very good reason for performing the operation soon after birth if it is to be done.

There are no compelling medical reasons for circumcising as a routine. Information on cancer of the head of the penis or of the female cervix is inconclusive. On the other hand, religious and aesthetic considerations (both highly personal matters) can dictate that the procedure be done. If a father and older brother are circumcised, this makes a strong argument for circumcising an infant just so he will not be different. However, the reverse is equally valid.

At birth, the foreskin, even when retracted, permits only the tip of the penis to have contact with the air. As time passes, the natural adhesions (or bands) that attach the underside of the foreskin to the glans dissolve, permitting greater and greater retractions. This developmental process is usually complete by the early teens, when the foreskin can be retracted completely. Washing is necessary only on the part of the penis that can comfortably be uncovered at any one time. With proper hygiene there is no need to be concerned about uncleanliness and proneness to infection.

IMMUNIZATION

In the first three months of life the only immunization shots the infant ordinarily receives are the *DPT*, which protects him against diphtheria, pertussis (whooping cough), and tetanus, and the *Trivalent OPV* against poliomyelitis (infantile paralysis). On the immunization schedule recommended by the Child and Family Health Division of the Children's Hospital Medical Center, he will receive the DPT and Trivalent OPV twice more in his first year and boosters at eighteen months and again before entering school. Thereafter boosters should be given at intervals for the rest of his life.

Any immunization is a deliberate stimulation of the body's defenses against a specific harmful germ. We know that many diseases occur only once in any one person's life. From this fact, observed over many years and among millions upon millions of people, the scientists who first developed vaccines concluded that when a person recovers from certain diseases he thereafter is immune to them. The basic idea of immunization is to set up these conditions artificially and safely, just as if the child (or adult, for that matter) were being infected by the harmful germ but without having to undergo the illness. The ideal immunization would stimulate the immunity without causing any symptom of sickness. Most of the vaccines we use do come close to this ideal but never quite achieve it. There are some vaccines with undesirable side effects, but, except for the very rare patient, these side effects are not nearly as serious as the disease that the vaccine has been developed to prevent.

The body responds to the vaccine much as it would to any foreign body; that is, it produces antibodies directed specifically against that foreign body. The antibodies react with or unite with the foreign substance (toxin, bacteria, or virus in this case) and inactivate either the germ or the germ's toxic product. By "tagging" the substance and sealing it off, the antibodies render it less harmful and mark it for removal from the system. And having once been produced to rescue the body from invasion by this specific foreign body, the antibodies thereafter remain on call, so to speak, to respond immediately to any new invasion by the same enemy. In other words, the body has organized a specific defense against a specific germ—it has become *immune*.

Many vaccines, besides stimulating the production of antibodies, also stimulate changes in the immunity of the individual cells of the body. A type of allergy develops such that mere contact with a microbe or its toxic product elicits a reaction capable of destroying the invader.

The vaccines for immunization are of two types, killed and live. Killed vaccines consist of concentrates of dead germs, which may be either bacteria or viruses, or of their toxic products. Certain bacteria produce chemical poisons that do the actual damage; these poisons are the *toxins*. The whooping cough vaccine, for instance, is made of the killed germs of the disease, whereas the diphtheria and tetanus vaccines are made of toxic products, not the bacteria themselves. The toxin is modified to stimulate immunity without causing the harmful effects of the unmodified toxin. In this condition it is called a *toxoid*.

Live vaccines consist of living viruses. These are harmless close relatives of the harmful viruses that cause full-blown disease. Because a close relationship exists between the two viruses, the body responds to both in the same way; exposed to either, it becomes immune. The difference is that whereas the harmful virus would cause a serious illness, the vaccine virus produces only a mild local reaction, sometimes with fever. Smallpox is a severe, disfiguring, even fatal disease. Smallpox vaccine (although no longer given routinely), in contrast, causes a single soon-healed sore, perhaps with low fever and mild discomfort. Yet both stimulate similar immunity. This is the crucial point. Another important difference is that vaccine viruses, in general, are not transmitted from person to person as disease viruses are.

For successful immunization it is not enough merely to stimulate production of antibody—a certain amount of the antibody must be produced. This amount is called the *protective level*. More than a single injection of certain vaccines (notably DPT) is required to stimulate development of the protective level of immunity. For others (notably the measles vaccine) one shot is enough. It seems likely that some vaccines (measles and mumps, for example) confer immunity for life. With others the immunity gradually wears off until it drops below the protective level. Then a *booster* injection is required to stimulate antibody production back up to the protective level. Immunization against tetanus and diphtheria requires regular boosters throughout the person's lifetime. Smallpox vaccination also had to be repeated when it was routinely given.

The following immunization schedule or a close variation thereof is standard for children in the United States.

The DPT, which is the only immunization that comes within the age limits set for this book, is given to infants by injection into the thigh. Children cry on being punctured, but most of them experience no ill effect from the shot. A small minority exhibit slight irritability and may have mild fever twelve or twenty-four hours after the inoculation. Occasionally there will be redness and some swelling at the site of the inoculation. These symptoms usually subside in a day or two. They should be reported to the doctor at the next checkup. He may lower the dose for the subsequent shots. Because whooping cough is mainly a disease of quite young children, boosters for this immunization are not given after the age of five.

We have gone into this subject at some length because immunization, which should be started in the infant's second or third month, is a lifetime undertaking. The parent's obligation is threefold: first, to see

(*Child and Family Health Division,*
The Children's Hospital Medical Center,
Boston. REVISED AUGUST, 1969.)

2–3 months	DPT (Diphtheria, Pertussis, Tetanus) and Trivalent OPV (Oral Polio Vaccine)
3–4 months	DPT and Trivalent OPV
4–5 months	DPT and Trivalent OPV
9–11 months	Tine (or other TB) test
12 months and above	Measles vaccine, mumps vaccine,* German measles vaccine†
18 months	DPT and Trivalent polio
1–2 years	Smallpox vaccination
2 years	Tine Test
3 years	Tine Test
4–5 years (*on entering school*)	DPT and Trivalent OPV
5 years	Tine test
6 years	Tine test, Smallpox revaccination (5 years postprimary)
8 years	Tine test
10–12 years	DT, Smallpox revaccination, Tine test
Thereafter	Smallpox revaccination every 10 years, DT every 10 years for life

* Procedure regarding mumps vaccine is not standardized. Usually given just before puberty to boys who have not had the disease.
† TB testing pregnancy is determined by risk of exposure.

that the child receives the full course of inoculations; second, to see that the record of the child's immunization is kept up to date and at hand for quick reference; and third, with older children, to do whatever possible to prepare the child psychologically so that the necessary injections will not be upsetting.

HOWARD S. KING, M.D.
RICHARD I. FEINBLOOM, M.D.

CHAPTER SEVENTEEN

Feeding

A. INTRODUCTION

Getting Started

IN A WORLD in which just about everything else has changed or is changing, milk remains the one best food for babies. This solution of sugar, protein, minerals, and vitamins in water answers most of the nutritional requirements for the first year of life.

The advances in the synthetic feeding of infants have given the modern mother a real alternative. In complete confidence that her baby will thrive whatever her choice, she may elect to nurse him, to feed him by formula, or to combine the two methods. Though the belief persists that human milk is "best for baby," science has failed so far either to sustain this contention or to disprove it. Some studies seeking links between the method of feeding and infant allergies have seemed to favor breast-feeding, but none of these findings is regarded as conclusive. For the family with a past record of allergies, particularly eczema, caution in the use of formulas based on cow's milk should be the rule. As of this writing, the prevailing impression in the medical profession seems to be that, on grounds of nutrition alone, a significant case cannot be made for one method of feeding versus another. (This generalization does not apply to primitive regions where ignorance of hygiene prevails; in those places breast-feeding is far safer.) The time may come when the balance will tip in favor of breast-feeding or bottle feeding in respect to nutrition and the baby's general physical health, but that day must await more comprehensive and conclusive study of the subject. Since we devote some space in a later section (see pages 302–304) to the psychological considerations involved in bottle- and breast-feeding, we will confine ourselves here to matters of nutrition and the feeding regimen, whether by bottle or breast.

At the Hospital

Regardless of his mother's plans for the long run, the infant born in a hospital ordinarily gets his first feeding from a bottle. Either twelve or twenty-four hours after birth, a nurse in the hospital nursery gives him a bottle of sugar water to make sure that he can suck and swallow without any difficulties. If all goes well, and in the overwhelming majority of cases it does, the next feeding will get him started on the regimen, at breast or by bottle, that will be followed for the next several months. This policy is changing and now more and more mothers who wish to nurse are given that opportunity right in the delivery room minutes after birth.

In their first three to five days of life, babies vary a good bit in appetite. Some from the very start are ravenous. More often, however, babies tend to be slow and seem uninterested in food for their first several days. They suck spasmodically and over twenty or thirty minutes may take as little as half an ounce. They often fall asleep. This pattern will be more noticeable and last longer if the mother has received more than the usual amounts of analgesic drugs in labor and delivery (see pages 184–85 and 301) . The drugs pass through the placenta and into the baby through the umbilical cord, and a baby will be slower than an adult to shake off the effects. One result of our appreciation of this phenomenon is to urge that less medication be given to mothers during labor. (See pages 197–98 on natural childbirth.)

The newborn baby's lack of interest in food worries a good many mothers, but there is no reason for concern. The baby comes into the world with enough extra fluid to tide him over for the first few days. Ordinarily a baby will lose some weight at first, and it may take a week to regain the weight he had at birth. This is one of nature's arrangements. In the first several days after delivery the breast-feeding mother produces only scant quantities of a thin, watery liquid rich in protein, called *colostrum*. Not until the third or fourth day does her real milk "come in," as the saying has it. And this is just the time, interestingly enough, when the baby's appetite perks up. It is good for the young mother to know these things in advance. Some familiarity with nature's operations can spare her worry, and worry at this time is something we can do without. Worry can interfere with the nursing mother's production of milk. Any questions about the baby's feeding (or any other source of worry, for that matter) should be taken up at once with the nurse or doctor. It is very important for the new mother to feel relaxed and comfortable with her child.

In the hospital, as at home, the ideal practice would be to feed the baby when he is hungry, not according to some arbitrary schedule. In this world, unfortunately, the ideal rarely is realized. For understandable practical reasons, hospitals see to it that babies are kept on a rigid schedule of a feeding every three or four hours. It inevitably happens that at times the baby will not be hungry when he is brought to the mother for breast or bottle, and at other times that he will have been hungry but has lost his appetite in a rage over having to wait for his food.

When hospital rules permit, the so-called rooming-in arrangement offers definite advantages in respect to feeding. Instead of staying in the central nursery, the baby is in the mother's room. She can do as much for him as her condition will allow but can call on the nursing staff for help. In this arrangement she has professional supervision at hand while she begins to learn the routines of caring for an infant. At the same time, she knows that if she becomes too tired or if she wants to store up energy before undertaking the full responsibility at home, she can always send the baby back to the nursery. Meanwhile, she has the baby with her and can feed him when his hunger peaks, not when the hospital timetable dictates.

Hunger Signs

Learning to recognize when a baby is hungry presents no problem. The hungry baby cries—loudly—and he "roots." Rooting is the searching movement the baby makes looking for something to suck on. If you touch a baby's cheek with your finger, he will swivel his head around and take your finger in his mouth. This is a reflex action, an automatic response to an environmental stimulus. Obviously, not all crying is a hunger signal, but if you eliminate all the other probable causes of discomfort without stopping the crying, you can be reasonably sure that it is time for your baby to eat.

Over the first week of his life the average baby feeds from six to ten times a day. From one week to one month of age the range is from six to eight times a day. By four to six months the number of feedings usually drops to four or five a day, and by one year it usually evens out at three. If you allow about one-half to three-quarters of an hour for each feeding, you can see that in the first months you are going to be spending a good portion of your own waking hours in feeding the baby.

At the hospital, if you have not had a rooming-in arrangement, you may have got the idea that your baby will stick to the four-hour schedule once you are home. Do not let yourself be disappointed. You should expect some irregularity. In the first few weeks it is not at all unusual for a baby to demand food every hour or two over several feedings and then perhaps go five hours between feedings. In time he will settle down to a more or less stable pattern, but at the start look for some irregularity. In general, introducing solid foods to stretch out the intervals between feedings has no effect, despite the popular impression, nor will they hasten the onset of sleeping through the night (see page 326). Early introduction of solids may also be related to obesity in infancy (see page 322).

On the average, babies take between two and three ounces per feeding in the first and second weeks, between four and five ounces for three weeks to two months, five to six ounces from two to three months, and six to seven ounces between three and four months. While there will be considerable variation from one feeding to the next, those numbers will give you at least a rough measure of what to expect. But remember, the numbers are *averages*. That is to say, the three-week-old who takes five ounces at one feeding and three at another is not straying very far from the expected average for his age. These variations hold also for breast-fed babies. Nursing mothers can tell by the feeling of their breasts and by the amount of time spent nursing whether the baby has taken more milk or less than his usual amount. One can get quite an accurate measure of the amount of milk taken at the breast by weighing the baby (plus diaper) before and after the feeding, but the information is hardly worth the trouble—unless, of course, you want to satisfy your curiosity.

Whether bottle- or breast-fed, your baby will himself be the best guide you can follow in judging when and how much to feed him. To state it as simply as possible, we suggest that you feed your baby when he is hungry and only when he is hungry, and that you give him enough to satisfy him. If you are breast-feeding, unusual hunger will stimulate extra production of milk (see page 309), and if you are bottle feeding, all you have to do is bring out another bottle. Do not let the baby's hunger dismay you. Even if he wants double the average for his age, let him have it. The answer to a hearty appetite is more milk. Making the formula "stronger" will have little effect. The baby will probably decrease his intake. As we said before, to begin giving solid foods early (see page 292) is not necessary. The best answer usually is more milk and a discussion of your infant's needs with your doctor or nurse.

Is it possible to overfeed a baby? Ordinarily the baby will prevent it. Once satisfied, he stops sucking. If you can persuade him to take more, he probably will spit it up when his stomach becomes too distended. On the other hand, it probably is possible to "fatten up" a baby by giving too rich a formula (see page 322). As best we can tell, the ideal formula has the same concentration of calories (20 calories per ounce) as human breast milk. Babies fed this formula usually do not gain excessive weight. There are always some who become quite chubby on this standard formula and on average amounts of milk but we do not know why. We are far from understanding the mechanism of appetite in all its implications. Regardless of what they are fed, some babies may become obese. All we can say is that a high-calorie diet will make a baby even more obese. Contrary to the old-fashioned view, obesity is not a desirable condition for babies. It is better to increase the quantity of milk and hold down the calories (see pages 292–93).

Getting on Schedule

Is it possible to stretch the time between feedings and accustom the baby to a regular and predictable pattern of eating? For the very young baby we do not recommend stretching the time between feedings unless he becomes hungry more often than every two hours and keeps it up over several successive feedings. This pattern would seem to lead into a vicious circle. At such frequent feedings the baby would eat less each time (or so it would be reasonable to suppose), his stomach would empty quicker, and the emptiness would stimulate fresh hunger sooner. To deal with this pattern, the mother might try the pacifier, holding and rocking the baby, or give a few sips of water (not more than an ounce) to take the edge off the hunger. If the feeding could be held off for forty-five minutes or an hour, the baby would eat more, his stomach would then take longer to empty, and hunger pangs would be postponed.

For obvious reasons it would seem particularly desirable to stretch the time between feedings at night. This situation is a bit different, however, from that of the baby who eats too often. Our problem here is not that the baby is hungry too often but that he wants to eat at night when his parents want to sleep. Our goal is to persuade the baby to adjust to the accepted pattern of sleeping through most of the night hours.

The first maneuver usually is to nudge the baby toward a feeding close to the parents' bedtime. Some parents try to stretch the time between afternoon feedings not only to have this one fall at bedtime but also to make the baby as hungry as possible. Some parents even awaken the baby to give him this final bottle for the night. If this works, fine and dandy, but do not be disappointed if it does not. The other tactic is to put the baby on solid foods early, on the theory that solids will satisfy hunger longer than milk does. Despite popular support for this school of thought, science seems to be against it. The subject has been studied rather carefully, and there is no evidence to support the theory that introduction of solids cuts the frequency of feedings or extends the hours of sleep at night. The average baby sleeps through somewhere between three and five months, if you are lucky, regardless of the kind of diet. For that matter, the first method is not conspicuously successful either. All these maneuvers have the drawback of interfering with the baby's natural rhythm. We believe that this natural rhythm should be reinforced, not broken. In time, his life will organize itself into an acceptable pattern. Trying to hasten the process rarely succeeds and may have unfortunate emotional consequences. The wise course is to accept the fact that as long as their children are young parents are going to lose some sleep.

Burping

On breast or bottle, babies tend to swallow air while feeding, and a large enough air bubble in the stomach will cause discomfort. To relieve the discomfort the baby must bring up the bubble. Sometimes the bubble will rise by its own buoyancy if you sit the baby up on your lap facing forward and rub or tap his back. Or you can support him, face down, on your shoulder and pat and rub his back. Success in either position is signaled by a belch, which may be of startling loudness. This operation is known as "burping" the baby. It is customary to burp the baby at least after a feeding and perhaps also in any long pauses in the course of the feeding. If nothing happens in five minutes of burping, it is all right to put the baby down unless he seems uncomfortable. In that case burp him again. Some doctors play down the need for burping. If left alone, the baby will bring up the air bubble by himself, they contend. They may be right, but burping has become so much a part of the ritual of having a baby that most mothers would feel deprived without it.

Air swallowing can be minimized with proper technique (see page 319). Disposable collapsible "bag" bottles are claimed to reduce air swallowing and probably do to some extent. Just how important a difference these make is not clear to us and we have no strong preference one way or another.

Sometimes babies spit up small quantities of milk while burping the air bubble. Spitting up of this sort should be viewed as an exaggerated burp and has no special significance. Remember, mere inches separate the baby's mouth and stomach. With every burp some quantity of milk undoubtedly comes up the food tube, and a little extra effort will lift it to the mouth and often into the nasal passages too. Regurgitated milk that has been in the stomach for even a few minutes may be curdled. Spitting up is not the same as the vomiting that accompanies illness. For one thing, the quantity brought up is much greater in vomiting. In spitting up it rarely runs over a couple of teaspoons though it may appear to be more.

Hiccuping often follows feedings, especially in very young infants. We do not view it as abnormal, nor need anything special be done about it. Occasionally, burping may stop it but we have known many babies who have hiccuped their way to sleep.

Spitting up may occur at a pause in the feeding or at almost any time after a feeding, even as long as half an hour afterward. You may find milk on the crib bedding near the baby's face. Spitting up rarely bothers babies, and they often sleep through it. If it occurs while you are holding the baby, gently turn him face down to let the regurgitated milk run out of his mouth and nose under the force of gravity. Sometimes a spitting-up baby will cough and gag. This reflex protects him from aspirating any of the milk into the lungs. The normal baby is in no danger from aspirating milk.

Some babies spit up and some do not, and why there should be this difference is a minor mystery. Some babies are harder than others to burp. Some babies spit up when they have been fed a bit more than they were ready to accept. When the baby seems satisfied and loses interest in the breast or bottle, he has had enough. If you are bottle feeding and the baby seems to be having difficulties with burping or spitting up, check the nipple. Too fast or too slow a flow of milk can lead to swallowing of air. Changing the formula, even to the point of thickening it with some cereal, may help with spitting up. Often keeping the baby in a semisitting position for twenty or thirty minutes after a feeding helps. Nevertheless, if your baby does spit up, you had better be prepared for the spitting up to continue. It is usually a feature of only the first few months, but it has been known to go on for over a year. The striking fact about these spitters-up is that they suffer no harm and do extremely well in general. In time the spitting up comes to an end.

We have said that a baby rarely spits up more than a teaspoon or two although it may look like more. If it should seem to you that the amount regurgitated is consistently greater than this over several feedings and if the baby then wants to feed again, you should call the doctor. You also should notify the doctor if over two successive feedings you notice a distinct falling off in the strength of the baby's sucking. (See page 344.)

The Need to Suck

To the parents worried about thumb-sucking, almost any explanation will suffice except the simple one that babies by nature need to suck. At the baby's stage of life thumb-sucking does not reflect inadequate nutrition or a physical or emotional insufficiency of sucking, nor does it foreshadow the development of a troublesome habit for the future. In his own time your child will quit. There is a drive toward growing up by imitating not only one's parents but also one's peers. Given half a chance, children will abandon an infantile habit unless they come to use it as a weapon against parental overreactions.

Some parents cannot abide the pacifier. The use of plastic for the ring-shaped handle and the circular guard that keeps the pacifier from slipping down the baby's throat is the only new thing about this dummy nipple, which goes back a fairly long way in history, in one form or other, and often has been prescribed for colic. Why should this gadget arouse such antagonism among some parents? Perhaps these persons have unpleasant memories of relatives or neighborhood children who clung to pacifiers long past the appropriate age. Or perhaps they see themselves having to pick up a wet pacifier and replace it every time it drops from baby's mouth, day or night. In any event, a good many parents reject out of hand any suggestion that a pacifier might reduce certain of their problems.

The baby's need to suck is probably most urgent in the first four months, and it is in this period that the pacifier can often be put to good use. Babies vary considerably in this regard. Some will reject the pacifier without qualification. Most will suck (on their hands, bedding, and so forth) whether you use one or not. If, an hour or so after an apparently satisfactory feeding, your baby seems unduly fussy or appears to be rooting about for something to eat or to find his thumb, you might consider the possibility that it is not actually food he is seeking but something to suck on. When these episodes recur regularly between feeding times, you might do well to try the pacifier. Its advocates maintain that pacified babies are less inclined to become thumb-suckers and that most babies give up the pacifier on their own at a quite early age without being subjected to any kind of duress or deprivation. Both assertions may be open to debate, but brief use of the pacifier in the early months is not likely to addict the baby, and it has been the experience of many, many parents and doctors that withdrawal of the pacifier at a relatively early age is not going to cause any serious emotional disturbance. By that time the vast majority of babies will have discovered their thumbs.

B. BREAST OR BOTTLE?

One decision you will have to make in motherhood is whether or not to breast-feed. Until this century the majority of mothers had little choice but to follow nature's method of nourishing babies. Now, thanks to formula (the magic word!), the situation is quite different. The woman of today has a choice between breast-feeding or bottle feeding or a combination of both.

Studies have shown that the percentage of women who breast-feed varies from region to region and according to socioeconomic class. Over the last few decades, however, in Europe as well as America, there has been one consistent trend that has overridden the local variations. A drastic reduction in breast-feeding is reported everywhere. In just ten years, for example, the rate for the entire United States dropped by a half. A similar rate of decline has been reported in British and French regional surveys. While no final count one way or the other exists, there is reason to guess that in our western society the formula bottle may now be nourishing almost as many infants as the breast does.

Yes, of course, some will say, and why not? If great-great-grandmother could have gone down the street for a six-pack of reliable canned baby formula, the switch from breast-feeding would have occurred long since. From as far back as we have records, at least from the time of the ancient Greeks, there has been a search for an adequate substitute for a mother's own milk. To avoid breast-feeding, women in favored social positions have hired (or bought) wet nurses to feed their babies. The wet nurse, a lactating woman with milk to spare, was a familiar figure in ancient Athens and Rome, in the London and Paris of the seventeenth and eighteenth centuries, in our own Colonial America. Her frequent appearances in the novels of Charles Dickens are a reflection of how numerous her kind must have been a hundred years ago. Fashionable women were not the only employers of wet nurses. Mothers without milk and the guardians of infants whose mothers died in childbirth also turned to the wet nurse for help.

Over the centuries, other substitutes, besides the wet nurse's milk, were tried but with much less success. The milk of goats and cows, mixtures of honey or sugar and water, various cereals ground and stirred with fluids into pap, foods prechewed by mothers or grandmothers—all these and more have nourished orphans, the infants of mothers without milk, or hungry babies in times of famine. In ancient Rome a research project was subsidized by the government to develop a satisfactory substitute for mother's milk, and the efforts of many individual physicians were applied to the problem from those days until our own time. One or two British physicians of the last century made international reputations with the formulas they concocted for babies.

Nevertheless, in spite of centuries of experimenting, development of the satisfactory substitute for mother's milk had to wait for our own era. Advanced techniques in chemical analysis were required. Respect for scientific methods had to be encouraged. When these conditions finally came about, science was able to produce an adequate formula for feeding babies. For the first time, there was a food other than mother's milk that could be given to the average normal baby in full confidence that it would not endanger his life.

Certainly, formula feeding has fitted in well with the times. The wet nurse has disappeared from our scene, but the baby-sitter is very much in evidence. Knowing that someone else is there to give baby his bottle, the new mother can in good conscience leave the home for longer periods of time. She may take up her social life again or even go back to her job. Baby will get his bottle just the same. He no longer requires her physical presence.

Formula feeding also has had appeal in the age of technology because it seems so scientific. We have been able to prescribe not only the kinds and amounts of nutrients in the bottle but also the times of feeding. Nevertheless, it is still impossible to duplicate fresh breast milk. The current formulas come very close, but there remains a significant difference. For instance, breast milk contains enzymes and antibodies (see page 303) not found in heat-treated cow's milk. To many parents and doctors, however, these shortcomings in the accepted formula mixtures seem less important than the positive side of the ledger. With formula the nutrients known to be of crucial importance—protein, carbohydrate, fat, certain vitamins—can be given to the baby in regulated amounts. In our technological age we insist upon measuring, weighing, sampling, charting, and wherever possible, substituting machines for human effort. Canned baby formula satisfies most of these specifications.

In thinking about our century's startling change in the feeding of babies, there are two possible avenues of approach. One can ask why so many mothers have given up breast-feeding for bottle feeding, or one can ask why, when bottle feeding has proved satisfactory, so many mothers still persist in breast-feeding. The second approach seems to promise more interesting answers, and it is the one Newton and Newton* have followed in their study of lactation as a phenomenon of human behavior. They find lactation sensitive to a variety of psychological influences that can be separated roughly into three classes. The first is the nursing mother's emotions and attitudes as an individual. The second is her emotions and attitudes as a member of a social group. The third is the interchange by which emotional and social factors influence her milk production.

The mother's performance in breast-feeding bears a close relationship to her attitudes toward breast-feeding, the Newtons found in a 1950 study they made of ninety-one mothers in the postpartum period. Mothers who had positive attitudes toward breast-feeding gave more milk than those whose attitudes were judged to be negative. The conclusions drawn from this original study of the Newtons have been confirmed by four subsequent studies by other investigators.

The data compiled by the Newtons in their study are of interest. When a mother with a favorable attitude toward breast-feeding was allowed to cuddle and suckle her infant as long as four or five hours a day, the baby at a feeding on the fourth day of life took, on the average, fifty-nine grams of milk. (In the metric system the gram is the unit of weight, a small fraction of an ounce.) In contrast, the baby of a mother with a negative attitude took only thirty-five grams of milk. Measurements such as these can be made very easily by weighing the baby, including diaper and clothing, before and after a feeding. The difference in weight is the amount of milk taken. In the case of the two classes of mothers in the Newton study the difference was significant, amounting to about one-third in favor of the baby of a mother with a positive attitude toward breast-feeding.

Breast-feeding has been inextricably linked with sex in the survival of the human race. Over countless thousands of years while humankind was developing a conscience, the physical pleasure to be derived from breast-feeding was the only incentive the mother had to suckle her young. Like coitus, nursing was a voluntary act. If it had not given pleasure enough, it would not have been performed often enough to insure continuance of the race.

A number of studies have confirmed the close alliance in the physiologic responses of coitus and lactation. In both suckling and sexual excitement uterine contractions occur, and so does erection of the nipples. Women have been observed to eject milk in sexual excitement. Stimulation of the breast, which is the essence of nursing, of course, is sufficient to bring some women to orgasm. Similar skin changes and changes of temperature have been observed in sexual intercourse and suckling.

Nursing women, according to Masters and Johnson,† show a higher level of interest in sex in their postpartum periods than do mothers who are not nursing. Individual nursing mothers report sexual stimulation from suckling, and as a group nursing mothers exhibit greater interest in a rapid return to sexual relations with their husbands.

Other studies, notably one concerning the attitudes of seven hundred English mothers toward breast-feeding, tend to confirm, though by a reverse implication, the existence of a link between breast-feeding and sexuality. Among many of the English mothers a preference for bottle feeding was expressed, and those women appeared to have feelings of aversion for nudity and sexuality. When Eva Salber and her associates studied patterns of breast-feeding among clinic patients, she found that many of the American mothers, on grounds of modesty, were repelled by the idea of breast-feeding. A relation between failure at breast-feeding and feelings of aversion has emerged from other studies. Most authorities are agreed that any woman who feels a very strong distaste for the idea of breast-feeding is not likely to be successful at it.

Since breast-feeding requires the cooperation of the baby as well as the mother, its success or failure will depend on the efficient or inefficient sucking and the responsiveness or lack of responsiveness of the infant. It has been established that in the first few days of life those qualities in the baby are related to the amount of medication the mother has received for labor and delivery. A study by T. Berry Brazelton, since confirmed by other research, showed that barbiturate medication in labor affected the baby's sucking up to the fifth day of life. On the first day he rated as only 30 percent effective the feedings of babies whose mothers were heavily medicated, against 65 percent for the babies of lightly medicated mothers. The differences for the second and third days were about as great, and it was not until the fourth day that heavily medicated babies were rated as 55 percent efficient in feeding. These and similar findings of recent years have had some influence on the obstetrician's attitude toward the use of certain drugs in labor.

If the baby is introduced to the bottle in his first ten days of life, his interest in nursing may diminish in comparison with the interest of babies who have been fed only at the breast. This finding seems to fit with the results of studies showing that supplementary bottle feeding may interfere with the mother's milk supply. Proponents of breast-feeding contend that a full milk supply comes only with the stimulation of sucking. Resort to supplementary feeding reduces sucking, which reduces stimulation. Reduction of stimulation reduces milk supply, and reduction of milk supply reduces baby's interest.

What decides a woman to breast-feed? A woman's attitude toward

breast-feeding is unquestionably linked to her role in society, as determined by geography, education, socioeconomic class, and the cultural
patterns of the particular peer group. Any number of surveys have
demonstrated statistically that breast-feeding varies from region to
region in the United States and from country to country elsewhere. For
example, whereas only 20 percent of the babies were still being breast-
fed when they left the hospital in Massachusetts, Maine, and Connecti-
cut in 1956, the figure for Georgia and a half dozen of the Western
states was over 50 percent. Marked national differences in breast-
feeding were found in a study of European countries.

Class differences count heavily in rates of breast-feeding in the
United States, England, Switzerland, and Sweden but not, for instance,
in France. In the United States at the present there is a higher rate of
breast-feeding among women with a college education than among
women with a high school education and the comparison holds also for
England. In a 1965 study in California, however, it was found that
while well-educated mothers were more inclined to start breast-feeding
they were not as likely as less-well-educated mothers to keep it up.

Among persons who have occasion to work with mothers scientifically
a strong suspicion exists that the attitudes of husbands, families, and
friends also have a significant influence on behavior in breast-feeding,
but Niles Newton has found the suspicion difficult to substantiate.
There is statistical evidence that the peer group has an influence on
whether a mother elects to breast-feed, and it seems likely that the
prevailing attitude among the doctors of a given community will have
an effect. For instance, a woman obstetrician in 1959 started a breast-
feeding program among her practice. In two years the rate went up
from 33 to 65 percent and 52 percent of them continued to breast-feed
for five months, as compared with only 15 percent prior to the program.
Lack of enthusiasm for breast-feeding among the medical community
was found in recent years in studies both in this country and in England, but the growing interest in preparation for childbirth and natural childbirth (see page 189) may prove to be a counterbalance, because physicians interested in natural childbirth are likely to promote
breast-feeding as well. Change is in the air and more and more young
women, most of them college educated, are returning to this ancient
method of feeding.

We think it helpful for mothers to know about the social and psychological factors influencing the decision to nurse and the likelihood of
success in the hope that with this understanding they can plot their own
course more effectively. For example, if you decide to nurse just

because "it's the thing to do" but deep down inside would rather not, chances are you are headed for trouble. Respect your own feelings; do not try to buck them. Our modern pace of living may not always support your interest in nursing. Friends, neighbors, and relatives may discourage you directly or by asking suggestive questions such as "Are you sure he's getting enough?" or "Why don't you just give him a bottle?" or, more frantically, "Do something, so I can get some sleep." Many young couples lack helping hands to relieve with some of the downright work of baby care. The new mother—home sore from the hospital, perhaps feeling a bit blue and unsure of her new role, over-sensitive to the mildest negative remark, tired from a seemingly endless number of feedings and with little chance to sleep herself, zealously committed to the ideals of nursing, and feeling that she is less of a woman if she cannot make the grade—may have some problems. Add to this a little financial insecurity, a move, some marital misunderstand-ing, and nursing—always so sensitive to emotional climate—may be an uphill struggle. Understand that these factors commonly operate and with your husband plan accordingly in a preventive way.

People debate endlessly the pros and cons of nursing. Only a very small percentage (well less than 1 percent) are physically incapable of nursing. Even the mother who wants to nurse but temporarily cannot because of physical illness or separation from her infant (for example, a small premature) can in most circumstances and with the right support from professionals maintain milk production by manual or mechanical expression until full nursing becomes possible. Enlightened hospitals are encouraging contact between mothers and prematures far earlier than was once the practice. Separations due to illness or unexpected trips need not stop nursing as long as milk production is maintained. In our affluent society there is, however, no overwhelming argument for or against breast-feeding. Babies thrive equally well, as far as we can tell, on human or prepared milks. There is no demonstrable difference in infections due to the kind of feeding offered (of course, the story is quite different in primitive unsanitary areas of the world, where nurs-ing has a clear advantage). It is true that human milk contains anti-bodies against some viruses and bacteria. These may explain some of the anti-infective qualities of human milk. However, in an environment in which, through high levels of sanitation and immunization, exposure to the microbes is eliminated, this quality of human milk takes on less importance. Regarding convenience, all bets are off. Some find nothing more convenient than carrying your own ready-made instant supply along with you, available at any time or place at the right temperature and without fuss of preparation. However, today's disposable ready-made bottles of formula, while contributing to the problems (and they are real) of solid waste disposal, cannot be said to be any less convenient if you can afford them. Regarding the shape and configuration of the female breast, an aesthetic object of considerable concern in our society, proper support with a well-fitting bra can guarantee return after nursing to previous loveliness. Put your husband's fears to rest.

Regarding development of allergies, there is fairly good evidence that infants on the older cow's milk formulas are more prone to eczema and other symptoms of allergy than are infants fed breast milk. These studies need to be repeated with the newer commercial formulas. Lacking this evidence and given a choice, we suggest breast-feeding babies who come from highly allergic families as a preventive measure.

The most unanswerable question is the difference in emotional well-being of the breast-fed versus bottle-fed infant. Here it seems that the kind of feeding chosen is of much less importance than the general quality of the relationship between parents and child, much of which is determined by the innate temperament of the baby. Pick the feeding mode that meets your needs most comfortably. Do not be a slave to ideology if you are unhappy with it deep down. Do not feel that you are neglecting your baby if for any of a variety of reasons you prefer not to nurse. Many successful nursing women report a surge of maternal warmth and closeness during nursing. They like the skin contact with their baby and the naturalness of the process. Others report, equally enthusiastically, similar feelings with bottle feeding. Who is to say which is better? And, remember, there is no rule that says you must either nurse or bottle feed exclusively. It is definitely possible to do both once your milk supply is well established. You are free to work out your own arrangement. Flexibility is the key.

If you do decide to nurse, you may want to contact the nearest branch of the La Leche League International (Franklin Park, Illinois 60131) for further breast-feeding advice.

Given the proper support and encouragement, many mothers who are "on the fence" in their decision can have a very positive experience in feeding by breast. We try to make it maximally possible for them to succeed by eliminating negative factors, such as rigid nursery schedules, and by encouraging a supportive climate free of tension and with knowledgeable, understanding husbands, doctors, and nurses. Setting into operation a positive momentum has a snowballing effect. Success breeds confidence and more success.

C. BREAST-FEEDING

The foregoing discussion, though not intended to be more than a brief sketch of some of the work done on the psychology and sociology of breast-feeding, has given enough facts to indicate that nursing a baby involves both psychological and bodily functions, operating together. In the language of medicine, psychosomatic (mind-body) mechanisms are brought into play (see below) .

The First Few Days

After delivery of a baby, whether or not nursing is planned, the female breasts (with exceptions) secrete a milky fluid called *colostrum*. Colostrum appears usually after the sixteenth week of gestation. This fluid is thicker and yellower than later milk and somewhat different chemically, but both colostrum and the later milk come from the mammary gland and are valuable for nourishment of the baby.

The biological changes that lead to secretion of milk are not known totally or exactly, but a decline in the levels of progesterone and estrogen (see page 215) appears to accompany a rise in the level of a pituitary hormone called *prolactin* or *luteotropin,* known as the *lactogenic hormone* from its influence on milk production. Prolactin activity is high in the blood of lactating women, and in certain complicated experiments prolactin has been shown to produce secretion and breast engorgement artificially.

The true milk appears from twenty-four to ninety-six hours after delivery, "coming in" so suddenly that many women are confident they could tell the exact moment. Others who have been breast-feeding from birth are not so sure, however, and it may be that the sensation of "coming in" is no more than a feeling that the breasts are too full.

The *letdown reflex* is the psychosomatic mechanism involved in expelling the milk that has been secreted in the mammary glands. This milk is stored in the *alveoli,* tiny sacs in the breast surrounded by special cells that contract as muscles do. The full process of milk expulsion can be described as follows: sucking stimulates nerves in the breast, and the impulses are carried to the pituitary gland at the base of the brain. A lobe of that gland releases a hormone called *oxytocin* (known in commercial preparation as Pitocin). The oxytocin reaches the breast by way of the bloodstream and acts on the contractile cells. These cells squeeze the milk out of the alveoli into large ducts leading to the nipple. The baby's sucking, of course, then empties the ducts. The letdown phase of this total process refers to the expulsion of the milk from the alveoli.

Other signs of the letdown reflex are strong contractions in the uterus. The oxytocin in the bloodstream acts on the uterine muscles as well as the tiny muscles in the breast. These uterine contractions, while sometimes painful at first, are a sign that the mother is letting down her milk and that breast feeding is working well. After several days the action of the oxytocin will have served its purpose. The uterus will have clamped down and become small. Thereafter there will be no uterine cramps or afterpains.

The letdown reflex is easily inhibited. When a mother is frightened or upset, she does not let down her milk as well. The milk is in the breast, but the baby cannot get it easily. In one experiment, inhibited mothers, after nursing their babies and being pumped by machine, received oxytocin by injection to set off the letdown reflex artificially. Mothers who had not had enough milk for their babies finally produced, and it was found that almost half their milk had not been available to the baby or the milking machine.

Fortunately, oxytocin can now be given by nasal spray instead of needle. Some doctors prescribe it to help mothers let down their milk when hospital routines disturb them or, later, when something at home upsets them. A tingling in the breast follows the squirt of spray and then milk begins to flow.

Newton and Newton have listed four symptoms of letdown:

1. The mother feels cramps or lower abdominal pain while nursing. (Oxytocin causes uterine contractions.)

2. Milk drips from the breast not being sucked. (Cell contractions stimulated by oxytocin are forcing milk from the alveoli.)

3. The breasts drip at expectation or sight of the baby. (The reflex has been established at previous feedings.)

4. Nipple pain ceases after the baby has sucked for a few seconds. (Sucking causes back pressure on the empty ducts; letdown fills the vacuum with milk, relieving the pressure and pain.)

It has been demonstrated experimentally that various distractions and actual physical pain can inhibit the letdown reflex in nursing mothers. Among mothers whose interest in breast-feeding is wavering from the start, the distractions of the usual hospital surroundings may be enough to inhibit the letdown reflex.

In pregnancy the breasts become larger in preparation for breast-feeding, and the nipples grow darker. Nature has provided for the nipples to keep themselves partially sterile. Sweat mixed with the oily secretions of the skin has an antibacterial action, and the nipple has the largest sweat glands of all. Further, newly secreted human milk is reported to have an antibacterial action. Thus, the nipples are ready for sucking whenever the baby needs comfort or food.

Although a few drops of fluid from the breast often appear in the latter days of pregnancy, the big boost in secretion comes at birth. The breasts begin to fill up. How long it takes for the milk supply to be ample for the baby depends on how much suckling is permitted during the first few days, as well as on individual factors. An experienced nursing mother who can have her baby in the room with her from birth and who suckles him for hours a day may find the baby gaining weight by the second day, especially if he is very vigorous and alert. But in the usual situation even with rooming-in, milk may not begin to appear in quantity until the third or fourth day. This delay is nothing to worry about. Babies are expected to lose some weight the first few days and most are a bit poky in the beginning, especially if they have received analgesic drugs transplacentally prior to birth.

About the time the milk comes in, the breast may become firm, full, and tender. This is normal. In extreme cases, fortunately rare, there may be fever and aching all over the body, as well as localized pain in the breast. These are symptoms of extreme engorgement, a condition not common when the breasts have been kept empty by frequent, vigorous nursing periods. Even with extreme engorgement, most of the discomfort goes away after a day or two. Wet packs of towels wrung out in hot tap water seem to help when placed on the sore breasts. A bra that gives good support is helpful.

Getting Started

If you are new at nursing, nothing is quite as useful in getting started as the coaching of an experienced nurser. She will show you how to use the baby's rooting reflex to get him on to the nipple, how to express milk manually (a useful maneuver to master) , how to soften an overly hard areola so that the baby can get his gums in place for the chewing action that expresses the milk, how to break the suction at the end by slipping a finger between his gums, how to hold him, and other fine points of the trade. Nursing is something like making apple pie, best learned in the doing, not in the reading.

Ordinarily there is a certain amount of nipple tenderness with nursing during the first week as the nipples toughen up to their new job. In most mothers this disappears after several days. The best approach is to "grin and bear it." The cornerstone of care for nipples is sound nursing, regular emptying of the breasts, establishment of mutuality between mother and infant, and a relaxed environment aided by rooming-in arrangements when baby's peaks of hunger and effective sucking can be directed at the mother.

There are many rules about length of sucking to allow. The best guide is the baby's behavior. When he slows down and seems full and your breasts feel deflated, it is probably time to stop. You will get the "feel" of this and become your own expert. We discourage watching the clock, but think—if you do better with figures—that about five minutes of actual sucking per breast is right for the first two days, building up to ten minutes at about one week. Ten minutes of sucking usually empties a breast and additional nursing is frosting on the cake. So long as a mother's nipples can tolerate it, we have no objections. If tenderness develops, better to redirect this sucking energy to a pacifier. These guidelines are for general or average situations. The key is flexibility, and we encourage every mother with help from her doctor or nurse to find the happy medium that works best for her and her infant. Some can nurse for ten minutes or more without batting an eye right from day one, while others with tender skin must be much more careful about the duration of sucking.

In the average situation we are inclined to do little to the nipples other than expose them to air following feeding. General cleanliness of the mother suffices, and while water will not hurt, no special cleaning before or after nursing is truly necessary. Sometimes an ointment is useful, and we usually recommend one containing lanolin. Again, how much one does for nipples depends in large part on the individual needs of mothers and babies. An analogy can be drawn to the care of the diaper area of an infant. How much you do depends on its characteristics. If nipples become cracked, an intensification of the usual precepts of care ordinarily suffices and healing occurs within two or three days. At times we restrict the duration of nursing temporarily but continue to empty the breasts by manual expression. Ointment may be helpful at these times. Nipple shields are sometimes used to permit nursing to proceed while reducing irritation of the nipple.

The lactogenic hormone, as well as oxytocin, is of great importance to continued nursing. Here again the behavior and environment of the mother are important. Her state of mind will have a lot to do with whether or not the lactogenic hormone is secreted. Secretion of the lactogenic hormone in the pituitary is caused by the stimulation of continued nursing. Just how is not clear, but research seems to indicate that repeated suckling does account for the maintenance of lactation, and the inhibition of ovulation and menstruation.

Babies allowed to suckle every three hours gain weight more quickly than those restricted by a fixed schedule to every four hours. This is a good argument for rooming-in arrangements. The implication is that the extra stimulation in the more frequent feedings leads to greater production of milk and hence to greater gain in the baby's weight. An increase in the number of feedings will often produce an increase of milk in about two days; a decrease in the number of feedings may be reflected in a lowering of milk supply in about the same length of time. Breasts soon dry up when no suckling is applied. In fact, this is the way weaning is accomplished (see page 312). Many mothers of twins find they can produce milk for two simply by permitting both babies to suckle, thus doubling the stimulation of the breasts. The best way to raise the level of the lactogenic hormone is to let the baby suck frequently.

In most hospitals babies and mothers still are kept in separate rooms. The baby is brought to the mother at scheduled times, usually every four hours. The first visit may be delayed until twelve to twenty-four hours after delivery to give mother and baby a chance to rest and recuperate. Some hospitals routinely feed babies sugar water or formula, which reduces the baby's interest in nursing. The mother who wishes to breast-feed her baby should not let this situation worry her. Once home, frequent, flexible feedings can be started, and an abundant milk supply will usually come in, provided the mother is relaxed and the baby sucks well. Under a "rooming-in" arrangement breast-feeding can have a better start in the hospital. The hungry or lonesome baby belongs on the breast every two or three hours and the sucking builds up the milk supply.

In the days when most mothers managed to nurse their babies successfully, doctors emphasized the importance of frequent sucking. For instance, Dr. Thomas S. Southworth, writing in a popular medical text, Carr's *Practice of Pediatrics,* published in 1906, recommended four nursings the first day, six on the second day, ten a day for the rest of the first month, eight for the second and third months, seven for the fourth and fifth months, and six a day for the sixth month through the eleventh. Night feedings were approved up through the fifth month.

The idea of having babies fed on schedules by the clock originated at about the same time bottle feeding was beginning to become popular, and at about the time hospitals started keeping mothers and babies in different rooms. Now the trend seems to be in the other direction. Physiologists have discovered sucking is *the* crucial factor in milk secretion, and psychologists have come to emphasize the importance of the physical closeness of mother and baby.

A good rule is to nurse the baby whenever he seems hungry or needs comforting. Breast milk, unlike formula, is easily and quickly digested and will not upset him. Sometimes the baby may want to nurse only a few minutes, but other times, especially toward the end of the day, he may want to nurse as long as half an hour or forty minutes. This is his way of visiting with you, and he is also building up the milk supply. As your baby gets older, and the milk supply is securely established, he will gradually cut down on the time he wants to take at each feeding.

You can increase the sucking stimulation by nursing the baby on both breasts each time you feed him. Doctors who studied one-breast and two-breast nursing found that the new mothers who gave two breasts at each feeding soon developed more milk than the others.

During the first several weeks, we emphasize nursing as often as the baby is hungry and prefer to postpone relief bottles until lactation is well established. For too frequent feedings we may allow a few sips of sugar water to space meals out a bit, but nothing works as well to build up milk supply as letting a hungry infant direct all of his appetite at the breast. The answer to hunger is more nursing, not a bottle. The same principle applies to excess hunger occurring after the newborn period. Many babies as they grow temporarily outstrip their mother's supply and let it be known by hungry crying. The answer is to nurse more often. The extra sucking and emptying stimulates increased production and a new balance is reached, usually in two to three days. Giving a bottle at these times will deny the mother needed stimulation, and she will go on producing to meet the needs of the baby's "old" appetite and become dependent on the bottle.

Occasionally when for any reason milk production markedly lags behind demand, we suggest small amounts of supplementary formula after nursing. Depending on the circumstances, we begin with one to two ounces and decrease the amount rapidly so that within two to three days we are off the bottle.

After nursing is well established, great flexibility is possible. Some mothers may want to nurse exclusively and this is fine for them. Others may want to combine nursing with bottle feeding, and this is OK too. We are impressed with how individual a matter nursing is. Some working mothers whom we know are able to nurse once or twice a day when they are with their babies and maintain production at this level. Others are able to rapidly build up their supply for a trip of several days when they nurse exclusively and then to decrease just as quickly on settling back into their old routine. The key is positive thinking, relaxation, and enjoyment of caring for baby.

Experiences such as these with many mothers have led us to believe firmly that each mother becomes her own expert on nursing her baby. Everyone does things just a bit differently, and we encourage mothers to experiment and to pass on their tips to us. It is OK to make a few mistakes along the way.

Breast Complications

Two complications are associated with breast-feeding. One is a general infection of the breast called mastitis. Another is a localized infection, an abscess. Both are part of the same disease process, which is caused by a staphylococcal organism and may be picked up in the hospital. Both problems tend to occur most frequently when the breast is overfull. This condition may arise from attempts to cut down on breast-feeding, or may be due occasionally to prolonged emotional upsets causing letdown reflex failure in the mother. A dramatic example of the latter occurred in Great Britain in World War II. At a time of prolonged strain under enemy attack a very high rate of breast infections was reported.

A favorite prescription for mastitis in the past has been to wean the baby, but now a growing number of doctors are of a different mind. The reasoning is that when nursing is stopped, the breast becomes increasingly congested and abscesses may be more likely to form. Doctors who do permit continued nursing usually insist on absolute bed rest for the mother and give antibiotics against the staphylococcal infection. The breast infection is likely to recur if the mother again becomes upset or tries to cut down feedings so rapidly that her breasts become overfull.

When a general infection becomes localized into an abscess, a surgical incision and drainage is usually necessary. Sometimes this operation can be minor, done with local anesthesia, but sometimes if the abscess is large and deep, it may require general anesthesia and hospitalization. Depending on the nature of the abscess, and on the doctor's and mother's feelings about breast-feeding, nursing can be stopped or continued.

A stopped-up duct in the breast sometimes causes pain in a small area and may be mistaken for an abscess. A change of nursing positions may help drainage.

Weaning

There is no set limit to the time nursing should continue. It depends on how much the nursing couple enjoy it. If nursing has gone well, with abundant milk and with evidence of a special feeling between mother and baby, then there is no harm in continuing to nurse for a year or more. American women of the nineteenth century usually did. Nevertheless, most American mothers nowadays do not nurse their babies so long. They usually stop in two or three months, if not sooner. Nursing to six months is often recommended, for at that stage the baby can theoretically be weaned to a cup.

When the time comes to stop nursing, it is well to do it gradually enough so that you are not uncomfortable. Remember that you can always let the edge off the discomfort of breast distension by expressing a small amount. How fast you go depends on your own comfort. The baby needs time to become accustomed to bottle substitutes, and the mother's breasts need to adjust to giving less milk. Dropping one or two additional feedings per day is a good rule of thumb to follow.

D. BOTTLE FEEDING

The Formula

Cow's milk differs from human milk in having a higher concentration of protein and salts. The kinds of protein and the salts are somewhat different too. The calorie content (that is, the number of calories per ounce) is about the same. Both milks contain adequate amounts of vitamin A but are deficient in vitamin D and may be lacking in vitamin C. Neither human milk nor cow's milk has enough iron. A continuing deficiency of iron through infancy can bring on anemia.

If we gave the newborn undiluted cow's milk, the higher concentrations of salts and protein would put a heavier load on his kidneys than he would get from human milk. In ordinary circumstances a healthy baby could carry this load, but some unusual stress might change the picture. By lowering the level of the bodily fluids, diarrhea, vomiting, or profuse sweating (all frequent accompaniments of illness) could increase the concentration of salts and protein. An undesirable accumulation of salt and protein waste products in the bloodstream would result. It is to prepare for such contingencies in non-breast-fed infants that we modify cow's milk before we give it to infants. Mainly, we want to reduce the concentrations of protein and salts in early infancy (three to four months) . Such a modification is known as a *formula.*

You can think of the formula your doctor will prescribe as a recipe for modifying cow's milk to a better approximation of human breast milk. There are three basic types, the first two of which you can make in your own kitchen. The first uses canned evaporated milk, which is cow's milk boiled to remove a certain amount of water. In the process, the protein is altered to produce a softer, better tolerated curd. The second uses fresh whole (usually homogenized) milk straight out of the dairy bottle. In both formulas water is added to reduce the concentrations of salts and protein. This dilution also cuts the calorie concentration, and it becomes necessary then to restore the proportion by adding sugar of some kind. The final result with either the evaporated milk or the whole milk is a product much closer to human milk than to the cow's milk with which we started.

The third principal formula, also based on cow's milk, differs from the others in being the product of a commercial factory. The protein, fat, and salts of cow's milk are altered to make it more like human breast milk. Vegetable fats are substituted for the animal fats of the cow (see page 320) . Vitamins and usually iron are added. The final preparation is packaged for sale as a canned liquid concentrate or powder to which water must be added, or as an already diluted, bottled formula all ready for the baby. Like beer, the bottle formula is offered in convenient, tidy six-packs, one more illustration of how the merchandiser's long arm reaches into our lives.

There are three major brands of the commercial formulas. While your doctor will have his own recommendation to make, there does not appear to be any significant difference among them. Indeed, in respect to nutrition, science has not been able to demonstrate any significant difference between these formulas and human breast milk. The average baby will thrive on any of them. This does not mean, however, that your own doctor will automatically prescribe a commercial formula for your baby. He may have his own reasons to prefer something else, or he may find that a particular baby does not tolerate standard formulas and needs something special.

Preparation

Thanks to the commercial preparations, there is a marked reduction in the amount of tedious work a mother has to endure in order to feed her infant by bottle. Until the development of these excellent preparations, the daily task of sterilizing and preparing formula was a time-consuming chore for a woman already hard pressed to keep up with a demanding schedule. The economy-minded may protest that making one's own formula in the kitchen saves money, but the woman who has tried both ways will probably conclude that the saving in dollars is not worth the extra trouble. On the other hand, some parents with real financial constraints may choose the cheaper method with the full realization that their infant will be properly nourished.

The preparation of formulas requires a small amount of equipment, some of which can be adapted to other uses when the baby is weaned. Nursing bottles come in two sizes, four ounce and eight ounce. Since the baby will begin with the small ones and grow into the larger size, you will need about eight of each. Any bottles you buy should be of heat-resistant, unbreakable glass or clear plastic, smooth inside and with a graduated scale in ounces plainly marked on the outside. You will need the scale to measure how much formula you are pouring. If early in the game you have occasion to buy a six-pack of commercial formula, you will be that much ahead, because those bottles can be used again for formula of your own preparation.

You will need caps, collars, and nipples for the bottles. All these components can be bought separately. Make sure that you have at least a dozen nipples on hand. Extra collars with the little disks that convert them into caps are always handy. You will want a bristle brush for scrubbing the bottles and a pair of metal tongs for handling them. You will find use for a heat-resistant glass measuring cup, a measuring spoon, glass funnel, can opener, standard tablespoon, strainer, and a glass jar with a tightly fitting screw top to keep sterilized nipples and collars uncontaminated.

The sterilizer, of course, is the main piece of equipment. This contraption need be nothing more complicated than a deep kettle (usually of aluminum) with a lid and rack for the bottles. Sterilizers come in a variety of styles (more accurately, in a range of prices), and you can suit your own taste and pocketbook. When the baby is weaned, you can add the sterilizer to your collection of kitchen pots and pans. Even the bottle rack will be worth keeping—you can use it for steaming asparagus.

The old ideas about sterilizing the formula and the utensils have undergone some modification in recent years. When bottle feeding was first attracting attention, infections among the newborn constituted a serious health problem. Since those days we have developed effective inoculations and medicines against some of the most dreaded infections, and we have greatly improved the sanitation of our water supplies. Under conditions of ordinary cleanliness, the majority of American babies probably could get by today without any sterilization of their bottles or formulas, but there is no point in subjecting them to needless risk. Unless your own doctor advises otherwise, you should sterilize at least for the baby's first two months.

The procedures for sterilizing are really quite simple. When the baby has finished a bottle, rinse it and the collar and nipple under the faucet. If you are not going to wash the bottle immediately, leave it filled with water until you do. For washing use either soap or a dishwashing detergent. Scrub the inside of the bottle and the screw threads of the collar thoroughly with the bristle brush. The brush will be more effective for digging into nooks and crannies if it has a hook on the bristle end. Wash the nipples by forcing soapy water through them. Hold the nipple between your first two fingers, fill it with soapy water, and then press down with your thumb. The water will shoot out in a fine stream. Use the same trick with clear water to rinse. Be thorough about rinsing bottles, nipples, and collars.

With the bottles, nipples, and collars washed clean, you have a choice of two methods for the sterilization proper. You can boil the utensils and the formula separately or (the simpler way) fill the bottles with the mixed formula and boil. The first method is called *presterilization,* the latter *terminal sterilization.*

In presterilization you simply put all the equipment—bottles, collars, caps, and utensils for mixing the formula—into a pot and boil them for at least ten minutes. You should not boil the nipples that long, for they will harden and crack. About five minutes is the limit for the nipples. After washing your hands thoroughly, you measure into a saucepan the amount of water needed for the formula, plus an extra half ounce to allow for evaporation, and bring it to a boil. If you are using whole milk, shake the bottle to mix the contents and wash the top of the bottle well with warm water before you remove the cap. When the measured water in the saucepan has come to a full boil, add the required amount of milk and, stirring constantly, let the milk and water boil for five minutes. Add sugar if the formula calls for it. If your formula specifies evaporated milk or either powdered or liquid commercial premodified milk, wash the top of the can well with soap and water and rinse thoroughly before you puncture the lid to pour. Since these products are already sterile, no further sterilization will be necessary. Just pour the milk into the pan of water that you have had boiling. Add the sugar, if necessary. The formula is then ready for bottling.

In terminal sterilization you wash all the utensils well but do not boil them before mixing the formula. Pour the mixed formula into the clean bottles. Place caps loosely on the bottles, but do not tighten them. Insert nipples into collars and place them in a jar with a screw top lid. Place the lid on the jar loosely but do not tighten. Now put the bottles of formula in the rack in the sterilizer and pour in enough water to cover them half way up. Cover the sterilizer, bring to a boil, and boil gently for twenty-five minutes. Remove the bottles with your tongs, placing them in a container of cool water, and tighten the caps securely. Remove to refrigerator. The usual sterilizer will have room enough for tongs, spoons, and so forth and perhaps a screw-topped glass jar for nipples in addition to the load of formula bottles. The easiest procedure for the nipples is to boil them separately after fitting them to collars. Five minutes in boiling water will be enough. Then remove them with tongs to the sterilized jar and cover tightly. When it is time to fix the baby's bottle, all that remains to be done is to take the cap off the bottle and replace it with a sterilized nipple. The most scrupulous will use a freshly boiled pair of tongs to handle the nipple. It goes without saying that you should wash your hands well with soap and water before handling any of the utensils or equipment for the baby's food.

The cans of formula base (including evaporated milk) come in the right size for making single batches of formula. If you should have some left over, you may store it safely in the refrigerator for forty-eight hours, covered tightly with plastic wrap. The bottled formula also can be kept safely in the refrigerator for forty-eight hours. A bottle can stand at room temperature for an hour without spoiling and, if unopened, go back in the refrigerator. If, however, the baby has taken some formula from the bottle, the remainder should not be kept for more than an hour (half hour in a hot climate) and should not be returned to the refrigerator.

The doctor or nurse will suggest the proportion of water to be used with the commercial formula bases (Enfamil, Similac, SMA, and so forth) or the proportions of the various ingredients for the homemade formulas. Two fairly standard formulas of the latter class are:

1. Evaporated milk . . . . 13 ounces
   Water . . . . 17 ounces
   Sugar . . . . 2 tablespoons cane sugar or
   4 tablespoons dextromaltose preparation

After several weeks the doctor may recommend reducing the proportion of water (to perhaps fifteen ounces) .

2. Whole milk . . . . 21 ounces
   Water . . . . 7 ounces
   Sugar . . . . as in first recipe

Corn syrup (Karo) , brown sugar, and various mixtures of dextrins and maltose are favored by some doctors and hospitals for the sugar content.

If the newer commercial preparations are as good as we have indicated, why, you may ask, do hospitals and some doctors still stick to the old favorites? Apart from the human tendency to rely on the familiar and the proved, and the concern about costs, perhaps the best explanation is that the professionals do not like to become involved in commercial competition if they can avoid it. The old formulas are simple and they work. Why change?

Until a very few years ago, it was taken for granted that the baby's bottle had to be served up warm. After all, isn't breast milk warm? Then a venturesome study demonstrated quite convincingly that there is no apparent medical reason to warm the milk. Not only can babies take cold milk without flinching, but many of them seem to enjoy it. Nevertheless, since the baby's natural milk would come warm from the breast and since so little effort is involved in taking the refrigerator chill off the bottle, why be innovative just for the sake of innovation? For the ordinary run of things we recommend giving formulas at room temperature or a little warmer.

There are babies, not many but some, who are on formula but cannot tolerate cow's milk at all. For them a satisfactory substitute for the cow's milk formulas must be found. On a different feeding regime these infants will show dramatic improvement. But for every one such case a score or a hundred others can be cited in which milk was wrongly blamed for excessive crying, loose stools, constipation, spitting up, fretfulness, skin rashes, and so forth. The milk is said to "disagree with" baby. While emphasizing that our understanding of this subject is still quite limited, we can state that in most instances juggling formulas will not provide the answer for the symptoms. We cannot deny that the few demonstrably intolerant babies do vomit and have severe diarrhea from cow's milk, but we also cannot overlook that the minor growing pains of infancy exhibit similar symptoms. The most satisfactory course is to eliminate all the other possible causes of the symptoms before blaming the formula.

Giving Baby His Bottle

There is no discernible reason why a baby cannot be cuddled as tenderly while having his bottle as he would be while nursing at the breast. Admittedly, the nipples are different and the milks too; still, all the other elements of the two situations are the same. We encourage this cuddling and discourage the practice of propping the bottle to let the infant suck on his own. The physical contact, perhaps mainly a matter of warmth and comforting pressure, is important to the baby. Indeed, there is ample evidence to support the notion that cuddling is vital to his well-being, even to his survival as a psychologically whole person. It is well-known that the babies of other primate species (notably gorillas) will pine away and die for want of mothering though they may have ample food. We do not suggest that what is true of gorilla babies is necessarily binding upon human babies, but we do know from experience with infants in institutions that they fail to thrive unless they have close contact with some adult in a substitute mothering relationship. The deprivation affects them physically as well as psychologically. The feeding period, whether at breast or by bottle, is the time for the mother to really get to know her infant. Every minute she can devote to him then will in the end be amply repaid by the feelings the mother herself will derive from the relationship.

If in the beginning you feel awkward holding the baby for a feeding, do not despair. Many mothers (and more fathers) are downright timid at the start but in just a few days become accomplished old hands. There is not a great deal to learn. After a couple of feedings, you find that the baby fits naturally in the crook of your arm. You can relax and enjoy the experience. The baby starts to suck as soon as you put the nipple in his mouth. Or, you can stroke his cheek with the nipple and let the rooting reflex (see pages 247 and 291) take over. Either way you will find him more than ready.

For a very small baby the nipple should not be so long that it touches the back of his throat and causes gagging. A premature baby or an ill baby, lacking sucking strength, may need a softer nipple, the so-called preemie nipple. You want the flow of milk from the bottle to be neither too slow nor too fast. Either situation may lead to swallowing of excess air. A good rule of thumb is that the milk should drip out slowly and steadily a drop at a time when you hold the bottle upside down. To tell whether the baby is getting his milk, watch for bubbles to appear in the milk still in the bottle. Since nipples harden under repeated boiling, old nipples may have openings that are too small. Either enlarge the opening with a punch of some sort or discard the nipple. If a new nipple has too large an opening, boil it a few times.

After a feeding, especially in early infancy, the baby is likely to fall asleep. Many young infants will pass a stool while feeding and you can hear and feel his intestines "rumbling." It is a good idea to change a wet or soiled diaper before putting the baby down. You will find that your baby will seem most comfortable lying on his stomach or on either side. In theory the right side has an advantage. Since the stomach opening is on the right, in this position gravity will assist in emptying the stomach. If the baby seems at least as happy in this position as in any other, we suggest you make a practice of putting him down on the right side, but which side he sleeps on is not a matter of prime importance. There is no need to raise either the head or foot of his crib.

E. THE DIET OF INFANTS

Infants' diets are now receiving some long overdue attention. Interest stems from two major public health concerns, coronary artery disease and obesity. Until recently, most interest in these two hazards to health has focused on adults, since older members of our society are the ones who actually suffer most. However, evidence is accumulating that these disorders begin far earlier in life, perhaps in infancy. Recent studies of the blood of newborns from families with a disorder of fat metabolism leading to high blood fat levels has shown elevation of blood fat at birth.

Although there is no proof yet that this blood finding is predictive of later disease or that reducing the blood fat by special diets or drugs will help, the likelihood of these relationships is quite great. If important clues such as these are linked to the strong suspicion that the average American diet, particularly regarding its heavy use of animal fats, contributes significantly to the development of atherosclerosis, it is understandable that interest is being directed to the diet of infants. Already, certain changes in infant feeding are occurring in keeping with this line of thinking, even though there is no conclusive evidence yet to prove their value. For example, there is a growing tendency to use low fat milk for older infants and children. More and more dairies are producing special milks with reduced fat content and added protein. These changes may be premature, however. Recent experimental work in rats has suggested that it may be desirable to expose baby rats to the animal fat of their own mother's milk. Exposure to this fat during infancy may "accustom" rats to using these fats effectively so that they are not deposited as readily in arteries. The blood cholesterol levels of human infants who are breast-fed are higher than those of infants fed commercial formulas with polyunsaturated fats. The long-range meaning of this observation is not known. Is this helpful or harmful? At present, we cannot answer this question. Accordingly, we cannot recommend any fundamental change in feeding practices regarding fat in milk.

Obesity

Babies of today are undoubtedly larger and heavier as a group than those of thirty or forty years ago. It is reasonable to suspect a connection between this development and our national problem of obesity.

An interesting experiment recently conducted in rats suggests an explanation for how obesity in infancy may set up a lifelong pattern. Infant rats in this experiment were fed average diets and then compared with other rats overfed to the point of obesity. When the rats were sacrificed and their fat analyzed, it was found that the ones overfed in infancy had more fat-containing cells. And the cells were bigger. Rats made obese as adults, on the other hand, increased only the size, not the number of fat cells.

The number of fat cells present at the end of infancy persisted throughout life, regardless of diet. Thus, the rats made obese by overfeeding as infants had more fat cells as adults. It appears that appetite is related to number of fat cells. If the number of fat cells increases, appetite may permanently increase. This increase in fat cells may be the way the food thermostat is raised by overfeeding in infancy. If the same situation applies to humans, it may explain in part at least why infants who become obese because of too many calories in their diet tend to remain so, why dieting to lose weight is often so difficult, and why a premium should be placed upon preventing obesity in infants when this is possible.

Why some babies are fat and others are thin is an intriguing question to which a satisfactory answer is not yet available. Paradoxically, thin babies consume more calories than obese ones under normal circumstances. The apparent explanation is that thin infants are very active and "burn up" energy, while chubby ones tend to be quieter, converting more of their caloric intake to fat. The basic appetite thermostat of a baby appears to be largely determined by his heredity. The number of calories that a baby is offered unquestionably plays a part, but probably more so for some infants than others. Variation in number of calories taken depends on the richness, calorically speaking, of the diet and the emphasis placed on food by parents. For some babies, it seems likely that chubbiness has resulted from "overfeeding" and/or excessive richness of the foods given. On the other hand, some infants seem to refuse adamantly any more food than they actually need despite coaxing. Nothing will put more weight on these epicures. Why some babies are more susceptible to influence by feeding practices has remained a mystery. It is an important question that deserves research.

While there are no clear rules yet, we are rethinking the old idea that a "fat baby is a healthy one" and are looking much more into obesity and feeding patterns of infants and children as the precursors of obesity in adults. Much additional research is needed on this topic. Our tentative impression is that we should, if possible, try to prevent obesity in infancy by avoiding excessive calories in babies' foods (perhaps by delaying introduction of high calorie solid foods such as fruit, high meat dinners and meats [see page 327]) and being willing to stop feeding infants when they give us the clue that they have had enough. Such an approach might minimize but not entirely eliminate obesity in infants.

Vitamins

Vitamins are organic chemicals that the foods we eat contain in minute amounts and that our bodies must have if we are to remain healthy. Deficiencies of the various vitamins are associated with certain specific disorders. Most people are aware that every child from birth on requires vitamins in his diet, but not everyone realizes that in the consumption of vitamins it is possible to overdo a good thing, although even in our overvitaminized society we rarely see any toxic effects of overdosage.

The vitamins to consider are A, D, C, and the B group. Since the B vitamins are well represented in the foods (including human and cow's milk) given to babies in the United States, we mention them only in passing. The child's diet may, however, be short on A, D, or C, and parents should have a little information about them. (There are other vitamins besides those we have mentioned, but they are widely enough distributed in the diet so that no conscious decision about them is necessary. We will confine our discussion to the three which are sometimes missing from the diets of children.)

Vitamin A is found in milk, butter, cheese, egg yolk, carrots, squash, sweet potatoes, and animal fats. Fish livers—cod, halibut, tuna—contain large quantities and are the most common commercial source. Human milk contains vitamin A, usually in adequate quantities if the mother herself has a normal diet. Cow's milk varies with the season, depending on the available forage, but in general contains adequate amounts for infants.

Vitamin C appears in almost all fresh fruits and vegetables, but especially in citrus fruits, tomatoes, berries, and leafy green vegetables. Overcooking tends to destroy the vitamins, but modern canning and freezing methods help to preserve them. Cow's milk is an unreliable source of vitamin C and supplementation is required. Human milk contains adequate amounts if the mother receives sixty milligrams daily in her diet.

Vitamin D is found in fish oils and (in lesser quantities) in eggs. It is manufactured by chemicals in human and animal skin under the action of sunlight. However, vitamin D is passed poorly into human or cow's milk and therefore as a general practice in this country it is added, both to cow's milk and to commercially prepared milk.

Vitamin A is important to vision. A deficiency of A causes night blindness and other disorders of the eye. Vitamin D is essential to normal growth of bones. The bone changes known as *rickets*, not seen as often nowadays as formerly, result from a deficiency of vitamin D. Vitamin C, whose chemical name is *ascorbic acid*, is essential to the healthy development of the small blood vessels and other bodily structures. Easy bruising, bleeding gums, hemorrhages around the bones are symptoms of deficiency of vitamin C. The medical name for this condition is *scurvy*. A couple of centuries ago the British Navy began requiring its sailors to drink lime juice to prevent scurvy, and Englishmen ever since have been known as "Limeys."

Many symptoms beyond those noted are commonly attributed to vitamin deficiencies. Among them are poor appetite, stunted growth, whining, and frequent colds. It is true that these symptoms are often seen among severely malnourished children, but the deprivations of these children usually go beyond vitamin deficiencies. In our affluent society we do not recognize any direct relationship between these symptoms and lack of vitamins. Though parents often pour vitamins into children exhibiting the symptoms, the children rarely respond. The parents are right to be concerned about the problems, but they should look in another direction for the solutions. As a general comment, it can be stated that we Americans, under the pressures of our high-powered advertising, grossly overuse vitamin preparations.

Because they occur in various plants and animals, vitamins can be harvested from natural sources. They can also be manufactured in the laboratory. They can be given in the form of drops or tablets, and many commercial preparations for the infant are available. The usual practice is to begin giving the vitamins a few days after the baby is home from the hospital. He takes his prescribed amount once a day from a medicine dropper. You will discover that he is quick to learn how to suck on the dropper and that he seems to enjoy it.

The baby's daily needs of vitamins are: fifteen hundred units of vitamin A, thirty to sixty milligrams of vitamin C, and four hundred units of vitamin D. How the infant receives these makes little difference. If his diet contains all of them, there is no need to give supplements. If his diet is inadequate, supplements for the deficient vitamins only are needed. By the time a child is on a full range of solid foods and juices and consumes vitamin D–fortified whole milk—usually no later than one year of age—he should receive all needed vitamins from his diet and additional vitamins are uncalled for. If you live in an area where the water is low in fluoride, a supplement of sodium fluoride is indicated until all of the primary and permanent teeth have erupted (from birth until mid-teens) .

Vitamin supplementation needed for following feeding programs:

1. Breast-fed infant whose mother consumes adequate amounts (fifty milligrams) of vitamin C per day needs vitamin D supplement of four hundred milligrams per day until this is supplied by vitamin D–fortified milk.

2. Bottle-fed infant taking vitamin D–fortified evaporated or homogenized milk needs thirty to sixty milligrams per day of vitamin C until diet (two ounces of fresh, frozen, or bottled orange juice) supplies adequate vitamin C.

3. Bottle-fed infant on commercial formula (SMA, Similac, Enfamil, and so forth) containing added vitamins needs *no* additional vitamins.

Vitamins may be supplemented selectively. For example, if only vitamin D is needed, there is no need to give C and A too. However, many infant vitamins are packaged as a group, containing A, C, and D and sometimes B as well. If individual vitamins are unavailable, it is safe to give the combinations even though the baby may be receiving more of some vitamins than are actually needed.

Iron

Human breast milk and unfortified formulas are deficient in iron. Iron should be in the diet no later than the three-month mark. As a baby grows he outgrows the supply of iron he was born with, and because of growth alone will become iron deficient. A reasonable precaution to insure iron intake is the fortification of infant milks with iron or the addition of iron drops to the baby's diet until he is eating sufficient quantities of iron-rich foods to meet his daily needs. Accordingly, more and more commercial formulas contain added iron. The breast-fed infant or the infant on *nonfortified* evaporated or whole milk formulas should receive iron drops daily. Check with your doctor or nurse for the dose. (Remember that iron tablets or drops taken in excess are extremely dangerous. Give just the recommended amount and no more. Keep the bottle in a safe place. Keep ipecac syrup on hand to cause vomiting for accidental ingestion.)

When it is clear that other dietary sources (cereals [see page 326], meats, eggs) are being taken in sufficient quantities, the iron-fortified formulas or supplemental iron drops may be discontinued and the baby can begin on regular milk. Check with your doctor or nurse.

Beginning Solids

The clear historical trend in this country has been to introduce solids at ever earlier ages until now many babies begin within one or two weeks of birth. Why this is so has never been adequately explained. There is no compelling scientific justification for this trend. No doubt manufacturers of baby foods who stand to profit by extended use play a part in the trend through their advertising. Also playing a role is the competitiveness of many mothers. We Americans have the bias that anything that is done earlier, including beginning solids, must be better.

A nutritional consideration, which has entered into the recommendations for the introduction of solids, particularly in the past, is the infant's need for a source of iron. Without dietary iron by four to six months, infants will tend to become anemic. Neither unfortified commercial milk formula, cow's milk, nor human milk contains sufficient iron for the baby's needs. Another source must be found. Traditionally, this source has been iron contained in fortified cereals, meats, and eggs, and the introduction of solids, particularly cereals, by three months of age was advocated on these grounds. While the need for iron is just as real as it ever was, there has been a shift in thinking about the best way to achieve this goal.

Cereals in general do not appear to be quite as reliable a source of iron as was once thought. The form of iron salt used in their enrichment is important. If a ferrous salt is used and the iron remains in the ferrous state, it is easy for the body to absorb and use. If a *ferric* form of iron is used, it is likely that little can be absorbed from the intestine into the body. Iron in this form is of little value. There is no uniformity in the iron salts added to commercial infant cereals, so the usefulness of cereals must be judged by brand. The emphasis and trend now is to bypass this uncertainty and to fortify milk itself with iron or to provide supplemental iron drops, relying less on solids for iron supply, particularly during the first six months (see page 328). Accordingly, the need for introducing cereal by two and one-half to three months on the grounds of providing a source of iron is less compelling.

Another consideration entering into the decision to begin solids, whether or not with a spoon, is the conviction that milk alone does not satisfy, as evidenced by short intervals between feedings and refusal to sleep through the night. Parents give solids in the hope that feedings will be stretched out and sleeping through the night will occur earlier. Milk becomes somewhat suspect because of its supposed inability to satisfy. This question has been studied, and despite the strong convictions of many parents, no connection has been observed between the age of introduction of solid foods and the daily number of feedings or the age of consistently sleeping through. In short, the studies say that if a baby seems hungry, giving him more milk (formula or breast) is just as effective as giving him solids. The average age of sleeping through is three to four months regardless and depends, as does *number* of feedings, primarily on the maturation of the infant. Solids, according to the studies, do not "hold" an infant's hunger any more than does milk. Besides, getting up at night is part of the job of parenting and should be accepted as such.

It appears from the above that there is no strong scientific argument for introducing solids at one time rather than another. Such is the case. No one should feel, according to the evidence at hand, that he must begin at one week, two months, or five months. Everyone agrees that it is desirable that by the time teeth are in, babies should have begun to take table foods. But it is less clear when to begin on pureed solids.

As we mentioned earlier in this chapter, there is concern about obesity in infants and the possible role that solids introduced early in life might have. Accordingly, because there is no evidence of special benefit in beginning early, we tend to be conservative on this question and suggest starting at about three months, depending on the "readiness" of the infant to take from the spoon. We see no advantage in giving solids from the bottle and advise waiting until the baby is able to manage spoon feedings.

Infants vary in their readiness to accept solids. Some may take readily to them at two and one-half months. Others at the same age are disinterested or even strongly opposed, spitting out everything you put in their mouths. If your baby is a member of the latter group (a perfectly normal one by the way), simply postpone the operation for a week or two.

When you do begin on solids, do not be discouraged if at first every spoonful of food comes out on the baby's chin as fast as you put it into his mouth. This is caused by the thrusting movement of the baby's tongue, used to express milk from the nipple. The behavior does not indicate stubbornness or lack of appetite. Simply scrape the food off and reinsert, being careful to get it over the tip of the infant's tongue. His ability to take in and swallow solids will improve as he gains better voluntary control.

The usual routine for starting solids is to offer cereal at the 10 A.M. and 6 P.M. feedings, somewhere between two and one-half and three months. You might start with a few small spoons of rice cereal heavily diluted with formula or, if you are breast-feeding, with ordinary whole milk. Gradually, you will strengthen the mix and increase the volume. If the baby continues to take it well, you can add oatmeal and barley. Then at intervals of two to four weeks, you can add fruits, vegetables, and meat, in that order.

It is a good idea to introduce new foods one at a time, separating them by at least two or three days. Then you have a check on which new food is tolerated. We usually begin juice around one to two months. You may find it convenient to give juice between feedings on a hot day. Then, if he is taking two ounces of fresh, frozen, or bottled juice containing vitamin C (check the label), and is getting adequate vitamin D from his milk, you can discontinue supplementary vitamins (see pages 322–25).

Our philosophy in general is to encourage parents to go slowly and keep things simple during the first few months. A number of quite normal events, colic or heat rash on the baby's face for instance, are likely to be a little disturbing to the new mother. If she proceeds a little slowly, she will be less inclined to attribute, mistakenly, these minor, transient problems to new foods, as opposed to things that occur naturally to most babies.

For those families who suspect a strong incidence of allergy or who might interpret rashes, discomfort, and the like as signaling allergy, it would seem desirable to hold up for a while on solids. It goes without saying, of course, that a genuine, existing allergic condition will influence, if not dictate, the diet.

After cereals, we add fruits, vegetables, and meats in that order. Generally speaking, we hold off eggs until six months of age and then begin with the yolk only. If this is well tolerated, the whole egg may be introduced a month or so later, in any of a variety of forms. The small amount of egg that is added to various other baby foods does not seem to be a problem before six months of age.

Water

Your baby will not in general need more water than the amount he is already getting from his formula or breast milk. Water may seem to quiet his crying, but it is probably the nipple that does it. The pacifier alone might have done the trick.

Feeding Program

To recapitulate, it would be a great mistake to regard any schedule for introducing new foods as ideal or sacrosanct. Every mother knows her baby best. Develop a menu or a program that is convenient and logical for you; it will be good for the baby. Do not be afraid to deviate whenever expediency dictates.

About two and one-half to three and one-half months (or earlier):

Milk at four-hour intervals. Again the period between feedings is very flexible, depending upon your evaluation of the baby's needs and your convenience. The 2 A.M. feeding usually can be discontinued between four and eight weeks of age. Give juice between feedings.

Rice cereal may be offered before the 10 A.M. and 6 P.M. bottle. The average baby may gradually take from one to three tablespoons of a progressively thickened feeding and eventually work up to at least ten tablespoons per day.

About three to four months (or earlier): By now you may have experimented with barley and oatmeal cereal. Parents often begin to introduce fruits about this time. This may be applesauce or banana, but nothing in these two is inherently preferable. If your baby takes them, well and good. If he or she seems to be fussy with them or has loose stools, discontinue them temporarily. Try another fruit perhaps and give the first fruit another chance a week or two later.

Now, if you are bottle feeding, you will probably have changed to whole milk (although, of course, you could use evaporated milk or commercial formula indefinitely) and have stopped sterilizing. Using a clean bottle and nipple, take the milk you use out of the refrigerator, merely warm the bottle, and discard whatever the child does not drink.

Four to five months: Over these next four weeks you may find it possible to reduce gradually the milk intake of the baby to about four bottles of milk per day, at approximately 7 to 8 A.M., 11 A.M. to noon, 4 to 6 P.M., and a bedtime bottle. Each family, however, will work out the best schedule for itself, depending upon when the parents get up in the morning and so forth.

You may find that the bedtime bottle is becoming less necessary, particularly if you have to wake the baby for it. If you find, however, that the baby is hungry during the 2 to 4 A.M. period, then convenience would suggest that waking him up at 10 to 11 P.M. is preferable. But particularly as they approach four months of age, many, perhaps most, babies will begin to sleep from nine to twelve hours a day.

For breast-feeding mothers who want to delay solids until after five months, we have no particular objections. A source of iron should be begun by three months in the form of iron drops, molasses, or fortified cereal (see page 326) .

RICHARD I. FEINBLOOM, M.D.

---

* Niles Newton, Ph.D., and Michael Newton, M.D., "Psychologic Aspects of Lactation," *The New England Journal of Medicine* (November 30, 1967) .
† W. H. Masters and V. E. Johnson, *Human Sexual Response* (Boston: Little, Brown, 1966) .

CHAPTER EIGHTEEN

Prematurity

*B*Y THE commonly accepted standard, premature babies (affectionately known as "preemies") are those born in or before the thirty-seventh week of gestation. You will recall that most babies (see page 75) are delivered after forty weeks of gestation, give or take two weeks. They are known as full-term or term infants. The babies born later than forty-two weeks are called postmature infants (see pages 340–41).

Most persons probably have a mental picture of the preemie as a tiny creature, almost a miniature, and indeed prematures usually do weigh less than five and one-half pounds. Until a few years ago doctors were inclined to pay more attention to the weight of a newborn than to the length of gestation. On the basis of the weight alone, they might decide that the baby was "premature" and consequently would need special care. There usually is a direct relation between the length of gestation and weight of the baby, but not always. We have come to recognize that many babies weighing five and one-half pounds or under nevertheless have been born at term—that is, between thirty-eight and forty-two weeks of gestation. Furthermore, some babies born before the dividing line of thirty-seven weeks do weigh in excess of five and one-half pounds. To make a judgment about prematurity on the basis of weight alone no longer seems to be warranted.

From the physician's point of view, the most important consideration is how mature developmentally the baby is at birth. In general, babies born prior to thirty-seven weeks of gestation, regardless of the birth weight, may be less mature functionally. That is to say, their kidneys, lungs, muscles may not work as well as we would expect of a term baby. It is the immaturity of the functioning of parts of the body that requires the special care given to prematures. To assess the degree of immaturity, the doctor will have to consider not only the birth weight but the length of gestation, as far as it can be determined from the date of the mother's last menstrual period. Human forgetfulness and the difficulty of relating the actual time of conception to the menstrual period make this calculation difficult.

Fortunately, the doctor has other indicators of maturity or immaturity to guide him. Prematures are likely to have thin skin with little underlying fat. The breast tissue is less developed than in full-term babies. The creases in the soles of the feet are not so prominent. The scrotal sac of the premature male baby is different, lacking the rough appearance of the sac of the term baby. The testes are more likely to be undescended than in full-term babies (see page 263). There also is a difference in the calcification of the growth centers of the long bones of the body, and this difference can be detected with X ray.

The main point here is that premature babies are not simply small babies but immature babies who may or may not be small at birth. It is quite possible for a baby to weigh seven pounds and still be immature, or for a five-and-one-half-pounder to be mature. Factors other than weight figure more importantly in our diagnosis nowadays. At any particular gestational age we can find a range of weights. Some babies are abnormally small. Some, having acquired a disease such as German measles (see pages 166–68) from the mother, fail to grow in utero. Or heart malformation or some other congenital disorder may be at fault. Inadequate nutrition resulting from a defect in the placenta is another presumed cause of failure to grow. We do not understand very much yet about prenatal malnutrition. Babies who have suffered nutritional deprivation of some sort in utero and whose weight in consequence is below normal are usually referred to as *dysmature*. In their behavior after birth these dysmature babies are very much like premature babies of the same size. One problem more common among the dysmature babies is the relatively frequent occurrence of lower blood sugar level, a condition known as *hypoglycemia*. Doctors and nurses watch dysmature babies carefully for signs and symptoms of hypoglycemia.

Prematurity occurs in 5 to 15 percent of all pregnancies. Despite all the advances in medical knowledge in the last generation, our understanding of the causes of prematurity remains limited. Consequently, our ability to prevent this common occurrence is limited. We can say, however, that several factors do seem to be related to prematurity. Some of these are preventable or correctable and others not. Chronic illness of the mother or such complications of pregnancy as toxemia (see pages 157–61), placenta previa (see pages 145–47), maternal infection (see pages 149–50), incompetent cervix (see pages 413–14), and Rh incompatibility (see pages 151–56), seem to increase the probability of premature delivery. In particular, we can cite the mother's diabetes or severe erythroblastosis fetalis (see pages 151–54) as known occasions of prematurity, because in these cases birth frequently is accomplished by elective Caesarean section at about thirty-six weeks of gestation to safeguard the life of the infant.

To a certain extent, high-quality care during pregnancy can hold all the so-called medical factors at the minimum, but by no means will it eliminate prematurity altogether. These medical factors, while important, do not explain all. Pregnancies complicated by potentially remediable medical factors account for only about 10 percent of the premature births. In the remaining 90 percent other factors as yet undetermined must be operating. There are indications that the baby's weight at birth may be influenced by the mother's smoking in pregnancy, by her size and weight, by her living at high altitude, or by her having an infection of the urinary tract (with or without symptoms) in pregnancy. Investigations are in progress, but it is too early to make definite recommendations, except to stop smoking (a wise idea for every woman, pregnant or not).

The woman who gives birth to a premature and does not rack her memory or search her soul for an explanation is probably the exception. As happens in so many situations where knowledge is limited, the imagination leaps in to supply answers. Was it something she did in early pregnancy, or even before? Did she go to the doctor early enough? Was she as conscientious as she should have been? If she had observed certain precautions, could she have carried the baby to full term? None can say, but too often the parents of a preemie blame themselves for real or imagined past behavior and see the premature birth as their punishment. This tendency is more pronounced when the baby has been conceived before marriage or when husband and wife disagree about having children or when the marriage is in trouble. People do see their misfortunes as punishment for alleged sins of commission or omission, and it is not always an easy task to persuade them to a more rational view. In the case of a woman who has delivered a premature baby or a baby with a handicap of any kind, the problem is magnified, for she is prone to interpret the event as a reflection on her fundamental capacities as childbearer and mother. The feelings of inadequacy and guilt so aroused can be overwhelming to the point of disturbing the mother's ability to deal with the reality, which usually is much better than she thinks. If a mother has feelings of guilt about her premature delivery, she should reveal them to her doctor. This is most important. The doctor will have encountered similar situations many times and out of his experience may be able to convince her that she is going through a very common and familiar psychological process.

PROBLEMS OF PREMATURITY

There are all degrees of prematurity, from mild to severe. The more immature the baby the greater the risk of early death. At a certain point, prematurity blends with miscarriage; the fetus is not sufficiently developed to survive. On the scale of birth weight we can give a rough idea of the expectations. A baby weighing between five and five and one-half pounds at birth has a better than nine to one chance of surviving, whereas only about 30 percent of the babies under three pounds will survive. But we repeat with emphasis that birth weight alone is probably not as important as the maturity of development. On the basis of gestational age (an indication of maturity) thirty-three weeks seems to be an important dividing line in terms of mortality. Nevertheless, the rule holds: the smaller and less mature the baby, the greater the risk of death, the higher the rate of complications, and the longer the stay in hospital under observation. Of course, there are prematures and prematures. To some babies premature birth seems to make no difference at all. For others it makes all the difference in the world. This variation from individual to individual has to be kept in mind in any discussion of the care of these early infants.

Compared to full-term babies, prematures are much more sensitive to the medications that are given in labor. As you have read elsewhere (see pages 185 and 197), these drugs are transferred from the mother's blood to the baby's through the placenta. Depression of nervous function, resulting in sleepiness, slowed respiration, and other physiological changes, is a side effect of pain-killers. Premedication of labor can depress all babies. Aware of this problem, obstetricians are more stingy now than they used to be in the amounts of pain-relieving drugs they give for childbirth. When they have a premature delivery on their hands, this reluctance may approach the point of total withholding. Whereas the full-term baby can overcome a mild degree of sedation, the consequences for the premature can be serious. Because of his lack of functional development, his ability to control his respiration may be no more than barely sufficient under optimum conditions; the sedation from even a small dose of pain-relieving medication given to his mother before birth might tip the balance. He could have real difficulty in breathing.

Immediately after birth the premature baby's temperature fluctuates in sensitive response to the temperature of his environment, whereas the full-term baby holds a fairly stable temperature regardless of minor variations in the surrounding air. Hot or cold, the environmental temperature strongly affects the premature's temperature. For this reason, we place the premature in an incubator, where the temperature can be regulated carefully. The incubator temperature is kept, usually, above the temperature of the room and close to what the baby's own temperature should be. While the nursery may be at only 70° Fahrenheit, the incubators will be kept around 88°.

The premature baby is susceptible to several types of respiratory difficulties. The very smallest prematures may undergo what are called *apneic spells*. In these periods the baby stops breathing altogether. He turns blue. These apneic spells can be very frightening, but fortunately most of them end spontaneously. The baby starts to breathe again. In dealing with the spells, we do not rely upon a spontaneous return to normal breathing but try to stimulate breathing the moment we identify the signs of onset. Sometimes just the flick of a finger on the baby's heel will be enough of a goad. The spells probably occur because the brain centers that regulate the respiratory movements are too immature for normal control.

In the other common respiratory problem of the prematures, the baby usually seems to be all right at birth but within a few hours begins to breathe heavily. His chest retracts, sucks in, and he turns a dusky color or blue. This coloring (or *cyanosis*) is caused by imperfect oxygenation of the blood. The condition is known by two formidable names, *hyaline membrane disease* or *idiopathic respiratory distress syndrome,* whose derivations are too technical to be explained here. Essentially what we see is persistence of the circulation pattern that is characteristic of the fetus but not of the infant after birth. In the fetus only a small part of the blood pumped from the heart passes through the lung whereas in the infant at birth all the blood passes through the lungs before being pumped out to the rest of the body. During fetal life oxygenation of the blood and removal of carbon dioxide occur in the placenta. The baby's mother literally does the breathing for him. The baby's lungs are collapsed and full of fluid. At birth the lungs expand with the baby's first breath. Henceforth they must do the work of respiration. Rerouting of the blood flow within the heart and in the great blood vessels then is necessary to pass the blood through the lungs. But for some still unknown reason, this redirection of the circulation within the heart and great vessels does not occur for the baby with hyaline membrane disease, and his blood flow continues in its fetal pattern. Now lacking the placenta for respiration, the circulatory process of the afflicted baby fails to oxygenate the blood adequately and to remove carbon dioxide from it. The blood simply does not pass through the lungs in sufficient quantity. Coincidentally, a proteinaceous material, glass-smooth, forms on the linings of the smaller air passages. (From this material comes the name hyaline membrane.) The condition appears in all degrees of severity, from mild to fatal. It rarely lasts beyond three days, but it is difficult to predict the outcome for a particular baby. In general, the more labored the breathing the poorer the chances of survival. The treatment is to give oxygen and antibiotics (to prevent secondary infection) and often intravenous fluids to supply water and correct imbalance in the acidity of the baby's blood. At some medical centers measurements now can be made of the oxygen, carbon dioxide, and chemical constituents of the blood, and this information may be helpful in efforts to manage the baby's distress.

As might be expected, premature babies are more prone than full-term babies to develop excessive jaundice (see pages 383–85) and to have it linger longer. The infant's ability to deal with jaundice depends to a large extent on the maturity of his liver, and since the premature liver is less mature, the difficulties are exaggerated for these small babies. It may be too that the premature's central nervous system is more sensitive to increase of bilirubin (the chemical that accounts for jaundice), and so the same degree of jaundice may have different consequences for the early baby and the full-term one. The treatment of excessive jaundice (see pages 385–86) is similar for premature and full-term babies. Since the premature does not tolerate exchange transfusion as well, the development of phototherapy (see pages 385 and 386) may prove to be a blessing for him.

Prematures are much more susceptible to infection, and they can have serious infections without showing signs more severe than poor sucking or mild vomiting. Early recognition of the symptoms is most important, and here, as in the other difficulties that may beset the preemie, the contributions of the nursing staff are invaluable. Doctors must be in and out of nurseries. It is the nurse or her aide whose watchfulness is crucial.

Feeding presents frequent problems. The smallest preemies may lack the strength and energy to suck. Immaturity of his swallowing mechanism may cause the preemie to choke, gag, or breathe in (aspirate) liquids. For these reasons we avoid feeding by nipple until the baby's general condition has improved. The principal alternative is feeding by tube, called *gavage*. A small plastic tube is passed through the baby's nose and down his throat into the stomach. The tube may be withdrawn after each feeding or left in place. At first the feeding is limited to several cubic centimeters of glucose (sugar water) every two or three hours. The amount is increased gradually and, in several days, a weak milk formula started. Mother's breast milk may be used for these feedings. The formula is strengthened by stages until it has the consistency of the milk a full-term baby normally would receive. When the baby's condition warrants, tube-feeding is discontinued or alternated with nipple feeding, bottle or breast. *Gastrostomy*, which is surgical insertion of a tube through the abdominal wall into the stomach, is an alternative procedure for the frailest babies, who, as they strengthen, will also be transferred to the nipple. When the mother wants to breast-feed, it is often possible to begin nursing before the premature leaves the hospital. She need only keep her milk flowing by manual or mechanical expression.

Because of these many anticipated problems, there is a growing tendency to develop specialized facilities for the care of premature babies. The care of the premature requires skillful nurses and elaborate machines to monitor the baby's status (his respiratory rate, for example) and to carefully regulate his treatment (the slow constant rate of an intravenous feeding, for example). Perhaps in the future there will be regional centers for the care of the premature, and most premature babies from the region will either be delivered in or transferred to these centers.

The weight loss (see page 290) that follows birth is more pronounced and more prolonged in the premature baby. Several weeks may pass before the preemie gets back to his birth weight. Here again, the degree of maturity determines the similarity of the preemie's pattern to the full-term pattern. Once the preemie has turned the corner, his weight gain usually is steady, but he will have to remain in the hospital until the doctors decide that he is mature enough to be cared for at home. Before discharge he should show a good gain in weight and be able to breathe and feed without any difficulties.

The premature's stay in the hospital will vary, depending on his maturity, from a week to several months. After a good weight gain has been established and any complications dealt with, he can be graduated from the incubator to a bassinet. At first he will spend only a few hours a day in a bassinet while his ability to regulate his own temperature is tested. Certainly he will have to demonstrate his ability to thrive outside the incubator before he can be taken home.

Unlike the full-term baby, who ordinarily is in his mother's arms within hours or minutes after birth, the premature may be separated from his mother for some time. In the first few days there is often a real question whether he will survive. He may be ill and all but hidden under the various tubes and other devices attached to him. Even when the first critical days have passed, the possibility of complications remains. At best, his worried parents will have no more than glimpses of him through the window. Physical contact may be out of the question, although earlier contact is becoming the rule. These first days or weeks of a premature baby's life, especially if there are complications, are a trying time for the parents. Various ways of reacting to the situation are repeated so often that they have become familiar to the doctors and nurses. Consciously or unconsciously, the parents may begin to prepare themselves for the death of the baby. Even when the initial critical period has been passed safely, they may behave as if the baby were about to die. Finding it hard in the circumstances even to look at the baby, they may stay away from the hospital. A common reaction is to seek someone to blame—the nurses, the doctors, or themselves. They become touchy and complain about the care the baby is receiving even when it is of the highest quality.

All these parental reactions are understandable. Parents have a hard time confronting the fact of prematurity. But these feelings can give rise to a severe and continuing problem. They may interfere with proper care of the infant at home and they may color the parents' attitudes for years to come. Many, if not most, parents of prematures persist in viewing their infants as more frail and more susceptible to disease than a full-term baby would be. They worry about keeping the baby warm and hover about to prevent a fall. They try to force down extra helpings of food. At the slightest sign of anything out of the ordinary they call the doctor, and they keep other people away to stave off infection. This concern, though it may seem exaggerated, is quite understandable, but it may persist long past infancy. Excessive protection can have a significant influence on any child's growth and development—too much babying can block his drive to become a truly independent human being. It is the experience of the medical profession that premature babies, once home safely from the hospital, do not in general require extra protection or special medical care. Parents who have these worries about their premature baby should by all means discuss them with the doctor. Most often, he will encourage them to disregard the prematurity and treat their baby as they would any other infant.

One promising change that can minimize these parental reactions is earlier involvement of the parents, particularly the mother, in the care of the infant. The trend is to let mothers handle, feed, and care for their infants as early as possible during the nursery stay, before the feeling of "strangeness" has a chance to set in. The wish to spare a mother from contact with an immature infant who might die does not appear to justify the separation rules of the past. Death of the baby when there has been early contact with his mother increases the mourning response of the mother, but not to such a degree as to justify avoidance of physical contact.

Because death does occur in a significant number of very immature prematures, it is worthwhile to note that we now have a clearer idea of what the normal mourning response of parents is and of steps to take to speed psychological recovery. For example, we try to move the mothers to another part of the hospital to avoid contact with mothers and babies. We point out what to expect in the normal grief response (insomnia, for example), and we encourage the parents to communicate their feelings, especially to each other. The mother's doctor ordinarily meets with the parents during the hospital stay and also several months later.

LATER DEVELOPMENT

The parents of a premature almost always want to know what he will be like when he grows up. Will he be handicapped in any way, physically, emotionally, or mentally? When the question is asked about a specific premature baby, it is next to impossible for physicians to predict the outcome. For that matter, no physician can really predict the outcome for any baby. But there are certain statements that can be made with respectable certainty. The first is that in general premature babies do very well. Though off to a slow start, they usually catch up with the full-terms and on the whole thrive no worse. The rosters of the most brilliant minds, greatest artists, and most influential statesmen in all history are studded with the names of preemies; Isaac Newton, Charles Darwin, Voltaire, Napoleon I, Renoir, Victor Hugo, and Winston Churchill are among them. So, in general, an optimistic view is justified. The second statement that can be made is less optimistic. It is that the more premature the baby has been, the more likely he is to develop handicaps that will have some bearing on his life. Among those possible handicaps are lowered intelligence, learning difficulties, impairment of hearing, visual troubles (myopia, astigmatism, and strabismus are the most common), physical awkwardness or clumsiness, certain kinds of cerebral palsy. Still, those are all conditions to which full-term babies also are subject. The degree of risk is the issue here; for the markedly premature baby it is significantly higher.

The task for everyone intimately concerned with a premature baby is to try to live as comfortably as possible with the statistical doubts and to deal with each situation as it arises, not before and not forever. Babies with the handicaps we have mentioned can be helped. Several large-scale studies are in progress to determine which characteristics of premature infants are predictive of normal or abnormal development. When this information becomes available, some of the uncertainty plaguing many parents of prematures should be removed. In the meanwhile, be assured that most preemies do very well indeed.

It is not quite fair to compare a premature baby with a full-term baby of the same age. A simple correction seems to be in order. If you subtract the number of weeks of prematurity from the preemie's chronological age, you will get an age more in keeping with his developmental progress. Thus, the six-months-old premature who was born two months early is more aptly compared with a full-term infant four months old. This correction will hold through the first two years. Development is very rapid in this period, and a month or so will make a big difference. On this scale most prematures will be found to be progressing quite normally. After two years the correction can be dropped, for most preemies will then be able to hold their own with their full-term peers.

As a group, prematures do seem to have some trouble learning to walk without help. While many full-term babies are walking quite steadily at a year or a little more, the preemie may be well into his second year before he achieves this mobility. Similarly, he may be later to talk. The point is, he will make the grade in his own time, given parental patience and confidence. The parents of prematures will have all the usual problems with sleeplessness, feeding, crying, and fussing and probably more of them. The premature will be slower to drink from a cup and may perhaps take longer to master the art of climbing stairs. But he, no less than the full-term, needs to earn his independence by mastery of the childhood tasks of development. The mother should try to curb her impatience at the clumsiness with which he transfers food from saucer to mouth, even though he may still be somewhat under the ideal weight given on the chart for full-term babies of his age. It is no more healthful for him to be confined to a playpen than it is for the full-term. He needs his share of falls, of bumps and bruises.

Maternal feelings of frustration and anxiety are no more to be discounted for the mother of a premature than for any other mother, but she perhaps should be less reluctant to discuss them with her physician. Premature births do generate special anxieties, which can persist for a long time. However negative these feelings may be, it is vital for parents to recognize them. Unrecognized feelings of guilt can induce behavior in the parents that in the long run will affect the child's development. To bring them out into the open, with the help of a physician, is the first step in creating a healthy psychological atmosphere for the premature infant.

POSTMATURITY

Just as the premature baby requires special consideration, so too does the baby whose birth comes later than the statistically normal time for delivery. We define *postmaturity* as a gestational age at birth of greater than forty-two weeks. (The gestational age of the full-term baby, you will recall, is between thirty-eight and forty-two weeks, and the premature's is under thirty-eight weeks.)

Though much investigative work has been done and is being done on the initiation of labor, medicine is still in the dark about the cause (or causes) of postmaturity. For that matter, we do not understand with any great precision why it is that most women should go into labor between thirty-eight and forty-two weeks after conception, or why some women should deliver weeks earlier. The primary importance of these investigations lies, of course, in the implications for the newborn who has arrived ahead of his time or after.

Except for their unusually wide-eyed alertness, the great majority of postmature babies cannot be distinguished from their full-term fellows. A small minority of them do show some signs of malnutrition. These are referred to as *dysmature postmature infants*. Their physical condition gives every indication of their having lost some weight from a high point in the womb. The skin has a sagging looseness that is characteristic of adults who have been on a crash diet; it must previously have enveloped an accumulation of fat. The characteristically fine hair of the full-term infant (the lanugo) is missing. The skin tends to be cracked and dry, parchmentlike, and within hours it may begin to peel, particularly on the hands and feet. The fatty vernix caseosa (see page 257) we expect to find covering the full-term infant is usually absent. The fingernails are long enough to need trimming at once. The nails, skin, and umbilical cord may all show yellowish green staining from meconium evacuated into the amniotic fluid prior to delivery.

The dysmatures may have some problems in establishing normal respiration, in maintaining normal levels of blood sugar, and in nervous function, but these problems are in general manageable. The baby too impaired by malnutrition to sustain life is rare in this very small percentage of all postmatures.

The explanation for the malnutrition in dysmature postmaturity probably is to be found in malfunction of the placenta. The amounts of oxygen and nutrients available for proper metabolism must decrease as the placental functioning slows or fails altogether. It is to be hoped that current research in these related fields of investigation will soon provide answers.

RICHARD I. FEINBLOOM, M.D.

CHAPTER NINETEEN

Is My Baby Sick?

A NEW FATHER, very anxious, calls the doctor's office. His baby has vomited several times. The doctor is out or occupied with another patient, and by the time he can return the father's call the infant has taken a regular feeding and gone to sleep, seemingly quite content. A day or so later the father calls again to apologize for having been so frightened when there was no reason to be. Then, in a manner almost pleading for the key to insight, he asks, "But how can you tell if your baby is sick?"

It is a good question.

In the foregoing chapters on the newborn, we have encouraged parents to expect good health of their newborn. Ill health is very uncommon in infants. Furthermore, it has been shown that much or most of what parents regard as abnormal is in fact normal. Rashes, lumps, spitting up, infrequency of stools all may occur in a perfectly well baby. If we could include all babies and all parents in a generalization, it probably would be safe to say that more anxiety arises from parents' overreactions to the normal deviations of their offspring than from their encounters with actual disease. Nevertheless, there is need to point out that babies can become ill. Sickness serious enough for the doctor to want to see your baby may be infrequent, but it does occur.

Our purpose at this point is not to discuss the diagnosis of specific diseases or the management of illness in infancy. To get down to details here would be inconsistent with the aim of this chapter, which is to give support to the development of a certain overall attitude in the parents of newborns. This attitude is composed, about equally, of intuition and of a willingness to communicate that intuition to the doctor.

TURNING TO THE DOCTOR

Whenever parents become concerned about their babies, they should turn to their doctors or nurses. They should heed the developing intuition that makes them uncomfortable when they observe behavior or appearance that seems odd or out of the way. Many times the observations they make will in fact fall within the normal range of infant behavior. But the ability to discriminate between the normal and the abnormal, the sick and the healthy, the important and the unimportant, does not come to us magically the day our babies are brought home from the hospital. It is acquired only over a long and sometimes painfully anxious experience of learning. This experience never really ends. Even for the professionals—doctors with children of their own—the process is never complete. We are all in the same boat.

Nevertheless, through continuous association with a baby or babies in states of both good and poor health the average parent does develop a great deal of confidence and insight in a relatively short time. But parents must feel able to ask questions! Never be afraid of "bothering" the doctor. You have a right to ask all the questions you think it necessary or instructive to ask. Do not hesitate for fear the question may seem trivial or even silly or may reveal your ignorance. Some parent before you has already put that same question to your doctor—and has had a civil and informative reply.

Without realizing, you may find yourself asking the doctor a certain question over and over again, though in slightly different forms. The superficial aspects of the question may alter from time to time, but they only conceal a single basic problem. This disguised repetition will suggest to your doctor, when he detects it, that you seem unable to accept or to assimilate certain information, and he should then try to find out why this particular problem should present you with difficulty. What is the doctor's goal in his relations with you? Of course, it is to deal with the specific health problems of your baby, but his aim should also be to guide you to the point where you can arrive at solutions of your own (within definite, understood limits) regarding future appearances of these same problems. "Do I need to call the doctor for this? Well, here are the facts. This is what I see. Can I solve the problem presented by these facts or do I need the doctor's guidance?" To help parents develop an increasing assurance in their ability to assess the baby's problems should be, at least in part, the aim of the doctor.

But how can you tell if your baby is sick? We come back to the basic question. Babies do not talk. They cannot tell you their "stomachs hurt" or that they do not "feel well." We have to rely upon another "language," which we must learn to decode. We look for the main clues here in their *feeding habits* and *activity*.

POOR FEEDING

Over the first four to six weeks of life most bottle-fed infants will take somewhere between two and four ounces at a time, increasing the intake as they grow. The amount, as we have noted (see page 292) , may vary from feeding to feeding, but you can look for reasonable consistency. When a marked change in a baby's appetite occurs, the mother should take immediate note. The significance is not so much in the number of ounces at any one feeding but in a *change*—from, say, three to four ounces every four hours to only one ounce or one and one-half ounces on a regular or irregular schedule. Though this change may merely reflect a transient decrease of appetite, it does call for explanation. At the least, you should telephone the doctor. Perhaps your alertness will at first stimulate a number of seemingly unnecessary calls to the physician, but you will have had a useful experience. If your baby resumes his regular pattern of feeding, well and good. You will have observed that deviations can be both transient and without significance. You will have begun to tune up your intuitive parental machinery.

Not only is change in volume important but so also is the *vigor* of feeding, especially if you are breast-feeding and cannot be sure of the baby's intake. One clue will be continued fullness of the breasts after feeding. If you observe that the baby has become poky all of a sudden, if you have to force him to eat, if he spits up half of what he has been obliged to swallow and takes an inordinate length of time to feed, questions to the doctor are in order.

LETHARGY OR LISTLESSNESS

The usefulness of the infant's general vigor as a clue to his well-being will depend, of course, upon his temperament. As we have said (see page 266), some babies from the start seem very active while others appear quite passive. Here again, it is a marked change in behavior that is important. If your previously active infant with a loud or piercing cry should suddenly or gradually seem less eager to move or thrash about, if his cry sounds weaker, and if you have to prod him to stimulate any response, take note. You may only be intruding upon his quiet time or he may only be settling down to sleep, but you will have to go through a number of these occasions before you will be entirely comfortable in distinguishing a quiet period from a symptom of something amiss.

To be able to tell when a baby of the quiet, inactive kind is sick may pose a problem. In him the lethargy of illness may not seem a striking change from his usual behavior. All you have to rely on is your growing intuition. The intuition of mothers of identical twins is somewhat comparable. Without having to look for the distinguishing birthmark or freckle, they know immediately which twin is which. It is a *feeling* they have developed.

IRRITABILITY

There is, however, another clue the parents can look for. Sickness does not always manifest itself in decreased activity. Sometimes sick babies become overactive or, more specifically, irritable. The irritability is almost like a change in personality. The baby may scream and arch his back; he may reject a feeding almost as if he were being jabbed with something sharp. The new mother looks at the "colicky" baby with consternation and thinks at once that he is ill. Not at all. But it will take time, experience, and telephone conversations with the doctor before the mother can recognize that the irritability of colic differs from that of genuine sickness. The irritability of the sick baby is persistent. In contrast, the colicky baby has periods of contentment when he feeds well. These periods, to be sure, may be interrupted with some consistency by spells of irritability during which nothing will placate him. There is a subtle difference here. The mother of a colicky baby may have to visit the pediatrician's office several times before she learns to distinguish between the cry of illness and the cry of fussiness. Some pediatricians, in fact, let the standard newborn fee cover these educational sessions prior to the regularly scheduled first visit at four or six weeks of age. The ability to discriminate between health and disease cannot be developed overnight.

SPITTING UP AND VOMITING

As we have noted earlier (see pages 295–96), spitting up is a disconcerting but very common reaction through the early months. The infant may drink four ounces with vigor and then, a few minutes or even hours later, bring up what seems to be an equally large amount. What distinguishes this regurgitation from the vomiting of a baby who is sick with infection or has some other serious problem? As the first step in this assessment parents might ask themselves the following four questions:

1. Is the baby sucking and feeding with vigor or have I had to force him, more or less, to take his milk?
2. Did he take in a good volume of fluid and really spit up only the last ounce, or did he take in only a relatively small amount and spit up most of it?
3. Does he vomit at every feeding or just once or twice a day?
4. Most important, how is he functioning otherwise? Is he alert, moving about? Is the pattern of his bowel movements typical and are the stools of "good" color (see page 347)? Or does he look pale, seem either lethargic or excessively irritable, and is he either producing no stools or having very frequent abnormally colored movements?

With factual answers to these questions in hand, the parent is in a good position to decide (if she feels that self-assured) whether she needs the doctor's advice, and she is also prepared to provide the doctor with useful information on which to base a judgment.

BOWEL MOVEMENTS

Parents should regard with suspicion any infant whose pattern of bowel movements changes suddenly, in particular if the color of the stools changes to green and remains so consistently (not just once or twice) and if the movements become very watery and explosive. Sick babies usually pass many stools. Two or three green, watery, and explosive movements may be sufficient to disturb parents. There are some babies, both breast-fed and bottle fed, who may have eight or even ten loose stools a day, but as long as the movements remain yellow in color and do not have much water content, the frequency is of little significance. At the other extreme, many infants have only one bowel movement every other day and some perfectly normal babies (especially breast-fed infants) may skip two or three days between movements.

It may be worth adding that the same illness that afflicts an older child or an adult with a cold may produce diarrhea in the infant. Furthermore, irritability and diarrhea may be the only manifestations of earache or sore throat in an infant. The intestinal tract of the infant can represent the main symptomatic pathway for a variety of stresses, infectious or otherwise.

Finally, diarrhea is relatively common in infancy. Usually it is a benign problem that will respond to dietary management alone. Nevertheless, there are good reasons for concern. At this very early age diarrhea can be associated with some degree of dehydration. Because of his smaller reserve of fluids, the infant develops dehydration more quickly than his older sibling does. Accordingly, if you become concerned about your baby's diarrhea, call the doctor early. He will have suggestions to prevent dehydration.

Whatever attitude one may have toward constipation (infrequent bowel movements), one should certainly not regard it as an illness in infancy unless it is associated with the following conditions:

1. Unexplained vomiting, usually persistent and projectile.
2. Distension of the abdomen.
3. Failure to gain weight.
4. Pallor, weakness, listlessness, or excessive irritability.
5. Excessive difficulty in passing a stool, including blood on the stool. Remember that most normal infants fuss and fume, and may grow red in the face for several minutes while expelling a stool.

PALLOR

Parents should not wait for or rely upon a dramatic change in the infant's coloring to alert them to deterioration of his health. Instead of being only an early warning, a significant degree of pallor or duskiness could be a sign of far-advanced disease. We would hope that before this condition appeared the parent would already have been alerted to the presence of disease by some earlier indication—poor feeding, lethargy, persistent irritability, frequent bowel movements, or coughing.

SNEEZING AND COUGHING

Sneezing is very common in well babies. A tiny particle of dust or lint can bring it on, or some other reflex action. It happens all the time. There is no occasion to brace yourself for an impending cold.

A cough, however, is something else. The cough too can be a minor occurrence, no more than a clearing of the back of the throat from a slight postnasal drip. But a cough, especially if it persists and is associated with other signs of ill health (nasal discharge, fever, and so forth), can signal the presence of infection. Parents may find it reassuring to know that coughing, to a certain extent, serves a defensive purpose in that it keeps mucus out of the baby's chest.

Your doctor probably will want to know how often the baby coughs and whether the coughing keeps him from sleeping or interferes with his feeding. Have you noticed any increase in the baby's rate of breathing? Does he seem to work harder at it? Does he seem more lethargic or irritable than usual? Does he feel warm? Has he a fever? The answers will help the doctor to decide what the cough means and what measures should be taken to manage it.

FEVER

Usually, an elevated temperature signifies the presence of infection, but in infants this again is an unreliable sign to wait for. A new baby could be quite ill without fever. In short, any fever in the young infant (under six months) probably warrants a discussion with your doctor even though it may not be indicative of a serious problem. On the other hand, if a new baby seems ill in other respects, the absence of fever should not be reassuring.

What is normal temperature?

Taken by mouth (older children and adults), the usual temperature is 98.6°. Rectal temperature normally is 99.6°. It is a waste of time and mental effort to try to convert one to the other ("It's 102 by rectum so it must really be 101"). Just compare the actual temperature you have read from the thermometer with the normal value for the method you have used. Leaving the thermometer inserted for two minutes is usually sufficient to give a reliable reading.

There is a common misconception that temperatures below normal are dangerous. Except for the patient actually at death's door, this is not so. A temperature of 97° or 97.6° is quite consistent with a state of well-being.

Over the whole range of childhood we probably take temperatures too often. While taking the temperature may be necessary now and then to check a subjective impression, you are not required to do it repeatedly unless your doctor has asked for an accurate record over a specific time for some particular purpose. Most of us soon develop by sense of touch a good idea of when temperature is normal and when it is "hot."

Too often a child's high fever frightens parents needlessly. It really makes little difference whether a child shows 103° or 104°. Children quite commonly run high temperatures with relatively minor infections. We have to differentiate here, however, between early infancy and the whole of childhood. The early infant's fever is more significant because he has so few means of communicating that something is wrong with him. In late childhood parents have more cause to be anxious about the child whose temperature is only 101 but who shows excessive irritability or lethargy with marked general discomfort or localized pain, than about the child with 104 who is happily coloring pictures in a book and voicing no complaint. On the other hand, children sometimes "overreact" with fever and the fever itself becomes of concern and requires steps to reduce it.

THE CHRONIC
OR PERPLEXING PROBLEM

It would be consoling if we could be sure that problems like spitting up, coughing, and diarrhea would disappear in a few days. Such symptoms, even when of brief duration, are worrisome enough in infancy. What happens when they persist, week after week? It goes without saying that a physician or nurse should examine all such children. Nevertheless, the average mother finds it hard to accept that her infant is not seriously ill when loose stools continue to appear day after day or when the nose keeps right on running despite the doctor's apparently thorough examination and confident prescription.

Two points can be made regarding persistence of problems of these kinds. Infants, like older people, take time to improve after contending with seemingly minor problems. Just as a parent will feel run down after a cold, so a baby may take a week to return to complete well-being. More importantly perhaps, as long as a child is sucking and feeding well, appears alert, smiles, coos, and in particular, gains weight, we can endure the chronic problem in expectation that ultimately all will go well. While a healthy baby may sometimes gain weight at a slow rate and even a sick baby may show some gain, it is very infrequent that a sick baby will gain in any regular way.

The perplexing problem is the kind that leaves you wondering, Where do I look this one up? For example, a mother with a baby five weeks old reports finding a spot of blood on the baby's sheet where his head rested. She has started him on solids and wonders whether at the last feeding she might have scraped his mouth on the spoon. She cannot find any raw or scraped place, but she cannot find any other obvious symptom either. He is cool, has been breathing and sleeping easily, has not vomited or shown diarrhea, has good color, has a healed navel, and seems normally active. Since the supposed accident he has been through a feeding period and consumed the usual bottle with gusto.

There is no particular reason to doubt the mother's diagnosis, but note that one reaches this reassuring conclusion only after running down a fairly comprehensive checklist of the child's functioning:

1. There is no history of previous injury.
2. The baby is sucking and feeding well with no vomiting.
3. The eliminatory functions appear to be working properly.
4. The skin and navel appear to be normal.
5. The baby does not seem feverish.

It is parental observations like these that form the raw material of your doctor's or nurse's reassuring judgments. Sooner or later, you too will find yourself making such observations almost automatically and more often than not coming up with logical conclusions about the condition of your baby. But when in doubt, call the doctor!

HOWARD S. KING, M.D.

CHAPTER TWENTY

Diseases and Disorders
of the Newborn

OBSTRUCTION OF AIRWAY

*A*NY OBSTRUCTION of the upper airway (nose, throat, larynx, trachea) can cause noisy breathing (*stridor*), which is a not uncommon symptom in infants. Resistance to the passage of air sets up vibrations, which cause noise, and severe obstruction can cause real difficulty in breathing. Severe stridor can be recognized shortly after birth, but the milder forms may go undetected until after the baby has been taken home from the hospital.

Whereas croup is the main cause of stridor in older children, the most common cause for infants is some congenital abnormality, or birth defect, of the airway. *Laryngomalacia* (literally, softening of the larynx) is perhaps the most common of these defects. The cartilages comprising the voice box should be firm and relatively inflexible but in this condition are overly pliable. In breathing they collapse and increase the resistance. Babies with laryngomalacia tend to improve as they grow older. By the age of one, the stridor in most cases will disappear.

Children with congenitally underdeveloped jawbones may have an associated displacement of the tongue resulting in partial obstruction of the airway and, of course, stridor. The breathing difficulty will be relieved when the jawbones have grown enough for the tongue to assume a more normal position.

In *choanal atresia* a bony overgrowth blocks the rearmost part of one or both nasal passages. If both sides are affected, the child cannot breathe through his nose at all and at feeding time will be in a great deal of difficulty. The definitive therapy is surgical removal of the bony obstruction.

Abnormal vocal cords can cause stridor. Instead of being separate, the two cords may be partially fused. There may be benign growths (*papillomas*) on the ends of the cords. Children with these defects have recognizably weak and peculiar-sounding cries. Neurological disease may paralyze the cords. There also can be abnormal growths in the trachea. A common form is *subglottic* (meaning below the voice box) *hemangioma*, which is a nonmalignant tumor of blood vessels. Abnormally positioned blood vessels or an enlarged thyroid can compress the larynx and so cause stridor.

Treatment of stridor varies with the cause. For many cases the passage of time is enough. For others surgery will be in order. In the most severe obstructions, tracheotomy may be found necessary to bypass the obstruction until the child is old enough for definitive treatment.

BILIARY ATRESIA

In *biliary atresia,* an uncommon congenital condition, the major bile ducts are either too malformed to carry bile from the liver to the intestine, or are missing altogether.

Bile, which is a thin yellow fluid, is a vehicle for the excretion of a number of body products, including bilirubin (see pages 382–86), the major component in the breakdown of aged red blood cells. Bile also contains chemical compounds that are important in the digestion of fats. Bile is produced in the liver cells. Microscopic channels carry the bile from these cells to larger tubes in the liver that, like streams joining in a river, come together to form the *common bile duct,* and this duct connects the liver with the duodenum, the uppermost section of the intestine. There is one major branch, the *cystic duct,* leading to the *gallbladder,* which is the storage place for bile.

Obstruction to bile flow, from whatever cause, can bring on progressive damage and scarring of the liver with consequent impairment of function. When the outflow of bile is blocked, all the substances normally excreted in the bile back up into the bloodstream. Bilirubin being one of these substances, jaundice is thereby an important symptom of biliary obstruction (although this condition will be rare among all the causes of jaundice in the newborn [see pages 382–86]) . The insufficiency of bile in the intestine results in incomplete digestion of fatty foods. Chronic diarrhea and the signs of poor nutrition will be the symptoms. If unrelieved, complete obstruction of bile flow causes so much liver damage that death results.

In infancy the common and cystic ducts and the gallbladder, any one or all three, may be involved in a biliary obstruction. There are two major classes of malformation: those in which some part of the common duct exists and those in which it is missing. If any part of the duct is present and in normal communication with the smaller branches and tubes within the liver, it is in theory possible to obtain normal flow of bile through surgery. If the duct is missing, a new linkage is impossible and liver failure, usually at between one and three years of age, is inevitable. Unfortunately, this prognosis holds for most of the infants born with defective biliary systems. (Remember, though, that this is statistically a rare condition among the entire class of newborns.) Experiments with transplantation of the liver offer hope for the future.

Although the symptoms are similar, congenital biliary atresia must be distinguished from *hepatitis* (inflammation of the liver) . The two conditions are difficult to tell apart, but it is important to diagnose biliary atresia as early as possible. The sooner a repairable biliary atresia can be corrected, the less liver damage will result. The diagnosis can be made only by taking a small specimen of the liver (biopsy) for examination under the microscope. While the infant is in surgery for this procedure an X ray is taken to determine where the obstruction is and whether it can be corrected. There is an unfortunate catch here, however. If the infant's trouble is hepatitis, there is risk that anesthetizing him will make it worse. As a compromise, it is common practice to wait from four to eight months in the hope that hepatitis, if that is the difficulty, will clear up.

BIRTHMARKS

Very many, perhaps most, babies are born with a birthmark. The cause of *hemangioma,* which is the medical name for lesions of this sort, is not known. Hemangioma is a cluster or growth of small blood vessels on or under the skin. It is not cancer and is usually no more than an inconvenience. Rarely requiring treatment, hemangiomas tend to disappear on their own, but the process may take many months, even years.

The commonest hemangioma is the *salmon patch,* a cluster of small red spots on the nape of the neck, across the bridge of the nose or on the upper eyelid (see page 257). It used to be said that the marks on the neck were left by the stork's beak. The salmon patch never requires treatment, but disappears so gradually over the first year of life that the parents may not even notice its going.

The *strawberry mark* is another very common hemangioma, occurring in as many as 10 percent of all babies, more frequently among females. Bright red, this mark looks as if a strawberry had been cut in half and stuck to the baby's skin. Most often it appears on the face or neck. Characteristically, it may be so small at birth as to be hard to find, but it enlarges rapidly, attaining peak size by six months. Almost without exception, this rapid growth signifies that the strawberry in time will wither away. A change of color to dark red and the appearance of small islands of gray in the red herald this involution of the strawberry mark. At age three a third of all strawberry marks have disappeared, at four 60 percent, and by six 70 percent. Altogether, 90 percent disappear on their own. For the remainder surgery is available and X-ray treatment, but time is on the side of the "wait and see" attitude, unless the mark becomes an acute emotional problem for the child. The rare mark that grows at an excessive rate or is on a site subject to repeated bruising may call for earlier intervention.

A minority of strawberry marks extend deep down in the skin. The visible portion may be only a small part of the total hemangioma. Some hemangiomas are completely submerged, recognizable only by the resulting lump or by the suggestion of a large blue mass under the skin. By and large, all these submerged hemangiomas follow the same pattern of growth and involution that is characteristic of the visible ones. The conservative approach is always in order.

A third hemangioma of relatively common occurrence is the *port wine stain.* These stains are areas of skin that appear to be normal except for the red coloring. The most common variety is a patch shaped like a diamond on the forehead extending to the bridge of the nose. When the infant cries, the diamond flushes, and even in adults the coloring of the patch gives a clue to the emotions. The port wine stain, which may occur elsewhere on the head or body, is especially prominent in blonds. There is no treatment for this lesion. It usually fades in time but sometimes will remain at least faintly visible. Cosmetics will render the mark less conspicuous.

CLEFT LIP AND CLEFT PALATE

Cleft lip and cleft palate are two often related birth defects. While not common in the United States as compared, say, with Vietnam, these defects appear frequently enough for most persons to have seen them or at least to know of them.

Cleft lip, also known as harelip, is almost always a defect of the upper lip, varying from a small notch in the lip itself to a sizable gap extending from the edge of the lip up to the nose. Cleft palate can vary from a small slit in the *soft palate,* which is at the back of the mouth at the opening of the throat, to a half-inch gap stretching from the soft palate across the roof of the mouth (the *hard palate*) or the upper gums. The gums also may be involved in these defects and the teeth too. There are rare cases of babies with chromosomal abnormalities who have had both cleft lip and cleft palate in association with much more serious congenital defects. Furthermore, the fact that there appears to be a disproportion of these defects in certain peoples would also support the hypothesis of genetic influence.

The soft palate, which has a conical body known as the *uvula* projecting downward at the back of the mouth, is composed mainly of muscle and moves when you talk or swallow. It acts as a valve closing off alternately the upper and lower parts of the throat. The soft palate keeps air from entering the throat in the act of swallowing and food from entering the nose in the act of breathing. The sealing action of the soft palate makes it possible to whistle, gargle, blow up balloons, and utter a number of sounds, including those for the letters *t, b, d, p, h, v,* and *f.* Obviously, a cleft impairs or destroys the sealing action of the soft palate. There will be problems of feeding and, later, of speech. Children with cleft palates are more liable than others to middle-ear infections. For the child with cleft lip there is the aesthetic problem that can be psychologically disturbing.

About one-third of the children with cleft lip or cleft palate will have one or more known relatives with the same defects. The hereditary influence seems stronger for cleft lip, but prediction on the evidence of a known family tree is not yet an impressively precise art. On the other hand, we have no evidence suggesting that these defects arise from anything mothers do in pregnancy or may have done prior to pregnancy.

The treatment of cleft lip and cleft palate is surgical repair. It is customary in this country to repair the lip in the first six weeks of life.

Repair of the palate is a more individual matter, but in most cases is accomplished by the time the child is one and one-half or two years old. The surgery may have to be done in several stages. The idea is to correct the defect early so that the development of speech will be interfered with as little as possible. For the majority of these children the results of the program of surgery and speech training are excellent, but speech therapy may have to be continued into the school years.

Until the cleft lip or palate can be repaired, feeding has to be done with a "cleft-lip feeder," which is a sort of syringe with a long tube in place of a needle, somewhat like the gadget used to baste roasting meats. After surgery, the infant's hands must be immobilized to prevent him from reaching into his mouth and damaging the repair. The parents will have to take an important part in speech therapy, and their role in coping with any psychological problems will, of course, be crucial.

CLUBFOOT

In clubfoot, which is a congenital deformity of unknown cause, the entire foot is bent downward and twisted inward. The foot is in a fixed position. The child cannot move the foot himself, nor can the doctor manipulate it through what would be the range of movement of a normal foot. This disorder, which is known to doctors as *talipes equino-varus,* may affect one foot or both. The clubfoot does not improve on its own. Left untreated, the deformity will seriously impair the child's walking.

A child with clubfoot should be taken as early as possible to an orthopedic specialist. The earlier treatment can be started, the better the prospects. A series of plaster casts is applied, beginning in infancy, and over a period of months the foot is stretched into the normal configuration. Casting alone, however, will not correct the most rigid forms of clubfoot. Surgery will be required.

COLIC

According to reliable studies, a large percentage of small babies (some say as high as 80 percent) cry from three to four hours every day for no discoverable reason or cause. In the extreme form, this regular crying every day is known as *colic,* and, as the statistics show, it is an unfortunately common disturbance of the first three months of life. It may begin any time between the second and sixth week and it gradually fades away by the age of three months. The regularity of the pattern is so marked that the disturbance is commonly known as the three-month colic.

Some babies (whose parents are the lucky ones) have their colic in the daytime and are peaceful in the evenings, but theirs is not the most familiar pattern. In the classical situation, the baby begins to stir uncomfortably soon after the evening feeding or even before it is finished. He draws his thighs up onto his abdomen as if in intense pain and shrieks and wails for three or four hours with hardly a respite. The belly may be distended, and the baby may pass gas. Neither rocking the baby nor burping him has any effect. The pacifier fails to calm and so does a drink of water. Finally, at 10 or 11 P.M., when mother's and father's nerves are raw and screaming too, he falls into limp sleep. He may or may not gulp down his 10 P.M. bottle before dropping off. The next morning he is again himself, seemingly happy and feeding well, only to repeat the performance come 6 P.M. But all through the day, by all the usual signs, he has been a perfectly well baby. In fact, it is characteristic of colicky babies that they seem to thrive exceptionally well and suffer no permanent impairment.

Until a few years ago colic was taken to be of intestinal origin. Enemas and various drugs were routinely prescribed. Even Dr. Benjamin M. Spock distinguished between true colic and "periodic irritable crying." Nowadays pediatricians are not so sure. When babies cry frantically, they draw in large amounts of air, whose presence could explain both the distended abdomen and the passage of gas by rectum. The contemporary opinion tends toward regarding the difference between "true colic" and other more or less regular episodes of irritable crying as merely one of degree. At that stage of his development the baby may have no other means but crying to relax tensions and let off emotional steam. The regular disappearance of colic at three months would seem to indicate a developmental explanation. Dr. T. Berry Brazelton, of the Children's Hospital Medical Center, has written in *Pediatrics:* "As other ways of discharging tension and of reaching out to the environment become available, there is a constant gradual reduction in the quantity of daily crying . . . Infants gradually seem to replace these crying periods with sociable interaction with their parents or with other activities, such as rolling over, watching their hands or other objects."

When it comes to colic, the temptation is to prescribe for the parents rather than for the baby. To be confronted night after night with a frantically screaming baby who rejects or ignores every effort to soothe him is a trial for the most saintly mother and father. Young parents encountering colic for the first time are almost bound to feel frustrated and angry to the point of rage at their inability to command the situation. The fact that the doctor can offer no guaranteed remedy does not help matters.

The best advice for the parent of a colicky baby is to arrange somehow to get away for a few hours from time to time. If you cannot find a sympathetic relative or a reliable sitter to watch the baby, take him along for a ride in the car. The change of scenery will do you good and the fresh air and motions of the car may even quiet the baby, though no one can give you an ironclad warranty on that. If you are stuck at home without chance of relief, you should not feel guilty about turning up the TV or hi-fi a notch or two to drown out the nightly shrieks.

Extremely conscientious parents have been known to develop a sense of guilt about colic. "Am I causing it?" they ask. The answer no can be given with some confidence. If the parents insist upon probing their feelings in relation to colic, a better question might be, Is there anything going on in our lives right now that makes us especially vulnerable to the baby's crying? Discussion centering on this question may bring to the surface some submerged factors that have been producing tension in the family scene. When they are out in the open, the parents may feel better able to cope with the colic, especially if they can convince themselves that it really will not last beyond the third month.

CRIB DEATH

In the face of all the progress in medical research and infant care, the sad fact remains that several thousand babies die each year in the United States without having exhibited any recognized symptoms of sickness. The annual figure for these *crib deaths* or *cot deaths* is put at somewhere between sixteen thousand and twenty thousand, depending on the authority quoted. In the typical case an infant is put to bed at night seemingly in good health and is found dead the next morning.

Various explanations are offered, none of them as yet statistically conclusive, but the opinion seems to be growing that these infants are the victims of sudden massive and overwhelming infections.

The age range for this *sudden death syndrome,* to use the professional jargon, is between five weeks and five months, the peak coming between two and four months. Rarely does the syndrome occur, if ever, prior to three weeks of age or after six months. This particular span would tend to give some credence to the old explanations of crib death—that the mother somehow "overlay" her infant in sleep or that the infant suffocated in his pillow or blankets. A younger baby would not be exposed to those hazards and an older one should be able to defend himself. But in point of fact, suffocation, though a common concern of parents, is very rare. The infant whose breathing is interfered with thrashes about and kicks up a considerable fuss. He would have to be severely constrained to keep him from turning his head sufficiently to get a breath of air, and unless his caretakers were callous to his well-being, it is unlikely his cries would not be heard.

In a sense it is a testament to medical progress that the condition is recognized for what it is. We have had such success in our attacks upon the old scourges of infancy that we can rule out of the picture here most of the diseases that used to take such a terrible toll of the young. Unexplained death now takes the spotlight because death has become so rare. In terms of statistics, your infant is in greater danger from traffic and various household hazards than from crib death.

The sudden death syndrome can strike the rich and the poor alike, the conscientious as well as the careless. There is no basis for a parent to blame himself or herself for such a calamity. Nor is there evidence of a genetic influence. The chances of a repeat occurrence with later born infants is not appreciably increased. This is one situation in which the educated parent is no better equipped than the uneducated to protect his child. Nevertheless, the parent who has had to bear this tragedy understandably tends to blame himself and may overwhelm subsequent children with exaggerated protectiveness.

The National Foundation for Sudden Infant Death (1501 Broadway, New York, New York 10036) was established in 1962 to stimulate research into this strange syndrome. Any parent whose child has been a victim would do well to get in touch with the foundation. It is almost always helpful for parents to associate with others who have been through the same misfortune or with those who have specialized information about it.

EMPHYSEMA

Emphysema is a condition we hear much of these days in relation to cigarette smoking, but it is found also in infants in association with a variety of lung ailments. The physician makes the diagnosis after he has examined a child (often with X ray) for a respiratory difficulty of some sort. When any part of the lung, large or small, is distended excessively with air, we call the condition emphysema.

The bronchial system, through which air is moved in and out of the body, resembles a tree with its branches in the lungs (*bronchi*) growing smaller and smaller the farther removed they are from the main trunk (the *trachea* or windpipe). The smallest branches, which are too fine to be seen with the naked eye, communicate directly with the lung's *alveoli,* tiny sacs that are the basic respiratory units. These sacs exchange gases with the smallest blood vessels, the *capillaries.* Across the wall between them, the alveoli give oxygen to the capillaries and take carbon dioxide from the blood. To complete our analogy, we can think of the alveoli as the leaves of the bronchial tree.

The air tubes composing the bronchial tree are all flexible and expansible, from the smallest to the largest. When we breathe in (inspiration), the cross section of the opening in the tube (the *lumen*) enlarges. When we exhale carbon dioxide (expiration), the lumen contracts. Now, suppose there is an obstruction of some kind in a tube. Because the diameter of the tube expands in inspiration, there could still be room for air to get by whereas the contraction of the tube in expiration might close it down completely and block the exhaling of carbon dioxide. Air would flow in but not out. The trapped air would distend the passageway and the alveoli at the ends of its branches. This is the condition we call emphysema. In adults this overdistention can destroy not only the lung's normal elasticity but even the lung tissue itself. Complete obstruction from any cause leads to collapse of the structure involved (see page 387).

Any inflammation from infection can narrow air passages and set up the conditions for emphysema. In infants hyaline membrane disease (see page 335) is a common cause. Another is aspiration of the amniotic fluid just before delivery in a situation of fetal distress. Emphysema in children tends to be less important than the disease or diseases causing it, and treatment is aimed primarily at the cause. There is one exception. Congenital lobar emphysema requires immediate relief by surgery. In this condition one lobe of the lung balloons to many times its normal size, compressing the normal lung and in extreme cases exerting pressure on the heart and great blood vessels. The normal lung may be flattened like a pancake. The only treatment is removal of the affected lung as soon as the condition is recognized, even on the baby's first day.

HEPATITIS

Hepatitis is inflammation of the liver, usually from an infection. Though relatively common in later life, the disease is rare among the newborn.

The hepatitis found in the newborn comes in two varieties. In the first it is part of a picture of widespread infection that may involve most of the body. For example, hepatitis is a component of rubella (German measles), or syphilis, of cytomegalic inclusion disease (a virus infection affecting the fetus cells), and of toxoplasmosis (a parasitic disease more common among animals than in man). In all these infections other organs besides the liver will be involved, but in the second variety of hepatitis the liver, if not the only organ involved, is certainly the site of the major attack. This variety resembles the hepatitis found in older children and adults.

The outlook for the baby with the first variety of hepatitis seems to depend not so much on the liver involvement as on the extent to which other organs, the heart and brain primarily, are affected. In the second variety, where the liver is the major site of infection, the prognosis will be determined by the amount of damage to the liver. Most of the babies will survive, but in the severest infections the outcome will be fatal. Though the majority will recover completely, a few will have a chronic impairment of the liver.

For most of the hepatitis in which there is an associated infection of other bodily parts, the causative germ has been identified. We have been able to isolate the viruses of German measles and cytomegalic inclusion disease, the bacterium of syphilis, and the amoeba of toxoplasmosis. The same cannot be said of the hepatitis in which the liver is the primary seat of disease, but we suspect that some virus or viruses eventually will be identified as the villains. The germs we have identified are passed to the fetus from the mother through the placenta, and although we cannot as yet prove it, we suspect a similar pattern for the others.

The treatment of hepatitis will depend, of course, upon the cause. Information is increasing rapidly. For the hepatitis from viruses or protozoa we have no effective drug and no preventive vaccine. Treatment will be aimed at proper nutrition and prevention of secondary infection. The symptoms of hepatitis (mainly jaundice persisting beyond the first week of life) are indistinguishable from the symptoms of biliary atresia (see pages 352–86). We count on the body's ability, under proper care, to clear itself of hepatitis in a matter of months. If there is no sign of improvement, steps must then be taken to exclude the possibility of biliary atresia, which may be surgically correctable.

DIAPHRAGMATIC HERNIA

Occasionally the diaphragms, which are the two thin sheets of muscle separating the chest cavity from the abdominal cavity, fail to form completely in embryological life, and a child is born with the quite rare congenital defect known as *diaphragmatic hernia*. An opening is left in the diaphragm through which the contents of the abdominal cavity (stomach, intestines, and so forth) can intrude into the chest (*thoracic*) cavity.

The abdominal contents pushing up into the thoracic cavity may thrust the heart and great blood vessels to one side and compress the lung. The understandable result will be severe difficulty in breathing. A second possible problem is the kinking of the intruding intestine with resulting obstruction (see page 380) and perhaps strangulation of a segment of the gastrointestinal tract. In the most severe forms diaphragmatic hernia becomes a medical (and surgical) emergency in the newborn nursery. Even in the best circumstances of early recognition and good surgical technique, many babies succumb. In less severe cases there may be no symptom, and the hernia may not be detected for several years. Fortunately, diaphragmatic hernia is so rare that it should not be an occasion for worry.

INGUINAL HERNIA

The protrusion or displacement of an organ of the body beyond or outside its normal confines is a *hernia*. For example, nature intends the intestine to reside in, and only in the abdomen. When a segment (usually called a *loop*) of intestine escapes its normal limits by protruding from the abdominal cavity and intruding into the groin below, we say that the wayward loop has *herniated*. Despite all the bad jokes of the TV comedians, the word hernia does not refer exclusively to the groin, although the groin or *inguinal* hernia is the most common type. Diaphragmatic hernias (see page 362) and umbilical hernias (see pages 280–81) are also seen in the early weeks of life, which are of particular interest to us here.

To explain hernia it is necessary to review a little anatomy and embryology. The *peritoneum,* which is the lining of the abdominal cavity, forms early in embryological life. Somewhere around the third month, a small saclike projection of the peritoneum (the *processus vaginalis*) extends down through the *inguinal canal* into the *scrotum* of the male or the labia of the female. At birth a process of sealing off this *peritoneal pouch* and dissolving it begins, to result eventually in the complete disappearance of the pouch between the abdominal cavity and the testis. But until this process is complete there is a communication between the cavity and scrotum into which the intestine could intrude. Further, the sealing-off process can be partial as well as complete. There are several variations of failure to seal off, and as long as any communication with the abdominal cavity exists a hernia can occur. One often hears hernia described as a "rupture" but this is a misnomer. In this hernia nothing tears; rather, the muscles of the inguinal canal under strain may loosen and allow the intestine to slip down into the pouch. There is reason to believe that the pouch never seals off in from 5 to 10 percent of males, and it is in this population that the hernias of adult life occur.

Inguinal hernia is a very common condition. It is often associated with hydrocele (see page 366), a collection of fluid in a pinched off section of the pouch. Though statistics are hard to come by, it is probable that hernia occurs in about 5 percent of children, with boys affected nine times as frequently as girls. Most cases of hernia in children are detected in the first year of life. Often the parents will notice the telltale bulge in the groin. The bulge may come and go, depending on whether the baby is relaxed or straining, and it may disappear under pressure from the parent's or doctor's hand. In this case the intestine is slipping in and out of the abdominal cavity and the hernia is said to be *reducible*. If the hernia persists under all conditions, it is said to be trapped or *incarcerated*. Then the intestine may be kinked, leading to obstruction, or the blood vessels may be compressed, bringing on progressive development of gangrene. Incarceration is regarded as cause of prompt hospitalization and surgery. It is likely to occur in children, and for this reason we tend to recommend surgical intervention when hernia is detected. The younger the child the more urgent is the need for correction. If the child has no fever, is not vomiting or screaming with pain, the hernia does not constitute an emergency, but if the child is exhibiting those symptoms along with a bulge in the groin, the doctor should be notified immediately.

Our recommendation for early surgery on inguinal hernia in childhood is not in accord with the accepted practice regarding hernia in adults. Though hernias do not cure themselves, the risk of incarceration is far less among adults than for children.

Hernia occurs more often on the right side than on the left, but in 15 percent of the cases it occurs on both. Detection of hernia on one side should always prompt thorough examination of the other.

Modern surgery has quite changed the picture of hernia in infancy. The operation, called *herniorrhaphy,* is performed under general anesthesia, but it is not at all unusual for the baby to be admitted to the hospital in the morning and discharged the same day. Babies tolerate the surgery well and within hours are behaving as if nothing had happened. This quick recovery contrasts with the adult experience, which is likely to be annoying or downright disagreeable. If prematurity or some other special condition requires postponement of surgery, use of a truss to hold the intestine more or less in place for the time being is recommended.

DISLOCATED HIP

In the language of the mechanical engineer, the hip is an example of the ball-and-socket joint. For a linkage of this sort one end of a movable member (a rod or a pipe or whatever) is held in a fixed position while the other end is free to swivel about in a full circle. A ball at the fixed end of the rod or pipe fits into a concave socket in the other member of the joint and is held there by some simple mechanical arrangement.

The ball of the hip joint is the upper end of the thighbone (the *head* of the *femur*). The socket (the *acetabulum*) is formed by the three major bones of the pelvis. The head of the femur fits snugly into the acetabulum and is held in place there by ligaments and the several muscles that activate the joint. If the femoral head is displaced from the acetabulum (ball out of socket), we call the condition displaced hip, partial or complete.

The hip joint is formed early in embryonic growth. Development of the acetabulum depends upon its receiving constant stimulation from the head of the femur. If the head is not in close contact, the socket fails to grow. It will remain underdeveloped, unable to accept the femoral head securely, and the head then will tend to slip still farther out of the socket. In this cycle the dislocation can be a progressive condition, and some babies at birth have hips completely dislocated. More commonly, the dislocation is partial, but in time a partially dislocated hip tends to become completely dislocated. The earlier the abnormality is detected, the easier the treatment will be and the greater the chances of complete cure. While fetal dislocation of the hip is far from rare, few parents will have heard of it.

Careful testing of hip movement is an important part of the physical examinations of the newborn and the infant. With the infant on his back on the table, the examining nurse or doctor *abducts* the thighs; that is, he rotates the legs and pushes on them as if trying to make the knees touch the table. A dislocated hip offers resistance to the movement. Asymmetrical folds in the thighs and shortening of one leg are also signs suggesting abnormal hip development, and X ray may confirm the suspected underdevelopment of an acetabulum. The nurse or doctor should be the one to make the finding of something wrong, but sometimes parents are the first to notice. If the condition escapes detection until the child begins to walk, there will be a distinct limp favoring the affected side.

To some extent, the stage of the condition will determine the treatment for dislocated hip. The guiding principle is to hold the head of the femur in normal relationship with the acetabulum. In early partial dislocation a heavy wadding of several diapers is put on the baby to hold the thighs apart and in a somewhat rotated "frog leg" position. For complete dislocation some form of mechanical traction is required to bring the head of the femur into proper position. The child wears a body cast for a period of days or a couple of weeks. The outlook is excellent if the dislocation is diagnosed and treated early. The longer it goes untreated, the more difficult the treatment becomes and the less satisfactory the results. Surgery may be necessary for older children and for marked abnormality.

HYDROCELE

In association with failure to seal off the peritoneal sac (see page 363) an accumulation of fluid around the testis often occurs. This condition, called *hydrocele,* is not painful or harmful and usually resolves itself. When the nurse or doctor is examining your baby, you may notice the procedure in which a flashlight is held behind the scrotum. If the beam of light is blocked entirely, a hernia exists, but if the scrotum lights up like a light bulb, there is a hydrocele.

For hydrocele alone a period of watchful waiting usually is in order. If the hydrocele persists for a year, and particularly if it is large, the chances are great that the peritoneal pouch is open still and that hernia sooner or later will occur, if it has not already occurred. In consequence, it is customary to operate on large hydroceles, especially those that have persisted for the better part of a year. In the course of the surgery, the remaining peritoneal pouch is removed, along with the hydrocele.

HYDROCEPHALUS

In the past twenty years, new treatments have been developed for hydrocephalus, which used to be known as "water on the brain" or "water of the brain." The head of the child with hydrocephalus grows at a faster than normal rate. It is a serious condition but not a common one. The doctor, not the parent, will be the one to discover it. When the doctor or nurse at a routine visit puts the tape measure around a baby's head, hydrocephalus is one of the possibilities he or she is checking against.

Essentially, hydrocephalus is a consequence of excessive pressure from spinal fluid, which is the clear liquid surrounding and supporting the brain and spinal cord. The fluid is contained in a membranous sac (the *meninges*), around the brain and spinal cord, and it serves to cushion those delicate structures of the central nervous system. The fluid flows from and into channels and cavities penetrating both the brain and cord. Specialized cells within the brain cavities (*ventricles*) form the fluid, which is in a constant state of flux, production and removal proceeding simultaneously. There are numerous filtering sites on the meninges where the fluid is resorbed. You can think of saliva as going through an analogous cycle, formed in the mouth, swallowed with the food, and in the intestine resorbed back into the body.

The infant's skull growth responds to brain growth. In hydrocephalus the brain is not increasing in substance but is expanding in form under pressure from an excess accumulation of fluid, just as the skin of a balloon expands from the pressure of the air you blow into it. The skin of the inflated balloon does not weigh any more than it did, but having been thinned out, it covers a much larger area. The similar process in hydrocephalus "thins out" and enlarges the geometry of the brain structure. The bones of the skull, not solidly joined at birth, spread apart, and the fontanel stretches out. If allowed to progress unchecked, the stretching can damage the brain to the point of death.

There appear to be two main causes of hydrocephalus. In the first an obstruction blocks the flow of fluid from the centers of production. The obstruction might come from some failure of embryological development or it might be the result of scarring from inflammation, as in meningitis. Production goes on as usual, but the fluid, unable to find an exit, backs up and exerts pressure on the brain. In the second type there is an imbalance, again probably a failure in embryological development, between the body's ability to produce the fluid and its ability to resorb it. It seems reasonable to suppose that filtering sites are missing from the meninges. The end effect, of course, is the same as in the first type.

In its severity hydrocephalus varies widely. Even with no treatment the mildest forms may cease spontaneously to develop (*arrested hydrocephalus*) and enlargement of the head comes to a halt. Some babies at birth have heads too large for vaginal delivery; others seem normal at birth but show abnormal skull development in the first year. The treatment in any case is directed at reducing the fluid pressure. The accepted approach at this writing is surgical. When the obstruction in a brain channel cannot be removed altogether, the cavity is tapped to remove excess fluid and reduce pressure. By means of a fine plastic tube inserted through a small hole in the skull, the fluid is carried down into the chest, where the other end of the tube is threaded into the large vein returning blood to the heart from the head, neck, and arms. This procedure, of which there are several variations, generally works well. In the case of imbalance between production and resorption of fluid, a tube is connected between the spine and the ureter of one kidney, which must be sacrificed. The excess spinal fluid runs off into the ureter and out in the urine. Neither treatment gets at the underlying cause but only relieves the symptoms. Research for a more fundamental attack is in progress.

HYPOSPADIAS

This relatively common birth defect appears in the external genitalia of both sexes, in various degrees of severity. As is the case with so many birth defects, the exact cause of hypospadias is not known.

In the male this condition has three main features: the urethral opening is on the underside of the penis and not at the tip; the shaft of the penis may be bent downward; the prepuce (or foreskin) may be defective or altogether absent on the underside, lending the penis a hooded appearance. In the most common form, which requires no treatment, the urethral opening will be just below the normal site, but in severe cases it may occur anywhere along the shaft to the juncture of penis and scrotum. In rare instances the scrotum is divided in two with the urethral opening between the sections. The most severe cases of hypospadias are likely to be accompanied by other disorders of the urinary tract. When marked hypospadias is present, X-ray examination of the kidneys, ureter, and bladder is in order.

In girls, displacement of the urethra is not so noticeable and may be discovered only in a gynecological examination. In the most severe cases the opening may occur in the vagina and make itself known by causing difficulties in urination. But for all practical purposes the nature of hypospadias makes it a problem primarily of the male.

Hypospadias does not constitute an emergency, but if the more severe forms are not corrected they may interfere with sexual activity in adult life and it has definite psychological implications for the boy. The treatment, of course, is surgical. The incompletely formed prepuce can be removed and the misplaced opening corrected. The results of surgery are usually quite good, but more than one operation may be required. The best time for surgery will depend on the individual condition and the personality of the patient.

INCOMPATIBILITY OF BLOOD TYPE

A common cause of jaundice in the newborn (see pages 382–86) is incompatibility of the baby's and mother's blood. In the chapter on diseases of pregnancy (see page 117), we already have talked about the Rh-factor incompatibility, but the subject of blood differences goes beyond the Rh difficulty and is of sufficient importance to warrant further discussion.

All human beings have distinguishing characteristics, such as the color of hair or eyes. These traits are not unique, but they do allow certain groupings to be made among our kind. That is, we will belong to the group of blonds, as distinct from brunets, or to the group of the blue-eyed, as distinct from the brown-eyed, and so forth. So it is also with the human blood cells. They are all blood but they fall into distinguishing groups or *types* determined by minute variations in chemical structure. The chemical composition of the walls of the red cells of one group of persons is different from the chemical composition of the cell walls of another group. Most of the variation involves only four or five different protein molecules, so the number of major blood types is not very large, but when it comes to the mixing of blood these minute differences are vital.

The four major blood groups are designated O, A, B, and AB. Types O and A are by far the most common. As we saw in chapter 6 (see page 151), there is the further distinction that some persons have (while others lack) the blood molecule called the Rh factor. In the United States the population is divided into 85 percent with the Rh factor and 15 percent without. The molecule takes its name from the rhesus monkey, in whose blood it was first identified. When we describe a person's blood, we give the type first and then say whether it is positive or negative with respect to the Rh factor. For instance, to say a person is

A positive means that his blood is type A and has the Rh factor. If he is O negative, his blood is type O and lacks the Rh factor.

Type O blood carries antibodies (see page 152) against the type A and type B red blood cells. Type A has antibodies against B, and B against A, but type AB has none against either A or B. The antibodies are proteins. You can think of them as attaching themselves to alien cells to mark or tag the cells for removal from the bloodstream and destruction. Thus, if a type O person should receive a transfusion of type A blood, his anti-A antibodies would react with the A red cells, which then would be removed from his bloodstream and destroyed. In contrast, a type A person can receive type O blood because he has no anti-O antibody. In fact, type O blood can be given to types O, A, B, and AB, but the type O person can receive only type O blood. The AB person, having no antibodies against O, A, or B, can receive blood of any of the four major types.

In the chapter on pregnancy, we saw how the blood of an Rh-negative mother forms antibodies when it comes in contact with the blood of her Rh-positive baby. That process is not the same as the one involving type O with type A or type O with type B. The existence of type O antibodies against A and B does not depend on contact. Type O has them from the start, and in consequence they are called *naturally occurring antibodies*. They come in two molecular sizes. The smaller of the two can pass across the placenta into the baby's bloodstream, but the larger cannot. While every person who has anti-A and anti-B antibodies will have them in both sizes, the O-type person will have the small ones in greater supply. Hence, type O mothers are more likely to transfer antibodies that can affect the red blood cells of their babies.

As we have seen, when an antibody (whether anti-A, anti-B, or anti-Rh) against a baby's red blood cells crosses through the placenta from the mother's bloodstream into the bloodstream of the fetus, *hemolytic disease* of the newborn (see page 371) occurs (hemolysis means destruction). The red blood cells tagged with antibody are removed by a special system of the fetus (known as the reticuloendothelial system) and destroyed. To keep up with this process of destruction, the baby must produce red cells at a higher than normal rate. In most situations the infant can increase red cell production to keep up with the losses. If the process is greatly accelerated, however, the destruction can exceed the baby's capacity to manufacture red cells. The number of red cells will be reduced, and the baby will go into the state we call *anemia*. The more severe this process is the harder the baby's hematopoietic system must work, and just as the biceps of the arm enlarges under training at weight lifting, so does the baby's hematopoietic system enlarge under this extra load. In the fetus major sites of blood forming and removing tissue are the liver and spleen. Hence, babies who have undergone excessive destruction of red cells are likely to have enlarged livers and spleens. In the section on jaundice (see pages 382–86) , we follow the sequence in which hemoglobin from the destroyed red cells is liberated and processed into bilirubin, which enters the fetal bloodstream. As long as the baby is in utero the placenta constitutes an escape hatch for removal of the excess bilirubin, which the mother's liver can handle. After birth, the excess bilirubin of the infant becomes a medical problem.

This sequence of events occurs in some degree for all babies whose mothers have the small variety of antibodies directed against the fetus's red blood cells. The condition can be so mild as to be barely noticeable, may show up as moderately intense jaundice (see pages 383–84) , or at the other extreme, it can cause anemia severe enough to bring on heart failure and death. The severe form is known as *erythroblastosis fetalis* (see pages 151–52) . Thus, the clinical problem presented by babies with sensitized red blood cells covers a wide range of severity. The public hears more about those problems in relation to the Rh factor, but there is also a much more common *ABO hemolytic disease of the newborn* that can come about from passage of antibodies directed against blood groups A and B. With rare exceptions, only the type-O mothers will have the anti-A and anti-B antibody in the small size that can pass through the placenta to react with the red cells of the type A or type B fetus. While type-A and type-B mothers have the antibody, it is of the larger size that cannot get into the fetal circulation. ABO hemolytic disease is not a severe problem. Anemia and heart failure are very rare. It does not require the amniocentesis or intrauterine transfusions that have become standard practice for severely affected Rh-positive babies of Rh-negative mothers (see pages 154–55) . In these ABO incompatibility cases the children of succeeding pregnancies may have jaundice, but it will not be more severe than the jaundice of the older sibling. The reserve, you will recall, is the case in Rh incompatibility (see page 154) .

There is no easy way to tell whether the red cells of an A or B baby have been sensitized. If the baby has enlarged spleen and liver at birth or develops jaundice early, we check the blood type and measure the bilirubin (as for an Rh baby) . If the blood is A or B and the mother is

O, we infer that maternal antibodies figure in the rising bilirubin. The procedure thereafter is the same as in other cases of excessive bilirubin and excessive jaundice (see pages 384–86).

INFECTION AND THE NEWBORN

Until just a few years ago, death from infection in the first year of life was lamentably common; in the undeveloped regions of the world it still is. Happily, modern medicine has changed that picture completely.

Antibiotics, which came into general use in the 1940s, have revolutionized the care of children with infections, and our knowledge of how to manage infection generally has made notable advances. Infant mortality—that is, the rate of death of babies under a year of age—is down to an eighth or a tenth of what it used to be. Of equal interest is the change in the ranking of the factors that account for infant mortality. At the turn of the century infection was far and away the leading cause of infant deaths. Now it has dropped to fourth or fifth place, lagging well behind prematurity, birth injuries, and birth defects (congenital malformations).

These changes become even more dramatic when we look at statistics on the causes of death after the first year of life. Mortality tables for the older children show that accidents compose by far the major factor, followed by malignancies (such as leukemia and tumors) and congenital malformation. The picture of the child struck down by a ravaging illness such as spinal meningitis or pneumonia, well one day and dead the next, is no longer a true one. In the modern world, instead of worrying about some fulminating illness, parents will be better advised to concern themselves about automobiles, about where the medicines and poisons are kept, whether the children have learned to swim, or about drug abuse. The chances of a child's succumbing to the onslaught of an infectious illness are not yet down to zero, but they are really quite slim. It is the lag in our thinking, not the state of medicine, that accounts for a persistent dread of infection.

Technological advance undeniably has raised our standard of living in respect to the control of infectious disease. Right now, most of us in America can count on drinking water that is free of disease bacteria and other harmful substances. We can bathe more frequently than our forebears did. We dispose of sewage more safely. We can count on finding the great bulk of the foods we buy uncontaminated by bacteria, though a good bit of it may contain additives or agricultural poisons that will turn out in the long run to be in some degree harmful to people. By law we require widespread immunizations that, in this country, have all but eliminated some of mankind's worst scourges. Since the introduction of the vaccine in the 1950s, the once-dreaded *poliomyelitis* (infantile paralysis), which crippled or killed thousands of children every year, has become almost a concern of the past. Measles, which almost any mother could diagnose on sight only a few years ago, is so rare that today's medical students cannot recognize it. Better obstetrical care, sterilization of artificial milk formulas, technological improvements in the hospital nursery, improvement of techniques of treatment—all those advances have checked the spread and reduced the seriousness of infections among the newborn. True, a number of important problems do remain unsolved, but in general our message for parents regarding infections is a reassuring one.

There is a group of children, fortunately small, for whom infections hold special risks. Some cannot manufacture antibodies properly (see page 374). Some have chronic diseases, such as cystic fibrosis. Premature babies (see pages 330–41) are especially susceptible to infections during their first weeks. But, on the whole, the chances of infection are much less for children today than they used to be, and the prospects of cure are excellent.

Shortly after birth, the baby begins to accumulate the host of microorganisms, his *normal flora,* which will establish peaceful germ colonies on his skin, in his nose, mouth, throat, and intestinal tract. If healthy, he is in good shape to live with this multitude of quite ordinary germs, unless they should multiply too rapidly or get into parts of his body where they do not belong. We all live with our normal flora. These germs are to be distinguished from the less common and much more dangerous ones that we classify as *virulent* because they are associated with disease. We try to shield the baby against these virulent germs by stimulating his immunity.

The baby's endowment of antibodies is somewhat higher at birth than the mother's own supply. Her gamma globulin antibodies pass from her blood to the baby's via the placenta but not in equal proportion. The baby gets relatively more of those that combat viral illnesses but is slighted in respect to those dealing with some kinds of bacterial illness. When some germ does gain a foothold, we usually find it to be one for which the baby has not received enough antibodies. Nature's bookkeeping seems to have been at fault here. Of course, if the mother herself is lacking in certain antibodies, she cannot pass that type or those types along to her offspring. For example, the infant whose mother has had measles or been immunized against it is born with a supply of antibodies that will protect him for his first four to six months. On the other hand, the infant whose mother never had the disease or immunization is susceptible to measles from his very first day.

The newborn's supply of maternal antibodies diminishes gradually until, at the end of four to six months, only a certain small quantity remains. This quantity will stay with him for another four or five months. At about three months, in response to contact with bacteria and viruses in his environment, fortunately, he will have on his own started manufacture of the same kinds of antibodies he received from his mother, and by the time he is three or four years old, his production of them will be up to the normal adult levels. From birth he has been manufacturing other kinds of antibodies, but resupply of the types in his maternal endowment does not begin in a major way before the age of three months.

As the infant comes in contact with the common and uncommon germs of his environment, he manufactures the appropriate antibodies, which then are added to his supply. This process is entirely normal. Every child plays host (see page 373) to colonies of microorganisms on his skin and in his respiratory tract and intestine. First contact with the microbial world normally is made during passage through the birth canal. There the infant picks up many germs that will form part of his normal flora. He encounters others through minor infectious illnesses such as colds and diarrhea. Some of these infections are so mild that no symptom is produced even though antibodies are manufactured. For those dangerous germs against which he has received little or no protection from his mother (*pertussis*, or whooping cough, is an example), he needs our intervention with our techniques of immunization.

The diphtheria, pertussis, and tetanus injection (the *DPT* that your infant will receive at an early visit to the pediatrician) stimulates him to manufacture antibodies against those microorganisms or their toxic products. Were we not to immunize the baby, he would be susceptible to infection by microorganisms with which he would be poorly equipped to cope. Some antibodies, such as the measles antibody, linger in the body for as long as nine or ten months, provide immunity during this period, and would interfere with the infant's response to measles immunization. For this reason, we delay giving these particular inoculations until the supply of maternal antibodies has dropped to a certain level (see page 374).

There are several points in the very early life of a baby at which he can become infected. First, it can happen while he is still in the mother's womb. Then there is the possibility of infection at delivery or shortly thereafter. Finally, the baby can be infected after he leaves the hospital.

We have known for a long time about the possibilities of infection in the womb, prior to rupture of the mother's amniotic sac (see pages 91–92). In these cases the infection has passed from the mother's bloodstream through the placenta to the fetal bloodstream. A classic example of this sort of systemic infection transmitted from mother to infant is, of course, syphilis. Though the disease is at this writing again on the rise in the United States, prenatal infection is a much less common problem than it used to be, thanks to better care in pregnancy. Another disease transmissible from mother to unborn baby is typhoid fever. Most of the transmissible bacterial diseases have been brought under good control.

Infections acquired in utero became the focus of heightened attention around the end of World War II, when it was learned that the German measles virus (see pages 166–68) could affect the fetus in the first three months of pregnancy. A significant number of the fetuses whose mothers contract German measles in the first trimester will themselves develop the infection. The mothers may or may not show symptoms themselves. Many of these fetuses will be so affected that the pregnancy will abort. Others will suffer damage in varying degree. The virus attacks the fetal organs in the period of formation, when the rate of growth is high, and may cause cessation of growth or subsequent misdirection of growth. Since the affected organ's *rate* of growth at the time of infection, not its absolute growth, is the critical factor, the timing of the onslaught will determine which organs are to incur the most damage. The organs growing fastest at that moment will be the worst hurt, since growth will be halted or interfered with when it should be proceeding most rapidly. Many infants escape with no difficulties, but others may be critically ill at birth and die shortly afterward, or they may have defects involving the heart, brain, eyes, liver, skin, and other parts of the body. Such permanent handicaps as mental retardation, heart malformation, cataracts of the eyes, hearing disturbances may be the lot of those who survive. The affected babies will harbor the virus for a year or more after birth and can pass it on to others. From the foregoing it is apparent that intrauterine infection is a very serious matter. Great effort was exerted to develop the vaccine against German measles (medically known as *rubella*), which once was dismissed as a harmless indisposition. Any woman in the first trimester of pregnancy who has been in contact with a known or suspected case of German measles should inform her doctor at once for appropriate testing (see page 167).

The fetus is also subject to attack by *cytomegalic virus,* which appears in the latter part of pregnancy and is transmitted through the placenta and probably also from infections of the cervix as the baby passes through the birth canal. This virus has a most unfortunate preference for the central nervous system and consequently can cause brain damage, the most severe cases resulting in death soon after birth. As in rubella, the affected infant may secrete the virus for many months after delivery and be a reservoir for infections of others. Cytomegalic virus is actually more common than rubella and is now receiving much needed investigation. The unborn baby is also susceptible to transmitted microorganisms other than the bacteria and viruses. One such is the amoeba *toxoplasma,* which can cause an illness in adults, *toxoplasmosis,* with symptoms similar to those of mononucleosis. The infection of the pregnant woman may be too mild to be apparent, but the baby may die soon after birth or suffer permanent damage of various kinds.

It is characteristic of the infections acquired in utero that several or many of the infant's organs become involved. He is not likely to simply have an ear infection or a throat infection. On purely physical findings, the physician often has a difficult problem differentiating the true cause from the various possibilities, but laboratory analysis can help. While these transmitted infections, except in epidemics of rubella, are not common, they deserve the attention we have given them here because it is an established fact that they do cause birth defects. Their existence raises the possibility that other, as yet unrecognized, microorganisms may be the cause of other congenital abnormalities, which, taken as a class, are near the top of the list of problems concerning the newborn. At present, there is no effective treatment short of abortion for these transplacentally transmitted infections (see page 375). The major hope lies in prevention. Interest centers on the development of vaccines to immunize the mother.

Infection of the amniotic fluid and membranes (see pages 91–92) can spread to the infant directly. Amnionitis is almost always a complication of premature rupture of the amniotic sac, which when intact forms an excellent barrier against invasion of microorganisms from the birth canal. For this reason, mothers with prematurely ruptured amniotic membranes are objects of particular concern often to the point of hospitalization.

We have mentioned that many microorganisms are acquired normally during the passage through the birth canal and become part of the natural flora of the infant. Occasionally one of these organisms multiplies excessively and sets up an infection. A very common example is the common fungus Monilia, which causes the condition of the tongue and mouth known as *thrush*. The Monilia fungus is a normal inhabitant of the vagina. The baby picks it up in transit.

Infections at delivery were once very common, but the precautions of modern obstetrical practice have greatly reduced the probability. Most babies are born nowadays in hospital delivery rooms under very clean conditions. They are transferred to nurseries where scrupulous cleanliness is the watchword. They are bathed in antiseptic solutions and their umbilical cords treated with chemicals to reduce growth of harmful bacteria. Attendants with any symptom of illness are excluded from the nurseries, and at the first show of illness a baby is removed to an isolation unit to protect his fellows from a dangerous microorganism. There is an occasional breakdown of procedure, of course, but the search goes on continuously in every hospital to find and eliminate sources of infection. From unpleasant experience we have learned that these sources turn up right under the nose, so to speak. For example, in one outbreak the aerator on the spigots of sinks was discovered to be a harboring place for certain microorganisms that, though harmless by and large for adults, are particularly dangerous for babies. Over the years, an elaborate set of rules of safe procedure have grown up to keep the dangerous microorganisms away from the newborn. Progress has come more from reducing exposure than from increasing the infant's resistance. Babies are less likely to become sick because we give them less opportunity.

Once home from the hospital the infant is in quite a different situation. All families are subject to various illnesses that can be passed on to the newborn. Fortunately those illnesses are not likely to pose problems of major concern. Viral colds and sore throats, viral diarrhea, viral flu and grippe are common, as we know only too well. The infant just out of the hospital is susceptible to them all, but for reasons that are still not clear, these ailments tend to produce milder symptoms during his first few months than later. While we should not go out of our way to expose the infant to these common afflictions, neither can we keep him from some contact with the rest of the household. For some time prior to the appearance of symptoms, any infected member of the family will have been shedding virus about the house. By the time he is actually sick, everyone under the roof will have had ample opportunity to pick up his germs. As every mother knows, short of resort to physical restraint, there is no way to keep a toddler with a cold away from the newborn. Face masks have been tried to reduce contagion but without conspicuous success. There seems to be no feasible safeguard. So, our recommendation is a simple one: avoid unnecessary contact with outsiders exhibiting symptoms of illness but do not try to isolate the baby from a sick member of the household. If someone has diarrhea, it makes sense for those attending the patient to be careful about washing the hands, but this is a standard rule, with or without a new baby in the house. The newborn comes home from the hospital with an ample supply of antibodies against the common contagious diseases of childhood, such as chicken pox and mumps. While it is a good idea always to discuss these circumstances with your own physician, there is little need to isolate the infant from another child with one of these ailments. But the unusual diseases, skin abscess or bacterial dysentery, for instance, are a different matter altogether. At the appearance of one of these ailments in the household, you will want the advice of your physician or his nurse on how to prevent spread of the infection to your new baby.

Newborns can have infections of the urinary tract, pneumonia, meningitis, and skin infections—in other words, the same kinds of infective illnesses older persons are subject to. (See various entries in this chapter.) The difference lies in the rapidity with which infections of the newborn can spread from the site of origin. Consequently, illness that can be handled readily in older children and adults arouses more concern when the patient is an infant. The doctor is much quicker to hospitalize the very young baby (under two or three months) who has a urinary tract infection or bad diarrhea or who is running a fever without any other particular symptom. Many infections of the newborn, even quite serious ones, may produce rather nonspecific symptoms—poor feeding, perhaps a slight fever or a subnormal temperature, listlessness, drowsiness, poor color. (See chapter 19, pages 342–50.) Often the doctor will be unable to locate immediately the site of infection, and he will want all the technological help available in a modern hospital.

On occasion the infection will be found only in the bloodstream, a condition known as *sepsis*. Another site of obscure but serious infection in the newborn can be the nervous system. *Meningitis* is the medical term for the resulting inflammation of the membranes surrounding the brain and spinal cord. When the lungs are infected, the illness is *pneumonia*. Another possible site of infection is the stump of the umbilical cord, which is normally cut off from the blood supply and is poorly equipped to resist heavy invasion of bacteria. This infection, which is a major concern in underdeveloped countries but not in ours, is known as *omphalitis*. Proper care of the cord, as routinely practiced in good hospitals, and sanitary surroundings have drastically reduced the incidence of this infection. Skin infection in the newborn is somewhat different. The affected area can spread rapidly, with peeling of the skin, until the sore resembles a burn, instead of the pimple or abscess an older person would have.

All the aforementioned conditions can be very serious, since the newborn's system is not yet as capable of containing infection as the older child's would be. They call for vigorous treatment with antibiotics. If the doctor even suspects the presence of one of them, he is likely to hospitalize the baby. Usually, it is unwise to rely on medication by mouth for young babies, and the doctor will give intravenous and intramuscular injections instead. It is possible for these illnesses to strike even in the clean surroundings most people provide for babies. Sometimes the source of the contagion cannot be found. The reassuring element all these infections have in common is that they usually can be brought under control quite quickly once the doctor has entered the picture. The important thing is for parents to report promptly to the doctor or his nurse any unusual symptom they observe in the newborn.

INTESTINAL OBSTRUCTION

The causes of intestinal blockage, even in young children, are numerous and varied. A foreign body, an area of inflammation or a tumor may block passage through the intestine, though tumors are a rare cause in children. If detected early, most forms of intestinal obstruction can be relieved with confidence in complete recovery. The long-range outlook depends on the underlying cause of the blockage but it is usually favorable.

When the passage through the intestine (the *lumen*) is blocked, neither the products of digestion nor air can get through. A sequence of events that depends somewhat on the point of stoppage but is reasonably predictable then ensues. In the small intestine, which is closest to the stomach, forceful contractions will occur just above the block; the intestine is trying to force the air and digestive material through. These contractions make themselves known to the patient in crampy pains. If the obstruction is complete, the intestine at some point will relax to many times its usual diameter under fatigue from the accumulation of fluid, air, and partially digested food. The patient will feel "bloated," and his abdomen will be distended perceptibly. There is a tendency for the contents of the intestine to be evacuated in the reverse direction— the patient vomits. Vomiting and the crampy pains are cardinal signs of intestinal obstruction.

For obstruction of the large intestine the picture is not very different. Again, predominant early symptoms are distention and crampy pain, but vomiting comes on later than it does when the small intestine is involved. The obstructed material has a much greater distance to travel.

Persistent obstruction, of course, deprives the child of food and water. He will become dehydrated, showing the usual signs—dry tongue, pasty skin, sunken eyeballs, and so forth. If not relieved, obstruction is eventually fatal. All forms of intestinal obstruction have one hazard in common. This hazard is impairment of blood supply to the point of interference with the respiration, nutrition, and waste removal of the affected segment of intestine. Under prolonged impairment of blood flow the intestinal tract will literally die. The erosion of gangrene will leak the intestinal contents, including bacteria, into the peritoneum, with resulting peritonitis.

One cause, by no means common but not rare either, of intestinal obstruction in the newborn is *meconium ileus,* which is a rare manifestation of cystic fibrosis. In this condition defective pancreatic function in the womb prevents proper digestion and liquefaction of the contents of the baby's intestine. This material becomes too gluey to be propelled through the intestine, which may become blocked at several points. Another cause is the twisting of the intestine upon itself or the kinking as is commonly seen in *incarcerated* (trapped) *inguinal hernia* (see pages 363–64). In young children one section of intestine may telescope into itself *(intussusception,* see below) . In all cases the diagnosis of obstruction is one for the doctor to make, not the parents. In the newborn the nurses or physician will recognize the symptoms in the hospital nursery. If the obstruction develops later, it will be the symptoms of pain, vomiting, and distention of the abdomen that will alarm the parents and send them to the doctor for help. X-ray studies will probably be made to identify and locate the obstruction. Treatment will vary according to cause. In general, first efforts are directed at reversing the side effects of the obstruction. Fluids given intravenously relieve the dehydration and antibiotics fight infection. A tube is introduced through the mouth or nose into the stomach and beyond to the point of blockage to draw off the accumulating material and decompress the dilation of the intestine. Once the child is in condition to stand anesthesia and surgery, the blockage is opened and associated defects, such as inguinal hernia, repaired. Where the blood supply has been impaired to the point of gangrene, it may be necessary to remove a section of the intestine.

INTUSSUSCEPTION

Intussusception is an unusual bowel condition that occurs mainly in infants and young children and requires medical attention, perhaps surgery. The child cries in severe pain and passes stools that look like gobs of currant jelly. It is blood-tinged mucus that gives the stools this unmistakable appearance.

The condition is a spontaneous telescoping of a section of the intestine. Think of a very flexible hose or tube that you are holding with both hands. Imagine you are bringing the hands together to force the tube into itself. In intussusception this is more or less what happens. A section of small intestine swallows itself and by continuing contractions (as if forcing fecal matter along the passage) sucks in more and more of the bowel. The blood vessels of the sucked-in section of bowel are compressed and the flow of blood shut off. There is swelling with obstruction of the intestine. Gangrene or death of the intussuscepted segment can follow, leading to peritonitis, which is fatal if not treated. Interference with the blood supply causes inflammation of the lining of the intestine, followed by a copious flow of bloody mucus.

The child's pain in intussusception is obviously severe, as might be expected. It is likely to come in short bursts with intervening periods of lethargy. The pain is usually signal enough for the parent to get in touch with the doctor; the appearance of the "currant jelly" stools is the clincher, if one is needed. In examination the doctor often can feel the swollen segment of intestine and may find a currant jelly stool in the rectum.

There are two treatments for intussusception, barium enema or surgery. The enema, which would also be needed for X-ray examination of the intestine, may push the intussuscepted segment of bowel out into its normal position. If this approach fails, then surgery is the only recourse. The enema would not be given if there was indication of gangrene or perforation of the intestine. In surgery an attempt is made first to manipulate the segment of bowel back into normal position; if that fails, the segment is cut out.

A small minority (under 5 percent) of the children who have had intussusception will have a recurrence.

JAUNDICE

A mild degree of *jaundice* is common enough among the newborn to be regarded as almost normal. Well over 50 percent of all normal newborns exhibit this "physiologic jaundice," as it is sometimes called. The characteristic yellowing of the skin and eyes appears on the second or third day and gradually disappears by the end of the first week. Physiologic jaundice does not bother the baby in the least and may not even attract the mother's attention. But the doctor and the nurses in the hospital nursery will be keeping a sharp eye on it.

Contrary to popular belief, jaundice is not a disease but a symptom. It can represent a variety of ailments and appear at any age. The actual physical cause is a yellow chemical called bilirubin, which is normally present in small quantity in the blood of everyone. This chemical is a breakdown product of hemoglobin, the oxygen-carrying red pigment in the red blood cells. To understand jaundice it is necessary to know a little about the bodily processes involving bilirubin.

Red blood cells are constantly being formed and constantly being removed from the bloodstream. Originating in the marrow of the bones, they have a life span of about 120 days. In old age (any time after 100 days) they deteriorate and are then removed from the circulation. Within the lymphatic tissues (more precisely, in the reticuloendo-thelial cells) these old red blood cells are destroyed, and their hemo-globin is altered chemically. A product of this chemical breakdown is the bilirubin that causes jaundice.

From the lymphatic tissues the bilirubin is carried in the blood-stream to the liver for further processing. The liver excretes all but a small amount of the altered bilirubin into the bile and sends it through the bile channels to the intestine, whence it passes out of the body in the stools. The small amount kept in the body goes back into the blood-stream from the liver. The amount of bilirubin normally present in us all is small but measurable, and chemical analysis can distinguish the bilirubin on its way to the liver from the bilirubin that has been pro-cessed in the liver and returned to the bloodstream. It is this measurable amount of bilirubin in the bloodstream that is critical in jaundice.

There are two rather obvious ways in which the amount of bilirubin in the bloodstream could increase. Some development could increase the production of bilirubin beyond the normal, or some other develop-ment could interfere with the normal process of removing excess bilirubin from the body. Sometimes both factors operate. In any case, after the amount of bilirubin in the blood attains a certain level, the skin and the whites of the eyes take on a yellow tinge. Jaundice has appeared.

Hepatitis is the disorder with which most people associate jaundice. In this disease the liver is inflamed and no longer can perform properly its work of dealing with the bilirubin produced in the normal destruc-tion of old red blood cells. The bilirubin therefore accumulates in the bloodstream, and the patient becomes jaundiced. If gallstones block the bile system, a common condition in adults, bilirubin backs up and jaundice results. In certain anemias red blood cells are destroyed at a rate that exceeds the capacity of the liver to deal with the bilirubin; the result again is elevated blood bilirubin and jaundice. In all these condi-tions, you will observe, jaundice is only a symptom, not the underlying cause. Jaundice alerts the doctor to the existence of a problem.

Because certain parts of the infant brain are sensitive to *excessively* high levels of bilirubin, jaundice has special significance in respect to the newborn. But note our emphasis on the adverb *excessively*. Even up to the point where they do cause some jaundice, levels of bilirubin short of the excessive will not damage the brain. We almost expect *some* jaundice; the problem is *excessive* bilirubin producing *excessive* jaun-dice. This distinction is important.

The mild jaundice seen so often in the first week of life has a ready explanation. The livers of these babies have a limited ability to process bilirubin. Because of immaturity of the liver, there is an insufficiency of the enzyme that directs the conversion of the bilirubin into the form that dissolves in bile. But in a matter of days, the amount available of this enzyme increases enough for the liver then to be able to take care not only of the bilirubin of current manufacture but also of the accumulated backlog. The degree of maturity of the liver at birth varies. As the percentage we have quoted shows, despite the large proportion of jaundice among newborns, there still are many infants who can handle the normal load of bilirubin immediately after birth and without any difficulty.

Doctors and nurses become expert at judging by skin color alone just how much jaundice a baby has, but if there is any question at all a laboratory test to measure the bilirubin level will be ordered. The test may be repeated several times to follow the curve, up or down, of the bilirubin level. The crux of the matter is at what rate the jaundice is increasing or decreasing. Most babies, as we have indicated, will require no treatment, but immediate intervention is required for severe jaundice.

The illness resulting from very high bilirubin levels (or, to put it another way, in excessive jaundice) is called *kernicterus*. Not all babies with high levels of bilirubin will develop kernicterus, but there is a strong association between the two conditions. In kernicterus there are severe neural (that is, nerve) symptoms and there can be severe permanent damage to parts of the brain. Cerebral palsy and deafness are among the handicaps associated with kernicterus. So, when the jaundice patient is a newborn, the doctor must not only find the underlying cause but also manage to keep the jaundice (that is to say, the level of bilirubin) within safe bounds. In other words, he has to treat the symptom as well as the disease.

Premature babies, because of the comparative immaturity of their livers, are prone to develop increased bilirubin. The newborn with an infection will be likely to have more than the usual jaundice because in his condition more of the red cells are being destroyed and the liver is not working as well as it should. (This is an example of the simultaneous operation of both possible factors in the causation of high bilirubin levels [see page 383].)

It may come as a surprise to hear that some breast-fed babies undergo not only an exaggeration but also a prolongation of this newborn jaundice. Their nursing mothers are producing a larger than normal amount of an estrogenic hormone and passing it along to the babies in their milk. The babies' livers remove this hormone, but the work has to be done by the same enzyme that is involved in the bilirubin processing. If the enzyme is busy with the hormone, it is less available for removing the bilirubin, which then backs up in the bloodstream. Even when the liver is mature enough to deal with the bilirubin under ordinary conditions, it may not be able to handle both these jobs at the same time. In these babies the jaundice may persist as long as breast-feeding continues. Usually it is mild, and nothing need be done. If the jaundice should become excessive, however, nursing would have to be stopped, at least temporarily. In general, excessive newborn jaundice will not preclude breast-feeding. For the first few days the mother who intends to breast-feed can express her milk to keep up the production until the difficulty with bilirubin passes with or without special treatment and the baby can begin to nurse.

Another cause of jaundice in newborns, often of the severe kind, results from differences in the incompatibility of blood types of the baby and the mother. This is a complicated subject, already discussed in regard to pregnancy (see pages 151–56) and developed in some detail in the section on incompatibility (see pages 369–72) .

The standard treatment for an excessively high level of bilirubin in the blood or for a rapidly increasing accumulation of bilirubin is the *exchange transfusion*. There is also a simpler but promising, though still somewhat experimental treatment called *phototherapy* or *light treatment*.

The exchange transfusion is just what the name implies. The baby's blood is removed and replaced with the blood of another. The theory is simple. When the baby's blood is taken away, the bilirubin goes with it, along with most of the red cells that have been labeled with antibodies from the mother (see pages 155–56) and any free-floating antibody unattached to red cells. The result is not only an immediate reduction of blood bilirubin but also a diminution of future sources of bilirubin— the labeled cells and the unattached antibody. At the same time, any anemia present will also be corrected. For the most severely affected infants, those with erythroblastosis fetalis (see pages 151–52) (who may have heart failure as well as anemia) , exchange transfusion can be life-saving.

Most infants tolerate exchange transfusion well; it carries little risk and is painless for the baby. The technique makes use of the blood vessels of the umbilical cord. A thin tube (catheter) is threaded up the umbilical vein and blood drawn out with a syringe. The baby then is injected with the donor's blood. Small amounts are thus exchanged for nearly an hour, and at the end over 80 percent of the baby's blood has been replaced. The baby is placed in an incubator under close supervision, which includes checking the bilirubin level. If the condition is satisfactory, he is started on feedings. A new rise in the bilirubin level (the *rebound effect*) is expected as bilirubin from the body tissues (for example, the yellowed skin) returns to the bloodstream, and sometimes the transfusion must be repeated. An occasional baby will require more than three exchanges before the bilirubin levels out.

In phototherapy the baby, naked except for blinders to protect the eyes, is placed under bright white fluorescent light and kept there most of the day, being removed only for feeding and cleansing. The babies in this treatment appear to be quite comfortable and suffer no burning or tanning from the light. The bilirubin level is measured every few hours. When it reaches a peak and starts to decline, the baby is removed from the light. If the bilirubin level should continue to climb, the baby would become a candidate for exchange transfusion. The theory is that the light, which is of the same wave length as daylight, by photoanalysis breaks down the bilirubin into harmless chemicals that can readily be excreted from the body.

LUNG RUPTURE AND COLLAPSE

In a lung rupture, air leaks into the thoracic cavity and is trapped between the lungs and the rib cage and diaphragm, a condition called *pneumothorax*. In the newborn, pneumothorax can complicate a number of respiratory difficulties associated with partial or complete obstruction of the air passageways. *Pneumonia* and *hyaline membrane disease* (see page 335) are among these disorders. Air in the thoracic cavity can also compress the lung and thus decrease the volume of lung available to the baby for respiration. Shortness of breath and in severe cases cyanosis can result. A continuing accumulation of trapped air and consequent increases of pressure can not only collapse the lung but may also displace the heart and great blood vessels, compromising their functioning and threatening life.

The doctor will look for pneumothorax (often with the help of X ray) any time an infant exhibits respiratory symptoms of any type. Treatment is directed at the underlying cause—for example, antibiotics for infection. Excessive accumulation of air may be relieved by inserting a small tube between the ribs into the pocket of air. The air leak in the lung usually seals in time. Most children recover completely.

Atelectasis is collapse of part of a lung, always discovered by the physician (and not by parents) when he is investigating symptoms of respiratory disorder. Often the diagnosis is made after X-ray examination.

In the lungs microscopic air sacs (the *alveoli*) normally contain some air even when you are breathing out. If the air is totally exhausted, the sac, like a deflated balloon, collapses. This situation is an important complication of hyaline membrane disease (see page 335), which affects the lungs of some prematures (see pages 334–35), babies of diabetic mothers, and to lesser extent, babies delivered by Caesarean section. The disease results from persistence of the fetal pattern of circulation after birth; there is a failure of blood flow to the lungs. The disorder takes its name from a deposit of proteinaceous material (*hyaline membrane*) on the linings of the alveoli and small air passages, with consequent collapse of the alveoli. Another cause of atelectasis in the newborn is aspiration of amniotic fluid in the birth process. Blockage of the smallest air passages results.

The symptoms and difficulties with atelectasis depend on the extent of the lung collapse, and treatment varies with the cause and severity.

MONGOLISM (DOWN'S SYNDROME)

Down's syndrome, also known as *Mongolism* or *Trisomy 21* is a common cause of mental retardation and is caused by a genetic abnormality of chromosomes whereby an extra chromosome is present in the cells of the body (see page 439). The term Mongolism (the old term for the disorder) refers to the superficial facial resemblance of affected individuals to Asians and reflects a certain racial bias of Caucasians in naming a disease after the appearance of over one-half of the world's population.

Down's syndrome occurs in about three births per two thousand and accounts for approximately 10 percent of retardates in institutions. Physical as well as mental growth is retarded. Characteristic physical findings include a small head, flattened in front and back, a lateral upward slope of the eyes, small ears, small jaw and mouth, protruding tongue, short flat nose, delayed eruption of teeth, and a short broad neck. In the infant and young child hypotonia (looseness and laxity of muscles) and potbelly are prominent. The hands and feet tend to be flat, broad, and square. Heart defects are relatively common, and the occurrence of leukemia, for causes not yet understood, is ten to twenty times greater than in the general population.

The diagnosis is confirmed by a direct analysis of the chromosomes. It is now possible to make this diagnosis during pregnancy (see page 439). Chromosome analysis of the mother is in order to exclude the possibility of the rare form of inherited Down's syndrome (see page 439).

There is no cure for Down's syndrome at this time. The question of institutionalization usually arises as the child reaches school age. This issue is handled differently by different families. Genetic counseling is in order after the birth of a child with Down's syndrome (see page 439).

PKU (PHENYLKETONURIA)

Though *PKU* is a comparatively rare condition (approximately one in ten thousand babies affected), we hear a good bit about it. In the first place, the practice of testing neonates for PKU is widespread and in some states required by law. Secondly, PKU is a textbook example of the transmission of defects by recessive genes (see page 437). Thirdly, the condition demonstrates dramatically the interdependence of mind and body.

Phenylketonuria is a disorder of the metabolism (that is, the bodily processing) of the amino acid phenylalanine. Amino acids are the basic building blocks of all proteins, and the process of digestion splits proteins into these constituents. After digestion, the amino acids are absorbed across the intestinal wall into the bloodstream. When they enter into the chemical reactions that occur in the cells, the amino acids may be incorporated into new protein or they may be broken down for conversion into energy or for elimination from the body. There are vitally important amino acids (including phenylalanine) that the body is unable to manufacture on its own and that it must therefore obtain from the protein in the diet. These are known as *essential amino acids*. Each of them is crucial to the accomplishment of some particular step in the normal process of growth and development.

In PKU the body fails to process phenylalanine because there is a deficiency or derangement of a certain enzyme. (Enzymes are very complex substances that act as *catalysts* in the chemical reactions of the body; that is, they are necessary in promoting the reactions but do not themselves enter into the chemical changes.) For want of this processing, the phenylalanine accumulates in the blood and tissues. The PKU test detects these abnormally high levels of phenylalanine. Alternate chemical processes then operate to convert the phenylalanine into chemicals that are found in large quantities in the urine, also detectable by a urine test.

Since specific genes control enzymes, the failure of the enzyme to process phenylalanine normally must be the result of a genetic defect. A small proportion of the population, from one in fifty to one in one hundred, carries a recessive gene (see page 437) for PKU. If two of these recessives mate, one-quarter of the offspring on the average will have PKU, half will themselves be recessive for the condition, and one-quarter will be entirely free of both the disease and the genetic trait. An infant inheriting the tendency will have enough enzyme to handle the normal dietary load of phenylalanine but not enough to cope with an extra load given by the doctor to test his system.

Excessive phenylalanine or its by-products can damage the brain, causing mental retardation and seizures. Further, it can interfere with overall growth and well-being. Severely affected infants may eat poorly, vomit, and fail to thrive. Since high phenylalanine also inhibits production of pigment, children with PKU will have lighter skins and hair than would be expected in their particular families.

The principle of treatment for PKU is quite simple. The idea is to provide a diet that contains the exact requirement of this essential amino acid and no more. Fruits and vegetables are low in phenylalanine, and a synthetic milk with all the essential amino acids but a reduced amount of phenylalanine has been developed. Since the total regimen of treatment is complicated, many communities have found it worthwhile to establish treatment centers for the affected children. At present, indications are that treatment for PKU can safely be concluded for most children by the time of their entry into school.

The current emphasis, of course, is on early recognition of the condition in order to catch it before irreversible brain damage has occurred. Breast milk, cows' milk, and commercial formulas all contain enough of the substance to elevate the level above normal in babies with the genetic trait. In the standard screening program a small sample of blood is taken from the baby's heel on his third or fourth day. The analysis does not positively diagnose PKU but does identify the babies who will need further watching. Conditions other than PKU can cause elevation of the phenylalanine level, but the idea of this testing is to avoid missing any baby who might have PKU.

PYLORIC STENOSIS

The pylorus is the muscular valve controlling the flow of food and gastric juices from the stomach to the duodenum, which is the beginning of the small intestine. In the condition known as *pyloric stenosis* this muscular valve thickens enough to obstruct the tract partially or completely. Since milk or other food then has no way to get out of the stomach except by the mouth, the baby vomits. Vomiting in the course of a feeding or soon after eating is the first symptom the parent will see. The vomiting tends to be projectile, coming out with force and traveling some distance. This is in contrast to normal spitting up, which is more of a drool. If the condition is allowed to continue for any length of time, the baby will lose weight, show signs of dehydration, and produce fewer stools. Pyloric stenosis is a condition that worsens progressively and gives the parent ample warning before serious malnutrition sets in. The persistent vomiting sends the parent to the doctor, who is the only one, of course, to make the diagnosis out of all the possible explanations of vomiting.

The vomiting from pyloric stenosis usually begins several weeks after the baby has left the hospital, rarely in the neonatal period. It may begin as not much more than the slight regurgitation common to burping, but with time it becomes greater in volume and more forceful. The physician can actually see under the baby's skin the outlines of the distended stomach's forceful contractions against the obstruction, and he often can feel the thickened muscle. About the size of an olive, the thickening is called a pyloric tumor, but it is never malignant.

The common treatment of pyloric stenosis is a surgical operation, which is a short one well tolerated by babies. With the baby under general anesthesia, the surgeon makes an incision into the muscle to the inner lining of the stomach to relieve the obstruction. In a matter of hours the child usually can be fed again. The patient may vomit at the first few feedings but will improve rapidly. For all practical purposes the condition has been corrected, and no recurrence is expected. In some parts of the world a regime of special feedings and antispasmodic drugs is followed for pyloric stenosis in the expectation that the condition will eventually relieve itself, but since the surgical approach is so simple and so successful, it is preferred in this country.

The underlying cause of pyloric stenosis is not known. It is more common among first-born children and much more common in males than in females. If one child in a family has had the condition, the chances for later siblings to have it are only slightly greater than for any other child. In other words, if there is an hereditary influence, it appears not to be a strong one.

DEFECTS OF THE SPINE

You can think of the spinal column as a stack of bony rings bound together with ligaments and so fitted that the structure can bend forward or back and to both sides. The spinal cord runs up the tube or canal formed by the column of stacked rings and attaches to the brain in the base of the skull. The cord is a kind of biological cable of nerve cells and long nerve fibers connecting the control centers of the brain to a network of nerves that spreads out all over the body. Messages in the form of coded electrical impulses travel along this cable in both directions. The brain's messages stimulate movement in parts of the body. The body's messages report to the brain on sensations in the skin, muscles, and bones. The brain's interpretations of these messages in terms of temperature, taste, pain, and so forth stimulate further muscular and nervous activity. At every level, from the neck to the lower back, nerves branch out from the cord through the spaces between the bony rings, which we call *vertebrae*. (A single ring is a *vertebra*.) The cord and the brain float in the *cerebrospinal fluid* (see page 367), which in turn is contained in the membranous sac known as the *meninges*. The fluid and sac together compose a shock absorber to cushion the delicate brain and spinal cord.

For reasons we do not understand, the bony processes of a vertebral body may fail, early in gestation, to fuse properly. The ring does not close entirely. This defect, known as *spina bifida* (literally, two-part spine) , results in an opening in the vertebral structure and may involve from one to five or six vertebral units. Its significance will depend on whether there is an associated defect of the spinal cord and nerves. In the most common type of this condition there is not. The spina bifida causes no symptom and may go undetected or be discovered only by chance on an X-ray film taken for some other purpose. There may be a small dimple in the skin of the lower back at the site of the defect. When there is no presenting symptom, the condition is called *spina bifida occulta,* the name signifying that it is hidden and of no significance.

In some less simple cases of spina bifida, there is an associated defect of the overlying skin, and the meninges protrude quite visibly. The spinal fluid can be seen through the transparent sac. If no segment of spinal cord or nerves is in the protruding sac, the condition is known as *meningocele;* when there is a protrusion of cord and nerves, the condition is *myelomeningocele.* The former is readily operable, but the latter is quite serious. The protruding cord and nerves are defective, and the parts of the body under control of the defective nerves will not function properly. There are all degrees of impairment from mild disability to complete interference with function. Specialized neurosurgery and programs of rehabilitation are required. For either condition the neurosurgeon should be called in promptly because he will want to act before the sac can become infected.

As is true of various other birth defects, we do not yet know the cause of spina bifida, nor have we any means of prevention. The appearance of spina bifida in some families would seem to suggest a genetic influence, but the inference does not appear to hold for other families. Fortunately, neither meningocele nor full-blown myelomeningocele is so common that it should be a source of worry for prospective parents.

UNDESCENDED TESTIS

The male reproductive glands, the *testes,* form early in embryological life but remain high in the baby's abdominal cavity until quite late in pregnancy. Each testis is attached to a flexible *spermatic cord,* which contains nerves, blood vessels, muscle, and the *vas deferens*. The vas is the tube for transportation of *sperm,* the male reproductive cells. You can think of the testes in the course of normal development as being lowered on the spermatic cord through the inguinal canal (see page 363) and into the *scrotum,* their proper location. In most baby boys this process of descent into the scrotum has been completed by the time of delivery, but in premature birth the descent has not always been accomplished. The condition in which one testis or both testes remain outside the scrotum is known as *undescended testis*.

There are all degrees of undescended testis, from the testis that remains in the abdominal cavity to the testis that has not completed its passage through the inguinal canal. Rather often a testis will have arrived in the scrotum but then been pulled back up into the abdominal cavity. This condition is known as *retractile testis,* which is not, strictly speaking, an undescended testis. The retractile testis can be manipulated back down into the scrotum and, almost without exception, will in time come to rest in the scrotum without surgery or other treatment.

We cannot say that we fully understand why the process of descent should go awry. In some cases the failure seems to be related to a maldevelopment that renders the testis defective from the start. The testis that remains in the abdominal cavity after the onset of puberty most likely will not produce spermatozoa, and even if brought down by surgery at that time, may not function properly. If both testes remain in the abdominal cavity after puberty, the boy will in all likelihood be permanently sterile, with or without surgery. Whether it is failure in the process of descent that affects the testis or a defect in the testis that affects the process of descent, we cannot say.

The surgery usually requires hospitalization of just under a week, although the boy is allowed out of bed on the day after the operation. In general, the outlook for a successful repair of undescended testis is good. Treatment with hormone has been tried as an alternative to surgery, but although it still is used at some medical centers, the results have in general been disappointing. In special circumstances ruling out surgery, a trial of hormone injections probably would be recommended.

Inspection and palpation of the scrotum to establish the location of the testes are essential in the complete physical examination of the infant, and the doctor or nurse in charge will almost always be the one to discover the condition of undescended testis. Parents should always report an unusual appearance of the scrotum to the doctor, but there is no occasion for alarm. If the doctor has satisfied himself at any point that the testes have once been in the scrotum, then the condition of undescended testis does not exist, and, as we have seen, there is no need to worry about retractile testis.

The timing of surgery for undescended testis depends on several factors. The accepted procedure in a case involving one testis is to operate no later than the onset of puberty but usually between the ages of five and nine. When both testes are undescended, the procedure is to repair one in infancy and the other by five or six, having thus given it a span of years to descend on its own if it will.

Psychological considerations are almost always important in cases of undescended testis. Some boys are very sensitive to the condition, and their peers may be brutal in their jibes and jokes about it. The best the doctor can do is to try to balance the psychological costs of hospitalization and surgery against the psychological trauma of having the defect. The answer will depend on the child, his family, and the doctor. Sometimes there will be a hernia in addition, and that combination, of course, will force the hand. While the hernia is being repaired, the testis will also be taken care of.

TRACHEOESOPHAGEAL FISTULA

Some babies are born with an abnormal connection between the windpipe (or *trachea*) and the *esophagus,* which is the tube conveying food and drink from the back of the throat to the stomach. This uncommon birth defect, known medically as *tracheoesophageal fistula,* can take several forms but always requires surgery.

If you press at the base of your throat, just below the Adam's apple, you can feel the trachea. It extends from the *larynx* (or voice box) into the chest several inches below the notch of the collarbone. At its lower end, it divides into the two major bronchi, which carry the air you breathe to the right and left lungs. Just behind the trachea is the esophagus. Under normal conditions, the two tubes are, of course, separate.

In the most common (but still rare) form of tracheoesophageal fistula the esophagus is divided into unconnected upper and lower parts. The upper part ends in a blind pouch in the chest; the lower segment joins the trachea at the bifurcation where the two bronchi normally begin. Obviously, nothing swallowed from the mouth, whether food, drink, or saliva, can reach the stomach, and a baby with this condition is in serious trouble. To make matters worse, gastric juices can be regurgitated up through the lower segment of the esophagus, into the trachea and thence to the lungs, setting up an intense reaction that results in pneumonia. The baby is both unable to feed and likely to develop lung infection. His drooling, choking, gagging, labored respiration, and poor color are sure to be seen in the hospital, and he becomes a candidate for surgery in his first few days of life. Unless he was very premature or suffers from some other illness in addition, his chances are very good.

The variations of this condition involve other abnormal connections between the two tubes. The symptoms will in general be similar except for the amount of drooling. Drooling is most pronounced in the form of fistula that we have described.

DEFECTS OF THE URINARY TRACT

Birth defects involving the urinary tract are relatively common. Since interference at any point in the tract will have important consequences for the whole system, and since urine is a principal vehicle for removing the body's waste products, the importance of this subject is obvious.

The urinary tract includes the two *kidneys* (and their *pelves*), the *ureters,* the *bladder,* and the *urethra.* Urine is manufactured in the *nephrons* of the kidneys and accumulated in the pelves, which are cavities, one pelvis to each kidney, drained by the ureters. The ureters are tubes that carry the urine to the bladder, where it is stored until it is passed outside the body through the urethra. The urethra in the female is very short; in the male it traverses the length of the penis.

The waste products disposed of in the urine are formed in the many complex chemical reactions that occur as the cells of the body undergo their normal metabolic processes. (Metabolism is the sum of all the physical and chemical processes affecting our fundamental living matter and the conversion of energy for its use.) One such waste product is urea, which comes from the processing of protein. Urine also carries off material that the body cannot use. For example, if you eat more salt than the body can use, the excess within hours will appear in your urine. In effect then, the urinary process, by siphoning off excess materials in the blood, keeps the composition of the blood stable within a range compatible with life.

The urinary tract forms early in embryological life, and even before birth the kidney is manufacturing urine. The baby excretes urine into the amniotic fluid, whence it passes into the mother's bloodstream to be excreted through her urinary system. Other waste products are transferred directly from the baby's blood to the mother's through the placenta. Since the placental route is closed after birth, the baby's kidneys then must take over the entire work. In the womb the placenta had served as an escape valve for any waste products a malfunctioning kidney had been unable to process.

It is easy to picture how an obstruction anywhere in the urinary system would impose strain on the other parts. Suppose, for example, a blockage existed between bladder and urethra. First, accumulating urine would stretch the bladder. The bladder's contractions to get rid of the urine would thicken its muscular wall. The ureters would have to pump harder in an effort to get urine into the already full bladder, and their walls would thicken. Urine would back up from this bladder and eventually into the pelves of the kidneys. The increasing pressure of retained urine, by stretching the kidney (*hydronephrosis*), would distort and destroy the nephrons, the microscopic ultimate units of the organ. If this chain of damaging developments continued unchecked, kidney failure would occur. The patient would die.

Very much the same sequence as in the foregoing would occur from an obstruction at any other point in the urinary tract, except that the parts immediately affected would always be above the blockage. There would be increased retention of urine, increased pressure, dilation, and stretching of the structures. The picture usually will be complicated further by infection. Bacteria can get into the urinary tract either by spreading up through the urethra or by transport in the bloodstream. Normally stray bacteria are cleared from the bloodstream in the kidneys and then flushed out in the urine without having had a chance to multiply. But the presence of these so-called tourists is not to be confused with true infection of the tract, such as would be likely to spread out from stagnant urine. From a point of blockage multiplying bacteria can spread throughout the entire urinary tract, and the ill effects will be compounded when the infection aggravates the blockage.

The birth defects of the urinary tract are obstructions that have come about from failure in embryological development. The most common sites for these failures are at the important junctions—between pelvis and ureter, between ureter and bladder, between bladder and urethra. As examples, we can mention the condition in which abnormally large folds in the urethra of a boy hamper flow of urine; an abnormal thickening of the muscle in the lower bladder that clamps down on the outlet in the act of voiding; duplication of a ureter, with one branch blocked somewhere and predisposed to infection.

There are other malformations than the ones we have mentioned. The obstructions resulting in all the conditions can range from partial to complete. With the passage of time, they may grow better or worse, and they may produce symptoms at any age from birth to senility. The longer an obstruction remains untreated, the greater will be the risk of a serious deformity, and sometimes deformity will progress to the point of rendering a section of the urinary tract useless even if the obstruction is surgically removed. In the stretching of the ureters and kidneys, there is a point of no return. Beyond this point they lose their capacity to function and serve only as reservoirs for stagnant urine. There may be kidney damage even before birth. If the blockage before birth is only partial, there is time to make repairs before irreparable damage has been done.

An obstruction in the urinary tract of the newborn can sometimes be detected by feel. An enlarged kidney, for example, can be felt in the flank of a baby. Partial obstructions, insufficient to produce symptoms in the newborn period, may cause no difficulty at all or may lead to trouble when the child is older. In some cases problems may appear only after infection has set in. Difficulties in voiding, dribbling, and complete failure to toilet train are signs requiring attention. Abnormal frequency of urination, fever, abdominal pain, nausea, vomiting, and passage of cloudy or blood-tinged urine are all symptoms of urinary infection. Urinalysis will detect pus cells, bacteria, and protein. Once a urinary tract infection has been documented, for boys particularly, the doctor's thoughts will turn very quickly to the possibility of an obstruction. Girls are more prone to infections without obstruction.

There are a number of tests for locating urinary tract obstructions. A dye injected into a vein is excreted in the urine, casts a shadow on X-ray film, and can give us a picture of the entire urinary system, from kidneys through bladder. Any abnormality of size or configuration will be revealed, as will abnormality in the rate of emptying the various structures of the system. Badly impaired kidneys will not concentrate the dye properly, but this failure too gives us useful information about functioning. In these circumstances a retrograde pyelogram is taken.

Under anesthesia, dye is injected through catheters passed into the ureters by way of the urethra and bladder. The dye fills all the structures of the tract and renders them visible on X ray. There are other procedures as well.

Treatment or correction of a deformity of the urinary tract depends, of course, on the specific problem. The first step is to control any infection present. Obstructions of the bladder outlet can sometimes be opened without surgery. In those cases instruments called dilators or sounds are passed up through the urethra to stretch open the passage. Other kinds of obstructions require surgery.

WRY NECK

When a baby with some consistency keeps his head tilted forward and to one side, a condition known as *wry neck* should be suspected. *Torticollis* (to use the medical term) is not a common problem or a serious one, but it does appear in some percentage of babies. It yields readily to proper treatment.

Torticollis may be recognized in the hospital nursery, but more likely will be seen first by the parents after the baby has been taken home. The cause is abnormality of the *sternocleidomastoid muscle,* which runs from the collarbone on each side to the skull just back of the ear and is one of the main muscles controlling movement of the head and neck. If you place your hand under your chin and resist a forward movement of your head with it, you will be able to feel the sternocleidomastoids on both sides tense up. The cause of the abnormality is not perfectly known, but it may be scar tissue left from a bruise or tearing of the muscle in pregnancy or delivery. Shrinkage of the scar tissue would contract the muscle and pull the head out of position. The imbalance of forces would also give the face an appearance of asymmetry. In any event, the condition is not likely to be overlooked, either by the parents or the doctor at a regular examination.

The treatment for wry neck is a course of exercises to stretch the affected muscle. If exercises alone fail to do the job, resort to surgery to relax the muscle will be necessary.

RICHARD I. FEINBLOOM, M.D.

PART FIVE

SPECIAL PROBLEMS

CHAPTER TWENTY-ONE

Infertility

*I*NFERTILITY—that is, the inability to produce children—is much more common than most persons think. The number of American married couples who at any given time are infertile has been put at one out of ten, which comes to a total in the millions. At the medical centers in our large cities there are doctors whose practices are confined to dealing with the causes of infertility, and every gynecologist comes on the problem in his day-to-day work.

The length of time normal couples require to achieve pregnancy varies widely. As the old joke has it, some wives seem to need only to see their husbands take off their pants. In contrast, many couples who never use any measures for birth control somehow manage to space their children three or four years apart. The accepted opinion among doctors is that most normal couples who want children will conceive within six months. If a year should go by without result, it would be reasonable to undertake an investigation. The first thing to be ascertained, of course, is whether the infertility is a temporary condition or permanent sterility.

When a husband or wife or both together inquire about infertility, two things need to be stressed. Pregnancy is a cooperative undertaking, to say the least. A study of one member of the couple without the other is often inconclusive. Some men refuse to have anything to do with these studies. The mere suggestion that they may be responsible for the wives' inability to conceive is an affront to their masculinity. In these situations doctor and wife should make every effort to persuade the husband to cooperate. Sometimes a patient will start an investigation but drop out before the study is completed. It is obviously worthless to begin if you do not intend to follow through.

The subject of infertility suffers from a lack of knowledge of the fundamental biology of reproduction. We do not know exactly how ovulation occurs, or how the sperm cells are transported. We cannot say that we know where fertilization occurs or why one particular sperm cell and not another fertilizes the egg. There are many puzzling questions. Until these are answered, the treatment of infertility will continue to be empirical rather than scientific. A lot of the advice given to infertile couples is probably worthless. There is a natural inclination for doctors to feel that what helps one couple will help another, whereas in fact the underlying causes of the infertility may be entirely different.

For a pregnancy to be established, a number of events must happen in a certain sequence. A normal egg cell must be cast off from the ovary and within a few hours be encountered by an interested sperm cell. Following the mixture of genetic material from egg and sperm cells, proper cell division must proceed. Within the first week the dividing ovum has to travel down the tube to the cavity of the womb and establish itself there in a favorable spot. There are many pitfalls along the way. If the proper event does not happen at the right time, pregnancy does not occur. When failure occurs month after month, we call it sterility. You can see that with so many factors involved there can be many reasons for infertility.

One of the fundamental causes of infertility is failure to produce a normal egg cell in the ovary each month. This condition is called *anovulation,* or lack of ovulation. It is usually thought to signify a hormone disturbance. The pituitary gland in the brain, which regulates all hormone glands, controls ovulation. We are just now learning how the pituitary accomplishes this control. The rashes of multiple births from previously sterile women result from the doctors' efforts to stimulate ovulation in women unable to ovulate spontaneously. That we still have much to learn about the pituitary's control of ovulation is obvious when we consider how unnatural it is to produce four or five egg cells all capable of fertilization at the same time.

Not all patients with failure of ovulation have hormone abnormalities. In some the ovaries seem to age prematurely: no more eggs remain to mature. Unfortunately, no form of treatment is successful in such instances. Another condition of unknown cause, characterized by infrequent ovulation, is known as the *Stein-Leventhal syndrome.* Here there is marked thickening of the ovarian surface. Whether it is the cause or result of infrequent ovulation is uncertain, but at any rate this condition is amenable to both medical and surgical treatment.

Ovulation may cease temporarily because of apparent emotional problems. It is common for young girls to skip two or three periods when they leave home for school or travel. During World War II many women in concentration camps did not ovulate. Of course, they were forced to exist on grossly inadequate diets as well as being subjected to unbelievable mental anguish.

Many patients who are trying without success to become pregnant will ask the doctor, "Do you think my emotions have anything to do with it?" While our emotional state has a great deal to do with the way we function in both health and disease, sterility problems are very rarely primarily emotional. In the opinion of many doctors, the correction of emotional problems results in very few pregnancies that would not have occurred anyway. The desire for children is so strong and so fundamental that failure to conceive after a reasonable time can become one of the most disappointing and frustrating experiences in life. It does not take a normal couple long in these circumstances to become fairly "emotional" about the whole subject of sterility. Emotional problems do have "something to do" with sterility, but they are more likely to be the result of this condition than the cause.

A common cause of infertility is obstruction of the Fallopian tubes following pelvic inflammation. (Those tubes, you will remember, transport the egg from the body cavity to the uterus.) There are numerous causes of pelvic inflammation, the commonest being *gonorrhea*. This disease, while no respecter of class or race, is more common in a culturally and economically deprived population, but at this writing it is on the rise across the United States at an alarming rate. The condition called *endometriosis,* a disease in which portions of the endometrium, or lining of the womb, travel to and attach to other parts of the pelvic region, is another common companion of sterility. Its cause is unknown, but it apparently has something to do with the postponement of childbearing that has become almost a necessity for girls who will finish college and maybe go on to graduate school. Endometriosis and pelvic inflammation seem to be almost mutually exclusive. Rarely are both found in the same individual. Pelvic inflammation is the common cause of sterility in city or county hospitals, while endometriosis is much more common in private hospitals catering to a more affluent clientele.

In studying infertile couples we sometimes find that in spite of ovulation, adequate sperm counts, and normality of the tubes, pregnancy still does not occur. The sperm cells do not seem to be capable of penetrating and surviving the mucus at the neck of the womb. Repeated examinations of this mucus after intercourse (the so-called postcoital test) fail to demonstrate any living sperm cells. This condition is called *hostile cervical mucus,* but just what makes the mucus hostile and what can be done to make it less so are at this stage moot points.

The conditions described are the commonest causes of sterility in women. Occasionally, inability to conceive reflects hormone disturbances in glands other than the ovary. It is difficult for women with underactive thyroid to become pregnant. Much less frequently, an excessive activity of the adrenal gland is found to be responsible.

Sometimes there are simple answers to seemingly complicated problems, which come to light as a careful history is taken. It is not unusual to learn that infertile couples are having intercourse only once or twice a month. Naturally, this restraint cuts down remarkably their chances of pregnancy. The other side of the coin is the question of the effect of frequent intercourse on fertility. Because there is somewhat of a drop in the sperm count for several days after sexual relations, some believe that the chances for pregnancy are greatest if several days of abstinence precede intercourse at the time of ovulation. This "precision bombing" technique can lead to difficulties. We have no simple means to determine the moment of ovulation. What the tests we have show is that ovulation has already occurred. By that time it may be too late. Couples anxious to conceive should have relations three or four times a week around the time the wife is supposed to ovulate. This effort should assure an adequate number of sperm cells for fertilization. More frequent intercourse should not reduce their chances of pregnancy. A doctor in England who has studied this question came to the amazing conclusion that the more often couples had intercourse the more likely they were to achieve pregnancy.

Some women douche immediately after intercourse. While douching is not a dependable means of contraception, it may reduce the chances of pregnancy in women of relatively low fertility.

Anomalies of the uterus do not interfere with conception but may be the cause of repeated miscarriages. The same can be said of the so-called incompetent cervix. Women with this condition are often not able to carry a baby for longer than four or five months. Most women with fibroid tumors have no difficulty in becoming pregnant or reaching term. There are, however, a few women in whom these benign growths appear to be responsible for infertility.

Infertility may especially distress women who already have had one baby. Often they have become pregnant the first time without difficulty but are unable to conceive again. A few of these women with so-called one-child sterility have pelvic inflammatory disease or endometriosis. More often, however, all the tests turn out to be perfectly normal. It has been suggested that the mother may become sensitized to the male sperm cells and form an antibody against them. There are numerous investigators working on the immunologic aspects of sterility, and there is certainly reason to hope that solution of some of these most difficult problems is in the offing.

In many infertile couples (at least 30 to 40 percent) the woman is perfectly normal. It is the husband who is responsible for the wife's failure to conceive. Normal males have sperm counts of 75 to 125 million per cubic centimeter and produce two to three cubic centimeters of sperm at each ejaculation. These counts vary considerably. With counts of 50 million and under, there is often difficulty in conception. On a count of 25 million we usually find infertility, and if "only" 5 or 10 million sperm are present in each cubic centimeter, pregnancy is most unlikely.

Some males with low sperm counts have a history of testicular injury or disease. The inflammation complicating mumps can damage the testicle permanently. But most males with low sperm counts have no history to indicate the reason for this difficulty. Some men are impotent; that is, they cannot maintain an erection or achieve orgasm and so cannot impregnate their wives. This is almost invariably a symptom of emotional disturbance. Occasionally, a simple tranquilizer will improve this condition remarkably. Most such problems, however, are so deep-seated that their solution requires a great deal more than just talking with an understanding gynecologist or reading a few books. If anything is to be accomplished, extensive (and expensive) therapy with a psychiatrist is in order.

In many couples no cause for infertility is ever discovered. In about 10 to 20 percent all the tests will be normal, yet pregnancy rarely occurs. The more we learn about this subject the fewer these cases become. The outlook, while dim, is not hopeless. The "spontaneous cure rate" among infertile couples is in the neighborhood of 5 percent.

Since the tests to determine the causes of infertility have to be done at the right time in relation to ovulation, a meticulously kept temperature chart to bracket the time of ovulation is the basis of the investigation. The fluctuations in temperature after ovulation are small, in the neighborhood of half a degree. It is therefore essential to take the temperature under exactly the same conditions each day. The only practical time is the very first thing in the morning, before getting up and going to the bathroom or anything else.

Oral temperatures are as satisfactory as rectal and a good deal easier to take, but many doctors feel that rectal temperatures are more accurate. If your doctor is of this school, follow his advice. A little practice will teach you to read the thermometer accurately. If you have persistent trouble, the special "basal body temperature" thermometers available at most drugstores are a good deal easier to read. Your doctor will give you a graph on which to record your daily temperature.

After ovulation there is a sustained rise in body temperature of about half a degree, which persists until a day or two before menstruation. If the temperature goes up and stays up for as long as twenty-one days, chances of pregnancy are excellent. The postovulatory phase of the menstrual cycle ordinarily lasts only about fourteen days. The hormone progesterone is formed in the ovary after ovulation to prepare the lining of the womb for pregnancy. This hormone is responsible for the elevated temperature in the last half of each menstrual cycle. Progesterone will cause a similar slight rise in temperature if given to males or to postmenopausal women.

One cannot tell the exact time of ovulation from a temperature chart. All that can be learned for sure is that ovulation has occurred and that progesterone is being formed. A short time before the temperature goes up there is often (but not always) a slight dip in the temperature. Many doctors think that this is the time of ovulation. Others think it occurs at the beginning of the sustained rise. When you are taking your temperature from day-to-day, you do not know if your temperature in the next day or two is going up or down. It is only by looking back at the end of the month that you can get a clear picture of what went on during that cycle.

One of the easiest and most informative of tests to determine the reason for infertility is the postcoital test in which the cervical mucus is examined after intercourse. In normal individuals the mucus about the time of ovulation becomes more abundant. Many women note an increase in vaginal discharge at this time. The mucus is thinner, more elastic, and more receptive to the sperm cells. Microscopic examination of a drop of the mucus at mid-cycle should reveal living sperm cells as long as twenty-four hours after intercourse. If none is found, it may mean that the male is not producing an adequate number to start with or that, in spite of normal sperm counts, the cervical mucus is hostile to the sperm cells. Whichever the case, it is obvious that pregnancy cannot occur unless adequate numbers of living sperm cells penetrate the cervical mucus and make their way up through the uterus and tubes. The results of the postcoital test vary considerably from time to time. If the first test is not satisfactory, do not run home to tell your husband—the next time the test may be perfectly normal. When the test is consistently unsatisfactory, a thorough investigation of the male, including a semen analysis, is in order.

The quality of the cervical mucus is evaluated at the time of the postcoital test. The mucus should be abundant, clear, and elastic. It sometimes contains many white blood cells, indicative of inflammation. In this case treatment of the cervix should be undertaken. Sometimes the quality of the mucus may be improved by tiny doses of female hormones.

Tests to determine whether the tubes are blocked are often done at the same time as the postcoital test. Most frequently this is accomplished by forcing carbon dioxide gas through the tubes under low pressure. When the tubes are blocked, the pressure builds up and shows that none of the gas is going through. The same information can be obtained by forcing a fluid, usually saline, through the tubes. All that either of these tests proves is that at least one of the tubes is open, but it does not give any information about adhesions or kinks, which may hinder chances of pregnancy without completely blocking both tubes. This test can be a little uncomfortable. Some patients experience a good cramp while it is being done. In addition there is often some residual soreness in the shoulder for several hours after a satisfactory test as the carbon dioxide gas gets up under the diaphragm as soon as the patient stands up.

The condition of the tubes can be evaluated further by X-ray studies. A dye that will show up on X ray is injected into the uterus and passes through the tubes if they are open. An X ray will demonstrate the outline of the uterine cavity and tubes. In addition to yielding information about the tubes, the X rays will sometimes disclose previously undetected uterine abnormalities that may have some bearing on the patient's inability to conceive. Such conditions may be uterine polyps, fibroid tumors (see pages 131–32) , or a partly bicornuate uterus.

Another helpful test is the endometrial biopsy. A tiny sample of the lining of the womb is obtained for microscopic examination. As described previously ₍see pages 101–02₎, successful implantation of the fertilized ovum requires proper preparation of the womb by the corpus luteum hormone. If this hormone is deficient, conditions for implantation are unfavorable and pregnancy unlikely. Administration of this hormone will naturally improve the chances for pregnancy. In addition to yielding information about the response of the womb lining to the corpus luteum hormone, an endometrial biopsy will sometimes disclose unsuspected inflammation or other abnormality that may be hindering implantation. Like the tests for tubal pregnancy, the endometrial biopsy can cause a hard cramp. Individuals vary greatly in this respect; many women will hardly know when it is being done. The endometrial biopsy must be planned for such a time in the cycle that a beginning pregnancy would not be disturbed.

A test of thyroid function is easy and informative. Deficiency in the thyroid hormone is often associated with difficulty in conceiving. In borderline cases it is worthwhile to try a course of thyroid hormone for several months to see whether it will do any good. Because they believe it may enhance the chances of conception, some doctors will give this hormone even to women with normal thyroid function. This is one of the many empiricisms in the treatment of sterility.

It goes without saying that anyone being treated for sterility should be in good general health. Common medical problems, such as anemia and obesity, should be corrected while the investigation is under way. Any specific diseases should be treated. A careful history and physical exam will sometimes suggest further studies. Since ovarian activity is so closely related to other hormone-producing glands, special attention is directed toward endocrine abnormalities. While the tests are being performed on the wife, her husband should be evaluated. He should have a complete physical exam and semen analysis. These are usually performed either by a urologist or the gynecologist who is treating the wife. If the semen analysis shows a lack of sperm cells, then a biopsy of the testicle may be performed. This will sometimes disclose that while the testicle is producing normal numbers of sperm cells, blocked ducts are preventing delivery of them. Surgical repair of the ducts then is indicated.

If, after all the tests, sterility still defies explanation, a further test is often done called the *culdoscopic* examination. This is a minor surgical procedure best performed in the hospital. The culdoscope, an instrument about the size and shape of a lead pencil, consists of a series of optical lenses and a light source. It is introduced into the pelvis through a tiny incision in the vaginal septum, which separates the birth canal from the abdominal and pelvic cavities. By peering through the culdoscope, the doctor can examine visually the tubes, ovaries, back of the uterus, and adjacent structures. This inspection will often reveal conditions that the doctor has not been able to feel in the internal examination. Endometriosis is often discovered and so are adhesions around the tubes, or ovarian abnormalities. Many doctors perform culdoscopic examinations under local anesthesia. It is usually not necessary to be hospitalized for more than a day for a culdoscopy.

Culdoscopic examination concludes the basic investigation of the sterile couple. By this time abnormalities usually will have been found. If correctable, and they often are, chances of pregnancy will be enhanced. Occasionally causes will be found for which we have no consistently effective treatment. For these couples there is little hope of pregnancy. They should consider adoption. There are a few couples for whom all the tests are normal and yet conception does not occur. They should not give up hope. There are always new drugs and techniques undergoing evaluation. There is about a 5 percent spontaneous cure rate in sterility that makes it most difficult to evaluate results in individual cases.

The past few years have seen great advances in the treatment of some types of infertility. For the first time we have drugs that will induce ovulation. They are so potent that several eggs are likely to be released. There have been numerous instances of multiple pregnancies from these drugs. Most of the quadruplets and quintuplets you read about in the papers have come about in this way. As we gain more experience with these drugs, the chances of multiple birth will decline.

Another recent advance in the treatment of infertility is the hormone treatment of endometriosis. This is a common condition, perhaps the leading cause of sterility in the female. Endometriosis improves if pregnancy does occur. This clinical fact has led to attempts to reproduce pregnancy changes by the continuous administration, for months at a time, of increasingly large doses of pregnancy-type hormones. Pregnancy is not possible during this pseudo-pregnancy treatment because ovulation is inhibited, as in normal pregnancy. After the drugs are stopped, chances of conceiving are improved.

Surgery is often advised for endometriosis. The decision to operate depends on many factors, the chief ones being the extent of this condition and the presence of other factors adversely influencing the chances of conception. When the disease is extensive, probably the best results are obtained by a combination of surgical and hormone treatment for endometriosis. Obviously, there is no point in operating on a woman for sterility of any cause if her husband is also sterile. It is doubtful that surgery for infertility is indicated after the age of forty. Chances for a successful pregnancy in previously infertile women beyond this age are slight.

Surgery is the only form of effective treatment for sterility resulting from pelvic inflammatory disease. In milder cases the tubes may be partially blocked or there may be pelvic adhesions destroying the usual relationship of the tubes and ovaries. In extensive disease the tubes are completely shut off. These cases tax the skill and ingenuity of the surgeon. It may be necessary to remove part of a tube and reconstruct the remainder. When chronic pelvic inflammatory disease is extensive and the tubes have to be all but rebuilt, the chances of pregnancy are then somewhere in the neighborhood of 25 percent. This may not sound like much, but without surgery the chances are for all practical purposes zero. When the disease is not so severe, the chances of pregnancy are much higher after surgery.

Surgery is sometimes advised for the removal of fibroid tumors if no other reason for infertility is apparent. Many women with these benign growths conceive and deliver without difficulty. There are some women, however, who have not become pregnant until fibroids were removed.

The treatment of the infertile male has lagged behind treatment of the infertile female, probably because, until recently, the male has been most reluctant to do anything about his condition.

It takes almost two months for sperm cells to mature. Any drug given to increase the sperm count has to be given for several months to be evaluated properly. Thyroid preparations are often given to men with low sperm counts. If it can be demonstrated that the sperm ducts are blocked, surgery can often cure sterility.

Sperm production is very sensitive to temperature fluctuations. This is why the testicles are outside the body cavity. If the veins at the side of the testicle become dilated, it appears to raise the temperature slightly and inhibits sperm production. Surgical correction of this condition, which is known as *varicocele,* is reported to improve the chances of impregnation.

Some of the techniques for dealing with male infertility have been borrowed from veterinary medicine, artificial insemination among them. This procedure is a satisfactory solution for a few couples whose infertility is due to a virtual absence of sperm cells in the male. But complex legal and emotional implications surround artificial insemination. Mature deliberation on the part of both the sterile couple and the physician involved should precede resort to this technique. For certain couples adoption may offer a more satisfactory solution. The procedure of artificial insemination is simple and painless. All that is required is to place a specimen containing a normal number of sperm cells into the vagina, shortly before or at the estimated time of ovulation.

Another technique borrowed from veterinary medicine relies on the storage of sperm cells by rapid freezing. There have been scattered reports of pregnancies achieved with frozen sperm when infertility had been caused by a very low sperm count. A number of specimens can be collected from the husband and frozen for indefinite preservation. When enough have been collected, they can be thawed and used to inseminate the wife artificially.

ARTHUR GORBACH, M.D.

CHAPTER TWENTY-TWO

Abortion

A. MISCARRIAGE

*I*N MODERN medicine the dividing line between, on the one hand, spontaneous abortion (or miscarriage, to use the layman's term) and, on the other, premature delivery has become somewhat vague. Dramatic advances in the care of prematures (see pages 330–40) enable us now to save little babies who once might have been described as aborted fetuses. For practical purposes, we can make a distinction by defining abortion as the termination of pregnancy in its first twenty weeks, when the fetus weighs five hundred grams (approximately one pound) or less. This is not to say that we can save every baby weighing more than one pound, but for a working definition this dividing line will do.

Miscarriage is very common. At least one pregnancy in ten winds up in spontaneous abortion. If this proportion seems high to you, remember that nature is extravagant. She always starts out with more individuals, whether of flesh, fish, or flowers, than can have any real expectation of survival to maturity. A woman can be perfectly normal in all respects, but if she has a history of several pregnancies, she is likely to have had a miscarriage.

Until rather recently, the true cause of most spontaneous abortions was not known. The majority of miscarriages occur between the second and third months of pregnancy. Usually the expelled material consists of placental tissue. If there is an embryo or fetus, it is at most a stunted one. The name *blighted ova* was attached to these specimens, but the reasons for the failure of some embryos to develop remained a mystery until the great explosion of knowledge in the science of genetics (see pages 428–41) provided an answer.

Genetic studies now have shown that an abnormal division of chromosomes (see page 433) has occurred in many of these cases of miscarriage. The fault appeared in the first cell division after the egg and sperm joined in fertilization. The pregnancy, in short, was doomed from the start. The germ plasm died and, between the second and third months, was cast off from the womb. The body tries to expel any foreign matter, and the process of spontaneous abortion follows the pattern. It gets rid of the dead material. An explanation of spontaneous abortion as a manifestation of "defective seed" had been offered for many years. Chromosomal analysis has finally pinned it down. This abnormal division of chromosomes in spontaneous abortion is not hereditary. In the great majority of cases spontaneous abortion does not recur.

There are other causes of spontaneous abortion, but these make up the minority of cases. Certain abnormalities or anomalies of the uterus can lead to miscarriage. The most common of these is the double or *bicornuate* uterus (see page 164) . Many women with bicornuate uterus have no trouble at all in pregnancy, but a few have repeated miscarriages or premature babies. Surgical correction of the bicornuate uterus offers these few a good chance of being successful in another pregnancy.

Certain other physical conditions of the mother have been associated with miscarriage. Among them are damage to the cervix from tears in childbirth or previous abortion or from surgery, fibroid tumors, uterine abnormalities other than the one mentioned, and some illnesses. Acute generalized infections sometimes will cause abortion, but it is astonishing how ill some women can become without losing the babies they are carrying. Malnutrition is also cited frequently as a cause of spontaneous abortion, but conclusive statistics to prove the case would be hard to come by. Large-scale malnutrition is found almost always in scenes of total catastrophe, such as war, where statistics do not exist. In contrast, we know that the poorly nourished do continue to reproduce. But to repeat, all these causes, or alleged causes, represent only the minority of spontaneous abortions.

A recent development in obstetrics is the concept of, and a treatment for, the *incompetent cervix*. There are a few women who repeatedly miscarry between the third and sixth month of pregnancy. In contrast to the more common situation where abortion occurs early, the fetus in these cases invariably is normally developed but too small to survive. It has been found that in these mothers the neck of the womb (or cervix) over a period of days or weeks dilates prematurely with labor ensuing shortly thereafter. Since the cervix is already dilated, the labor is rapid and relatively painless. Often the mother has no knowledge that anything is wrong until labor begins. Sometimes, for several days before labor begins, there is a heavy pink or brown discharge, along with a vague backache or sense of pressure. These symptoms should alert the pregnant woman to see her doctor at once, especially if she has lost an earlier pregnancy between the third and sixth month. Even though the cervix is partly dilated, the pregnancy may be salvaged.

In these cases of incompetent cervix, it is necessary to perform an operation and place a ligature (or tie) around the circumference of the cervix. After the ligature is in place, the opening in the cervix is reduced to the normal size for the stage of pregnancy. The operation is done "from below" (that is, through the vagina) so that no abdominal incision is necessary. The patient is hospitalized an average of four or five days after surgery. When she gets to term, or if labor begins before term, either the ligature is removed and the baby delivered normally, or the ligature is left in place and the infant delivered by Caesarean section. In making the decision whether to perform a Caesarean section or pelvic delivery, the doctor considers a number of factors, including the patient's age and the capacity of her pelvis. The operation is not done until after the third month to avoid the possibility of a spontaneous miscarriage, of a "blighted ova," after the surgery. If the ligature is left in place and a Caesarean section is performed, the ligature does not interfere with subsequent menstruation or conception. The results of the surgical treatment of the incompetent cervix have been dramatic. Formerly, infant survival was practically zero. Now some 80 percent of infants survive if the operation is done in time.

There are some women, fortunately few and very far between, who each time they conceive miscarry in the early months of pregnancy. This condition is known as *habitual abortion*. While the cause of habitual abortion usually remains obscure, any woman who has had two or more miscarriages in a row ought to be examined thoroughly in the hope of finding some condition that can be corrected to improve the chances of success in a subsequent pregnancy. Occasionally, some anatomic abnormality, bicornuate uterus, for example, will be discovered. A few women with hormonal abnormalities can be treated successfully. A great deal of research on possible links between hormone deficiency and abortion has been done, but the problem is still with us. In more than half the patients with habitual abortion no abnormality is found and the chances of another miscarriage are great. Nevertheless, the outlook for success in future pregnancies is never hopeless. Every once in a while a woman who has had a large number of miscarriages will conceive again and have a perfectly normal, trouble-free pregnancy.

It may be helpful at this point to list some events and activities that do not cause miscarriage. Whenever a woman has a miscarriage, she asks why. Some women are plagued with feelings of guilt. They are convinced that they must have done something or failed to do something that caused the miscarriage. But once a pregnancy has got started properly, it is all but impossible for the woman to do anything to influence its development. Certainly everyday activities are perfectly innocuous, and even strenuous sports can be engaged in with impunity. Traveling does not cause miscarriage, nor, in the opinion of many obstetricians, do emotional upheavals. Some women (or their husbands) feel guilty after a spontaneous miscarriage, because they erroneously believe that sexual intercourse has precipitated the accident. If having sexual relations in pregnancy resulted in miscarriage, the human race would have become extinct aeons ago. Women occasionally ask if some deficiency or abnormality of the male sperm cell can cause a spontaneous abortion. There is some division of opinion among doctors on this point, but the majority feel that abnormalities of the sperm cell are not the cause of miscarriage.

The symptoms of spontaneous abortion or miscarriage are cramps and bleeding in the first three months of pregnancy. Many women who have spontaneous abortions do not "feel" pregnant, or else they notice that the subjective symptoms of pregnancy abruptly disappear. A few days later the accident occurs. Not all bleeding in early pregnancy terminates in a miscarriage, however. Many women have slight staining for a day or two at the time of the first missed period. This is known as *implantation bleeding*. It is perfectly normal and innocent and, incidentally, is seen in some of the higher primates. Quite a few women in early pregnancy have bleeding that subsides with or without treatment, the pregnancy developing normally thereafter. This bleeding is thought to come from the *decidua,* which is the tissue that lines the womb during pregnancy. The decidua becomes congested and may bleed without any harm to the developing embryo. If a mother has bleeding in early pregnancy but does not miscarry, she has no cause to worry that the baby will be malformed or abnormal. Such accidents have other causes.

Bleeding in early pregnancy is never a good sign, however, and frequently it heralds impending miscarriage. If a miscarriage is in the offing, the bleeding is likely to start as a dark red or brown staining. Over the course of four or five days, the bleeding increases to an amount larger than a normal menstrual period and becomes bright red. When the miscarriage does occur, the bleeding becomes even heavier, and large blood clots usually described as looking like pieces of liver are passed. In addition, the pregnancy tissue itself is expelled. This is pale gray in color, often with a bluish or reddish tint, and in the usual miscarriage is a formless mass an inch or two in diameter. Along with the passage of blood and tissue, the patient will experience severe lower abdominal cramps and backache similar to menstrual cramps or labor pains. The doctor's examination at this time will disclose that the uterus is not as large as it should be for the stage of pregnancy and that the neck of the womb is open. It is important that any tissue expelled be saved for the doctor. By examining the tissue he can tell whether the entire products of conception have been expelled or if some remain in the uterus. If everything has been expelled, the miscarriage is said to have been complete, and no further treatment is ordinarily necessary. If only part of the tissue has been passed, the abortion is said to be incomplete. It is then necessary for the patient to be hospitalized and the uterus completely emptied by means of an operation known as *dilatation and curettage,* or D and C for short. This procedure is described in the section on induced abortion (see pages 416–27). This operation requires no incision. Recovery is usually rapid. Most patients are in the hospital only overnight.

After a D and C, there is usually slight vaginal bleeding for four to five days. The patient ordinarily is back in her normal routine in less than a week. Normal menstruation is to be expected in four to six weeks. Many women are anxious to conceive again as soon as possible, and there is no reason why there should be a long waiting period. Before attempting another pregnancy, however, it is advisable to wait until after the first normal period following the abortion. The entire lining of the womb was removed at the time of the D and C and a new one must grow to prepare a proper bed for development of the new pregnancy.

B. INDUCED ABORTION

Induced abortion, which is to be distinguished from spontaneous abortion or miscarriage (see pages 412–16), is the interruption of normal pregnancy by artificial means, almost always a surgical procedure.

Doctors tend to apply the noun *abortion* to all interruptions of pregnancy, natural as well as artificial, but when a layman uses the word, induced abortion ordinarily is what he has in mind.

Methods of inducing abortion have been known for centuries and practiced all over the world. Some societies have not merely condoned but encouraged abortion. In contrast, the Christian tradition has condemned it. Both the law of the church (notably the Roman Catholic Church) and the criminal law of the state have expressed this condemnation. In its extreme position the church has regarded abortion as the murder of a human being, the fetus. The secular criminal law, however, while taking its lead from the church, has not prosecuted on those terms. In practice, the police make arrests only when a woman dies of a bungled abortion or when some crusading group with political power demands action.

While we now seem to be on the threshold of drastic change, all the states of the United States had until quite recently restrictive (some would say punitive) laws regulating induced abortion. The prevailing pattern of law has limited induced abortion to those cases where, in the certified opinion of qualified doctors, childbirth would imperil the mother's life or endanger her mental health. Since modern medicine can preserve the life of almost every pregnant woman, these provisions boil down to a woman's being able to get an abortion on grounds of mental health or not at all. In many states, perhaps most, it has not been easy to obtain consent on this argument, and in any event the procedure has been available only to those who could afford the services of psychiatrists. The consequence has been that legal abortion (called *therapeutic abortion*) has constituted a very small percentage of all the induced abortions performed each year in the United States. The rest, estimated at a million or so a year, have been obtained outside the law. They are lumped together in the category of *criminal abortion,* which, at least in theory, is always liable to police action.

Exactly how many illegal abortions have been performed annually in the United States no one can say. Some investigators believe that the induced abortion rate for some segments of the population may approach 10 percent of all pregnancies. At this rate the total would be staggering. And in dealing with numbers there is another unexpected aspect of illegal abortion. Contrary to general belief, unwed mothers do not make up the majority of women who resort to abortion. The evidence suggests that as many as four out of five aborted women are married and have more than one child.

In view of the numbers involved and in recognition of the fact that highly respectable women are among those seeking illegal abortions, it is pertinent to ask whether the law has been in keeping with the times. The answers now beginning to be heard would suggest that it has not. Colorado, several years ago, became the first state to change its law. While the Colorado reform on abortion did not seem to produce startling results, the later and more drastic reform of the New York State law, which now makes abortion a matter between a woman and her doctor, can be expected to have more sweeping effects. It is historical fact that in major social legislation the country as a whole has tended to follow New York State.

If we in the United States are due for a nationwide change of attitude on abortion, we will only be catching up with others. The Soviet Union, though by all reports a very puritanical society, continues to provide abortion for its citizens, as it has done for many years, and has exported its official position on abortion to the Eastern European nations composing the Soviet bloc. Even in Roman Catholic Hungary the state maintains abortion clinics. Sweden, which has always been advanced in social legislation, has allowed abortion for some time, and in Great Britain, not long before this writing, a permissive new law was adopted. Japan has experience in legal abortion. For more than a decade after World War II the Japanese government promoted abortion in an effort to slow down the population explosion. In 1969, according to government figures, at least a million abortions were performed in Japan, whose population is only half that of the United States. Abortion has contributed to a slowing of the Japanese birthrate, but no one in that country (or elsewhere) advocates abortion as an ideal or even satisfactory method of birth control. On the other hand, if in all the countries with permissive laws anyone has been able to trace social disaster to freedom of recourse to abortion, he has kept his findings secret from the rest of the world.

Liberalization of the attitude toward induced abortion can be described as being in the trend of one line of twentieth-century thinking— away from ecclesiastical law and religious restraints in relations between the sexes and toward the emancipation of the woman. Those are sociological considerations outside the scope of this book. But induced abortion must also figure in any discussion of the welfare of the unborn child and of the mother.

In other sections of the book (see pages 136 and 428) we emphasize the great progress that has been made in very recent years in understanding genetic abnormalities and diagnosing damage to the fetus. Using the techniques of amniocentesis (see below) and chromosomal analysis (see page 439), it is now possible to diagnose with certainty, before birth, every known disease caused by defective chromosomes including, of course, Mongolism (see pages 387–88). Overall, several children out of every thousand are affected by one of these chromosomal disorders. Further, it is also possible at this writing to diagnose prenatally about a dozen inherited chemical disorders, some of which inevitably result in early death. Chemical problems appear less frequently than chromosomal abnormalities but are no less poignant for the affected families.

These diagnoses are made at prenatal genetic diagnostic laboratories, which have or will have the elaborate equipment and specialists necessary for this highly technical work. A network of these laboratories is being established across the country at this writing. If you have any reason to think that you should be tested, you should speak to your physician, who will have or will be able to get the pertinent information about applications. The Prenatal Genetic Diagnostic Laboratory of the Massachusetts General Hospital, first in New England, in its initial year of operation was accepting only pregnant women who met definite requirements: they had a family history of serious inherited diseases such as Mongolism, Tay-Sachs disease, or hemophilia, or they were forty years old or older.

Amniocentesis was first tried in the 1930s but for a long while was used only in management of the Rh disease, erythroblastosis (see pages 151–52). The procedure requires insertion of a needle through the pregnant woman's abdomen into the amniotic sac surrounding the fetus. A small amount of the fluid is then drawn off with a syringe. The procedure is carried out under local anesthesia and is best done around the sixteenth week of gestation.

Since the fluid drawn off from the mother contains fetal cells, the chromosomal and chemical analyses can be done as they would be after birth. Hundreds of these procedures have been carried out with only rare complications for either fetus or mother. It is emphasized, however, that the mother who undergoes the testing should be prepared for abortion if the results establish severe and incurable abnormality. Otherwise, the test is pointless.

That this newly developed ability to diagnose fetal abnormality (and the fetal sex too, incidentally) must have a profound effect on the attitude toward abortion goes without saying. For a mother to know for certain that the child she is carrying is defective is quite different from knowing only that there is a chance of abnormality, or from not knowing at all. Now parents must decide whether they want to bring such a child into the world, and the decision will have to be based not only on the possibly disastrous psychological consequences for the mother, but also on the implications for the child, as well as for society. At this writing the cost of caring for institutionalized Mongoloids in Massachusetts alone has been estimated at over $10 million a year. While human life is not to be valued in dollars, the figure does give some measure of the enormous burden imposed by genetic abnormalities, which now can be circumvented through abortion. The human tragedy, of course, is beyond measure or description.

Certainty of genetic abnormality of the fetus is not the only occasion for seeking abortion. There are also drugs that can cause fetal deformity. The thalidomide tragedy of a few years back was a sensational example. Mothers who had taken this tranquilizing drug at a particular stage of pregnancy were delivered of badly deformed babies. In one case reported on the front page of all the newspapers, an American woman carrying a thalidomide baby had to go all the way to Sweden for an abortion. The evidence from hundreds of previous cases in Europe made the odds overwhelmingly against her having a normal baby, but the law still prevented her from obtaining an abortion in the United States. The publicity given to her plight has provided the crusaders for abortion reform with powerful ammunition.

Then there is the relation between German measles (rubella) and fetal deformity. When an epidemic of the disease appeared about twenty years ago in Australia, the majority of the women who contracted it in the first three months of pregnancy delivered malformed babies. Subsequent investigation indicated that a woman's chances of having a malformed child are multiplied by a factor of four or five if she has German measles in those critical months. While the recent development of an effective rubella vaccine can be expected to cut this hazard substantially, still it will be a long while until every young woman in the world can be rendered immune. Mothers will continue to be faced with the choice of giving birth to probably deformed children or undergoing abortion.

Besides the genetic and chemical disorders of the fetus that medicine now can diagnose, there are various pathological conditions of the mother that have been regarded as ample cause for abortion. Among these are certain cancers of the reproductive apparatus (see pages 123–24), certain chronic conditions of high blood pressure with kidney involvement. As stated before, any condition that makes childbirth dangerous to the mother's life is a justification for therapeutic abortion, but the advances of modern medicine have cut into the list of those conditions.

The psychiatrist, who now plays an increasingly important part in the applications for therapeutic abortion, has his own list of conditions that in his opinion require therapeutic abortion for the mother's mental health. Heading the list, of course, is any psychotic state or depression so deep that suicide is to be feared. But his professional concern is not limited to the desperate situation; he will also have in mind the unborn baby's rights—the right to be a wanted child in a loving family, with at least an even chance to enjoy a healthy and happy childhood. The law does not take these considerations within its purview, but more and more modern medicine is beginning to look on them as *its* proper business. In the coming years we can expect much greater involvement of the medical profession, pediatricians as well as psychiatrists, in many matters that in the past have been held to be the concern of lawmakers and law enforcers exclusively.

Large-scale studies of pregnant women have revealed great variances in the attitudes of the women toward their unborn children, depending on their ages and on the number of children they already have. Many women who have three or more children and who are getting on in years approach a new birth with considerable reluctance, those studies have shown. Such an attitude is not surprising, nor is the reluctance of many young wives to rush into pregnancy before they and their husbands have had a chance to become established.

It is a simple fact that many pregnancies come at awkward times, too early or too late. The baby is conceived out of wedlock. Or a baby just at this time would interfere with important plans, be too great a burden to assume. These are realistic situations capable of complicating any woman's life (or man's) to the point of seeming unendurable. Such misfortunes can occur even to married couples who have agreed to practice birth control in the interest of planned parenthood. Sometimes, it is almost as if the woman's biological drive to fulfill her reproductive destiny is too much for her to subdue. Though she may conscientiously have intended to be faithful in the use of her chosen method of contraception—the IUD, the pessary, or the Pill—a slip somehow has occurred, and she is pregnant.

In the opinion of those who propose radical reform of the abortion laws, all the persons who unwilling find themselves in such situations should be legitimate candidates for abortion. They feel that the decision for abortion is the private business of the patient alone. The American Medical Association, long opposed to liberalized abortion laws, did an about-face in 1970 and went on record as regarding abortion as a matter between a woman and her physician. Nevertheless, it should be emphasized that a sizable and influential segment of the medical profession continues to disagree. To what extent this opposition is directed at the idea of abortion or is a reflection of professional indignation over the conditions under which most illegal abortions have in the past been performed is, of course, a matter of speculation. Certainly, none would question that it would be in the best interest of society to drive unqualified abortionists out of business. Though abortion is not among the most difficult surgical procedures, it is strictly an undertaking for qualified persons working in properly equipped and maintained premises.

It is very important for those seeking legal abortions at places distant from the home communities to secure them at reputable, reasonably priced facilities. In the absence of direct referral from a personal physician, we recommend contacting the office of Planned Parenthood, either in the home community or in the locale where the abortion will be performed. We discourage using commercial abortion referral services, which collect a fee for their services until these come under much closer governmental and professional regulation. Also, we think it is important for those women (or couples) who wish to discuss their feelings about abortion to have the opportunity to do so with a health professional, be it a physician, nurse, or social worker. In general, exploration of feelings before the fact is a healthy step.

Once a normal pregnancy has become established, nothing short of an actual manipulation of some sort within the womb itself can be counted on to cause abortion. Some experimental after-the-fact pills for birth control, now in various stages of development, may in a technical sense disprove the foregoing statement, but we will except them from our discussion. Despite all the folklore about methods to produce early abortion, the opening sentence of this paragraph still stands. Not any amount of hot baths or cold baths or of jumping downstairs will cause an abortion unless spontaneous abortion (see page 412) already is in the cards.

Among the many nostrums proposed for home cure of pregnancy is ergonovine, an old standby, which is capable of producing powerful uterine contractions at the end of pregnancy. This is one of the drugs given after delivery to contract the uterus and so protect against excessive postpartum blood loss. Taken in early pregnancy, ergonovine will bring on a few cramps, but the pregnancy nevertheless will proceed undisturbed.

Another old favorite undeserving of its popularity is potassium permanganate. This deep purple crystalline chemical is used in solution as a disinfectant or antiseptic, but many women who do not know any better are persuaded to insert the undissolved crystals in the vagina for abortion. Being strongly caustic, the chemical then produces deep vaginal ulceration. Profuse vaginal hemorrhage results but, of course, without effect on the developing embryo.

There are some drugs under investigation for treatment of malignant tumors that are slightly more toxic to rapidly dividing cells than to normal cells. As you might expect, rapid cell division is a property characteristic of developing embryos as well as of malignant tumors, and administration of some of these drugs on occasion has been followed by miscarriage in a cancer patient who happened to be pregnant. The results are not consistent, and the margin of safety is small. Because of almost universally severe reactions, the drugs can be given safely only in hospitals equipped and staffed to deal with the problems. No individual doctor would think of using one of these drugs for a therapeutic abortion.

Since an infected uterus tends to empty itself, anything capable of producing an infection, even a minor infection, of the uterus might be looked upon as an instrument or agent of abortion. In this way the introduction of a catheter, knitting needle, or the traditional slippery elm can lead to interruption of pregnancy. Once the bag of waters is broken (see pages 91–92) intrauterine infection becomes inevitable with the passage of time since the very efficient membranous barrier to bacterial invasion from the lower birth canal has been destroyed. The trouble with these techniques of inducing abortion is that the minor infection of the uterus sometimes becomes an overwhelming infection. The medical literature has reported an increasing number of cases of septic shock complicating improperly performed abortions. In such cases blood poisoning occurs and a state of shock supervenes. There is a high rate of mortality. Sometimes, removal of the infected uterus, if done in time, will be lifesaving.

The overwhelming majority of women with pelvic infections recover from them, but there can be a number of remote complications. Adhesions following the inflammatory process have been the cause of chronic pelvic pain and many cases of sterility. Some persons think that a uterine infection can be safely contained if the woman at the same time is taking penicillin or some other antibiotic. Doctors in all the fields of medicine have found the antibiotics very useful in the cure of disease but not always effective in its prevention. Infection has a way of appearing just the same, only now the germs involved are not the ones that are sensitive to the supposedly preventive antibiotic.

For a final exhibit in the chamber of horrors of the amateur abortionist, the introduction of soap or an abortifacient paste into the uterus can be lethal. If such substances gain entrance to the maternal circulation and are carried to the kidneys, the results are devastating. Then the usual course of events is shock, kidney failure, death.

The method most doctors prefer for emptying the uterus in early pregnancy is the scraping of the placental tissue away from its attachment on the intrauterine wall. The instrument used is a spoon-shaped scraper called a *curette,* which is about the size of a fingernail. Since the opening in the neck of the womb is smaller than the instrument, it is necessary first to stretch or *dilate* the cervix. Hence, the procedure and the instrument give the operation its name, *dilatation and curettage,* or *D and C.* Not all D and C's by any means are done for abortion. The D and C is also performed in a diagnostic procedure to determine the cause of abnormal menstrual periods or of bleeding after the menopause.

As pregnancy advances, D and C becomes progressively more difficult and dangerous. The enlarging uterus has softened and can be perforated easily. Should this happen, the operation must be halted at once. An attempt to complete the abortion will only result in injury to the intestines and serious complications.

The blood supply to the uterus increases manifold in pregnancy. Consequently, rather brisk bleeding always accompanies D and C as the placental tissue is being scraped away from the intrauterine wall. Naturally, the larger the placenta the greater the blood loss. So, if the pregnancy has passed beyond the third month, D and C is no longer the safe way to empty the uterus. In the worst of the illegal abortions hemorrhage is a common complication since most of the unqualified abortionists leave part of the placenta tissue behind. In these circumstances bleeding can be heavy and persistent. In addition to perforation and hemorrhage, infection, of course, is a hazard of the illegal abortion performed under primitive conditions. Any placental tissue remaining in the womb is an ideal site for growth of bacteria.

When the conservative gynecologist, operating legally, is going to perform a therapeutic abortion, he does the D and C if the pregnancy has not progressed beyond the third month. If it has gone much beyond the third month, he performs an abdominal operation much like the Caesarean section (see pages 207–11) . This operation is called *hysterotomy*.

In meeting the rush for abortions in New York City in the first few months after adoption of the new law, two techniques of abortion newer than D and C were put to some use.

One technique is known formally as *saline induction* or popularly as "salting down." It can be performed only after the sixteenth week of pregnancy. A small amount of salt solution is injected by needle through the abdominal wall into the uterus to kill the fetus. In theory the introduction of the alien substance and the death of the fetus should induce labor at once, but in fact induction does not invariably follow. Women who had been salted down in New York City were being received in Boston hospitals days later still carrying dead fetuses. The procedure to take care of them was similar to any induction of labor by administration of pitocin (see page 207) , the patient having to remain in the hospital for perhaps as long as four or five days, depending upon her condition and complications.

The salting-down procedure, which was imported from Europe, came to public attention in the 1950s and was at first received enthusiastically. Then a number of sudden deaths were reported, and the enthusiasm cooled. The cause of the deaths was taken to be excess concentration of salt in the blood. While saline induction is now considered a safe procedure where full hospital facilities and staff can be brought to bear in emergencies, the risk of complications, including blood clotting, is said to be higher than in other procedures. The psychological trauma from knowingly having to carry about a fetus that was killed at the mother's own behest is said to be devastating in many cases.

The other new technique used during the first trimester is also a European import, which may have originated in the Soviet Union and has been used extensively in Sweden. It is similar in technique to the D and C and is becoming increasingly popular in this country. A plastic instrument known as an *aspirator* with a suction pump attached is used. It is a rigid tube of small diameter, like a catheter, with a cutting edge at the leading end. It is introduced into the uterus by way of the vagina. As the material is scraped from the uterine wall, it is sucked away through the instrument, but the apparatus is said to have problems with plugging. Another even newer approach, still experimental but offering great promise, is the injection of prostoglandins (a type of hormone) into the uterine cavity. Prostoglandins cause the uterus to contract and expel its contents.

Whether the great increase of legal abortion under liberalization of the law will bring drastic change in medical or surgical procedures remains to be seen. A good bit will depend, of course, on developments in the contraceptive pill, especially of the so-called morning-after pill. The woman who is about to undergo abortion can take comfort in knowledge that the operation, when performed properly under proper conditions, carries little risk and few implications for a future pregnancy. Concerning the psychological consequences, there has been some debate, but since religious conscience and current morality will be an influence on those consequences, it would be rash to expect the answers to be either universal or simple.

Some authorities writing from the psychological point of view contend that abortion brings with it an inevitable sense of loss. This may be so, but it is likely that for most women the sense of relief in being freed from unwanted pregnancy will counterbalance the sense of loss. Dr. Grete Bibring has suggested that the sense of loss may not be felt until the menopause, when any hope of childbearing comes to an end. This exception would be the extreme example. Undoubtedly a woman who wanted children but had to have an abortion for some medical reason would feel loss, especially if some physical condition thereafter precluded pregnancy.

It unquestionably is a fact that many girls after unsuccessful attempts at abortion have come to change their minds and look forward to giving birth. Nevertheless, one should not assume that the sequence inevitably would hold for every girl in an initially unwanted pregnancy. The hundreds of babies given up for adoption immediately after birth every year offer only too poignant evidence to the contrary. And in a world that seems to be racing mindlessly toward totally destructive overpopulation, we can look for more and more change in the public attitude on all matters concerning unwanted children. Questioning of all our previous attitudes on abortion, as well as contraception, will figure prominently in the changes.

While abortion may be coming into greater favor, all agree that it is an undesirable and costly way to control populations. It is not a substitute for effective family planning, which includes family life and sex education as well as contraceptive techniques. The occasion for an abortion is an excellent, if somewhat belated opportunity, to take personal stock of these matters.

ARTHUR GORBACH, M.D.
RICHARD I. FEINBLOOM, M.D.

CHAPTER TWENTY-THREE

Genetics

*F*ROM TIME immemorial man has known that he resembles his ancestors. Whom does he (or she) look like? is almost our first question about every newborn. We say that the blue eyes have come from so-and-so and the brown hair from somebody else and so on. Further, it has long been part of the lore of our species that temperament and ability, as well as looks, can be inherited, but our ideas on this score have been more in the nature of an article of faith than a demonstrable scientific fact. Concerning physical inheritance in living things, however, there has been no doubt. For centuries man has been manipulating physical inheritance to his own advantage in the selective breeding of his domesticated animals to perpetuate certain desirable characteristics. Nevertheless, it has been only in the last one hundred years that the processes of heredity, the biological mechanisms by which certain characteristics are passed from parents to children, have been understood at all.

The study of heredity is the comparatively new science called *genetics,* which in recent years has been taking enormous strides. In no other branch of biology or medicine has progress been more rapid or the discoveries of greater fundamental importance. The geneticist already has revealed the origin of many obscure conditions and has opened the way to developing corrective measures for some of them. He has enriched immeasurably whole fields of thought in biology and psychology, and it is not extravagant to say that he may be on the edge of solving the biggest mystery of all, the mechanism of life itself.

[428]

Each branch of science, genetics like the rest, has its own vocabulary. To gain even casual acquaintance with genetics, you need to know the meaning of several technical words and to understand one or two elementary technical operations. This article is intended as a primer. You will not find it difficult if, as you read along, you keep turning back to the basic definitions until the comparatively few technical names become familiar. You should find the small effort amply rewarding. Genetics is a truly fascinating subject. Even this very elementary introduction will give you a better understanding of how your baby acquires the characteristics that make him an individual but still relate him to the long family trees of his parents.

The science of genetics began amid rows of pea plants in the garden of a monastery in what is now Brno, Czechoslovakia. Its author was a Moravian monk, Gregor Johann Mendel (1822–1884), who lived in obscurity and died without acclaim for discoveries that rank among the great contributions to science. In a paper published in 1866, he spelled out in great detail his findings on the crossing or breeding of different varieties of garden peas, but he was too far ahead of his time. The rest of the world did not grasp the significance of his reports.

In the everyday sense Mendel's life was one of frustration and defeat, but it makes a poignant and inspiring story. He was born in a small village in what was then Austria and is now Czechoslovakia. Like the poor peasant farmers who were his ancestors, he grew up close to the soil and had an almost instinctive familiarity with plants and gardens. It was not by chance that he turned to ordinary garden peas for his experiments on heredity. Because he showed promise, his parents at great sacrifice sent Mendel away to school. He often went hungry, but he excelled in his studies and hoped to go on to Vienna to pursue a career in science. Under privation and hard work, however, his health failed when he was ready to enter the university. At this point, he decided to abandon his bitter struggle for existence; he entered a monastery in Brno, which then was known as Brunn. In 1847, he was ordained a priest.

Mendel obtained a temporary position teaching, which he enjoyed. He felt he had at last found his niche in life. But his hopes were dashed again when he failed to pass an examination that would have given him a permanent position. While flunking, he nevertheless so impressed his examiners that they arranged for him to go to Vienna to the university and complete the higher education in mathematics and science for which he had always yearned. After graduation in Vienna, Mendel returned to Brunn, where he taught science in the local high school. This not too demanding occupation left him ample time to pursue his favorite hobby, experimenting with plants. After years of painstaking experiments, Mendel was ready, in 1866, to present his findings to the scientific community. The scientists, however, were not in the least stirred, or even interested. His revolutionary theories about the mechanism of heredity were not accepted. He was advised to forget his work. Mendel apparently had failed again. Fortunately, his reports were published as a matter of routine in a scientific journal, so they were not lost to the world. But when he died, in 1884, his great work was still utterly ignored, apparently consigned to oblivion.

In Mendel's lifetime, the evolutionary theories of the great Charles Darwin dominated the scientific world. Darwin thought biological inheritance was accomplished by a simple mixing of parental "bloods" or "serums." Individual characteristics of the parents were thought to be blended in the preparation of a new individual, much as modern man mixes four parts gin and one of vermouth when he wants a good cocktail. It was Mendel's genius to have seen, on the contrary, that there was no blurring or dilution of individual traits in heredity. Instead, inherited characteristics are transmitted from parent to offspring as separate units, which maintain their identities from generation to generation. Specific characteristics may fail to appear in some generations, but inevitably at some point in the future they will again express themselves.

Like many other great scientific advances, Mendel's experiments were disarmingly simple. A garden of ordinary pea plants was his laboratory. Mendel noted that not all peas were alike. Some were tall, others short; some had green seeds, others yellow seeds, and so forth. Mendel found that when he crossed a pure strain of yellow-seeded peas with a strain having green seeds, the first generation of *hybrid* plants always had yellow seeds. In the second generation, however, which he obtained by crossing the first-generation hybrids, about three-fourths of the plants had yellow seeds and one-fourth had green seeds. Because the yellow seeds "covered up" green seeds in hybrid plants, Mendel said the yellow was a *dominant* trait. The green, which was "covered up," he called a *recessive* trait.

Mendel concluded that the first generation received a dominant hereditary unit from one parent and a recessive unit from the other. We now call these hereditary units *genes*. When the offspring has obtained a combination of a dominant gene from one side and a recessive gene from the other, the dominant gene always prevails in the offspring. Individuals with such a combination of a dominant and a recessive gene are said to be *heterozygous,* having two unlike genes for a particular characteristic. If they receive the same type of gene from both parents they are said to be *homozygous* for a trait, whether the trait is dominant or recessive. For the recessive trait to become manifest, the offspring has to receive the recessive gene from both parents and to be homozygous for the recessive trait.

Mendel's theories are usually expressed in symbols. Dominant traits are shown in capital letters while recessive traits are designated by the corresponding lowercase letters. Mendel's pure strain of yellow-seeded peas is symbolized as YY. This genetic formula is known as the *genotype.* The pure recessive strain of peas with green seeds is shown by the genotype yy. When these two strains are crossed (YY by yy) all progeny will have the same genotype Yy. You will see how this works if you think of the first Y as combining with the first y to produce one Yy and then with the second y to produce a second Yy. Then the second Y combines with the first y to produce the third Yy and with the second y for the fourth Yy. These are the heterozygous hybrids of Mendel's first generation, and all have the same demonstrable characteristic, which is known as the *phenotype,* in this case yellow seeds.

When Mendel's first generation of hybrids is interbred in the second generation, Yy by Yy, there are four combinations (two of which are the same), having the following genotypes, YY, Yy, Yy, yy. The offspring will consist of one homozygous yellow seed (YY), two heterozygous yellow seeds (Yy), and one homozygous green seed (yy). The Y of the first hybrid combined with the Y of the second to form the YY, and with its y to form one Yy. The y of the first combined with the Y of the second to form the second Yy and with the y of the second to form one yy.

The colors of pea seeds are of little moment to those having babies, but the much publicized Rh blood factor will bring the significance of Mendel's peas closer to home. The Rh blood factor is inherited by exactly the same process. The Rh factor is dominant. All Rh-negative individuals lack this dominant trait. Rh-positive people may be either homozygous or heterozygous. If the father is an Rh-positive homozygous and the mother is Rh negative, which also is homozygous, all the children will be Rh-positive hybrids similar to Mendel's first generation of yellow-seeded peas. If the father is heterozygous Rh positive with genotype (RH rh) and the mother Rh negative (rh rh), there are four combinations but not all of them different. Two will be heterozygous Rh-positive children with the genotype (RH rh), and two will be homozygous Rh-negative children with the genotype (rh rh).

Inheritance can be studied only when individuals of the population have contrasting traits; for example, yellow seeds versus green seeds, or Rh-positive blood type versus Rh-negative blood type. Such inherited contrasting conditions, called *alleles,* usually exist in pairs. A number of important genes, however, exist in three or more *allelic states* and are called *multiple alleles.* In man the inheritance of the ABO blood group system is an example of this latter type of inheritance.

Many important characteristics (height, intelligence, and special aptitudes, for example) appear to be transmitted not by one but several genes. These determinants are known as *multiple factors* or *multiple genes.* In predicting the outcome of mating when multiple genes are involved, we follow the Mendelian laws but find that the problem rapidly becomes very complex. The number of possible combinations soars. The inheritance of skin color is a good example. In the mating of a pure strain black with a pure strain white, all first generation are hybrid or, in this case, mulattoes. When mulattoes mate there are sixteen possible combinations because two pairs of genes are involved. When only a single genetic pair is under consideration, you will recall, there are but four possible combinations in the second generation.

Even before Mendel's time, scientists knew that all living things were made up of cells. It was believed at first that these cells were empty, but improved laboratory instruments and techniques revealed that within each cell there is a tiny lump. This blob became known as the *nucleus,* from the Latin word for "nut" or "kernel." We now know that the nucleus is the headquarters for each cell and that the cell (with exceptions) does not exist without its nucleus. Progress in the study of the cell was slow until it was found that certain dyes stained the nucleus, which could then be seen under magnification. About the same time, microscopes were improved and machines perfected to slice biologic preparations much thinner than previously had been possible. In the very thin slices a great deal more detail could be seen through the microscope.

Some years after Mendel's work, biologists discovered dark-staining rods in the nucleus of cells undergoing division. They gave the name *chromosome,* or "colored body," to these structures. It soon became apparent that the physical basis for heredity must lie in these chromosomes. It was shown eventually that the chromosomes did indeed carry the heredity units, or genes. The remarkable thing about Mendel is that, long before anyone had ever heard of a chromosome or a gene, he postulated the existence of some kind of hereditary unit coming from each parent. The behavior of chromosomes fitted nicely into the laws that he had proposed.

While the individual chromosome can be seen and studied, genes are much too small to be visible under even the most powerful microscopes. Genes determining a certain characteristic are located at the same spot in a chromosome. Chemically, a gene is the complicated compound known as deoxyribonucleic acid, or *DNA*. The threadlike structures we call chromosomes are individually visible only at cell division, when *daughter cells* are getting chromosomes from *parent cells*. Chromosomes have a definite size and shape, and each species of plant or animal has a definite number of chromosomes characteristic for the species. Man, for example, has forty-six. Just a few years ago man was supposed to have forty-eight. The true state of affairs has only recently been brought to light.

Ordinary cell division is called *mitosis*. By splitting in two, each chromosome makes a copy of itself, one copy going to each of the two daughter cells produced by the division. Each daughter cell thus receives exactly the same number and kind of chromosomes the parent cell had. In the formation of egg and sperm cells, a unique type of division occurs, called *meiosis* or *reduction division*. In meiosis, each daughter cell winds up with only half the number of chromosomes. Human egg and sperm cells have only twenty-three chromosomes each. When they combine, the new individual formed by their union has forty-six chromosomes, the characteristic number for the human species. If the chromosomes were not halved before fertilization, they would double with each succeeding generation.

On rare occasions in meiosis there is an uneven apportionment of chromosomes to the daughter cells. Daughter cells may form with an extra or missing chromosome. This is called *nondisjunction*. Another accident that may happen in meiosis is *translocation,* where a segment of one chromosome shifts to another chromosome. Egg and sperm cells having either nondisjunction or translocation of the chromosomes may be incapable of fertilization. Or if the egg is fertilized, the combination may give rise to an abnormal individual.

The heredity factor or unit we call the gene determines such properties as eye and skin color, type of hair, body configuration, blood type, and all the other physical characteristics passed from generation to generation. Genes are thought also to have a large part in determining for the individual such qualities as intelligence and special aptitudes and the relative immunity or susceptibility to some diseases that appear to run in some families. A combination of genetic material from the mother and the father gives rise to the new individual, who will resemble each parent in certain characteristics. It is estimated that the fruit fly, which has been used extensively in genetic experiments, has between one thousand and five thousand genes on each of its four pairs of chromosomes. Assuming that in man the number of genes is of proportionate magnitude, one must conclude that the comparable number of human genes would be somewhere between twenty-five thousand and one hundred thousand. You can easily appreciate how the mixing up of such great numbers of genes will give rise to almost limitless variations in the offspring.

Until just recently the study of genetics was confined largely to predicting the frequency of different inherited characteristics. The fruit fly has proved to be an almost ideal experimental subject for the study of genetics because of this insect's short life cycle and its relatively simple genetic apparatus, consisting of only four pairs of chromosomes. Modern genetics is concerned with the mechanisms of heredity on a molecular level. A great deal has been learned about the chemical composition of genes and about their influence on the development of individual cells. The secrets of inheritance appear to be contained in the remarkable biological chemical called *deoxyribonucleic acid,* or DNA. As the prime clue in the unraveling of those mysteries, DNA has turned out to be the Rosetta stone of genetics.

The discovery of the importance of DNA took many years. Like almost all scientific discoveries, the tracking down of DNA was the work of several scientists, each adding to the groundwork of previous investigators. DNA was discovered way back in 1868 by the Swiss biochemist Johann Friedrich Miescher, who isolated it from the nucleus of the white blood corpuscle. At the time, no one had any idea of the significance of DNA; until 1946, it was just another obscure biochemical compound. But by 1946 the study of genetics had come a long way. A great deal had been learned about the inheritance of transmissible characteristics. Most of the information came from studies of those thousands of generations of fruit flies. Still the chemical nature and action of genes remained a mystery. Then, in that year, scientists at the Rockefeller Institute in New York who were trying to elucidate the nature of this substance transferred the DNA from one bacterial strain to another. When these organisms reproduced, the new generation was like the bacterial strain from which the DNA had been taken. This experiment proved that DNA controlled heredity, but it did not explain how DNA worked.

First, it would be necessary to learn what DNA looked like, a very difficult task. DNA, while a huge molecule as molecules go, is still too small to be seen with even an electron microscope magnifying over one hundred thousand times. All substances have a molecular structure made up of a collection of atoms that are arranged in a special pattern for each substance. Some molecules are simple: water has two atoms of hydrogen and one of oxygen. Others, like DNA, have thousands of atoms arranged in chains of submolecules that keep repeating.

Maurice Wilkins, a British biochemist, received the Nobel prize for taking an X-ray picture of DNA in 1952. He used a process called X-ray diffraction, bombarding DNA with X-ray beams. Like all atoms, those making up the DNA molecule have inner nuclei with outer shells of charges of electricity known as electrons. When a beam of X rays strikes an atom, it is bent or "scattered" by the electrons. The pattern of scattering is determined by the atomic arrangement of the bombarded substance. This pattern can be recorded on film. By making appropriate measurements of the recorded pattern, scientists can identify the structure of the bombarded substance. While Wilkins's work was a great advance, it was still only a two-dimensional picture of DNA. Linus Pauling, the renowned California chemist, suggested that DNA could be a long spiral chain, looking like a coiled bedspring.

Another Englishman, Francis Crick, working with a young American, James Watson, showed that in structure DNA was actually a double coil or "helix" held together by many short cross members, suggestive of the rungs of a ladder. The paired coils of DNA are made up of two alternating chemical substances, a sugar and a phosphate. The transverse members, the rungs of the ladder, so to speak, are made from four relatively simple chemical bases. According to Watson and Crick, each species has its own sequence of rungs. Nature achieves her great variety through multitudinous arrangements and sequences of the relatively simple units making up the large DNA molecule.

As more knowledge has been gained about DNA, it has become apparent that this substance, located in the nucleus of all cells, carries the pattern of life. The structure of DNA makes possible the duplication of living cells from generation to generation. DNA serves as the blueprint or template for determining the form and function of each individual cell in the body and thereby the entire organism as a whole.

Someday it may be feasible for scientists to change this genetic code by altering the DNA; the possibilities of changing an individual or the entire human race would be unlimited. It becomes increasingly clear that DNA is the carrier of genetic information and that the arrangement of the different parts of the DNA strand composes the code by which genetic factors are passed along in the process of heredity.

In this age of computers, when we are surrounded by cards that must not be bent, stapled, or mutilated, DNA might be likened to a biological punch card. The DNA determines how the cell will grow and what proteins or enzymes it will elaborate. When a daughter cell forms, it gets a DNA punch card identical to the parent cell, and this card predetermines the new cell's structure and function. It will be exactly the same as the cells from which it was derived. When egg and sperm cells join, a new punch card is made that determines how the embryo will develop.

Occasionally the DNA molecule is changed when it is passed on to the daughter cell. Consequently, the new cell has different characteristics. Possibly one of the units of the complicated structure gets turned around or lost altogether. When the new cell undergoes division, it will pass on the altered DNA, and all the progeny will have the different characteristics. In this manner *mutations* arise.

Mutations are permanent transmissible characteristics in the offspring. If the right mutation should occur, it would be possible, in theory at least, for a couple of redheads, both from families where there had been only redheads, to produce a black-haired child. Furthermore, this child would pass the gene for black hair on to all his or her children. Mutations are going on all the time. Unfortunately, the great majority are detrimental and result in inferior structures or functioning. On occasion, a favorable mutation will occur and a superior individual results. It is the natural selection of these favorable mutations that is thought to be responsible for the gradual evolution of man over the aeons of time. We do not know much about why these mutations occur or how to control them. We do know, however, that the *rate* of mutation can be increased by exposure to certain factors. Most of the knowledge in this field has come from experiments in which fruit flies were exposed to radiation. It has been shown conclusively that exposure to radiation increases the rate of mutation. Furthermore, the rate of mutation is proportional to the amount of radiation exposure—the more the radiation the higher the rate of mutation. While this work has been done with insects, there is no reason to believe that the conclusions are not equally applicable to human beings. This possibility does not suggest that X rays or other sources of radiation should or could be avoided entirely. Radiation, properly used, is a great help in the diagnosis and treatment of many diseases. But exposure to radiation should be regarded at all times with respect and avoided when it is not necessary.

Many factors other than radiation must also be responsible for mutations. It seems almost a certainty that some chemicals are capable of altering DNA, and it is quite likely that some viruses that grow and multiply have this property. Cancer is a mutation of certain body cells. Mutation suggests DNA involvement. Can we find a way to change the DNA of the cancer back to normal or alter it somehow to render it incapable of further cell division? These are big questions, but when the cure for cancer eventually is discovered, as it certainly will be, it will lie in some such biochemical process, not in bigger and better surgery or X-ray treatments as we now know them.

There is a growing list of diseases that are now known to be inherited. One that has gained a great deal of publicity is *phenylketonuria* or, in this age of abbreviation, PKU disease, which can lead to mental retardation. As we have seen (see pages 388–89) , PKU is characterized by the appearance of phenylpyruvic acid in the urine. Because a necessary enzyme is lacking, the essential amino acid phenylalanine cannot be processed in PKU patients as it is in normal individuals. PKU disease is the result of a genetic defect that is inherited as a recessive trait. It occurs only about once in every ten thousand children but is important because we have easy tests to determine its presence and a dietary therapy against its effects. The mental retardation that accompanies the disease can be prevented if the diet is restricted to foods from which the processes of metabolism will produce only small amounts of phenylpyruvic acid.

Galactosemia is another rare inherited disease. Like PKU, it is due to a recessive gene. There is lacking an enzyme that prevents the conversion of galactose into glucose, and in this condition too there is likely to be brain damage. Several types of anemia are inherited. These have a high incidence in populations of particular racial backgrounds. *Sickle-cell anemia,* inherited as a recessive trait, is a serious disease found usually in the Negro race. *Thalassemia,* similarly inherited, is a fairly common anemia in countries bordering the Mediterranean Sea and is often called *Mediterranean anemia.*

A number of diseases are due to chromosome abnormalities. The study of these conditions is called *cytogenetics*. In recent years there has been a veritable explosion of knowledge here. For a long time it had been known that *colchicine,* used in the treatment of gout, had the peculiar property of arresting cell division during mitosis. (You will recall that only during cell division can the individual chromosomes be seen.) Biologists used colchicine for years in preparing specimens for study, but the chromosomes always appeared as a jumble piled one on top of another, like a handful of straw. It was virtually impossible to count them, to say nothing of being able to make out individual differences in size and shape. Quite by accident, it was discovered that subjecting the cells to a certain saline solution forced them to absorb water. The chromosomes were then scattered and could be identified easily and counted. Using this method, Dr. Joetlin Tjio and Dr. Albert Levan, in Sweden, startled the biological world in 1956 by announcing that human beings had forty-six chromosomes, not forty-eight.

Newer chemical methods of separating and staining enable geneticists to work from photographic prints of the chromosomes enlarged three or four thousand times. The pairs of chromosomes are assigned numbers (from 1 through 22) according to the length and position of the *centromere,* the sharply constricted region joining the halves of the pair. The pairs through number 22 are called *autosomes.* There are in addition the two chromosomes determining sex, making the total of forty-six chromosomes per person. The generally accepted *Denver Classification* assigns the autosomes to seven groups, designated by letters of the alphabet. From the section on embryology (see pages 94–116) you will recall that the sex chromosomes are of two types, X and Y. The female has two X chromosomes, the male an X and a Y. In fertilization the X type determines a female child, the Y type a male. It is the father, therefore, who determines the sex of the baby.

All the diseases now known to come from chromosomal abnormalities appear to stem from either too much or too little genetic material. By far the commonest of these is Mongolism, also known as *Down's syndrome,* in which chromosome number 21 is involved. Children with Mongolism have definite physical characteristics that make early recognition possible. These children have a very limited intellectual capacity and almost invariably are severely retarded. Many have associated heart anomalies. It appears that this abnormality arises in meiosis, the unique type of cell division that prepares the ovum for fertilization. Instead of half the chromosomes getting to each daughter cell, an ovum is formed that has two number 21 chromosomes, instead of just one. When this ovum subsequently is fertilized, the result is a cell with three number 21 chromosomes.

We know how Mongolism comes about but we still do not know why. The abnormality is more common as the mother's age increases but does not appear to be related to the father's age. This observation leads us to assume that Mongolism results when an abnormal egg cell is fertilized by a normal sperm cell, rather than the other way around.

In about one Mongoloid child in fifty a different type of chromosomal anomaly has occurred. Instead of one daughter cell getting two chromosomes number 21 and the other none (an example, incidentally, of *nondisjunction,* see page 433) the process of *translocation* occurs. A segment of chromosome number 21 joins another chromosome, usually one of the D group in Denver Classification. When fertilized by a normal cell, a normal-appearing individual results with the normal complement of genetic material, albeit in a peculiar location. This individual may be a carrier of Mongolism, however, because of the translocated chromosome number 21. When a Mongoloid child is born, a cytogenetic analysis is in order to determine whether it is the nondisjunction type, which is a chance phenomenon related to the mother's age, or the translocation type, which may be inherited and passed on to future generations.

The foregoing discussion probably goes into more detail than the frequency of Mongolism warrants. It does, however, illustrate the mechanism of chromosomal abnormality and gives you an idea of how chromosomes are studied. The future will undoubtedly reveal other types of chromosomal abnormality. We already know that a number of rare syndromes usually involve chromosomal abnormalities of the sex pair of chromosomes. Many miscarriages are thought to be due to chromosomal abnormality. It is not unlikely that some cases of sterility will be traced to chromosomal structure because the fertilized egg may fail to divide if the chromosomal abnormality is a severe one.

One immediate application of our present knowledge about chromosomes is analysis prior to birth. A small sample of amniotic fluid is obtained by needle aspiration. The fluid contains a definable number of free-floating cells shed from the fetus. The chromosomes of these cells are like those of the infant from which they originated and show any abnormalities. In patients of a high risk for having infants with chromosomal abnormalities, this procedure gives an early warning of trouble, and always raises the question of performing a therapeutic abortion if defective cells are detected. In fact this examination is done with abortion in mind.

As new techniques are developed, we will certainly make great strides in the field. Investigators will be able to construct scanning instruments to search a chromosome preparation and to analyze the individual chromosome by computer much more accurately and rapidly than is now possible. These advances will make large-scale studies both feasible and cheap. Possibly in the next generation, a premarital chromosomal analysis will be as routine as the premarital Wassermann test is today.

All the recent work with DNA and chromosome analysis is fascinating and seems to portend limitless possibilities for the next generation. At the present, however, the surface has only been scratched. PKU disease is a medical curiosity; Mongolism occurs in something like one birth in five hundred. We still know nothing about the cause or prevention of most congenital abnormalities—clubfoot, cleft palate, or congenital heart disease, to name just a few. With rare exceptions, such anomalies come like a bolt from the blue. Combing back through the family history usually does not reveal similar cases. A review of the prenatal course fails to uncover any facts about strange drugs administered to the mother or virus disease. When a baby with a congenital anomaly is born, the parents are naturally distraught and want to know the cause of the condition. All that we can say now is that in most cases we just do not know.

These parents also want to know about the future and what, if anything, they can do to prevent recurrence in a subsequent pregnancy. Before another pregnancy is undertaken, several steps would appear to be in order. The parents' general health should be optimum. If there is any question, a complete medical checkup is indicated. Any abnormalities found should be attended to. In this age of hormones, there is a tendency to look on endocrine factors as the possibly responsible agents. If there is even a suspicion of hormonal abnormality, appropriate tests should be done. A careful study of the family history should be undertaken following the birth of a congenitally abnormal child. Perhaps a chromosomal analysis should be done, although the analysis in most cases will add nothing.

Genetic counseling will undoubtedly become more common in the future. Physicians are now able to screen, for instance, for sickle-cell anemia, a serious and still untreatable disease. Marriage partners with the sickle-cell trait will thus be able to decide whether or not to have children. Of course finding a cure for sickle-cell anemia would make such a preventative genetics approach less important.

After all is said and done, the great majority of mothers who have had a congenitally abnormal child are healthy young women without any evidence of endocrine malfunction or genetic abnormality. While no one has a crystal ball, these young women can be told in all honesty that their chances for a perfectly normal baby in a subsequent pregnancy are excellent.

ARTHUR GORBACH, M.D.
PARK GERALD, M.D.

INDEX

Index

Dribbling, defects of urinary tract and, 397

Drinking, premature infant and, 340

Drooling, trachoesophageal fistula and, 394–95

Drugs
analgesic, *see* Analgesic drugs
for depression, 126–27
nonprescription, 88
during pregnancy, 87–88
See also specific drugs

Dry birth, 202

Duodenum, 352, 390–91

Dysmature, 257, 331

Dysmature postmature infants, 341

E

Early care of infants, 277–88
babies' eyes and, 277–78
breathing and, 283
circumcision, 284–85
head and, 279–80
immunization and, 285–88
navel and, 280–81
skin and, 281–82
sleeping position and, 283–84

Ears
development of, 105–107
earlobes of newborn, 260–61, 279
Mongolism and small, 388
See also Hearing impairment

Eating during labor, 178

Ebbs, J. H., 18

Eclampsia, 158, 255

Eclamptogenic toxemia, 158

Ectoderm, 103

Ectopic pregnancy, 73, 161–62

Eczema, 289, 304

Edema, 129–31

Education on childbirth, 191

Egg yolk, 323

Eggplant, 81

Eggs
development of, 65
arresting, 66
division of, 67, 100–101
fertilization of, 66–67
implantation of, 67

Eggs, pregnant women need, 78

Ejaculation, 405

Elective induction, 175

Electrocardiograms, fetal, 140

Electrodes, 201

Electrons, 435

Embryo
inner cell mass forms, 101–102
miscarriage and, 412
See also Fetus

Embryology, 438

Emotional attitudes
toward children, through history, 49
toward pregnancy, 7–12
of career women, 9
financial problems and, 9
with planned pregnancy, 7
premarital pregnancy, 8–9
previous children and, 8
satisfaction of motherhood and, 11–12
social customs and, 9–11
with unplanned pregnancy, 7

Emotional support during labor, 25

Emotions
effects on prenatal environment of, 246
impotence and, 405
milk production and, 291
miscarriage and, 415
ovulation and, 403
See also Emotional attitudes

Emphysema, 360–61

Endocardial fibroelastosis, 169

Endrocrine abnormalities, 408, 440

Endrocrine gland, 65

Gums, 355
  of newborn, 261
Gut, development of, 105

H

Habitual abortion, 414–15
Hair, 113
Halibut, 323
Hands
  devlopment of, 106
  mongolism and, 388
  rhythmic motions of, 30
  swelling of, 130
Hard palate, 355
Hardening (calcification) , 279
  of premature infants, 331
Harelip, 46, 107, 355–56
"Harlequin sign," 258
Head
  early care and, 279–80
  embryonic, 106
  shape of newborn, 259
  swelling of newborn, 259
Headaches, 92, 132–33
Hearing impairment
  of premature infants, 339
  prenatal infections and, 375–76
Heart
  development of, 103–106
  malformation of, 375
  mongolism and, 388
  of newborn, 262
  pregnancy and, 13, 70
Heart disease, 133–34
Heart surgery during pregnancy, 70, 134
Heartburn during pregnancy, 71, 133
Hemangioma, 352
  birthmarks, 353–54
Hematopoietic system, 155, 370–71
Hemoglobin, 74, 382
  anemia and, 117

Hemoglobin (cont.)
  in women's blood, 118
Hemolysis, 117
Hemolytic disease, 370
Hemophilia, 243, 419
Hemorrhoids, 134–35, 217
Hepatitis, 353, 361–62
  jaundice and, 383
Heredity, 46–47, 88
  genetics and, 428–41
  newborn infant, environment and, 241–54
Hermaphrodism, 108
Hernia
  diaphragmatic, 362
  hiatus, 71
  inguinal, 363–64, 380–81
  of newborn, 263
  umbilical, 280
Herniorrhaphy, 364
Herpes simplex, 168
Heterozygous, 431
Hiatus hernia, 71
Hiccuping, 295
High blood pressure, 12, 93, 157, 420–21
Hindgut, 105
Hip, dislocated, 264, 364–66
Homozygous, 431
Homunculus, 241
Hopi Indians, 6
Hormones, 408, 440
  abortion and deficiency in, 414
  anovulation and, 402–403
  behavior changes and, 12–13
  corpus luteum, 408
  infertility and imbalance in, 404
  morning sickness and, 68
  ovulation and, 406
  pituitary produced, 65, 305
  placenta produced, 70, 115–16
  postpartum, 215
  See also specific hormones

O

THIS BOOK WAS SET IN
BASKERVILLE AND PALATINO TYPES.

DESIGNED BY JULIAN HAMER